BLOOD TRAITORS

ALSO BY MARQ DE VILLIERS

The Heartbreak Grape: A Journey in Search of the Perfect Pinot Noir

Down the Volga in a Time of Troubles

White Tribe Dreaming

BLOOD TRAITORS

MARQ DE VILLIERS & SHEILA HIRTLE

HarperCollins*PublishersLtd*

http://www.harpercollins.com/canada

First edition

Canadian Cataloguing in Publication Data

de Villiers, Marq, 1940-
Blood traitors

ISBN 0-00-255424-0

1. Dorst, Anna.   2. Frietz, Katy.   3. Strum, Heinrich.   4. United States - History - Revolution, 1775-1783 - Biography.   I. Hirtle, Sheila.   II. Title.

E206.D4 1996   973.38   C96-930747-0

---

96 97 98 99 ❖ HC 10 9 8 7 6 5 4 3 2 1

Printed and bound in the United States

Contents

Sources and Acknowledgments

The genealogical information and family lineages and histories herein were derived from many sources, listed below as well as in the general Sources list. The group of families we follow in this book went through many hard times (among them a grim recession in Germany, the theft of all their belongings in England, disease and lawlessness in the Carolinas, the Revolutionary war itself and, for many of them, a second exile to Nova Scotia) and it is not surprising that in such circumstances there are gaps in the information. Even in the best of times, family record-keeping is not always impeccable, and it is in the nature of the information recorded that much of it is speculative and conflicting, necessitating some (albeit plausible and informed) interpretation. And so it is with some of the lineages recounted here: there may well be family members with information that amplifies, corroborates or at times appears to contradict some of what we have recounted here. If so, we would be pleased to hear from them.

With that caveat, and with the usual warnings that the good people below who furnished us so generously with information should not be held responsible for its use, grateful thanks to the following:

Individuals
Dorothy Maider Barrow, Merle Blakney, Danny Bower, Carl Boyer, Darlene Brine, Barry Cahill, Mrs. Merlin (Audrey) Crawford, Cal Creaser, Katie

Creaser, Mrs. Joan Crise, Priscilla Haines, Emily Harris, Alice Jones, Charlotte Lane, Clifford L. Merck, Pat Mickler, Eric Miller, Linda Mitchell, Sarah H. Parker, Janie Revill, Richard Rogers, Eleanor Smith, Virginia Smith, Wilma Stewart, James A. Strohm, C. L. Strom, Earl and Kim Strom, M. Strom, Randy C. Strom, Samuel T. Strom Sr. and Martha J. Strom, Helen Meister Strum, Herbert Strum, Senator Strom Thurmond, Diane W. Timmerman, Ray Timmerman, Murray and Muriel Webber, Willie Mae G. Wood, Hilda Zinck.

Institutions

Church of the Latterday Saints, Archives; Public Archives of Nova Scotia; the Nova Scotia Museum; the British Library; Cultural Affairs Library, Department of Tourism and Culture, Halifax; German Lutheran Church of St. Mary Le Savoy, London; Goethe Institute Historic Immigrants Office, Hamburg; Library of Congress, Local History and Genealogy Section, Washington; National Archives, Washington; Genealogical Research Recording, South Carolina Library, Columbia, South Carolina; South Carolina Department of Archives and History, Reference and Research Department; South Shore Genealogical Society, Lunenburg, Nova Scotia; Westdeutsche Gesellschaft Für Familienkunde E.V., Cologne; Shelburne County Museum, Shelburne, Nova Scotia; Shelburne County Genealogical Society, Shelburne, Nova Scotia; Mahone Bay Settlers Museum and Cultural Centre, Mahone Bay, Nova Scotia; United States Senate; the Robarts Library, University of Toronto.

And grateful thanks to the following for their help with the research:

Audrey Crawford; Lynn Cunningham; Honor de Pencier, The Sigmund Samuel Collection, Royal Ontario Museum; Hikmet Dogu (director) and Claire Petrie, the Adam L. and Sophie Gimbel Design Library, New York; Christina Freeman, librarian, German Historical Institute; Goethe Institute, Toronto, Mrs. Habekost; Gwyneth Harrison; Pat Hash, guide, Charleston; Lynda Heffley, historian, Council Chamber Art Gallery, Charleston; Rita Jones; Michael McCaffrey, Robarts Library; Mary McTavish, Robarts Library; Mills Memorial Library, McMaster University; Metro Toronto Public Library, History Department; Pastor A. B. Muller, St. George's Lutheran

Church, Whitechapel, London; Nova Scotia Department of Lands and Forests; Sarah Parker; Kenneth Paulson; Peter and Monique Pook; Richard Rogers, Four East Publishers; Rev. James Slack, former pastor of Zion Evangelical Lutheran Church, Lunenburg; Eleanor Smith; Jill Keddy Smith; Martha Keddy Smith; Virginia Smith; Susanne Steinmetz, London; Eric K. Williams, Park Ranger, Ninety Six National Historic Site.

And a special thanks to Iris Tupholme, for her gift of confidence in the project.

Preface

This book is nonfiction, in this real sense: there are no invented or composite characters; events have not been telescoped or adjoined for dramatic effect; words attributed to historical figures are, as closely as we can discover, the words they actually used, as recorded by contemporaries or recounted in histories published soon afterward. The people portrayed herein lived the lives we say they lived, suffered through the agonies we say they suffered, fought the battles herein described, were exiled, betrayed, lived, loved and died as we say they did.

However, as will become obvious from the context, the conversations and interior monologues have been imagined.

A note on the town of Shelburne:

The town of Shelburne, Nova Scotia, is in reality a pleasant and photogenic little place with a wonderful natural harbor, an energetic local museum and archives, an attractiveness to Hollywood filmmakers looking for unspoiled locations, and a population friendlier and much less fractious than appears in this book.

So when you read what follows, bear in mind that while Shelburne might have started badly, it has finished rather well.

The Principal Characters

THE PRINCIPAL CHARACTERS ARE:

•The sisters Katy and Anna Adolph (Katy married Abraham Frietz, a Loyalist, Anna, Peter Dorst, a Patriot).

•Heinrich Strum, eldest son of Peter and Maria Strum.

•Maria Elizabeth (Dorst) Adolph, sister of Peter Dorst, married to Heinrich Adolph, brother of Katy and Anna. It's her death at seventy-five that brings Katy and Anna together for the first time since the Revolution, and so begins the story.

THE PRINCIPAL FAMILIES ARE:

The Adolphs:

Maria Elizabeth (Dorst) Adolph, twenty-seven when she came to the Americas with her husband, Heinrich, thirty-nine. Heinrich was denounced as a Tory in the run-up to the Revolution, and killed at the siege of Savannah. Their eldest daughter, Katherina, and second daughter, Elizabeth, were both "distressed refugees" with their mother as the Revolution wound down. The third daughter, Margaretta Rosena, married the American Patriot David Rush (1760-1839). Heinrich Junior, or Henry, was the youngest.

The Bauers:

The patriarch of the family, Adam, was forty-one when he came to America. He married Katherine Elizabeth. Their children were Angelica,

Karl, Maria, Susannah, Alizabetha, Henry (who disappeared on the way to Savannah about 1779), Philip and Margaret.

The Dorsts:
Anna Maria (Adolph) Dorst, thirty when she came to America with her husband Peter, is our pro-revolutionary heroine. Peter was an active Rebel. Their children were Peter (born on the voyage to the Americas), Magda, Anna, Rachel and George.

The Frietzes:
Katharina (Katy) (Adolph) Frietz was thirty-five when she arrived in America. She is the principal Tory-side narrator of the story. Her husband was Abraham Frietz; her brother, Heinrich Adolph, was married to Maria Elizabeth Adolph, whose funeral begins the story. Their children were Catherine (Katy Jr.), Mary, Anna, Peter, Rosannah Margaretha, Charles and John.

The Merks:
Johan Balthazar Merk, forty-seven when he came to America, and his wife Elizabetha Katherina, thirty-nine, had several children important to the story, among them Susannah Margaretha; Conrad, who later married one of Katy Frietz's daughters; Elizabetha; Lorentz; Anna Maria, who later married Peter Mehl; Rosina, Johan and Jacob.

The Rupperts:
Heinrich Ruppert, forty-three, a widower, was father of Friedrich and Christoph, and a neighbour of Peter Strum on Beaverdam Creek in South Carolina. Friedrich married Anna Maria (Barbara) Strum, Peter's youngest daughter.

The Strums:
Peter Strum, sixty-seven on his arrival in America, and his wife, Maria, who was fifty-one, had several children, among them one of the main characters in this story, their eldest, Heinrich.

Heinrich was twenty-five when he arrived in America; by the end of the war he had lost two wives and six of his eight children. He died "of his wounds and a hard life" in Halifax at forty-two. Of Heinrich's eight children

Henry was the only one to survive to adulthood. Heinrich was married to: Elizabeth (who died in 1768, raped and killed by outlaw marauders/horse thieves); Catherine (Kiess); and Isabella, who took up with Heinrich while he was stationed at James Island.

Peter and Maria's other children were Anne Elizabeth; Anna Maria (Eva), married to Daniel Michler; Jacob; Anna Maria (Barbara), who later married Friedrich Ruppert.

The Webers:
Georg Weber and Katharina had several children: Georg Jr., Friedrich, Thomas, Henry, Suzanne and Barbara.

The Zanges:
Christian Zange was forty-one when he came to America with his wife, Juliana. He fought for the British at Ninety-Six and was imprisoned but released "because of his advanced age."

The Zimmermanns:
Philip Zimmermann, thirty-seven when he came to America, was a Rebel. His brother, Friedrich, and his son, Henry, were Tories.

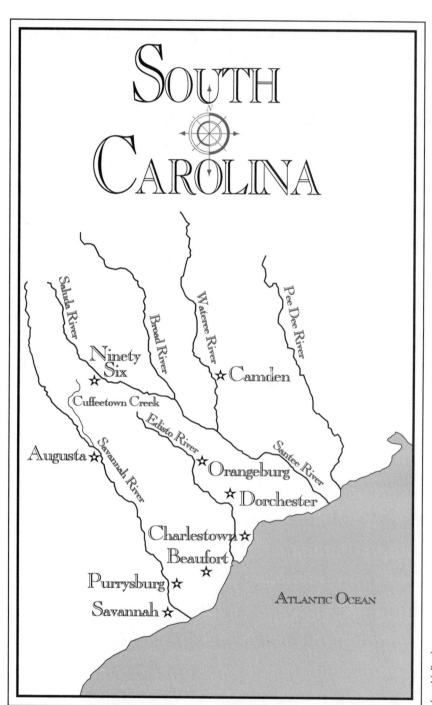

SOUTH CAROLINA

Saluda River

Broad River

Wateree River

Pee Dee River

Ninety Six ☆

Cuffeetown Creek

☆ Camden

Edisto River

Santee River

Augusta ☆

Savannah River

☆ Orangeburg

☆ Dorchester

Charlestown ☆

Beaufort ☆

Purrysburg ☆

Savannah ☆

ATLANTIC OCEAN

Mona M. Barakat

BLOOD TRAITORS

Prologue

June 1813
The Rush Farm, Cuffeetown Creek, South Carolina

The flesh hung heavily on her bones and her hip ached, and Katy sat stiffly, warily, on the end of the bench. She'd sat here at the edge of the creek often enough before, but always with dear, sweet, calm, kind Maria Elizabeth, her sister-in-law, dear, sweet, *dead* Maria, fresh in the ground up there in the meadow behind the farmhouse, boxed and buried, another war widow finally at rest, joining her husband, wherever he might be.

There'd been some kind of service at the church, held by the deacon, but she hadn't gone. She'd waited at the farm until the cart with Maria's body arrived, and had gone up to the meadow to see her clasped and enfolded by the red earth on which she'd lived for so long.

She wanted to pray for her friend, but there was no more prayer in her. God had taken Maria's Heinrich away thirty years too soon, had left poor Maria to spread her sweetness where she could, alone. That wasn't right. She felt giddy from the heat, and sat stiffly on the bench, conscious of the figure at the other end.

The pair of us, sisters in black, two old crows, what a history, what a time we've had! So much anger! So much heartbreak! Years without end, without grieving, too much anger to grieve.

The boards of the bench pressed into her legs, and she picked at the wood with her bony fingers. It was worn and weathered from the long years. The creek flowed sluggishly by, murky from the red soil, bits of leaves, seeds, skippers. Cuffeetown Creek. Where its name came from no one knew, any more than they knew the creek's source, but it would wind its way down to join Hard Labour Creek, then Stevens Creek and thence to the Savannah. Savannah! A name of grim memory . . . She used to paddle with her babies in Cuffeetown Creek, so many eons ago . . . Before everything . . .

Her mind was wandering, and she wrenched it back. She could feel the sweat running down, pooling in her clothes. When you're eighty-three, it's easy to live in the past. Husband gone, children gone, scattered, so many dead . . . A tear squeezed from her eye, surprising her. She was parsimonious with her tears these years. She had used up her allotment, decades ago. The heat really was getting her down. She glanced quickly at the figure on the other end of the bench. Anna was staring straight ahead, intent on the creek, as though she were trying to decipher its meaning. Little sister Anna. Little! She was seventy-eight years old.

Little Anna! We played together, once, and then the killing came, and we went our ways. She had angry eyes, I remember that, I remember the accusations and the angry eyes, and now you can barely see them, they've shrunken into her face, hidden by folds, wrinkles, pouches. A little maliciously, she thought, *Time has not used her well. She's a bag of bones, shriveled up.*

She sighed, and shifted on the bench. Her thoughts touched on her dead husband, Abraham Frietz, twice a refugee, a victim of recession, then a victim of war, dead so long ago on the rock-ribbed shore of New Scotland, buried in the sour soils of Shelburne, and a wave of bitterness swept through her.

Little Anna!

She sighed again. The bitterness faded quickly, her thoughts confused, as they usually were these days. How much of it had been Anna's fault, really? But . . . She'd had angry eyes, then, very angry eyes, eyes to shut everyone out. A sudden coldness came over her as she remembered what that anger had wrought.

There were screams from the house, childish yells, and a small form raced around the barn and vanished. One of Rosannah's grandchildren, Rosannah's and Conrad's. Conrad himself wouldn't come here, not now that David Rush owned it, but he let the children visit, this once. Probably the young ones had been told not to go down to the creek, warned to stay away, not to bother the old women. *They've not seen each other for nigh on forty years, let them talk, don't go near them* . . . Of course, in the way of children, they were curious. They wouldn't understand about the war and how it ripped us apart, families tearing at each other in that terrible cannibal rage . . . Children have no memory, no idea of time, of the endless years. They just want to poke at the *old crows*. They were probably staring right now, from behind a tree. No matter, they'd get bored soon enough.

"Well, sister," she said, looking along the bench.

"Well, sister, indeed."

"Forty years is a long time . . . Forty years!"

Anna said nothing, stared at the creek.

I have nothing to say to her! Katy thought, dismayed. *It's been too long.*

"We used to sit here, Maria and I, sometimes in the summer, I'd come to pay a call, after we came back, after the war. Adolph had his father's land by then. He let her stay with him, and David, after Heinrich sold the land to him . . ."

I'm blathering, she thought, *blathering and blithering. She knows all this.*

"We'd sit here by the creek, talking of how things were, and the children, talking of what had happened. We were always on the same side, you see."

She got a guilty pleasure from saying that. But Anna only shifted on the bench, and said nothing.

"Then she told me you and she visited too, here by the creek. I was angry with her for that, but she said you were her friend and she would hear none of it. So I said nothing. Because I loved Maria."

I was jealous, though, bitter. Didn't she remember what had happened? Why didn't she remember the dead, nurse the anger? Our brother, Maria's husband, poor Henry, bled to death in the muck of Savannah, shot . . . By her people, Anna's people!

Anna was still looking into the creek. She stirred. "I don't want to talk of all that," she said.

They sat for a while without saying anything. The heat was already oppressive though it was barely mid-morning. The childish screams had stopped. A cow lowed mournfully once, but there was no other sound. A horsefly buzzed and settled on the bench. Katy watched it apprehensively. A water spider flickered across the creek, vanishing behind a log. It was very quiet.

Gunfire is just an echo in my memories, Katy thought. *I don't want to hear the rattle of armies, not any more.*

"So what do you want to talk about?" she asked, more sharply than she had intended.

Anna was still staring at the sluggish creek. "I was remembering the Nahe," she said. "The river Nahe. In the spring, when it seemed to skip past the village. Do you remember? As if it couldn't wait to join the Rhine? Just like me. And the village? I was remembering the day Stumpel came. Oh, how I loved that man!"

"You loved Stumpel?" Katy asked, appalled. Stumpel was where it all began!

"Not him, but what he meant. I was twenty-nine! Don't you remember why we wanted to leave, why Stumpel seemed so blessed? The stories he told of the new age of possibilities? Where everyone would start fresh? Peter and I would have gone with him, even if no one else did, even with our first baby on the way . . . Peter was as ready as I was."

They sat for a moment, in silence. Katy said nothing. She hadn't thought of Peter Dorst for many years. Anna's husband . . . Dear Maria's brother, dear, *dead* Maria . . . Her mind skittered away. She wasn't ready for those memories.

"Anna," she said, "Anna . . . It is too late?"

"Not unless it always was," Anna said.

One

Anna looked over at her sister, but Katy was staring at the creek in her turn, fixedly, as though she could see God there. *We were so unhappy in that place. It was like an iron band squeezing my heart. So when the Seducer came, we would have followed him anywhere.* She peered at Katy again. She wasn't sure, from this vantage point, whether Katy had been unhappy or not. *When did the we become I?* How could you tell with Katy? She was wrapped up in her children and her man. She lived in the everlasting present. *Just like the savages.*

September 1763
Idar-Oberstein, German Palatinate

Johan Heinrich Christian, the Sieur de Stumpel, self-styled, appeared in town one day late in summer, or early autumn—in any case, it was after the apples had turned color but before the harvest, so the air was still warm. He clattered past the "new" castle, built about six hundred years earlier but now, like the old, abandoned and in ruins, its damp stones a convenient locus for vile sin and fornication, as the minister reminded them every Sunday, unwittingly encouraging that which he would suppress, and past the church below, embedded in the cliff, a white carbuncle in the black rock, with its stubby towers and two great windows like astonished eyes.

Stumpel made his way down the steep streets, his horse slipping occasionally on the damp cobbles, past the holes pierced in the cliff face, where the townsfolk had for centuries extracted agates from the rock, until he reached the Nahe River, at low water after a dry summer and stinking from the town's latrines, shallow and black, oily, with tottering old houses built tight to the banks, their stone skirts trailing in the fetid water. There were narrow alleys between them, and steps down to the littered shallows of rotting nets, broken punts, a jumble of glistening sewage-stained rocks and discarded parts of water wheels that had powered the small mills where the agates and gemstones were polished. There was an air of irredeemable shabbiness to the whole place.

Stumpel, by contrast, cut quite a figure, a semi-precious stone himself in a town of dull gray rock, like a knight back from the Crusades, a veteran of foreign wars and many hard campaigns, tall, very fair, dressed in knee-capping black boots, light breeches, and a somewhat worn but gentlemanly display of gold frogging across his chest. He doffed his tricorn as he dismounted; his chiseled face had a weary but kind aspect.

Anna Dorst, née Adolph, had watched him pass, seduced by his presence.

Huh. Weary but kind, indeed. So we thought, sister Katy and I. And we weren't girls any more, girls with their secret passions. We were grown women, mothers or about to be mothers, with husbands. But what an air he brought with him! Of foreign parts and new beginnings, of ships on the open ocean and a virgin country, of land for the taking, of great forests and savage people. New beginnings! Away from the priests and the castle, away from the tithes and the taxes and the endless demands. Away from drear!

A kind face. We all thought so. But behind that face, behind that flesh, was a skull like any other.

Adam Bauer adopted him and squired him about the village—my good friend Sieur de Stumpel this, my good friend Sieur de Stumpel that . . . With Adam in tow, Stumpel visited the pastor at the church, the schoolmaster in his nearly empty classroom (the children were in the fields—there was work to be done) and the tavern, where he drank a stein of hoppy froth in the taproom in the presence of his host. He visited the smith and then the cooper, poking about among the staves. Oh, he was busy! He hovered around the entranceways to the mines, and rolled the semi-precious stones between his fingers under the cold and suspicious eyes of the gem-polishers. He was invited into houses, nearby farmyards and, rumor had it, the occasional hayrick by the occasional randy young beauty—or was that just the pastor's suspicious nature speaking?

Stumpel stayed for a few days, displaying his papers, elaborate with scrolling signatures and red wax seals, pulling them out of his leather wallet with an air of bemused pride, as though he were just their custodian and they had an independent existence of their own, their own irrefutable personality. He showed these papers around, but because most were in the foreign English, no one could read them except the schoolmaster, who could puzzle out a phrase here and there.

He was a Hanoverian, Stumpel said, and in the late war had been captain in a corps of Walloon mercenaries in the service of the English king, George II, and before that, with the Prussians. He was an erudite man, a man of learning, and had traveled to Sweden, even to the Americas. He'd been with a company of Hessians in Halifax, and had helped in the exportation of the French Catholics of Fundy Bay, herding 'em like cattle to the ships going he knew not where, burning their houses and taking their beeves, some of which he drove down to the market and garrison at Halifax at a nice profit to himself and his regimental masters. The Catholics were expelled, he said, because of England's war with France, and now Protestants were needed to take their place, and would be treated well because of it, and this was why he was here.

He thumped the table in the tavern and shook his curls and spoke passionately, eloquently, of the great continent to the west. It seemed a marvelous place, the best of land but empty of people, virgin. There were a few English yeomen here and there, and the garrisons, of course, but the land yawned empty, immense, open, inviting, waiting for the plow and the ax to yield up its bounty. No one knew how far it reached—maybe forever. And through the gracious generosity of His Majesty King George of England, he, Stumpel, was in a position to offer each man here, and his wife and children too, land as much as he could till in a lifetime, a hundred acres for each man and single woman, fifty acres for each married woman and each child. He, Stumpel, could have had two hundred thousand acres for his new settlement if he'd wished. More even, much more, as much as you could wish for. But he was a prudent man. So he asked for and got twenty thousand acres. Twenty thousand acres! Enough for a very large townful of people. It was hard to imagine. And each family would have tools, and arms and ammunition to defend themselves or kill wild fowl and game, the beeves of the forest. They would have seeds and the where-withal to acquire all and any necessaries, and food for the first year, at least. And he, Stumpel, would take them there, and set them on their estates. They could entrust him with their households, with any valuables they might possess. These would be carried safely with him to America. They had his guarantees because he had the formal, gracious permissions of King George and his Board of Trade, as the papers plainly showed.

Well, so it was a shell game, how were we to know? The papers he carried likely said nothing of the sort, containing only pious promises and what ifs. What a trickster! He had to convince them he had us, and us he had them, and smear his lies with honey, the hard facts covered in syrup.

Someone, the schoolteacher perhaps, said he had heard the winters in the Americas were savage, that it was a howling wilderness, packs of wolves . . .

It's a calumny, Stumpel declared. In the summers, the crops grow of themselves, to the height of a man's shoulder. The winters . . . He couldn't tell a lie. The winters were hard, but there was wood for the taking, so much wood it was impossible to believe. Why, he said passionately, trees are so thick on the ground you can barely push through 'em, they belong to no one—just there for the taking, and they grow like weeds, you have to hack 'em back . . . Wood for houses and barns, for boats, for warmth in the winters.

Peter Dorst, uneasy about Stumpel's enthusiastic tales of the expulsion of the Catholics from this paradise, and in any case a quick-tempered and suspicious person, asked him about churches.

"This is where you're favored," Stumpel said. "You are Reformed, are you not? That's . . ."

"Followers of Luther," Dorst said, with some asperity.

"All the better!" said Stumpel. "Why . . ."

"No," Dorst said. "We've had too many wars here. We want no more. We just want to be left alone, to pray in our own way."

Stumpel shook his head, impatiently. He was a soldier. He'd pray the way his colonels wanted him to pray. Modern times called for modern practices. These people were worse than the Papists, with their endless wrangling! "If you come with me, you'll never have to worry about any of that again. You can be what you want. You can build your own churches from native wood, your own pastors will preach the way you want."

"These Catholics who were expelled . . . Maybe they thought they'd be safe there," said Dorst, not letting it go. "Then the English came, and drove them from their homes."

"You don't have to come, if you're afraid," said Stumpel. "Soon England will own all of the Americas . . . And the land is there, for the taking."

"I don't want another war," someone said, into the ensuing silence.

Late that night, after the dogs had quieted and the lamps had been lowered, Stumpel sat with Katy and Anna on an upturned skiff, sat close to them, his boots in the muck and his sword propped against the hull, talking of his travels. The men were in the tavern, arguing. Everywhere, Stumpel said, people were throwing in their lot with him, exchanging everything for a chance at a new world. He'd been all through the Hunsrück, all through the Palatinate. The people were ready. There was a weariness with the *corvée*, the tithing, the constant and increasing taxation, the grinding down—hardly paradise on earth, was it? He squeezed Anna's thigh, and she too thought of paradise, but not the kind his squeeze implied. Then she thought of the great emptiness of the new world, and a sadness filled her. Why was there not more happiness on this earth?

"Anna," warned Katy, "they may be watching."

"No matter," said Stumpel, grinning. "I'm all innocence."

He sat for a while.

"Everywhere I go, they are weary of weariness," he said, "weary of the old ways, of the old ways and the wars."

He'd been south to the winelands of Kirchheim and the orchards of Jacobsweiler, he said. He'd been to Stromberg and Baumholder, and up the Nahe to Bergen Birkenfeld and down to Kirn and Merkheim and Heimweiler, and to Kreuznach, where the salts were. Everywhere it was the same.

He sighed. It was lovely country. What a man could do with twenty thousand acres here!

He loved it all, but what a mess it was in! The hills to the north, the Donnerbergen and Thor's Hill, the crag-girt ruins of Falkenstein. So many ruins! Castles, abbeys, churches, their stones broken in forgotten wars. So much anger! Near Kusel he'd seen the largest ruin of them all, the enormous Burg Lichtenberg. Even in the smiling meadows around Kreuznach, the home of the celebrated necromancer, Dr. Faustus, there were ruins, relics of ancient blood-feuds. He'd made a detour to see the magnificent castle of Dhaum, an eyrie on a crag, restored only thirty years earlier, where an ape was said to have run off with the Wildgrave's child, and was seen nursing the infant in the forest, offering it a breast, an orange, an apple, a quince, some fruit, the stories varied. And he'd seen the ruined fortified abbey called Disibodenberg. Was its history not the history of this whole place, and also the history of poor, war-weary, recession-wracked Europe? Disibod came to spread light among the Teutonic gloom; Charles Martel, of all people, reduced his monastery to rubble; it was rebuilt and was again destroyed by Siegfried III of Mayence and the Wildgrave of Kirburg; once more the Cistercians repaired it and around 1500 it was plundered by the Prince-Palatine Philip V; the Cistercians again returned until Gustavus Adolphus finally drove them away . . . Stumpel had spent a fruitless hour contemplating the graying stones, then he passed into the forest called Soonwald at Pferdsfeld.

"So you passed the cave of Schinderhannes," said Anna, a little breathlessly, "passed by without harm?"

"Who?"

"Schinderhannes, Johann Buckler, Cruel John. The highwayman. He kills merchants, steals from travelers, even went to Mainz and took from the church . . ."

"No, fortunately for him, I missed him." He smiled.

"He doesn't steal from the villagers, only the rich," Anna said.

"Perhaps I am your Schinderhannes," Stumpel said, grinning again.

"Who are these people who have agreed to go with you?" Katy asked, curious.

"You won't know their names," said Stumpel, "except for some." He thought of Philip Zimmermann and his plump Apolonia from Bergen Birkenfeld, Balthazar Merk with his stolid sons and heavy daughters from Jacobsweiler, and in Berschweiler the Henns and Webers, especially the daughter Barbara, still only fifteen but very, very ready . . . He stroked Anna's knee, very lightly. The names that sounded to his Hanoverian ear like sneezes: the Kiesses, Kleins and Cruhmmenallers . . . And here in Oberstein, the amicable Adam Bauer, and Peter Strum with his brood, especially the son Heinrich, whose cold, black eyes had disconcerted

Stumpel a great deal. "You'll get to know them all, if you go along," he said.

"Oh," said Katy, almost involuntarily, "we'll go."

Stumpel clambered to his feet, ramming his toes into his boots. He looked down at the sisters in their small white caps, dark aprons and black skirts, sitting there on the boat. The moon shone on their faces, eager faces, eager bones, eager flesh, trusting eager eyes . . . It was almost enough to make a man change his mind, turn aside from his own destiny.

Weary of weariness, indeed.

They met the following day without Stumpel, after Stumpel had gone but before his agents had arrived, met in the drafty hall that served as a schoolhouse when school was in, which wasn't very often.

Much had been changing in the Hunsrück and the Palatinate, but not nearly enough. So many were so poor. Too many children ran about half-naked, demanding alms from travelers; their parents were dressed in rags, their barns empty, their cottages near collapse. Even those not destitute were bound as vassals to the Wildgraves and Raugraves of the Palatinate, a fixed *corvée* of a dozen days in return for military protection. That was a bitter joke. The Wildgraves spent their time in drunken revelry and fornication in their strongholds, or on great hunts in the Schwarzwald, or abroad, at other kinds of play in the fashionable towns, and were never there when the gloomy Swedes or the evil French or the Prussian armies rolled through. In truth, the peasants gave as little as they got, for the *corvée* was more honored in the breach . . . Compulsory labor . . . Well, they had to work anyway. But the ground-rent tax and the tithe on top of that . . . The tithes were supposed to be for the church, but the priests discounted them to the warlords in return for not having their churches burned down around their ears. The debt burden increased every year, rent and taxes, taxes and rent, arrears to be paid in seed and stock, until it sometimes seemed there was nothing left, and no way out.

The school was entirely empty this day, the schoolmaster himself absent, no doubt on some devious errand. They were all there, the miller and the innkeeper, the butcher, baker, dyer, wagon-maker and saddler, the chirurgeon, that cheerful butcher of human limbs, the shoemaker, smith, tailor and the bulky linen weaver, rank and damp from his work. And of course the pastor, whose job it was to put a stop to all this talk of abandoning their leftover feudal duties, as well as his more normal round of performing marriages and baptisms. It was his task and his duty, but everyone knew he wouldn't do it. Maybe he himself would slip away one day. It wasn't a sin to dream of a new church in the heathen wilderness. All those fresh new souls to be gathered in for the Lord! He could smell the new wood, and see the shiny faces upturned in the pew-boxes, and the coffers would be full, plentiful, easily replenished . . . Well, he knew he'd never go, but who was he to stop the dreams of others?

If they went with the Sieur de Stumpel, it was clear they would all go for different reasons. Adam Bauer, of course, said he'd go because his faith demanded it, but others believed that if he went, it would be because his native curiosity drove him. Others would go because they were in trouble—maybe for poaching, maybe for liberties with a Wildgrave's stock or a Wildgrave's orchards or, on occasion, with a Wildgrave's daughter. Others would go because their spouses had died, or their parents, or a child had perished of fever or hunger, or because they were afraid of new wars and of death on a battlefield far from home. Many, many, many would go because it was the only thing they could think of to avoid being ground down by the burdens of debt.

Katy would go because she wanted the lives of her children to be rich with promise, and she'd drag her Abraham with her if he balked; Anna because she needed a grand adventure to drown the anger she sensed in herself and her husband. Peter Strum would go mostly because he knew that great events were afoot in Europe; he didn't understand what they were, but his dominant emotion was foreboding. His wife would go with him because she had no opinion of her own. And their children? Heinrich, the eldest son, would go because he had a hunger for adventure and because he would commit some violence if he stayed—everyone knew that. Heinrich's wife, Elizabeth, would go because she was the tail to her husband's comet.

"Will they let us go?" someone asked. "When we're gone, who will pay their rents?"

"I'm going," said Peter Strum. "I'm going if I have to steal away in the fog. Who is to say me nay? I'll sail with Stumpel down the Rhine to this New Scotland."

"They'll seize everything we've got if we go!" someone else said.

"I have little, but what I have I'll entrust to Stumpel. They'll have to take it from him, and he has patents from the English King . . ."

There was silence for a moment, then young Heinrich Strum spoke.

"I want no man's permission," he said.

July 1764
Bingen-am-der-Rhein

The *schippers*, the Rhine-scouts, the laconic rivermen with their know-it-all attitudes and seen-it-all world-weariness, were waiting for them in Bingen, where the Nahe empties into the river that was to take them to the sea. The Rhine! It swept by, serene and uncaring, symbol of the world about which they knew so little and which knew nothing at all about them. On the right bank, opposite the Nahe, was the wall of terraces that marked the beginning of the central German highlands, the wall and the river, the river and the wall, as far up as anyone could see, toward Mainz. The wall was steep, precipitous in places, and vineyards clung to it, and paths, with here and there a castle, or the ruins of a castle, or a church. To the left, whence many of them had come, the wall continued as the brooding forest of the Bingenwald, the beginning of the Hunsrück, land of hidden villages, wild boar, highwaymen and outlaws, secretive and poor. Through this wall the Rhine abruptly plunged.

They'd come in a ragged procession, the oxen plodding as oxen do, bundles and baskets strapped to their swaying backs, children and adults on foot, a few of the old people on mule-back or in a donkey cart, cradling the babies. There were more than two hundred of them, but few had ever been to Bingen, with its crush of tall, gabled houses jostling with markets and churches, dominated by the spires of the cathedral. Still, not many paid much attention to the town; there was too much anxiety—would the arrangements hold? Would the boatmen be waiting? Where would they be? Were they in time? It had taken them longer to get here than they had believed possible. Could something have gone wrong?

They'd left Oberstein several days before, early in the morning, openly, not slipping away under cover of dark or fog as so many others had done. The castle's man was there, watching incuriously. He said and did nothing. He could have demanded payment in lieu of manumission, but he knew they had no money and would go anyway; he'd have to chain them to their houses to keep them there. Besides, who needed them? They were a burden, and one should be grateful for their going . . . The pastor, who was supposed to have discouraged them, instead had written certificates of baptism for each one, with his blessing, and these they had packed into their meager bundles, along with what food they could carry and the letters from Stumpel's agents.

It had been no secret that they were leaving. Debate and discussion had been under way since Stumpel had come and gone like a comet the previous autumn, and his agents had been back several times collecting names and promises. These were generally hard men, who seemed to know nothing and care less about Stumpel's great vision—all they wanted were promises, and they went through the houses with furious contempt, counting and sorting the goods to be taken or left, pushing people aside in their own dwellings. All through the winter the arguments had gone on in kitchens and taverns—not so much arguments about *whether*, or *why*, but exactly *who*, and *when*.

They'd started to collect in Idar-Oberstein not long before. It was past spring, and the planting should have begun. Already the trees were in bloom, and the wildflowers, and the wild grasses were springing up in the unplowed fields. To some of them, the unkempt fields were the first sign that they were really, really going.

They'd come to Bingen from all over, from small rural villages, high up and isolated in the forests and fields surrounding the river valley; they came from Stromberg, just a few hours' walk away, and from villages near Trier far to the west. They came down the Alsenz from Dannenfels and Jacobsweiler to the south, from the broad meadows and generous sweep of Berkenfeld and Baumholder, from the slate roofs of Berschweiler, Hennweiler and Merkheim; one family walked down from Pferdsfeld, a hamlet not near anything except the lair of Schinderhannes. They traveled overland along the footpaths or along the many meandering supplementary streams down to the Nahe River itself, which, though too shallow to allow water traffic, supported a string of villages and towns connected by rural trails.

Katy looked at the people trailing along behind them. She tried to imagine these weary souls at their destination, the wild woods of America. They'd be neighbors, then, they'd help each other in good times and succor each other in bad. That's what they all said.

Anna, she thought, would have no fear of the future. She wanted it too much to fear it.

She could make out Peter and Maria Strum with their son Heinrich, he of the black hair and the cool, assessing black eyes, striding along with his wife; and behind them the rest of Peter's children, the pale and wan Anne, the boy Jacob, Eva and the others, walking with Georg and Katharina Weber and Georg's sister Anna Alizabetha with her husband Adam Henn and their daughter Anna. Somewhere behind them, still hidden by a curve in the Nahe, were Philip and Apolonia Zimmermann and Philip's brother Friedrich, with his wife Margaretta. At the back of their little convoy were Adam and Katherine Bauer and their children.

In Bingen they met the Merks, Balthazar and Elizabetha, and their children, among them Conrad and Lorentz, and with them Peter and Anna Maria Mehl, who had traveled down the Alsenz to meet the Nahe just above Kreuznach. They came from Jacobsweiler, which tucks itself into a dimple in the south-eastern cheek of the Donnerbergen.

There'd be more, too, as they moved down the Rhine. At Duisburg they'd pick up Christian and Juliana Zange, and Heinrich Ruppert with his son Christoph and younger children; Philip and Katharina Knaab with his ninety-year-old mother, setting off to make a new life in the sunset of her own. People said it was the *Alte Frau* Knaab who was the driving force in the family; it was she who bullied them into going. In any case, they trailed behind her, her elderly will as tight as any rein. At her age, she was still hungry for something new!

The names were a litany in her mind, then just a blur. So many names, so many stories.

Why do I think of the names on the stones in the graveyard?

"How many more?" Balthazar Merk asked the captain of one of the waiting river transports.

"Altogether?"

"How many are going to America?"

"Everyone in the Palatinate," the man replied. "But this time? Two hundred, four hundred, six hundred, who knows? The agent says six hundred, but I don't think you're that many."

The Oberstein party swarmed on board and milled around. Many of them settled on the deck, others crowded the rail. They were all thinking of home.

By this, some of them meant Oberstein. Others meant . . . America.

Once they were in the Rhine scouts, the scows that were to take them to Rotterdam, the scale of their journey changed. They were no longer with a small group of intimate friends, a few of whom they had known all their lives, but one much larger, made up of anxious emigrants from numerous villages. The scowmen, who had seen many such make their way down the Rhine, were impersonal and uninterested.

The emigrants watched as the boats slipped away from Bingen and the spires of the churches faded from view in the smoky haze.

The boat stopped briefly at a toll station called Der Mauseturm, then the river turned sharply right and became a churning maelstrom as it squeezed through the gap in the massif.

It's the door to Somewhere, Anna thought. *Portal to the unknown.* She looked forward, but could see only waves, looked back, but there was nothing, only the wall of the massif. She felt captured by the future.

Will we leave a hole in the story of this place, now that we have gone? And fill up the bucket in the story of the new place? At least our journey has truly begun. There's no turning back.

The journey was slow, taking almost two weeks before they reached the Netherlands. Most days they'd have to stop at another of the dozens of customs and toll stations on the river. The *schippers* put their feet up while the captains snarled and complained and the tollkeepers, functionaries of this small principality or that tiny duchy, searched the boats, looking for who knew what—anything forbidden, anything that would give them a reason to delay further, to hold them hostage against time, to squeeze another small contribution to the Landgraf's well-being. These tollkeepers were uniformly hated by the Rhine rivermen, but no one ever tried to evade them—as well try to escape the relentless movement of the seasons or the first snow of the winter. The emigrants' meager baggage was hardly touched, except by those few customs officers who were resentful of their going; it was pitifully obvious that they were carrying neither contraband nor valuables of any kind.

At the frontier, at Emmerich, they were stopped again, this time on account of the emigrants themselves.

A small, worried-looking man in a brown frock and too-big boots fetched one of the captains and took him ashore. They were gone several hours before they returned. This time the captain looked as agitated as the shippers' agent.

The agent represented the "merchants in the Palatine trade" (as the shippers of human cargo were called) at Rotterdam. These merchants were licensed by the States General of the Netherlands to do their business, and were under heavy bond to ensure that they would truly ship overseas any emigrant brought into the country. The last thing the Dutch burghers wanted was ragged camps of benighted Palatines on the waterfront, destitute, needing to be fed, a burden on the public weal, which meant, in effect, the burghers themselves. They were cargo, and cargo had value only when it was moving through to its destination. The agent's job was to demand to know precisely who was responsible for them from the time the border was crossed. Before the ship could proceed, the captain and the agent had to be certain the emigrants were truly pledged to an American colony. Even with all the papers in order, the emigrants would remain on board the Rhine scows in Rotterdam harbor until their ships were ready to embark them, at which time they would be transferred directly. Once on board, the agent would hold a muster of "his" immigrants in order to make a list for the Board of Trade and Plantations in London; only then would the ship drop down to the Hellevoet Roads to await a favorable wind for putting to sea.

From there, the ships had to call at an English port for customs clearance. This was usually Gosport or Cowes. After that—America.

But now, a problem.

It appeared the papers were in order, duly signed by the Board of Trade and their sponsor, this Sieur de Stumpel. Oh, there were irregularities—Stumpel's co-sponsors, whoever they were, had not signed anything—but generally all the seals were in the right places.

"We went into the Customs House," the captain grumbled to his crew later, on the way down to Rotterdam. "I showed him mine and he showed me his. We slapped 'em down on the table like two gaming gents used to trickery and quackery of all kinds. My papers were perfect—signed, sealed, the wax as thick as apples, signatures everywhere, bonded and tolled and housed till a mouse couldn't slip through the wherefores and therefores, a thicket of advocatin' language. His were good too, mostly, exceptin' for the other gents who were to have signed. All he didn't have from this Stumpel was the money."

"So?" someone asked.

"So what could he do, 'cept look even more worried?" the captain responded, by now greatly relieved at not having been turned back at the border. "He couldn't pick holes in my papers, nor really in his own. So he had to let us go on."

"What about the money?"

"Well, don't tell them," he said, jerking a thumb toward the knots of emigrants crowded on the deck. "Don't tell them, but no money, no America. If this Stumpel doesn't pay up by the time we get to Rotterdam, they'll never get to see the promised land." He laughed, not an unsympathetic laugh, but the carefree laugh of one who no longer bore any burden of responsibility.

The following morning the boat slipped into Rotterdam harbor. To the Palatines, it was a glorious sight—the next staging post for their adventure. They saw a mass of red-brick houses with lofty gables, green gardens everywhere, often half-hidden by the rows of elms and maples, straight avenues intersected by canals and water streets—a commercial town, wealthy, and vast beyond imagining. The harbor was crowded with ships of all kinds. There were boats from the Rhine, the Moselle, the Main and the Neckar, sent to take in and carry home the produce of distant climes, brought here by the three-masted East Indiaman lying yonder, a forest of masts from exotic places. There were so many barges gliding about, laden with goods for the warehouses, it was hardly possible for a lighter to thread its way among them.

They knew nothing of the agent's worries. They didn't know why they stayed in Rotterdam for almost two weeks without being allowed ashore. They didn't know that, when they were eventually transferred to the ocean-going ship that was to take them to the Unknown, the precise location of the unknown was unknown even to the authorities. They didn't know that the agent waited in vain for the money to arrive from Stumpel, or rather that some of it finally did arrive, but not enough. They knew nothing of the furious arguments in the counting house of one of the great merchants. They certainly didn't know that their ship would take them not to Cowes and then America but to London, there to await developments. It was the pragmatic Dutch way; if there's an English problem, let the English solve it.

Stumpel would meet them in London. Or so the Dutch maintained. It would be settled there.

The ship slipped down the roadway, the last of the Rhine, the last trickle from their homeland, and they finally entered the sea through the canal and sluices at Katwyk and stood out for open ocean. Their journey was truly under way.

So they believed.

Two

The Rhine, Katy thought, *was our river of hope, but as we left the Rhine, the ship slipped from light into darkness and we from hopefulness to despair.* She was still staring intently at the creek, her fingers picking nervously at the wood of the bench. *And yet, from this vantage point, how quickly that one small black tempest passed.* She tapped her thigh, feeling the brittle bones beneath the skin. Brittle, but heavy, like lead . . . She risked a glance at her sister. Anna didn't look heavy, only . . . used-up. She sighed. *Here we are, in our black plumage, just beak and claw and fiber. Where was the sun, when we needed it most?*

Anna watched her sister fidgeting. She was thinking similar thoughts, but for her, as she remembered it, the despair had soon changed to anger. *It took hold of me and wouldn't let go.* She looked over at her sister. *That foolish, empty-headed creature! She never could see the obvious.*

August 1764
Whitechapel, London

Anna Dorst listened to the moaning that filled the ship's hopelessly crowded below-deck. It reminded her of something she'd once seen in the castle near the village, a tent in the courtyard, barbers in blue with sharp hatchets and clumsy saws, strong men screaming, the wounded of war having their limbs hacked off, soldiers chewing on rags to keep from biting through their tongues as the barber butchers tried to save their miserable lives. After the cutting, they were wrapped in linen and left to live or die. That was almost ten years ago, when she was not yet twenty, but she could still feel the shrieks on the edge of her teeth.

Well, there were no wounded here in the black belly of the ship, but it was somehow just as bad, a rumble of sorrow and pain, with every now and then an eerie howl as someone gave in to panic, or the wailing of a child. Why did it sound so awful? It was the crush of bodies, she thought, the terrible deep, black dark, and the unknown, the fear of being locked in, of being able to see nothing, to know nothing . . . She felt panic rising in herself, too, and fought it back. She couldn't afford panic, she owed it to the child she carried, if not to herself. Nobody would tell them anything. They were supposed to be on a peaceful voyage to a new home, but instead they were locked—imprisoned!—in the stinking black hold of the ship that had brought them from Old Home, or at least from Rotterdam at the end of the Rhine. An Indiaman, the seamen had called the boat, a vast thing, the biggest boat she'd ever seen. They had docked somewhere—London, someone said, it must be—a day ago, but the hatches hadn't opened. The slops buckets hadn't been emptied and the stench was like a physical blow. Where was everyone? Where was the man who had promised them a new life? Why weren't they let out into the air, to see the city of London, or to board the ships that would carry them across the Great Sea? She drew her shawl more tightly about her shoulders and hunched down, hugging her swollen belly. She leaned into her sister, Katy, pressing against her. Katy was hugging her babies, soothing them.

Why don't they quieten down? This moaning is madness! Why don't they come? Where is the man Stumpel? Why don't they let us out?

All four hundred and more of them were aboard, she'd been told. At least two hundred were crammed into this stinking hold, with hardly any room to move, to turn about, and no room to lie down except for the few, like her brother Heinrich's wife Maria Elizabeth. But then Maria would find a space to be calm even in hell, she thought ruefully—she was the calmest person Anna had ever met. You wouldn't think I'd married this person's brother, she thought. My Peter, my poor Peter . . . Not a calm person at all.

Peter Dorst was somewhere across the hold. He was small and nervous and energetic, always had been. How comforting Maria was, how close the families had become. She reached out in the dark to touch Maria's solid person, felt a child sleeping peacefully in her reassuring arms. The blackness and the stench pressed in, heavy, threatening; no one was heeding their cries. She started to whimper, but caught herself, squeezing it back.

Why doesn't someone come?

A banging sounded from the middle of the hold, near the stairway, and for a moment the moaning and the fretful crying stopped, as they wondered what it was. Anna knew. It was her Peter. He had been one of the first to break out of the inaction, to do something, to move. A few hours after they had docked, after the ship stopped shifting and the hatches hadn't opened, he had found a piece of wood somewhere, maybe a barrel stave, maybe a piece of an old oar, and had started banging on the underside of the hatch. How did he have room to swing the wood in this crowded space? But swing he did. Bang! Bang! Bang! It made a hollow booming sound in the hold. Bang! He'd banged for an hour before he grew exhausted, but no one came. Now he was starting again.

Why doesn't someone come?

The maddening banging went on for more than ten minutes. Then there was a rumble and a crash and the hatch was flung back, blessed light flooding into the hold, and a damp fog, damp but clean and refreshing, curled over the frame. The crowd surged forward, stopped. There were three sailors with boat hooks and belaying pins at the head of the steps.

Peter Dorst climbed up toward them.

"Why are you keeping us here? We must get out! Where's Herr Stumpel? We must meet with Herr Colonel Stumpel!"

He was speaking German, the only language he knew. The sailors stared at him stolidly.

"They don't understand you," someone shouted, a deep voice. It was his brother-in-law, Anna's brother Heinrich Adolph, calm husband of calm Maria. "Ask for the captain. He spoke something like our language."

Peter went up another step, a crush of bodies surging behind him. "Cap-i-tan," he said, speaking slowly and carefully, trying for what he thought was their language. "Bring cap-i-tan."

One of the sailors laughed harshly. "Capitan ain't here," he said, and prodded downward with his boat hook, pushing backward.

Peter caught the hook, pulled. Cursing, another sailor swung at him, catching him a heavy blow on the ribs. He let go, tumbling back down into the crowded hold. The sailors' heads disappeared and the hatch was dragged into place, plunging them back into the terrifying darkness.

About an hour later the first of the slops buckets overflowed, and a stinking puddle began to spread across the planking. The moaning had started up again. A child was shrieking, a shrill, nerve-tearing sound. Despair and weariness welled up inside Anna, and she began to weep, quietly at first and to herself, then with unrestrained sobs.

No one is going to come! We'll die here, in this terrible place!

Her brother Heinrich and her husband Peter stared at her, or at where they thought she was, there in the black, impotent, unable to do anything but stare blindly, as though that would help. Her sister Katy was huddled into herself, too miserable to care. The darkness seemed to press in forever.

The captain of the Indiaman, he who spoke "something like our language," was at that moment leaning against a railing near the wheel with his first mate, watching a stream of distraught Palatines from the stern hold filing down the gangplank to the crowded quay below, clutching their pathetic bundles. The wharfingers and the laborers manning a clumsy wooden crane swore at them and tried to move them on, up into the alleys past the rotting warehouses, but there were too many of them, two hundred, maybe three, who was counting?

"Packed 'em in pretty good," the first mate conceded. "But why're ye letting 'em go?"

"What would I to do with 'em?" the captain demanded. "Pack 'em in salt and lay 'em down for the men and their dinner? Haunch o' Hessian?"

"What about that lot, there?" The mate jerked his thumb to the midship's hold where the Dorsts and Adolphs remained imprisoned.

"Them? They stay till I get paid."

He stared resentfully at the stream of bewildered and dejected Palatines on the wharf. They didn't know why they were being summarily bundled off the ship. But who cared what they thought? Why should he go on feeding them? He'd got enough of 'em left to keep hostage. He'd keep those until

Stumpel or his agents arrived, if they ever did. He'd been promised a premium fee for getting the whole sodding crowd out of Rotterdam to London, and he wanted his money. Pay up, or they'll never get ashore.

"Take the money off them as remains," the mate suggested.

"They ain't got no money! What trinkets they had I got, but they dint have much in any case. Nah, get rid o' some, let his royal blessed majesty worry about 'em, keep t'others."

"Where d'you think this Stumpel's gotten hisself?" the mate asked.

"Ah! Colonel John Henry Christian de Stumpel? Gives himself airs, calls himself Sir Stumpel?" The captain spat. "Johan Stumpel he really is. Fought for Prussia, he said he did, till the war there ended. Just another discharged soljer with bigger-than-hisself ideas. Nah, he's a scoundrel and now he's absconded for sure. Promised his agents fancy estates each in the Americas if only they'd become shepherds to the Palatine sheep. And the sheep? Gave him their money and their goods, and he gets it and off he goes. Nah, they'll not hear again from him, I reckon."

"He give you any money?"

"Some, enough to get me going. Just enough to turn me head. The rest was to be here, in Lunnen." He smacked his head. "And I b'lieved 'im!"

The Palatines who had been thrown off the boat formed a milling crowd on the wharf. Most simply stayed where they were, not knowing what else to do, but after a while a small straggle of people began to move, rounding the dirty brick warehouses and flowing into the road that led from the Iron Stairs past the Tower, up toward Tower Hill. The captain could see them disappearing around the corner, already lost in the throng that boiled so readily out of the rats' nest of alleys to the north and east. Above the warehouse in front of the Indiaman was the steeple of a church, the home church of the nuns of St. Katherine. Behind that, though he couldn't see it, was the Angry Dragon Tavern, which held many a night of rum memories.

The captain sighed. "That's that, then. Won't let 'em back on board. They're gone and good thing too." He shook his head. "No one else leaves till I get paid."

"Where'll they get money, locked in the hold like they are, if this Stumpel doesn't come after all?"

"I don't care. I get my money, then they leave. If they all perish in there, the miserable sods, it's nothin' to me."

He looked for'ard. Three sailors were sitting on the hatch to the hold where the damned immigrants were kept. They were waiting for a signal from him. He shook his head and gave the order to cast off for a mooring in the deeper water of the Pool. He went below for a rum. Let 'em wait.

Heinrich Strum, who was twenty-four, was the last to leave the ship. His wife Elizabeth had gone ahead with his father and mother, and he'd stayed behind to scavenge what he could. He knotted a hunk of slightly rancid cheese inside a cloth, with a piece of bread so hard he believed he could trim his whiskers with it. He slung a large bundle of clothing on his back, as large as he could carry. The day was raw, with a cold wind blowing in from the sea, and they were going to need whatever they could manage. Where was this Stumpel? Heinrich felt a tight lump of anger growing inside him. Why was the man so late? It should be better managed than this! At least it wasn't raining.

His family was waiting for him on the quay, by the warehouse. His mother, looking weary, was sitting on a bollard, with his father standing by her. Elizabeth was holding the baby. His brother and all his sisters were there—wan Anne, just a few years younger than he was, Eva, a scrawny but determined sixteen, Jacob, who was a noisy and obnoxious twelve, and solemn little Barbara, who was just five. With them were some of the Rupperts, Adam Bauer and his son Karl, a thoughtful little lad of eight, Balthazar Merk with his sons Conrad and Lorentz.

Where was this Sieur de Stumpel?

There was no one to be seen on the quay except seamen, coal-heavers, laborers, malingerers and malefactors of all sorts. There was no sign of the smooth-talking Hessian who had persuaded them to leave their homes, nor was there any sign of his fellow officers, investors in his scheme, or any other who might represent them. Heinrich looked down the quay. There were piles of ropes, barrels, cranes, tumble-down wooden buildings, others of brick, stone, crumbling plaster. Another forest of masts, a thicket of rigging, ships moored as far as he could see, beyond the curve of the river, in the channel and on both banks. No sign at all of an agent who might be working for Stumpel, or a merchant, or anyone else they could ask. Not even a customs and excise man. Well, they'd had a surfeit of those on the journey down the Rhine. But shouldn't someone be here?

"What are we going to do?" Adam Bauer asked. "We can't just stay here."

"We can't just leave!" said Peter Strum. "Where'll we go?"

"Perhaps we can find the ships that will take us to America," Bauer suggested hopefully.

"We can't leave!" insisted Strum. "How is Sieur de Stumpel to find us? We have to be here when he comes."

If he comes, thought Heinrich. If. *If he ever comes.*

"I don't know. All I know is, we can't stay here."

Bauer looked at the river. There must have been a hundred ships, more. How could they possibly find which one was theirs? They couldn't ask anybody, no one knew their language. It could be up river, or down, or in the middle . . . A search could take days. He knew they didn't have days. They would have to be fed and sheltered before that, or they would surely perish. Some of them were already looking ashen from exhaustion.

They huddled for a time on the quayside, milling anxiously, shivering from the cold, the children tired and cranky with hunger. Once a gentleman pushed through them. They grabbed at him but he brushed them off impatiently, not understanding what they were saying.

An hour went by, another. It was clear no one was coming. Still they waited.

Then a gang of seamen armed with boat hooks and staves drove them off, as though they were so many beeves, into the drear and stony pastures of London.

They moved, just moving, not knowing where they were going, which way to turn. The alleys were dark, fetid, narrow. Slaughterhouses and tanneries were mixed in with tenements, the sewers were open pits. All around them were people, a huge throng, beggars, drovers, workmen, mechanics, drunks, artificers, carters, idlers, no one paying them any mind; there were horses everywhere, cattle on their way to slaughter; the cobblestones were slippery with dung. They had to pick their way through the offal, the debris. Wherever they looked, there were men urinating into the open gutters. The whole place stank.

Though there must have been three hundred of them or more, they seemed lost in the throng. They pressed through the network of rookeries and thieves' kitchens, moving numbly through the worst slums in the city, hovels and rotting tenements spreading up from the river to the Ratcliff Highway.

After an hour or so of aimless wandering, they came upon a white-washed church near the edge of a common, an imposing building with a large, covered portico.

Surely the church would give them aid?

Heinrich pulled on the door, but it was barred and there was no answer to his hammering.

Disheartened and exhausted, they made their way along to the common, called Whitechapel Fields, and sat down on the unkempt grass. Except for a few incurious sheep tethered to one side, it was otherwise deserted, in contrast to the teeming warrens that surrounded it. The blank walls and rat's-eye windows of the tenements stared down on them. The air was thick with smoke. There was a tavern nearby, off to one side, but none of the Palatines had any money or valuables left to pawn or barter; they'd be unable to buy anything. Nor could they have explained what they wanted—their importuning seemed like incoherent mumblings to the few Londoners who stopped to listen, and they soon hurried away. Wasn't there anyone among them who could speak this tongue-twisting language? It appeared there wasn't.

Where was Stumpel, the bastard?

By mid-afternoon the presence on the Common of a large and ragged band of foreigners had attracted knots of onlookers. They were being gawked at, like apes at a fair. Some of the families tried to make the gaping crowd understand their plight, but their unkempt appearance, and the anxious, persistent way they plucked at sleeves, made the English shy away, as though they were, indeed, a species of dangerous animal. A few youths threw stones from a safe distance.

By dusk, Stumpel had still not appeared.

As it grew dark, their dismay and weariness turned to deep anxiety, and then to something approaching panic.

What were they to do? They had nothing! Stumpel's agents had taken everything, all the little they owned; it was to have joined them in the Americas, the promised lands, their Promised Land. If he never came, they were destitute. No money, no food, no clothing, none of the necessaries of life, and no way of communicating with these people who gaped at them from afar but offered them no help. They huddled miserably together in the middle of the common. The children were crying from hunger and cold. Old Frau Knaab hunched into her shawl and petticoats on the bare ground, her family huddled around her. What were they to eat? How were they to keep warm? What of the pregnant, and the sick? What would happen to them? Some of the frail ones would surely die by the morning. Instead of their new life, their fresh start, they'd been abandoned, plundered, deceived.

Stumpel had stolen their future.

At around midnight, it started to rain.

And then, just before dawn, one of the women died.

Heinrich Strum, who saw her go, didn't know who she was. She'd joined them on the Rhine a few days down river from Bingen, and he had never learned her name. She was a thin, bony woman with a pinched face and knobby hands. After their expulsion from the hold of the Indiaman, she'd been silent, her grieving husband said, and never uttered a word again. She'd sat in the rain, her knees drawn up to her chin, and she'd died there, without a sound, not even a death rattle as she let go her grasp on life, not even a gasping breath, but just . . . stopped.

Her husband sat with her, holding her, as the sun continued its course, up there somewhere behind the gray clouds, and the chill mud she was sitting on leached into her bones, and she grew cold.

Then he left her, and Heinrich could see him walking toward the perimeter of the field, staring up at the tenements.

His dead wife sat upright where he left her, her hands clutching her skirt as he vanished into the maze of offal-filled alleys to the southwest, through Slaughterhouse Yard, past the victualing office for the Tower, and into the dank, sunless spaces of Savage Gardens and Seething Lane. Thence, he never returned. Perhaps, overcome with grief and despair, he threw himself into the river. Perhaps he was robbed and murdered, the robbers taking his shoes, for he had nothing else. Perhaps he was given a sound roof and a warm bed by some woman, taking pity on his travails.

Yes, and perhaps he has been transported by an angel up to Paradise. No one went to look for him. No one any longer had the animation of spirit that a search would have demanded.

The families gathered round the poor dead woman, laid her out, sang a psalm and said the prayers for the departed, but it was all they could do, except weep. Eventually some men carried her body to Whitechapel church, where a few of them had sheltered in the doorway the previous night, and laid her among the gravestones, on the grass.

Later, when they returned, she had gone. Scavengers had cut away her clothes and taken her to the Poor Hole near Spittle Fields church, which was where all the nameless paupers rotted, where the rats got 'em.

Their fortunes began to change because of an English baker with a heart and because of the Reverend Gustav Anthon Wachsel, the pastor of the newly commissioned German Lutheran church called St. George's on Ayliff Street, Goodman's Fields, a bit south and west of Whitechapel. The church had been built in 1762, just two years earlier, with money provided by Wachsel's uncle, a rich German pastry cook named Beckmann, who had become concerned with the souls of the many Germans working in the sugar refineries of the neighborhood.

On Thursday, August 30, there appeared the following item in the *London Chronicle*, low down on the second page, after the news from Paris of murder in the streets and before the advertisements for remedies of divers maladies, ranging from Purple Air to Secret Diseases:

"Saturday last as a baker was passing, with a basket of bread by a field in the Bow-road, where a great number of poor Palatines were lying, being informed that they had had nothing to eat for two days before, immediately threw down his basket saying, 'If that is the case, some of my customers must fast a little longer than usual to-day,' and immediately distributed the whole contents of his basket; consisting of twenty-eight two-penny loaves; and ten rolls, among them; telling them at the same time that he would call and see them again in a few days; for which generous and seasonable donation they could only thank him with signs and tears of joy, not being able to speak English."

Destitute Germans lying in a field near the Bow Road? And a great number of them, as the *Chronicle* said? How great was a great number? The baker, whose wife was a parishioner of Wachsel's, told the reverend that there must be upward of three hundred of 'em. Within the half hour, Wachsel was at the fields behind the Whitechapel.

By this time the Palatines had gone several days without any food except the baker's loaves, and many of them had sunk into apathy and misery. Even the children had ceased to cry and had taken refuge in fevered whimpering.

Few noticed as Wachsel came toward them, a small, well-filled figure with a benign aspect, marching determinedly from a gate near the church.

First there was a ripple of movement on the periphery of the crowd, an eddy of motion. Then a sound was added to the motion, a little wavelet of sound that washed over the common and swelled soon into a larger noise, with a few hoarse shouts, a shrill keening from a woman, as the news of Wachsel's arrival spread through the multitude. Most of them struggled to their feet and pressed inward, to where the reverend was surrounded by a throng. He was gesticulating and shaking hands and hugging the children, and men were crying. One woman just stood silently, her fingers on Wachsel's arm, touching him lightly to make sure he was real, that he wouldn't fade from view like a dream. Soon there was a babble of voices, a tumult, and the sound cascaded over him as he stood there, too many voices coming at him at once, stumbling over each other to make themselves heard, to pour out their pitiful tales, their fear and their anger, the fear receding now and the anger growing like a knot in the stomach as they all tried at once to tell him what Stumpel had done to them.

He held up his hands, shaking his head. He called for quiet, but no one heard. They were plucking at his garments and crying out, and pity filled his heart.

He finally quieted them, and began to talk.

By afternoon his parish had been mobilized and the relief work had begun.

There was too much to do, however, for one small congregation, no matter how diligent, and no matter the persistence and energy of its pastor.

So the Friday following, August 31, a few days after Wachsel discovered their presence in London, the *Chronicle* published his hastily scrawled letter, with a small preamble from the Printer:

"The following melancholy account of the truly distressful situation of the poor Palatines, come over here in order to be shipped off for our new-acquired settlements, has something in it so very affecting, we have inserted it as much on the behalf of those unhappy people as for the information to our readers of their deplorable necessity.

"To the Printer

"I hope you will permit me, by means of your paper, to inform those who have the power to redress it, of the very deplorable situation of the poor unhappy Palatines lately arrived here from Germany. They are in number, men, women, and children, about six hundred consisting of Wurtzburgers and Palatines, all Protestants, and were brought hither from their native country by a German officer, with a promise of being immediately sent to settle, at his own expense, in the island of St. John and Le Croix, in America; but, by inability, he has been obliged to decline the undertaking; so that instead of their being shipped off for those places, some of them have lain, during the late heavy rains, and are now lying, in the open fields adjacent to this metropolis, without covering, without money, and in short, without the common necessaries of this life; others lie languishing under the complicated evils of sickness and extreme want, at the Statute Hall in Goodman's Fields; and more than two hundred remain on board the ship which brought them over, on account of their passage not being paid for, where they are perishing for food, and rotting in filth and nastiness. Collections have been made at the German churches and chapels here, several times, to afford them some relief; but as the number of these poor creatures is so considerable, it is impossible, by such means to furnish them with a regular and continual supply, adequate to their wants; so that unless some provision is speedily made for them, they must inevitably perish. These unfortunate people would think themselves impressibly happy, if the English Government would be graciously pleased to take them under its protection; to allow them, for the present, some ground to lie on; tents to cover them; and any manner of subsistence, till it shall be thought proper to ship them off, and settle them in any of the English colonies in America; where, I doubt not, they will give their protectors and benefactors constant proofs of their affection and gratitude for such kindness, by behaving as becometh honest, industrious, and dutiful subjects to the British Government. I take the liberty of thus expressing the hopes and wishes of these wretched beings, as they have no friend to intercede for them who has interest sufficient for such an under-taking, or even the knowledge of the proper method of application.

"That their distresses are unutterably great, I myself have been too often a mournful witness of, in my attendance on them to administer the duties of my function; with one instance of which I shall conclude this melancholy detail. One of the poor women was seized with the pangs of labour in the open fields, and was delivered by the ignorant people about her in the best manner they were able; but from the injury the tender infant received in the operation, it died soon after I had baptized it; and the wretched mother, after receiving the sacrament at my hands, expired, from want of proper care and necessaries suitable to her afflicting and truly lamentable condition.

"That the almighty may, of his infinite mercy, incline the hearts of the great and good of this kingdom, distinguished for its charity and hospital-ity, to take under their protection these unhappy fellow Christians (who did not intrude themselves into this country, but were invited hither) and send them whithersoever they in their wisdom and goodness shall think proper, is the most ardent prayer of their and your most obedient servant,

"G. A. Wachsel, Minister of the German Lutheran St. George's Church, in Little Ayliff-street."

There was a small postscript:

"A subscription is opened at Batson's Coffee-house, in Cornhill, for the relief of the above poor Protestants."

Those still languishing on board were not forgotten. *The New Daily Advertiser* worried about them. On September 1 the paper wrote:

"As there are said to be 200 poor Palatines on board one ship, likely to perish for want, it is submitted to the gentlemen in the physical way, whether the long confinement of such a number of miserable objects, in so close a place, may not cause a dangerous epidemical disorder among these poor people."

Katy and Anna and Maria sat in the darkness in the dreadful hold of the Indiaman, shoulder pressed against shoulder, huddled up against each other, hugging the children. Not far away in the dank space their hus-bands crouched. Maria's Heinrich, who had said nothing for two days.

Anna's Peter, silent now, his restlessness sunk into apathy. And Katy's Abraham—where was he? She didn't know. Somewhere there, in the blackness. *Which matches the blackness in my heart*, she thought. Her black thoughts were filled with the golden curls of the deceiver, Stumpel.

How beautiful he was! And how the fairness deceived! Hadn't the pastors always said so? Beelzebub was the master of masquerade, the Changer, the face-dancer. She squeezed Anna's hand. *But I don't believe in the Tempter. I never have. It was Anna who was so taken with the man. So what was this yearning I felt after Stumpel had come, and then gone?*

In the blackness, eyes dry, the well of tears used up, she thought of their old home, and of Stumpel, and of the promised New Home, with its endless, endless forests. Then she thought of the thin gruel in the filthy buckets that the seamen brought them, once a day. *We've been in here a week! Will this ever end?* Her eyes were dry, but she cried anyway, in frustration and disappointment. She squeezed Anna's hand again.

Anna didn't respond. She was afraid of the dark, and her fear made her angry. She was near her time—what if the child came into the world in this black hell-hole? It would be born and die in the stench of shit—it wasn't fair! She was remembering her husband's banging on the deck, and his feeble bluster, and his inability made her angry too. She thought not of Stumpel but of Heinrich Strum, he with the cold black eyes, and she felt a little guilty pang, driven by her anger. How would he have reacted, struck down the gangway by a harrying, venomous rat of a sailor? She touched her belly. The baby was quiescent. *Not yet*, she whispered to herself. *Not yet.*

How many were dead, here in the black? She knew of one, at her feet; it didn't move when she nudged it, didn't move when she kicked it. Other bodies had been passed down to the end of the hold and stacked like firewood; she guessed there were rats in the dark, to gnaw at them . . . She had helped pass down one such; she didn't want to think about the flesh, so cold to the touch. A dozen, two dozen dead, lying blank-eyed in the dark.

Half an hour before noon, though none of them knew the time in the hellish blackness, there was a crash, and blessed light flooded into the hold, hurting their eyes. Wisps of cool fog again curled over the hatchway, smelling of damp and sodden wood and pitch. Maria stayed where she was, but Katy and Anna surged to their feet. The same sailor who had pushed Peter down the stairs a week earlier (had it only been a week?) peered at them from heaven. He looked angry, and he was yelling. The words were a meaningless jumble, but his intentions were clear. He jerked his thumb at them, and motioned upward.

The people in the hold surged up, clawing at the railings, unconscious of their stiff limbs, painful from stillness for days on end. The sailor was pushing and gesturing and driving them to the side of the ship, where several planks lashed together with ropes led to another ship, which in turn was tied to the quay. They stumbled over the planks onto the decking of the second ship, where more grimy sailors leered at them and jeered at their filth. Across the ship and down another gangplank to the quay itself. At the foot of the plank were three men, grinning hugely, not the malicious grin of the sailors but the welcoming smiles of family. These were Wachsel's deacons. As each of the prisoners passed, one of the deacons held out a reassuring hand, touching lightly, steadying the women, patting the children. To each as they passed, a phrase was spoken. "*Es ist alles vorüber. Ihr seid unter Freunden.*" It's over, you are among friends.

"Are you from Stumpel?" Katy asked, dazed, but the man didn't seem to understand her, and only smiled reassuringly and motioned her onward. "*Freunde!*" he called to her. "Friends!"

With Wachsel's men in the vanguard, the newly liberated Palatines stumbled through the streets of London toward Whitechapel Fields. To them, the city smelled sweet and clean, despite the coal smoke, the sewers, the pressing throng; anything would be better than the black hole in which they had been confined; anything would have smelled better.

Katy's mind swirled, like the wisps of fog that tugged at the corners of the buildings ahead of her.

The streets passed in a blur. As they rounded the corner into Whitechapel and turned onto the common, they saw the rest of their compatriots milling about. There were soldiers in the field, too, in tunics of dull blue, and a few horses, and tents were being raised. A hundred tents had been sent over from the Tower, in response to Wachsel's poignant letter, courtesy of the Marquis of Granby, or at least at his expense. Well, the tents had been moldering in the Tower in any case, not being needed for any campaign at that time, and had been sent over in care of a small company of

Dragoons who had nothing more urgent to do, no quarrelsome duchy to put to the torch, no festering nest of assassins and traitors to root out. These Dragoons, better with a blade or a halberd than a rope, were struggling to erect the tents in the dense throng of happy well-wishers and grateful Palatines; soldiers were not used to grateful hands clutching at them, especially when the hands were female, even if they were only dank and wild-eyed from want and excitable from gratitude. Still, the tents got themselves up somehow, and no sooner was one up than it was stuffed with prone bodies, drying out now, squirming and twisting to test the covering, before they wriggled out to join the throng and a new set replaced them.

Katy stared about her. What had happened here? What had happened to let them out? She saw someone she knew, young Eva, Peter Strum's girl, and demanded to know. Eva told her all, of the heroic baker, and of Wachsel, the general of the succoring army, and how some of them had been taken away to an infirmary somewhere in town, and many, no one knew how many, had died of exposure and the cold and hunger, and much more, some of which was right, and some the product of a mind still struggling from desperation toward joy, and therefore filled with what-might-bes and what-should-bes as though they were what-will-bes. Katy caught enough to understand the broad outlines, and discounted the notion that they would soon be visiting the Palace. She looked down at herself, her clothes stained and rank. Palace indeed.

Anna walked heavily toward the center of the field, her hands folded in front of her, holding her belly. She saw Philip Zimmermann, solid and solemn and reassuring, with Apolonia and their brood, four, no five, children, the youngest only two. Philip was standing with Peter Strum, who looked wearier than his sixty-six years. They were watching young Heinrich Strum, who was doing something with a tent pole. He was leaning his weight on it, straining.

Like a knight with a lance, shining black hair in contrast to Stumpel's gold, but a golden boy anyway, he's just a boy, five years younger than me. She suppressed this unexpected thought. *Why was she looking with longing on this . . . boy?*

She moved into the middle of the field and found a patch a little less muddy than the others, and sat heavily on the ground. Her husband trailed behind, and so did Katy and her Abraham, Abraham carrying the three-year-old, Rosannah.

Maria and her Heinrich joined them a few minutes later; little Katherina, who was named for Katy, her aunt, was asleep. It would be her fifth name day the following week, but no one had thought to tell her. It was not yet time for celebrations.

Before another hour had gone by, a cart pulled up. It was the same baker who had first sent out the alarm. The cart was full, bought and paid for with collections by the German congregations and a promissory note from Batson's that whatever money was needed would be promptly forthcoming. A chain of Palatines helped unload the cart of loaves and bags of beef dripping and pease porridge and mutton pies. The pies were a little elderly, but since they met their intended fate in minutes, it scarcely mattered. It was wonderful what a pie could do for morale; with a piece of pie inside and the miracle-working Reverend outside, anything began to seem possible.

The field had begun to resemble an army encampment. The hapless party of Dragoons were now set to digging a pit for a proper boghouse in the furthest corner of the common, still downwind, it should be said, from the earlier dung pile now spreading out perilously closer to the Palatines' drinking water.

Even the sun came out for a few minutes.

Wachsel was in the middle of the throng, as happy as a squire at a village fête. He had touched the hearts of Londoners. He felt giddy from the influence of his printed words.

Most of those newly released from the rank hell-hole of the Indiaman's hold sat in the middle of the field, still stunned, speechless, unbelieving. Anna started to cry, and her sister cried with her. So did their husbands, Peter and Abraham. And the children. Almost all of them wept.

These should be tears of joy, Katy thought. *Why are they not?*

The September issue of the *Gentleman's Magazine* gave what it called "Some Account of Col. Stumpel, by whose persuasion the Palatines were seduced to leave their country." Wrote the chronicler (rendering up yet another version of Stumpel's slippery military history):

"The article in our last concerning the deplorable condition of the poor Palatines, & the advertisement copied from the foreign prints discrediting Col. Stumpel, are thus accounted for: Stumpel was a captain in the British Legion during the late war, and being a soldier of fortune, offered himself to the Prussian service on the conclusion of the late peace; and was told, that if he could raise a regiment, he should have the command of it. This he undertook to do; and, by making a tour through Holland, where he had formerly been an officer, acquainting himself with the subaltern officers, and making himself agreeable to the men, he seduced many to desert, and some to enter volunteers, with promises of good encouragement. With these and some other recruits, disbanded soldiers, and idle young fellows, he presented himself to Prince Ferdinand, who recommended him to his Prussian majesty, and he received his commission; but the peace which soon followed in Germany, again reduced him to the necessity of applying elsewhere, and he came over to England, and solicited employment in the English Service. This could not be granted to a foreigner, when so many natives were dismissed; but on his boasting of the number of his countrymen he could carry over to our new settlements, provided a suitable tract of land was allotted him, the ministry was prevailed upon to grant his request, and a patent was actually made out at the proper offices for that purpose.

"With this grant he returned to Germany, and by the credit of it, and the advantageous offers he made to some young gentlemen who had credit with the common people, he prevailed with them to engage in the same project. Having so far succeeded, an association was formed, and these joint adventurers were active in the prosecution of it. By everywhere giving out what fortunes were to be raised, and estates acquired in the new settlements, many people of wealth were prevailed upon to sell their effects, and transport themselves, at their own expense, into America. The poor who offered, were either neglected, or referred from one to the other for the promised encouragement, till their number increased so fast, and their importunities became so pressing that no other shifts remained but to ship them for England, and leave them to the mercy of government. On their arrival, application was made in their behalf to the board of trade; but the forms of office prevented immediate relief; and, in the mean time, Stumpel came over, with a view to endeavor to justify his conduct and to know how his people would be received; but finding the ministry incensed, his patent revoked, and writs out against him to make good his engagements, he watched his opportunity, left the kingdom, and returned to the continent, but to what part is not yet publickly known."

Wachsel translated this dispatch for those Palatines who cared to listen. To them, the errors in the *Gentleman's Magazine* article were obvious enough. It was possible, of course, that a good many "persons of wealth" had indeed transported themselves to America at their own expense, as the dispatch said. If so, Stumpel had undoubtedly stolen their goods, and they were presently camped on the banks of some wilderness river in the Americas, waiting for a provisioner who would never come. In their own case, no application was made to the Board of Trade, as the dispatch asserted, unless it referred to some earlier unfortunates, or to Stumpel's disgruntled officers. Wachsel later showed them an article torn from *The New Daily Advertiser*, which quoted a Dutch newspaper as saying that the same Stumpel had "also engaged some young Dutchmen of good family to follow him, giving to one the title of Captain in chief of 20 families, to others those of Lieutenant, Secretary, etc." So he was still up to his tricks. Certainly he had never "come over" to England, for if he had, mayhem would have ensued, as Heinrich Strum pointed out, and the real story would have been beaten from him with cudgels. In addition, Stumpel himself had recruited them, coming himself to their villages . . .

"How do you know this was Stumpel?" asked the Reverend.

"Of course it was," said Philip Zimmermann.

"But how do you know it was him?" Wachsel persisted.

"It was clear, he made it clear himself. And he had papers . . ." Zimmermann fell silent. Which of them had read the papers Stumpel had so grandly waved at them? They had believed him because they wanted to believe him.

Could it be possible, Anna thought, *that it wasn't Stumpel at all in our village, but one of his dupes acting in his name? Could Stumpel have had a dozen false Stumpels doing his devil's work? No, it couldn't be!* She remembered him so clearly, his smell of leather and sweat, the fineness of the hair of his beard, the way he had put his hand on her thigh, there by the Nahe River, not meaning anything by it, not really.

Katy, for her part, remembered mostly his golden hair, silky as a kitten's. She looked at her sister, who looked away. *Does it matter? Does it matter if Stumpel were a chimera? We are going to America now!*

On Sunday afternoon at five o'clock, Katy stood in the middle of Whitechapel Fields singing her heart out. Her voice was shrill and she could feel its quaver, but that only made her sing the harder. The sun was out, and the Palatine encampment had a festive air, with its white tents and the new blue clothing of the men, courteously supplied by the charitable committee: blue jackets for the men, and for the boys, short blue coats; the women and girls in strong stuff gowns and petticoats. Hundreds of people lifted up their voices in the singing of thanksgiving psalms, hundreds of lusty voices soaring over the din of the capital, stopping the traffic on Whitechapel Road and quietening, for once, the raucous cawing of the whores. Katy lifted her voice and sang the glorious psalm "With God's Good Grace," squeezing out the words in English (for she was learning to mimic the language in her singing); it helped her close her heart to the past, to the dreadful days in the Indiaman, and to her apprehension for the future. Anna stood beside her, singing too. She was very near her time. Katy squeezed her hand.

Anna didn't respond. She stood quietly, her pregnancy looking oddly . . . external . . . on her bony frame.

Will the child come on the voyage? Will Anna have the space she needs? Will my sister be my neighbor in our new home? Will we be happy?

Wachsel passed on to his friends at the newspapers, who found him every evening at Batson's, an accounting of every small contribution made to the welfare of his charges. On Friday, September 7, he was able to tell them this: "Their Majesties have been graciously pleased to give £300 towards the relief of the poor Palatines."

Within ten days of the Rev. Mr. Wachsel's first intervention, a committee of eminent persons had been struck, to conclude what to do about the hapless emigrants and to decide their long-term fate. This committee was drawn from members of many coffee-houses as well as the gentry and Parliament.

One of the committee's first resolutions, taken at a meeting at Batson's, was to agree to apply to his Majesty in council, "stating their case, and praying his Majesty's directions for their settlement in such of the American colonies as shall be thought proper."

"To the King's most Excellent Majesty, The petition of Peregrine Cust, George Prescott, William Fitzherbert, Robert Nettleton, Esquires and others of your Majesties most loyal Subjects, whose names are hereunto subscribed.

"Most humbly sheweth, The upwards of 400 industrious foreign Protestants of the Palatinate, and other parts of Germany, having been seduced, from their own country, and brought into this Kingdom by the Sieur Stumpell a German officer, upon promises and assurances of encouragement and support, which he had neither authority to declare, or ability to execute; the said foreign Protestants abandoned by the said Stumpell, were reduced to great distress, and very deplorable must have been their fate, had they not been relieved by the charitable contributions of many of your Majesties loyal and well-disposed Subjects, excited, and animated thereto, by your Majesties great example.

"That the said Contributions have already amounted to a very considerable sum, and your petitioners who are a Committee chosen to manage the said Charity, are humbly of opinion, that the intention of this Charitable Contribution, cannot be answered in a manner more advantageous to the interest and happiness of the objects of it, and for the public utility, that in applying what shall remain, after their immediate wants are supplied and their support here provided for, to defraying the expense of their passage, to such part of your Majesties American colonies, where your Majesty shall, in your great wisdom, think they be settled, with the greatest advantage and propriety.

"Your Majesties petitioners, therefore with all duty, and humility, submit their intentions to your Royal Consideration, humbly beseeching, that if your Majesty shall be graciously pleased to approve thereof, your Majesty will issue your Orders, to what colony they shall be sent, and also to signify your Royal Directions to the Governor of such colony, that he do forthwith upon their arrival, give them all possible countenance, protection, and support, and cause a proper district of land, in a convenient situation, to be surveyed and allotted to them . . ."

They had raised £4072/8/9, more than four thousand pounds, not to mention the eight shillings and nine pence, and still the money poured in.

"Where are we to be sent?" Adam Bauer asked Wachsel later.

"It's not yet settled," said Wachsel. And he added, cautiously, "But not improbably South Carolina."

"Why there? Why not Nova Scotia after all?"

"I don't know," said Wachsel. "I understand the colony there is not inclined to pay for and support new immigrants at present."

"And South Carolina? What manner of place is it?"

Wachsel thought it prudent not to mention the gossip he'd heard at Batson's about the Carolina aborigines, the Cherokees, and their unfortunate habit of pillage and plunder; he judged it unwise to regale his new parishioners with vivid tales of violence. "The climate, I hear, is more salubrious than that of New Scotland," he said.

In the end, Carolina's willingness to contribute to the well-being of immigrants won the day; and the governors of that province were careful not to make too explicit their belief that one use for immigrants was to place them between the Cherokee Indians, so recently on the warpath to such disagreeable effect, and the comfortable plantations along the coast, whose proprietors had so much influence on the governance—and the prosperity—of the colony.

At Batson's, the committee responsible for finding ships to transport them, and for devising contracts with the ships' masters, drew up a list of minimum requirements, which they shopped around to those places where such men were wont to congregate. Eventually, two ships accepted the conditions, the *Dragon* and the *Union*. On September 24, the committee met again at Batson's and stipulated that the vessels would depart a fortnight hence. The committee agreed that it was necessary to "continue the subscriptions, that care may be taken in America to procure provisions for those people, till they can support themselves; and also to carry them to the lands set out for them by his Majesty's directions, that they may not be separated by private contracts, but be kept together, or in proper numbers, and settled as most useful to themselves and to the publick."

After that, the newspapers still kept an eye out for news of the Palatines but, now that their distress and want had, to the papers' own satisfaction, been relieved, their attention was more cursory.

"Thursday, Sept. 27 - Next Monday fortnight the Palatines are to embark for South Carolina."

On October 5, several members of the committee traveled down to Irongate to view the vessels they had contracted to carry the Palatines. They returned saying they feared there would scarcely be room for them all unless some modifications were made below decks. However, they knew there was no time for this: the embarkation date was a mere week away.

And so it came time to depart.

They crowded through the same cobbled and chaotic alleys they'd passed those bitter weeks ago, but their mood was utterly different. They'd become used to the reek and the poverty, and yet they noticed it more now that their own misery had abated. The cries of the street vendors, the hoots of the ragamuffins, the curses of the reeling drunks and the hard, predatory eyes of the young men had become part of the landscape they thought of as London. Their procession wound past the Shambles in Slaughterhouse Yard and the nunnery of St. Katherine's, the carriage of Mr. Cust in the lead, then several gentlefolk on horseback and then the round and beaming figure of Wachsel, his not-so-melodious voice leading the rest in song, hymns they had sung daily for so many weeks. They walked by Tower Hill, its gibbet temporarily empty of corpses, and down toward the Iron Stairs, where lighters were waiting to take them downriver to Blackwall, ten miles oceanward. Out in the stream, at anchor or floating placidly on the incoming tide, were dozens of other small boats, skiffs and gondolas filled with the idly curious gentry of the West End, come to see the conclusion of the episode that had titillated them for so many weeks.

Wachsel beamed and wept some more, Katy hugged him and wept, Maria hugged him and wept, he was hugged by so many that his ribs were bruised and so many tears fell they would have moistened the Great Desert of the Sahara. Almost two score of the Palatines were ill, some of them gravely so, and to those Wachsel said words of comfort.

To Anna and her nearly born, he said a special blessing.

She herself felt little joy, or even sorrow, only that she must endure.

The Dorsts and the Frietzes, together with their friends the Strums, the Adolphs and the Bauers, boarded the barque *Dragon*, in charge of Master Francis Hammot.

It was a pathetically small vessel for its purpose, only one hundred and eighty tons mass and ninety feet long, and in the terse notation of Lloyd's, had "a plain stem, no head, and square transom wales, flat floors, hard bilges and vertical sides." It was, in short, a broad-sterned ship with no ornament, a copper-bottomed but utilitarian vessel, nothing in it to stir the heart. Its two forward masts were square-rigged and its rear mast rigged fore and aft. It was expected to do twelve to eighteen knots in a good wind, even deeply laden as it was.

Just a hundred and eighty Palatines crowded into this fragile little home.

The other vessel, the *Union*, was also classified as a barque and was smaller yet, only one hundred and sixty tons. It, too, was sheathed in copper. It drew thirteen feet. Its master, James Smith, had a hundred and forty-five people under his care.

Twenty-five of them were judged too ill to make the voyage and were left at Gravesend, an ominous name, until or if they recovered; they would be shipped in a third vessel, the *Planter's Adventure*, under Captain Lonley, along with the entire party's baggage, meagre as it was.

Of the five hundred or so adults who had left their homes with such optimism those few short weeks ago, only three hundred and fifty actually embarked. A hundred and fifty had perished or vanished.

Forty more would die on the voyage.

High tide at London Bridge that day was just before noon. Less than two hours later, both vessels lifted anchor and caught the ebb.

They were, once again, on their way.

Once again, Katy Frietz, once again we go. She felt the first faint stirrings of optimism, overlaid with apprehension. *No more storms, no more setbacks, Stumpel consigned to history . . . Can it be true?* She wondered where the rogue had gone. Did she any longer resent him? He was slipping away, as surely as the water beneath their hull.

But . . .

She remembered that the Reverend Wachsel, in telling his tales of the cities now arising in the western colonies, had described the earliest mariners' maps of the Western Hemisphere, on which there were large blanks representing the Unknown; in these blank spaces on the map could be seen the forbidding phrase, "Here Be Dragons." She had laughed, then, at those timorous cartographers. Now she wondered. *We have faced monsters of our own,* she thought. Then she shivered, and went to look for her sister, Anna, so pregnant with promise.

After that, silence in the London papers. The Palatines were to become an American story. Wachsel fell back to his regular life's work, that of attending to his parishioners' souls. The King, undoubtedly, thought no more of his new Carolinian subjects, if indeed he ever had. But his benevolence, or at least the benevolent interventions of his ministers, would have a lasting effect on the fate of the persons they had so generously rescued, and color their attitudes toward the momentous events they were to undergo. Heinrich Strum in particular kept in his mind a picture of that Royal benevolence that was never to be shaken, even long years afterward, when he lay dying in another tent on a faraway shore, after giving everything for a hopeless Royal cause.

There was one small footnote to their London sojourn. In December, Baron Behr of Ansbach wrote to his esteemed friend the British Secretary of State that one Stumpel had been arrested, and that the British minister at Hanover had taken steps to see that "there should be taken from him the English documents of which he had been making such bad use."

Three

Katy looked over at Anna, began to speak, thought better of it. *If I ask her what she remembers first about America, she will say, "Breathing the free air after the stench of the voyage." But that won't be right. It will be a lie. As for me, I remember only fragments: words of English, the crack of the overseer's whip, glaring red eyes, the trees they called palmettos, snatches of German in foreign parts, dust, always dust, heat, always heat. No thought then of freedom.*

But Anna was not thinking of freedom. The weight of her years was focused on two bony buttocks pressing into the bench. *I feel as old as the rocks, twice as heavy. And what do I remember? I remember the serpent's tooth, the treacherous killer in its bright disguise. How much, I wonder, is that picture colored by what followed? How politics perverts memory.*

February 1765
Charlestown, South Carolina

The *Dragon* slipped across the bar on the rising tide and into Charlestown harbor at very first light on December 14, 1764. The weather was clear, just a few degrees above frost; there was a brisk chill wind from the north, perhaps the least complicated direction for a ship to enter the harbor; the morning watch had to do little but alert Captain Hammot and drop sail, leaving aloft just enough to waft the boat toward the town.

The vessel lurched once as it crossed the bar and then was steady; a soft plap, plap, plap replacing the uneven thumping of the open sea. Even the creaking of the rigging seemed dampened, muted. The headlands to the right and left were low, flat, gray-brown behind lumpy, pale dunes. The bay seemed broad and featureless. The town itself lay ahead on a peninsula between two sluggish river estuaries.

Below, the emigrants were waking. Most lay, in the sleep of the exhausted, on their tiered bunks. Broad as these were, they were crowded, three bodies, four, sometimes more to a bunk, a family to a tier, such privacy as there was gained behind canvas curtains crudely spiked to the decking above. The air was fetid and rank, though few of them noticed it any more. It had grown worse over the nine weeks of their crossing, the stench of fever overlying the sourness of infantile dysentery, the reek of unwashed bodies, the dusty smell of the aged and the other odors of a small vessel on a long voyage—slops buckets, canvas and tar, moldy food.

When the fevers had come, they took these smells for the smells of death. By now they were commonplace, and the dead and dying seemed no more rank than the living.

Eva Strum was the first to sense they had arrived in America.

She reached through the canvas and shook her father awake. Heinrich and Elizabeth were intertwined with the baby, Anna, snoring softly. There was no sign of Jacob.

Katy was lying awake in the next bunk, her arm around Rosannah, Abraham against her back. She was thinking of nothing very much, except what she called her "rutting thoughts."

Well, there are worse ways to greet a new world!

She heard the Strum girl.

"Papa!" said Eva, "Papa! We're here! We are where we're going!"

Irritated, Peter shook her off. After nine weeks at sea, and as many deaths and more among his friends, the voyage had taken on its own more than malevolent character. It seemed as if it would never end. They sailed on, and on, and on, ennui punctuated by the prayers for the dead. He closed his eyes.

"Papa!" Eva said again. "We've arrived!"

"Go," he mumbled.

"No, a sailor told me . . ."

"I told you to stay away from them," he said, automatically and without heat. He swung his feet to the deck and stood up, clutching a stanchion for support. By God! She was right! The battle with balance, the struggle to stand upright on a lurching deck, was over. He made his way to the gangway, still half expecting the sway of a swell that never came, the rise and fall of a floor that was never still. She was right! The voyage was over! They were in America! He pushed aside the hatch, flinching slightly at the chill air, and climbed up.

At his cry, half the people jammed into their bunks came awake, startled. Katy swung her legs down and ran to join him.

Charlestown was approaching fast, gliding to embrace the ship in an amber, early-morning glow, gold and coral and greenish blue brightening to white and pink and cerulean as the sun cleared the horizon. The sailors were lowering the remaining canvas; blocks squealed and tackles creaked. The wharves loomed, the slimy weed of the tideline, the heavy log fenders in coils of rope, here and there a person going about his business. Americans, going about American business! Heinrich and Elizabeth, still groggy, climbed up beside Peter. Heinrich wondered what it was these Americans were doing, when they had come, how they had felt, what their lives were like, how they would be toward newcomers. Then the last of the heavy canvas dropped to the deck and the ship nuzzled in with a slight jar and a shudder.

A crewman threw a looped rope at a heavy wooden bollard, and missed. A stranger, who had been sitting on a pile of planking, strolled over to help. The vessel was secured fore and aft, and a gangway lowered. An official party of some sort climbed up and disappeared in the direction of the captain's quarters.

They could see nothing but a few warehouses, the town itself now obscured by the ships, sixty or seventy vessels, some standing out in the harbor, most secured to the mile or so of timbered wharves and quayside. There were piles of coiled, tarred rope, puncheons of some sort of fish.

One by one, then in twos, in families and finally in a rush, most of the rest of the emigrants tumbled onto the deck, crowding to the railing to see what they could see.

A colonist, a Carolinian, one of the boarding party, stood by the gangway to make sure no one got off. He carried a weapon slung over his shoulder. He didn't look much like a soldier—he wore the same homespun clothing as others on shore—but he acted like one; he had the mistrustful eyes of a professional guardian.

"*Sind Sie von hier, von Amerika? Sind Sie Amerikaner?*" one of the emigrants asked, getting only a blank look in return.

It's over because it's over, Katy Frietz, she told herself. *It's over. America!*

She stood in the middle of the deck and stared toward the town, smudgy with morning smoke and patchy mist. Somewhere up there, beyond the edge of the world, was the great land mass in which they'd find their new home. Everything looked somehow different. But how? The men were men, the wharf was a wharf, ropes were ropes . . . But the air smelled different, and the men walked with a purposeful air that seemed different, and the clothes . . . the clothes were quite different, less . . . what? She couldn't quite put her mind to it. They somehow suited the purposeful men; some were made of chamois the color of old butter . . .

She thought of fetching her sister, but resisted. Anna was lying downstairs, the newborn, little Peterkin, on her belly, folded in her bony arms.

So he came into life in the hold of a ship after all. Not the stinking black hold of the Indiaman, but the stinking hold of the Dragon *instead.*

She laughed quietly to herself.

Well, he was born neither in the Old Home nor the New. She wondered what his life would be like.

What a difference knowledge makes to mood! In the Indiaman, Peterkin would have been born in stench and shit and would almost certainly have died in the blackness, nobody knowing anything, or caring. In the Dragon *. . . He had been born in stench and shit here, too, but we knew where we were going, on our way to Home. And so the pain and the blood of birthing meant nothing.*

Anna crooned over him as if he were baby Jesus himself.

Not that this voyage hadn't held its own terrors. After two weeks at sea, the fever had come, the ship's fever, "Palatine fever" as the seamen called it, grumpily dumping the bodies overboard, typhus as it would later be called. Twenty of them had died at sea of this distemper, and another twenty or so were at death's door.

For a time, they'd feared they might all be taken.

The victims burned with the fever, and ached, and then for a while the demons entered and they shrieked, not knowing what they were shrieking, then they lapsed into the silence from which they never emerged.

And when they died their vermin left them for warmer hosts.

Katy scratched and itched, as they all did, but otherwise had suffered only from seasickness.

They had made a good swift passage, nine weeks in all. This was not a record—one of the sailors told them he'd once crossed in twenty days—but many vessels, unlucky with the wind, took three months and more.

And, of course, some never arrived.

The *Dragon*'s captain sent for Frederick Meyer, one of those who had learned passable English in London and had soldiered for some years in the elector's army and who had, because of it, more or less appointed himself spokesman for the group. While they were at sea, Meyer had spent many days in the captain's cabin, probing him for information on Charlestown, on America and especially on the wild place to which they were consigning their lives—the place the captain called the Back Country. Meyer had learned a great deal, mostly about the coast. Of the interior the captain had little knowledge, and of the Indians, only lurid rumors. These, Meyer, like Wachsel before him, prudently kept to himself.

He stayed in the captain's quarters until mid-morning, taking instruction, he explained later, from the agents appointed by the London committee to look after their arrival, two Charlestown merchants, William Woodrop and Andrew Cathcart. They were all free to visit the town, he reported, but they should be back before nightfall. They were to sleep on the ship until they were ready to leave for their new land. There'd be formalities to fulfill the following day. Everything was going as planned.

The other ship, the *Union*, was already here. It had arrived a mere two days earlier. The passengers were still on board. They would all be let off together.

The sick, however, would have to stay where they were. The town wanted no sickness visited on it.

The soldier who wasn't a soldier stood aside to let them ashore, but it was a few minutes before anyone ventured to take him up on it. Finally, most of those who could made their way gingerly down the gangplank to the cobbled quay, unsteady on the unfamiliar firmness.

The wharf was alive with noise and smells. So many voices! There were French voices, and Portuguese, and the vowel-full sounds of Spain, rolling sibilants among the clipped, short familiars.

One of the children squealed and pointed. She'd seen a man burned, like coal, and oiled, so the charcoal glistened. His eyes were red and rolling, red eyes . . . He was only half dressed and shoeless in the chill air, and was carrying a heavy burden up the wharf.

Of course they'd heard of the blacks, but had never seen one.

He was the first slave they saw.

There were others like him, many others. Some were unloading a ship just west of the *Dragon*; they'd formed a human chain to pass down heavy sacks from the deck, piling them carelessly on the wharf under the desultory supervision of a white man; the gang was chanting, a deep and melancholy baritone. The sounds were exotic and alien, and pierced like a wound.

There was a sickly-sweet smell in the air, and too much dust, and horses and many, many carts. Almost sixty years later Katy still remembered the plaintive cries of the slaves at the impromptu slave market further up the wharf, and the banter and joking of the factor and the merchants and the plantation agents come to see what new breeding stock was to be had (for they had heard a Malagasy ship was unloading, the meanest but strongest of slaves) and though it was just a jumble of incomprehensible sounds and smells then, a bucket full of newness, when she was old she could still see the chains and smell the fear and hear the shuffling of many bare feet, so like the restless shifting in the cow biers at night, and sometimes it gave her nightmares. A few of the immigrants stood and gaped as the slaves were loosed from their shackles one at a time to be prodded and poked and their gums examined, their aprons whisked aside so the factors could assess their sexual parts.

Beyond the docks was the pretty, pastel town, which had been lost temporarily behind the chaos of the wharf; many of the houses were framed by the oddest trees of stiff, spiky leaves, a round clump of spikes on a thick, coarse, hemp-like trunk.

Charlestown was one of the three or four cities of North America whose level of sophistication could actually rival much of Europe. Its inhabitants envied the British, and emulated them in everything, and the town, though colonial, had an urbane air.

Peter Strum, along with Adam Bauer and Balthazar Merk, spent the morning on the dockside, trying to find out where they'd be going, and when. Others—Heinrich and Jacob, Elizabeth and Eva, along with the Frietzes and the Dorsts—explored the town. The babies stayed with Maria Strum and her daughter Anne, who refused to leave the ship.

The town itself was small, no more than a mile by half a mile, just beginning to spread beyond its old walls. Jacob and Eva ducked into an alleyway and disappeared. Heinrich and Elizabeth continued up the main street into the heart of activity. Anna and Katy went with them. Their husbands had wandered off elsewhere.

Well-named, Broad Street was a thoroughfare grander in scale than the town would seem to justify. It was lined with substantial houses, many of them rising three or more floors. Some were of plain brick. Others were of stucco or clapboard. They jostled the street; shop fronts displayed their wares in multi-paned, eye-level windows. Others, more reserved, were raised above the hoi polloi. These were the offices of the merchant traders, of lawyers, shippers, town agents of the great planters. There were many inns and taverns, all of them crowded, pouring their beery conviviality, so familiar to the German immigrants, onto the sidewalks.

Around the corner, on Church Street, they passed some of the homes of the gentry, close to the street, their formal gardens, courtyards, kitchens and liveries tucked tidily out of sight behind. The face they showed the public was neat and severe, despite the light-hearted pastels. Some of the front doors were elegantly trimmed in brass, with three or four steps descending directly into the traffic. Some houses, newer and narrower, had entrances that let into the ends of vast, double-storied verandahs to the side that overlooked their gardens. Though they were more "colonial" than the mansions of London the Palatines had glimpsed as they poked timidly about the West End, they seemed no less grand, no less affluent, no less gracious, no less comfortable. Obviously there was great wealth in the Carolina colony. Heinrich felt himself filled with the richness of possibility and opportunity—*we could live like this in a few years!*

Two steeples dominated the skyline, those of St. Michael's and St. Philip's, both of them tall and slender and tiered like wedding cakes.

There were other churches, of course, mostly just beyond the town's perimeter, smaller and less grand. Later that morning, they sought St. John's Lutheran, reaching it by a tiny lane between walled back gardens overflowing with lushness—palms and palmettos, leathery hollys, towering magnolias and azaleas, tea-olives and other exotics. Although it was well into February, everything was still very green. A few trees were in flower, one burdened with scarlet berries. A lush, spicy smell lingered in the air. The little Lutheran church was severely plain, made of white clapboards. The curious grave-markers of the Lutheran dead surrounded the building—two posts with a sort of bedstead affair between them, on which were carved or painted the memorial and comforting words to the deceased.

Anna and Katy, Heinrich and Elizabeth met Jacob and Eva in the graveyard garden. There were others from the *Dragon* there, too. Philip Knaab and his mother, and two of the Merk kids, Conrad and Lorentz.

A group of women strolled by, and one of them called out: "*Seid Ihr Ankömmlinge—jetzt erst angekommen? Wilkommen in Charlestown!*"

They were speaking German!

The colonials, smiling widely, knew exactly how the newcomers felt—that smothering, deadening gag of incomprehension gone, vanished for the first time in months, the frustrating struggle for new words to describe new experiences in a foreign tongue. So they were not surprised when the words came pouring out, many talking at once, the sentences tumbling over each other; memories of their fright at being abandoned in England, of the dreadful days in the ship's hold, of the miserable wait in the tents, of their uncertainty as to their destination . . .

"We were rescued by the King!" one of the children chirped.

"By the King himself, is it true?" One of the women, comfortably German like a burgher from Kreuznach, raised her eyebrows skeptically.

"Well," said Katy, "maybe not himself, but with his permission. We're grateful to the King for letting us come here."

"We'll see," the woman said, "if you're so grateful after a couple of years in this place."

She caught a warning glance from one of the others—it was not yet common to be openly skeptical about the unalloyed benefits of his gracious Majesty—and smiled. "Come," she said. "There are not so many Germans here, but there are some. And we live together, and make our way in the world. We're going home. Will you follow?"

She led them back in the direction of the waterfront and turned into Stoll's Alley, a roadway little wider than a cart. This narrow alley was edged with small, two-storey houses in brick, stucco and wood, mimicking the grander houses on Church Street. The grand piazzas were missing, but the tall garden walls were overflowing with trees and flowering shrubs. Some of them shared an arched cartway leading to a courtyard, and in a few cases, the house proper could only be entered through a workshop or storeroom on the ground floor.

They stopped at a small house freshly painted in a pastel pink; the stone step was polished and the brass knob gleamed. From a shop next door came the pungent smells of sauerkraut and smoky sausages and hard yellow cheese; more German voices could be heard from within.

"This is where we live," the Charlestown woman said, her arm taking in the neighborhood. "We live, and we work, and we do well. Are you going to be staying in town?"

"*Nein*," said Heinrich. "We've been granted land. They told us it's in the Back Country."

The woman, catching another warning glance (this one a plea not to disillusion the emigrants to no purpose about their new home), said nothing.

"We're from Hesse and the Rheinpfalz mostly," she said, opening the door to her house. "Where do you come from?"

"Hunsrück," Anna said. "Oberstein."

"No wonder you're here," she said. She smiled to show she meant no offense, and shepherded her sisters inside. "I hope things go well with you," she said as she closed the door.

Heinrich, thinking of the decaying stores of food in the *Dragon*, went into the shop to get some cheese, but he had no money and he found the storekeeper, though cordial, flint-hearted about samples, and came away empty-handed.

On their way back to the boat, they passed the charred ruins of one of the great houses. Young Jacob Strum was standing in front of it, staring into the debris.

"One of the black ones burned it down," he said. "One of the slave persons. A German boy told me. Made a fire too hot and burned the whole thing down. Told me they do that all the time, the black ones. That's why the kitchens are not in the house."

"If the kitchen's not in the house, how did the house burn down?" someone asked reasonably.

"That's what they told me," Jacob said. "Took coals into the house and just burned it down."

"On purpose?"

"They didn't say, but I think so. They flogged her until she died."

"Jacob!"

The remonstrance was half-hearted. The black masses, so unknown and unknowable, made them uneasy. Only dangerous animals were chained, and they chained the blacks here when they could . . . They thought of the strange scene on the wharf, the huddled bodies, the cries and the wailing, the whips and fetters. Were these blacks poor, pathetic creatures or demons? Anna thought back to the sailor on the *Dragon* who'd told them yarns about the naked savages of the great American interior. Or so he had described them. He'd implied there were endless thousands of them, who lived in thoughtless cruelty and who would kill and burn houses and carry off the women whenever they could. The sailor hadn't mentioned slaves, a hostile force imported into the very households of the colonists. Danger without and danger within . . . *Some American customs we should never, ever adopt.*

When they returned to the ship, they found most of the passengers from the Dragon and the Union milling about the dockside. Frederick Meyer was standing on a bale of something, yelling to make himself heard. No one was paying much attention. A cart rumbled by, piled high with cargo. Men climbed up and down the gangways with fresh water and provisions. Peter Strum was sitting on a crate nearby.

"They buried another five today," he said grimly. "Among them both the Kunold boys, Mathew and Johans. I suppose that's just as well. They were the last of their family left—the whole family gone. Another five gone, and more to follow, I fear. A dozen, at least. And my wife has taken to her bed. Says she doesn't feel well, that her hands and feet are aching . . ."

He pointed to a lumpish, sullen-looking boy standing nearby. "Henrick," he said, "Henrick Sanbrick. He's the last of his family. Told me today he's not going with us. Not going to claim his land, the poor fool. He's seventeen, quite old enough. I told him we'd help him, do everything we could to set him up. But he's staying here. Already got work as a drover."

He called the boy over. "Tell them what you told me," he said.

"I'm not the only one who doesn't want to go," the boy said, his face red and puffy from days of crying. "There are many others. The Stanhold family aren't going. They've already decided to set up as bakers here. I think some of the Webers want to stay if they can—Georg will go, but the rest want nothing to do with Indians. I think Rachel is also going to stay. A family came down and offered her a place with them. She'll work for them. It's a good family."

"Which Rachel is that?"

"You know, my friend Rachel," he said, unhelpfully. "She came with her mama, but her mama's gone off."

Katy remembered her then, though she couldn't recall the family name. She was a determined, plain girl of sixteen or seventeen, whose bunk had been three or four over from theirs. Her mother had "gone off," as the boy put it, early in the voyage, one of the first to catch the fever. She supposed the Charlestown family, whoever they were, would get good work out of her. She was strong and not at all frivolous. She wondered how they'd learned about her.

The boy wandered off as Meyer, finally getting through in a lull in the hubbub, yelled at them to be quiet.

"Unless you listen," Meyer shouted, "we'll never get anything done." He waved his arms for emphasis. "Tomorrow morning we go to the Governor's offices. We have to be officially received, say the oath of loyalty to the King. Those of you who can sign must do so. I'll help, and some others. Unless you take the oath, you won't get any land. You won't get anything—money, wagons, tools, guns, seed, plows, anything."

"How do we know what land we're getting?" someone yelled.

"Quiet!"

He explained that the Assembly had recently incorporated four new townships on the frontier. He recited the names, and though they meant nothing to anyone, they cherished the resounding English polysyllables: Boonsborough on Long Cane Creek; Hillsborough, near the junction of Long Cane and the Little River; Londonborough on Hard Labour Creek; and Belfast on Stevens Creek, a little to the south-east. Hillsborough was to be their new home.

"As soon as the oath-taking is over, a small party will leave for the place where our land is. Each family should name someone to represent them, to look after your concerns and your needs. This party will begin preparation for your arrival, meet the surveyors, start to lay out the farms, build some shelters. There will be guides, people who know the place . . . The main party will wait here until the *Planter's Adventure* arrives with the rest of the baggage and those who had to stay behind. Or those of them," he amended, "who survived. It should be here within a few weeks."

There was an uproar, and he shouted it down. "Argue about it later, but pick someone you trust. Everybody must be here on the wharf after sun-up tomorrow. We will go from here to the Governor's place."

Easy enough, Katy thought. *Abraham will go to find our land. Peter will go for Anna. Heinrich for the Strums. Someone for everyone. Off on the wilderness road.*

The road to the edge of the world. Or is it the road to where the world begins?

In the morning, the plans had changed somewhat. Frederick Meyer, who had gotten himself appointed Justice of the Peace by the Lieutenant Governor's office and so would represent the majesty of the law in the interior, such as it was, called upon the men of the advanced party to accompany him to the Governor's mansion, where they were somewhat curtly refused admission and redirected to the Provincial Council. This Council was, in the absence of the Governor's veto, the effective governing body of the Carolinas; it represented the planters and Charlestown itself. The Back Country, despite a growing population, was hardly represented at all, which was, as they would find out, a source of considerable grievance.

"They wouldn't let us in," Abraham told Katy when they returned. "We sat outside. Afterward, someone came out and told us what had gone on."

"And?"

"Mr. Bull was speaking about us."

"Who's he?"

"The Lieutenant Governor. As far as I can see, he governs more than the Governor. Then his man came to Meyer, who told us Mr. Bull had sent a message to a man called Patrick Calhoun to go where we are to be settled and to build us a shelter against the weather and that a Mr. Fairchild, the Deputy Surveyor, is to proceed with us and lay out our lands for us. Oh, and he also said this Calhoun, who he called Captain Calhoun, had orders to meet us along the way with a detachment of Rangers, which I suppose are soldiers, and guide us to our land. The advance party will go on horseback and should be there in a few days. The rest will stay here, sleeping on board until the third ship comes and the wagons are ready."

"What happened next?" Katy asked.

"We took the Oath of Allegiance," Meyer said. "We were called in and we took it."

"To the King," Abraham said. "An oath of loyalty. Then we marked papers where Meyer told us."

As the Council minutes later put it, "Several of them attending they were called in when they were sworn to their petitions and also took the Oath of Allegiance."

"I suppose," Abraham added ingenuously, "we're now Americans."

There were many questions: how would they know whose land was whose? What could they do if they didn't like the land selected for them? What would they be given to take with them? Would they have seed? Guns? Plows?

Katy and Abraham would get at least a hundred and fifty acres, that was clear. Maybe more—how much for a daughter? Catherine and Mary were surely eligible. And Anna was eleven, wouldn't she get some? And young Peter, who was nine? Or was sixteen the age at which a person was given land? Someone had said fifty for each child, but others said no. Which was it? Anna and Peter would only get the hundred and fifty, that was easy. Newborns wouldn't get land, and little Peterkin was so far their only child. What about Maria and Heinrich Adolph? Their eldest was six, young Katy. Elizabeth was only four and the baby just a baby.

Charlestown paid no attention when the advance party clattered out of town a little after noon. But a few of the more curious did gather when the wagon train carrying the rest of them left several weeks later. Even Charlestown didn't have convoys of thirty laden wagons leaving every week.

Those wagons were laden with produce that had been carefully measured, rationed to the ounce. Twenty years earlier, the Carolina Assembly had passed a Bounty Act, offering immigrants transportation to the frontier, provisions for a year, tools and livestock. Everything was spelled out, and rich though the colony was, the factors made sure minimums weren't exceeded. Each family received £10 in gold to help build a house. Each person over twelve was given three hundred pounds of salted beef, fifty pounds of pork, two hundred pounds of rice, eight bushels of corn and one bushel of salt. Under twelves got half these quantities. Tools and seeds for the first year were also supplied. Each man received an ax and two hoes, one wide and one narrow; there was a crosscut saw for every five people. And every family of five persons got a cow and a calf.

"And bulls?" Heinrich asked.

Meyer went to ask.

"One bull for ten cows," he reported.

"What about pigs?" Katy asked.

Meyer sighed, went off again.

"No pigs. Plenty of wild pigs to shoot. And there are people already in the Back Country who have pigs. Persuade them to part with a pregnant sow."

Just before they left, guns and ammunition were distributed from the Royal Stores "as needed." Every household received at least one firearm.

They would need more, many more, in the years to come. Guns, and ammunition too. Ammunition without end.

There were some two hundred and thirty people in the party, if you didn't count children or the carters and drovers and guards, almost a hundred fewer than had set out from London those many weeks before. The fever that had killed so many on board ship had carried off another four dozen in Charlestown.

It was a great relief to be on their way at last. It was an admirable day, pleasantly and surprisingly sunny and dry. As slowly as they moved, the wagons threw up clouds of fine, gray dust. The road was straight and firm and warm under foot, and the walking was easy. The walled yards gradually gave way to fields and plantations, most with avenues of spreading live oaks, still in leaf though it was winter, and draped with pale mosses and lichens. Down these avenues the curious could sometimes spy the sprawling houses of the plantation gentry. The black faces at work by the side of the road, by now familiar, no longer even exotic, hardly looked up, paying no attention.

The sun was warm; its light dappled through the moss-draped old trees, many of them huge. In a while these ancient forests thinned, replaced by towering pines and nearly naked gums. The spiky palms of the coast had already vanished. There were flocks of exotic birds; a flight of bright blue jays, noisy and quarrelsome, skimmed past, to settle in the stubble of a field. Here and there the settlers caught a glimpse of the river's reeds, lush and abundant, promise of future fields of waving wheat, heavy and golden, ripe for the sickle. Occasionally the convoy made a detour to skirt a swamp, where bare trees spread downward into the brackish water as fluidly as they did upward into the sky, branches and tendrils in a crazy jumble. One of the children, Philip Zimmermann's thirteen-year-old, the exotically named Adalalia, reported that a drover had told her huge lizards lived in the swamp, large enough to swallow a man. Nobody believed the story. High above, vultures wheeled and circled. The party passed a few on the ground, tearing at a hare's carcass. They were ugly and wrinkled, with bare heads in raw red and dusty gray; they regarded the travelers without fear. Peter Strum tried out his new weapon and shot one of them; the other birds paid no attention and continued their meal. The drovers advised the proud shooter to save his lead for more necessary game.

In mid-afternoon, Strum left the roadway to scoop up a handful of soil. He fingered it, rolling it on the ball of his thumb, shaking his head. It felt too fine, too dry, dusty, without texture, useless for crops. He hoped it would be better where they were going.

"How far it is?" he asked one of the drovers, trying out his rudimentary English.

"'Bout two hunderd mile," he said.

"How much is mile?"

"Take couple weeks," the drover replied.

He advised the men not to worry about the soil. The land would change character several times before they reached their stopping point.

"This is mostly swamp down here. We'll be out of it, maybe in a day. Then we'll be on the plain for seventy-five mile or so. Then there's some mile of sand, then we climb up to a plateau. That's where your land will be."

"What it like there?"

"Good land. Rolling hills. Farms and villages on the flat tops. Beyond that . . . Indian lands. And beyond that, mountains. More Indian lands. You won't be going there."

They camped that night by a swamp, sleeping uneasily despite the fires tended by the drovers. The forest felt oppressive and heavy. The woods were too . . . *busy* . . . with crashings, slitherings and rustlings, furtive movements, sudden cries and an occasional howl. Katy lay awake most of the night, the *sense* of the place whirling around in her mind, mixed with dreams of swamp and fever. The strangeness of the port, of the town and its people, the outlandish and secretive blacks of the slave markets, these exotic woods, where nothing was familiar and everything over-ripe, rotting . . . *Is this what we left our homes for?*

She fell asleep just as the drovers yelled to get them all awake again.

In the morning, the mood lightened. But just after midday, something happened to plunge them back into gloom.

It began in child's play. Young Jacob Strum precipitated it. He was wearing a knee-length "beard" of stringy gray moss he'd pulled from a branch and tied over his ears and was clumping about with a staff, bossing some of the smaller children. Christian Beckman, half his age and half his size, had been darting between the slow-moving wagons, as skittish and unpredictable as a puppy. He clambered onto a rotten stump, reaching for a strand of the moss, and crashed through, scraping his ankle on the bark. His bare foot brushed the outer coil of a sleeping snake, a pretty little red-banded thing that resentfully nipped him on his large toe before sliding away. Christian, frightened and howling, was taken up on the cart with Anna Barbara, his mother, to comfort him.

She washed his cut and bound it.

"It was a snake," said Jacob. "I saw it and it went off."

"It's just a cut," Christian's mother said.

"What kind of a snake?" asked the boy's father, Albrecht.

"So long," said Jacob, holding his arms out. "As long as an arm."

"What color?" one of the drovers asked.

"Red," said Jacob, who knew his colors in English.

"And yellow too? Striped? Red and yellow and black?"

"Red. No yellow," the boy said. He hadn't remembered any yellow but couldn't explain that he wasn't sure—he'd only caught a glimpse before the creature had rustled into the leaves.

"Better hope so," the drover said. "Bad otherwise. Very bad. Coral snake as bad as it gets."

The bite didn't hurt, Christian said, but he complained of a headache. After a while his face started to swell, his lips ballooning until they looked like uncooked bread dough.

He slept with difficulty, breathing rapidly. An hour later he woke, and this time his throat hurt, and his back, and his skin, it hurt to touch, everything hurt, and he started to cry, the sobs wracking his little body. He closed his eyes, because the light hurt too.

"Coral snake for sure," the drover said, and then he spat and walked off. "Better dig a grave," he said. "Coral snake."

Shortly Christian began to thrash about, in pain and frustration and anger, and then he started to vomit, retching in great, heaving sobs. After which he quieted and lay still, and great quantities of saliva ran through his puffy lips onto his mother's lap, and a few minutes after five he shuddered once, and his body quivered like a sail missing the wind, and then he died.

Anna clutched baby Peter to her. Her dominant emotion was anger. *Nothing can take him from me!*

The days went by, somehow. The sun was warm at noon, but at night they huddled around the fires, filled with gloom and foreboding. The boy's death affected them all severely; the sickness on the ships had been dreadful but, in its merciless way, normal; they didn't want to think of a serpent's poisoned tooth as a symbol of their new home. They could take no comfort from the night sounds and queer sights of the forests, and the bright snake, as pretty as a child's plaything, made them all afraid.

They had left behind the rice and indigo plantations and were traveling through pine forests, with occasional tall, leafless hardwoods. From time to time a field or opening in the woods suggested the presence of a farm, but there were no houses to be seen, only the occasional hut. Just as often they saw the ruins of a farmstead or a charred clearing.

Several times the convoy passed a tavern, a rude structure in the woods, sometimes doubling as a general store of some kind, and once or twice attached to a meeting hall that itself served as a church. They stopped at one such, and poked about. The "church," which was made of logs, wasn't chinked, and the roof had holes in it. Everything looked crude and unfinished. There was rubbish in the forecourt and a weed-entangled broken wagon blocked the side door. It was dispiritingly primitive.

Every few days they were passed by a train of carts loaded with deer-skins bound for market in Charlestown. The drovers invariably exchanged words, but what they said no one knew. If it was news, they kept it to themselves. Once, a dozen or so Indians strode silently by; the drovers were wary and watchful, but again, they said nothing. The settlers were fascinated, especially Jacob, to whom the Indians had already become figures of romantic menace. None appeared to be armed, except with crude axes of some kind, and they passed without expression or greeting, vanishing down the road behind them, swallowed by the emptiness.

The advance party had made its way up-country without incident.

On the evening of the fourth day after they had set out at a gallop from Charlestown, Heinrich Strum slumped wearily on the ground, his back against a rock. He could see nothing of his surroundings except a jumble of rocks. It was late dusk but not yet dark, everything a flat gray, without definition or perspective. Fairchild had pushed them very hard; he wanted to make his rendezvous with Calhoun, for Calhoun was an impatient man who took unkindly to being kept waiting. This morning they'd risen before sun-up and had crossed a curious inland desert at a dead run. Then, where the sands ended, Fairchild abruptly halted them, and they stopped at the entrance to a small defile, tangled with deadfalls and craggy rocks, damp and oozing, as though the cut were a wound and earth were leaking.

"We'll wait here, without fire, for Calhoun," he said, stripping the saddle from his horse.

Heinrich had ridden the four days with Peter Dorst and Heinrich Adolph; directly behind them were Abe Frietz, Adam Bauer and the Zimmermann brothers. The other twenty or so were strung out behind, and Fairchild had ridden alone in the vanguard. None of them had exchanged more than a few sentences the whole trip; by day they were pushed too hard to speak, and at night they were exhausted. Each man kept his thoughts to himself; Heinrich's revolved around his land, his child and his companions. He'd ridden side by side with Dorst for four days, and though he didn't warm to him, had come to admire his quickness and his readiness for confrontation. He sighed, leaning back against the rock. He'd seen Dorst's wife looking at him, but had paid no attention. Anna's gaunt, bony face had no attraction for him. Her sister, now, little Katy . . . He'd once held a sparrow in his hand, feeling its silky feathers and tight, quivering tendons ready to take flight, and watched its bold eyes, both brave and afraid, looking up at him, and then he'd released it, and it flew away without a sound or a glance, fluttering into the trees, gone. Katy would be brave like that, and quick, soft and tough in the hand, hungry and busy in her pleasure . . . So different from his wife Elizabeth, solid in her virtues, fleshy, her belly filling his two hands as she lay against him at night, soft and comforting.

He wrenched his mind away to Fairchild, squatting silently on his haunches a few yards off.

"Where this Calhoun?" he asked, picking carefully through his meager stock of English words.

"Always where he says he'll be," the surveyor said cryptically.

"And these Rangers . . . they are what?" Dorst asked from the other side of the rock.

Fairchild was silent for a long time, long enough for them to think he hadn't heard. But he was gathering his thoughts. How to explain the Rangers to these people? *Wild men of the forest!* He sighed. *Wild enough for the Indians, certainly.* They were woodsmen, turkey-shooters, hunters, men of the country, white Indians . . .

"All I can tell you of Calhoun," he said after some minutes, "is that not three years past, his whole family was viciously attacked and scalped by a horde of Indians as they prepared camp for the night, in a spot just like this. Not very far from here." He jerked his thumb in a westerly direction, though it was by then too dark for the others to see what he was doing. "It was, I believe, only a mile or two from where Governor Bull allocated your land. It's one reason we're not going there."

Heinrich, still wrestling with his English, understood about a third of this. "How had it happen?" he asked.

"They'd come from Ireland, settled in the Long Canes, not far from here, with four friendly families. The uprising came, the savages on the rampage, the settlers outnumbered. Calhoun with his friends tried to remove their families and some of their goods to Augusta." He jerked his thumb again. "That's about forty miles that way, a town, too big for the Indians to attack."

"This happen just now?"

"No more than three years back. They were set upon as they stopped to make camp at a creek, at a place called Patterson's Bridge. Fifty of them, mostly women and children, were murdered, hacked into pieces."

He stopped. The night had turned black; there was no moon and they hadn't lit a fire, at Fairchild's instructions. They tried to picture the huddled families, also in the black, in this immense wilderness, endless and menacing; elemental, uncaring . . . And out of the shadows, like spirits from a primeval past, came leaping the copper-colored killers, the Cherokee . . .

"Afterward, they found many children wandering in the woods. Calhoun, when he returned to the place of the massacre, to bury the dead, found twenty bodies mangled, in a heap, his own wife among them, and several of his children, scalped. Another man found nine children, cut and left for dead. Calhoun's brother William saw two of his little girls carried into captivity. The elder of them they found later, demented but alive; the other was never heard of. The few who escaped had cut loose the horses and fled into the night."

He fell silent. There was no noise from the forest. The evening before, they'd heard a savage howling in the wilderness that Fairchild had said was a wild cat, a puma. They'd also heard the mournful echoes of the wolves among the ravines. Tonight there was nothing, and the silence was even more unsettling than the noise. The Cherokee war was supposed to be over, but these stories of massacres, of Indians materializing from the night, these tales of piles of pathetic corpses, reminded them as nothing else could that this place to which they had committed themselves was a much more savage place than the ancient forests of the Hunsrück.

In the morning, Calhoun was . . . there.

Sitting, as quiet as a weasel.

No one heard him arrive. They woke at sun-up and there he was, squatting on the ground a dozen paces away with six Rangers, staring at them. He didn't move when they started up from their bedrolls, and nor did his men. Even the horses, tethered a hundred paces off, made no noise. But if Calhoun sat like a ghost, he was a solid, raw-boned, leathery ghost, unshaven, with a craggy face, piercing eyes, a hawk's brow and a thick mane of gray hair. He waited, unmoving, until the party had saddled their horses and then, in a few seconds it seemed, he and his men were mounted and ready to go; everything they did seemed effortless, expert. Heinrich was more than slightly awestruck. Calhoun jerked the reins and led them into the defile, upward through the tangle, toward the plateau above.

They rode all day, without respite, stopping only once for a quick meal, eaten cold, then remounting and pushing on. Eventually, they halted about an hour before sundown.

Heinrich, still too awestruck to approach Calhoun directly, asked Fairchild to ask him where they were going.

Fairchild pulled from his pouch a parchment map of the Back Country, as much as it had been mapped, and called Calhoun over. He spread the map on the ground.

"Here," he said, "is Charlestown. And here"— running his finger on a rough line from the coast up to the left—"is the Savannah River, biggest river in the province. Here is the town of Augusta." He stabbed his thumb at the river, about halfway up the map. "Now, the Indian line is here . . ." This time his finger slashed a line from the Savannah River northeastward, more or less parallel to the coast. "Right near that line, there where it crosses the river, is Hillsborough Township. That's where they wanted you to go. Only people there are a few French Protestants, newly arrived, and the Indians. Oh, they're quiet now," he said, with a sidelong glance at Calhoun, "but who's to say they'll be quiet long?"

Calhoun, expressionless, grunted.

"Captain Calhoun won't take you there. He says it's not safe."

"Even if Governor demand it?" Heinrich asked.

"Mister Calhoun makes up his own mind," the surveyor said quietly.

"Not take land away because of it?"

"They won't, no. There's land aplenty."

"So where we going?"

Fairchild stabbed once more at the map. "East of Hillsborough. Some way from the Indian line there's a fort called Ninety Six. South of there"—his finger smeared a small east-west patch—"are a series of creeks running down to the Savannah. Here's Hard Labour Creek. A few miles east, Reedy Creek, Cuffeetown Creek, Horsepen Creek, all in a cluster. Another few miles, Sleepy Creek. There's land all about there. I'll show you to it. Take your pick."

"You be with us?"

"I told you," Fairchild said impatiently.

"And Calhoun?"

"No, he has other business, then later he'll go back to meet the main party. They'll be along in a few weeks. We have much to do before then. There's a hut being built for you here"—he pointed to Cuffeetown Creek. "It should be ready when your families arrive."

"You're very kind," Abraham Frietz said.

Fairchild smiled, a little humorlessly. "It's my duty," he said, "to make sure you settlers make it through to the next winter."

One afternoon, almost two weeks out of Charlestown, the road the main party was following changed, began to rise and fall, weaving this way and that around bare hollows and dunes. The earth, which had been getting sandier and sandier, resembled more the shore at Rotterdam than farm country. It looked like a beach, the only vegetation being clumps of stunted, scrubby pines and brush and sharp, short grass, with here and there some outcroppings of coppery red soil and no water. Peter Strum had already fretted about the quality of the soil; this was much worse. He plagued Meyer to determine what they could expect of the land where their farms would be. Meyer could only glean that their journey was more than half over, but that they had much farther to go. This news mollified him somewhat, though he remained anxious.

There was little shade or shelter among the scrub, so the party rested during the day and walked long into the night and early in the morning. Even with a pale moon, the sand reflected enough light for travel, and in another five days they reached forest again. There they were met by the taciturn Captain Calhoun.

With their new guardians they began to climb through the oaks and beeches of the ridge. The road deteriorated to a rough track, curving to the left, then to the right, occasionally dipping to cross a creek by a crude bridge or a shallow ford. It was cold, even at midday. The trees towered over the ravines, their matted branches holding back the light.

Once the Rangers came upon a small group of Indians who were camping for the night and drove them away, beating them brutally from horseback, lashing out even at the children; their anger seemed raw, vicious, inexplicable to the travelers who hadn't yet heard the story of the Calhoun massacre.

After another day of hard slogging, the road leveled once more across a gently rolling plateau. The worrisome sand had been left behind, replaced by soil redder than anything any of them had seen. The shut-in feeling of the ravines had disappeared; the trees were tall and open, and the road, what remained of it, was blanketed under a bed of needles longer than a man's hand, needles mixed with fallen oak leaves. Peter Strum began to shed his pessimism.

Mid-morning one late February day, Meyer announced that Captain Calhoun had informed him they were nearly at their destination. A few hours later there were excited shouts from the Webers and Schildnachts, who were walking ahead of the main party. Within minutes the first wagons broke from the forest into a clearing, where many trees had been felled.

Katy looked up. There was Heinrich Strum, bolting over logs and through tangled brush, running toward them.

They were . . . home.

Four

Do you remember, she said, gesturing over to Katy, who wasn't looking, *do you remember how I galloped down to Charlestown? You stayed with the children and I got on a horse and rode, and rode, and rode! How American I felt then! But Charlestown was still the Old Country in spirit, and I felt much less American there. That was the moment I slipped away from the King.* She didn't mention the boy, Heinrich. She'd never mentioned Heinrich, not to anyone.

August 1765
Cuffeetown Creek, South Carolina

They came down out of the defile an hour before sunup, and set off at a dead gallop. It had been hot enough in the Back Country; here on the sand in the lonely desert the heat would beat at them like the wings of a carrion fowl from the underworld. Or so Peter had said last night as they lay in the sultry stillness of the forests, and Anna saw no reason to doubt him; yesterday's heat still radiated from the ground, the earth in the dry sweats of fever.

Peter wanted to reach the pines by mid-morning and rest there, to travel again as the sun went down.

Until they reached Charlestown.

When would that be? Four days from now? Five?

What am I doing here?

The four of them were riding ahead of her, riding hard. She watched the horses' hooves kicking up, their rumps, the rumps of the men, up and down, up and down. Peter's narrow rump, the sack that was her brother. Peter Strum. And the rump of the black-eyed boy, Heinrich. She looked away quickly.

For an hour, she concentrated on the drumming rhythm of the hooves, on the leached beige sand and the scrub bushes as they swept by, clinging to the saddle, keeping up with the men, keeping on.

Why had she insisted on going?

Peter was driving them. His energy, or his anger.

He had called them together at Maria's house, Maria's and Heinrich's on Cuffeetown Creek, near the Strums. There were thirty or forty of them, representatives of the community and its various pockets. The Bauers came, and the Zimmermanns, the Merks and the Webers. Christian Zange was there, and Georg Schildnacht.

They had all come at Peter's summons, because they knew things weren't going as well as they should.

They gathered at the Adolph house, a two-room cabin made of logs hewed on two sides and notched at the ends, roofed with pine shingles ripped with a froe. The doors and window shutters were made from rough, undressed boards; the chimneys were built of stones with clay mortar. There was rammed clay for the floor. It was a cabin such as they'd all built, if better wrought than most, and already filled with comfortable things Maria had made. But outside . . . too many of what should be fields were not yet stumped—the forest still rudely intruded. Heinrich Adolph, like the rest of them, had got some crops in on time, more than most, but not enough. They were afraid that food would run out. And so would their meager supply of money.

Bull, the Lieutenant Governor, had done his best to abide by the spirit of the Bounty Act that had permitted the German immigrants to settle in the Carolinas. He'd provisioned them and victualed them and counseled them and outfitted them and given them books of advice and law and custom. He'd even given them a set of colors, as he called the flags of identification, and sent with them an introduction "to some of the best English in that neighborhood for instruction in agriculture of our climate tho', I put them upon going well with their whole strength next year upon raising hemp by giving . . . several bushels of seed now and advising that they should prepare for a future staple of silk by planting mulberries."

True, he'd been thwarted in his earnest desire to settle them alongside the French Protestants near the Indian line (several times referring in his dispatches to their "obstinacy" on the matter). He never quite understood that this thwarting had been as much at the insistence of Calhoun and the Royal surveyor as at the Germans' prudence at not putting themselves in harm's way, and he confused things further by maintaining that they'd chosen land "not so good" and had refused to go to their lands "'till it was too late to expect the Crops," but this was hardly their fault, as he'd made them wait for their meager baggage, and the choice of site had really delayed them not at all.

The seventy-eight families who had made it to the Back Country had pulled back from the frontier, moving a little closer to the fort (such as it was) at Ninety Six, and spread out along the various headwaters of Stevens Creek. It was on Sleepy Creek that Peter and Anna found their land. Others, a mere dozen or so, including Katy and Abraham, established themselves on or near Hard Labour Creek. Another score of families chose Cuffeetown Creek and its branches, Horsepen and Reedy; that was where the Strums and the Adolphs found themselves. They were all within a few miles of each other.

It wasn't a bad location they'd chosen. First, it was more secure from Indian attack. And the land itself was rich enough, there on the fertile plateau with its network of streams. Meyer kept Bull's silk banner, but no one paid it any mind, nor Bull's exhortations about manners. They were too preoccupied clearing their land and trying to plant before high summer—so much time lost in London! So much work to do! By high summer, few of them had cleared more than an acre or two, and the rest of the seed was rotting in its tubs.

By the time they'd cleared more land, it would be too late to plant.

They would need help from the authorities at Charlestown. Peter Dorst volunteered to petition the Lieutenant Governor. Heinrich Adolph would go with him, carrying the platts, or deeds, of many of the community for registration. Heinrich and Peter Strum would take their own families' and those of several of their friends. Anna would go because . . . because she would go. She left the baby with Maria, mounted her borrowed horse and paid no mind to the sidelong glances of the other women.

And here I am, in the dust of the men. Behind the quick rump of my husband, up and down, up and down!

Well, he'd always been quick, her Peter. He was thin, with quick humors, and he'd always dreamed of rubies in the rock as he walked behind the plow. He had never been suited to the plow, she knew that. Plowing the fields called for patience, an ox-like devotion to the soil; there were those who loved the smell of fresh earth, the sight of a straight furrow, the feel of a meadow ready for the seed, ripe with promise. Peter loved more the smell of change. He'd seen a ruby once, buried in the rock, or so he told the others. They'd only laughed. He'd wanted to be a miner, but only spent a week in the caves, hating the dank, and the dark, and the endless chipping . . . He'd found nothing at all in the week, only a pile of broken rock to show for all that work; he'd work furiously for an hour but have nothing to show for it, and then he'd lean on his hammer, hearing the sharp, metallic taps of the other miners in the dark—endless, endless tapping, as steady as the steady step of the ox. They were as bad as farmers, worse! He thought he'd seen his ruby, somewhere there in the rubble, and he scrabbled for it but never found it.

After that he took his horse and rode to the Rhine, and from the Rhine to the Saar, or so he said, at a gallop most of the way, galloping for several days to the point of exhaustion, the horse and himself in a lather, and Anna had seen him as he returned, clattering into town, the horse stumbling and he wild-eyed and weary. She had married him shortly afterward.

She didn't really know why. He was ten years older than she, and an angry man, but he was also quick-witted and had heard of the ideas of the Frenchman, Voltaire, and had a theory about everything . . .

I liked his quickness, she thought. *As unpredictable as a mouse under the kitchen table. I liked that.*

They'd tried to have children, but nothing happened. She became pregnant only after Stumpel had brought the wildness with him. Her first child, born on the route Stumpel had chosen for them. Well, there had never been anything for Peter in the Old World. Perhaps he'd find his ruby here yet.

Next to Peter rode her brother Heinrich, Maria's husband. For him, Anna felt a mixture of affection and contempt. He was so nice! So slow! As shapeless as a sack. She watched him ride, the saddle thumping his rump at every stride, jarring him. Maria adored him, of course, and so did the children, young Katy and Elizabeth and the baby, Rosena. She felt a quick stab of jealousy that Maria had named her first-born for her sister and not for herself. Heinrich was the ox to Peter's ferret; he worked from sun-up to sundown and never appeared tired; his cabin and stockades were trim and clean, his fields, those small patches he had been able to clear, were plowed straight, their fences neat. In that way he was a little like Peter Strum . . . Big, slow, amiable, nice, thick-skulled . . . So unlike the boy, Heinrich . . .

She looked at Heinrich again.

Well, he's not really a boy. He's twenty-five. Five years younger than me.

Black hair, black eyes, did he have a black heart? Anna didn't think so. She watched him through the dust, riding easily in the saddle, effortlessly, none of the thumping of the elder Heinrich or his father Peter, none of the tension of her own Peter. The muscles of his legs, flowing with the rhythms of the gallop, rocking on the pivot of his rump . . . She thought of his wife, Elizabeth, broad-beamed as a saddle, fleshy, always tugging at her clothes, she never quite fit into her bodice; she'd been hugely pregnant on the journey to America . . . Well, Anna was already two, and the baby, Eve, was now suckling on that ample body. She felt Stumpel had been a little afraid of Heinrich, and she was, too, though he had never given cause, he was never threatening, he just seemed so . . . sure . . . She stared at his rear through the dust, adjusting to the jarring rhythms of the ride.

One morning after sun-up, three Indians came to Katy Frietz's door and demanded . . . something. Or did they demand anything? It was so hard to tell. How could she understand them?

There'd been no sign they were there. No sound of horses, no knock-ing, no footsteps. They were standing so close to the door that when she flung it open, they all leapt back, startled, and she saw their faces grimac-ing and smelled the odor of animal fat and old sweat.

One of them said something, but she shook her head. She understood none of it. He repeated it, more loudly.

She tried to remember what she could about Indians. Would these be Cherokee, or Creek, or Choctaw? Or were all those the same? What were they doing here? The Indian line drawn after the war was more than ten miles west of here. It was why Calhoun had advised them not to go where Bull wanted to put them; Calhoun hadn't wanted them to be vulnerable to Indian raids.

Well, this wasn't a raid, was it? They seemed peaceable enough.

She backed into the house, and they followed her in. The same one, who seemed to be a leader of some kind, spoke again.

Katy called to little Peter, who was only nine. She spoke in German, as calmly as she could. "Fetch your father! He's in the fields. Tell him there are Indians here." She patted his head, trying to communicate calm and hurry at the same time, calm to the Indians and hurry to Peter. *Run!* her hands were telling him, *run quickly!* She smiled reassuringly at the Indians, and made eating motions. They squatted on their heels, smiled back. She gave them bread.

Maybe they want to be my friends!

She felt giddy, from fear.

She didn't know what to say, to do. The three Indians stared at her, without expression.

She wished she had paid more attention to the stories of the Indian wars, but she'd put them out of her mind—so much killing, so much hatred! And for what? There was so much land.

Of course, this had been Indian country, once. Then the settlers pushed inland, further and further into the interior, away from the coast, at first just a few huts and cowpens here and there, then communities, families huddled together against the wilderness. Then there were the squabbles between the British and French, who claimed territory clear down the Mississippi from Quebec. The French were always trouble, any German knew that. She remembered that Calhoun had told them how what he called the "Indian savages," incited by the French, had descended on the frontier, tomahawk and scalping knife in hand. The Cherokee had not yet formally broken with the English colonists in Carolina, Calhoun said, but they had already been "tampered with" by the French. That's what set off the war.

But why? The Indians didn't own the land, did they? Savages didn't own land!

And in any case, that war was long over. They had signed a treaty!

The three Indians didn't look threatening. They simply squatted on the floor and stared. She supposed they wanted tobacco, but she had none.

She tried not to panic. She recalled only too vividly a story she'd heard from a few years ago, before the most recent Indian war, of an atrocity that had occurred just a few miles down the road, toward Charlestown. Or was it further? She wished she could remember where. Frederick Meyer had told it to them. It concerned Mary Cloud, a neighbor, of Cloud's Creek, which was a branch of the Saluda, and how she had ridden one day up to the house of Martin Fridig, all bloody and distraught, and told him the following tale, which he wrote down: "That on the 4th Instant two Indians came to my House about Half way between the Congarees and Savannah Town. The Indians were Savannas. They came there about dark, and sate down very civilly; and my Husband being able to talk their Tongue they talked a great while together. And I gave them Supper. And they asked my Husband for Pipes and Tobacco, and he gave it them. And we sate up until Midnight, and then we all went to Sleep; and they lay down too and pulled off their Mogassens and Boots. One of them broke his Pipe and came to the Bed to my Husband, who handed unto him his Pipe out of his Mouth, and laid down again; and we all dropt into Sleep; and when the Cocks began to Crow they came, as I suppose, to the Bed, and Shot my Husband through the Head. And a young Man liying upon the Floor was Shot in the same Minute. And the Indians, I suppose, thinking the Bullet had gone thro' my Husband's Head and my own too, struck me with a Tommahawk under my right Arm; and afterwards they struck me two Cuts upon my left Knee. I lying still they supposed I was dead, and one of them went and killed both my Children; & then they came and took the Blankets from us & plunder'd the House of all that was valuable and went off. And in that bad Condition I have lain amongst my Dead two Days. And by the help of Providence one of my Horses came to the House; and so I came to Martin Fridig's House."

She'd seen Mary Cloud once, that time a preacher had visited the Back Country. The English preacher. Mary had looked . . . ordinary. Just a widow, like many others.

Katy stared at the impassive Indians on the floor. Did they have names? Who were they? Calhoun would kill them if he found them here. So would many others.

And I have lain amongst my Dead two days.

The tableau held, frozen in time. The Indians squatted, stared, Katy smiled, trying not to make her smile look like a death's-head grimace.

After an eternity, Abraham returned with his musket, bristling with hostility, and the Indians rose and filed out the door, striding swiftly, and were soon lost in the woods.

A few days later, having recounted, to much acclaim, her own story, Katy approached Andrew Williamson, who lived on the nearby estate called White Hall and who had helped them build their first rude shelter, and timidly asked how the Cherokee wars had started.

It was a project for which Williamson lacked great enthusiasm. How do you explain to these people how far back the hostility went? Ask Calhoun, get one story. Ask the Cherokee chief Occonostota, get another. Williamson had traded with the Indians, and had ridden with them against the French, and had come to know them. Surely, they were savage. But whose was the fault here? However, he kept these opinions to himself. Too many of his neighbors had perished from an Indian tomahawk.

So he merely said, "Almost every Cherokee has lost a friend or relative, just as we have. A raid follows a raid, reprisal follows reprisal, a massacre is answered with a massacre, and always, defenseless families die. This has happened all along the frontier. Not very far from here. All around here. Within miles. Close."

He paused. Katy remembered the three Indians, with their unreadable faces. Had they suffered some relative slain? Some uncle, some brother? It was possible.

Early in February 1760, Williamson said—*only five years before now!* Katy thought—the Indians attacked Goudy's Fort at Ninety Six. It happened that they were provoked, he said mildly. "A scouting party surprised two of 'em, and took 'em prisoner. Their friends attacked the next day. They were dispersed, but burned down Mrs. Goudy's house. None of the guards was hurt except my good friend Samuel Bean, who was slightly wounded in the head."

"You were there?" Katy asked.

"Right enough, I was shot." He laughed. "I was mounting my horse. Shot through the sleeve of my coat, in at the shoulder and out at the elbow. No hurt whatever."

"And was that the end of it?" Katy asked.

"What do you think?" Williamson asked. "Do you think Calhoun has forgotten? His family was massacred a year after the peace pipe was smoked. Has Attakullakulla, the Cherokee chief, forgotten? His hunting land gone and his family dead? Would you?"

"Is this why Mr. Bull wanted us at the Indian line?" Katy asked.

"As to that, I couldn't say," Williamson replied carefully. He had no great love for the Governor or the Council at Charlestown, but he was a prudent man. "In any case, you're safer here."

"Would those Indians have killed me if my man hadn't come?"

"Who's to say? Perhaps"—he was trying to be encouraging—"they merely wanted to see who the new people in this land were."

"In this land! In their land! That's what they must think. We're living where they used to hunt!"

"Not theirs. Not any more. Yours."

They passed by the grave of little Christian Beckman without stopping—indeed, without even seeing it—and clattered through the gates of Charlestown in mid-afternoon, the hottest part of the day. There were no sentries, no sign of military activity, no guardian presence, no sign even of inhabitants, who were all probably fanning themselves on their piazzas. Even the few slaves they saw were sprawled on the grass under a tree, insensate. Anna had gone beyond feeling uncomfortable to feeling not very much at all; the sweat and grime pooled in her shift, and everything felt sticky with the heat.

They tied their mounts to a rail and went into an inn. There was no one there. The room was shuttered and dark. A hatchway was open to the cellar, and Anna smelled hops and the heady aroma of fermenting beer, and its air felt cool, as if by some miracle of alchemy there was ice somewhere in the earth under the inn.

They sagged to a bench while her brother went off in search of the innkeeper.

Anna closed her eyes. The smells were no different in the inns of Idar-Oberstein, not that she'd spent much time in inns. Hops were hops and beer was beer, and places where men went to talk were all the same, she thought. She felt a sudden longing for the bubbling waters of the Nahe in the spring. Cuffeetown Creek just wasn't the same . . . *No, but it's ours, after all, rude as it is. Rude as it was* . . . The cabin she and Peter were building was a rude thing, too. You could see daylight through the chinking where the logs had twisted or warped and the roof still leaked when it rained—she pushed little Peter back and forth at those times, depending on where the water wasn't dripping inside that day. But she remembered once, toward the end of April, when the cabin was newly finished, she and Katy and Maria had gone down to the quiet creek and tucked up their skirts and stepped into the water. Well, so it was barely knee-high, but it was cool and clean, and afterward they'd lain on the grass and stared up at the sky through the oak and the beech leaves, green and yellow against the blue, and had laughed together, happy that finally their journey was over and they were home. A year after they had left the Nahe, all those acres of land seemed pregnant with possibility; they had a home that was theirs, no matter how unfinished it was, and the slums of London seemed as far away as the stars, and so did the fine houses and the grandees of Charlestown, which . . . She caught herself. *Happy, yes, we were happy.* Lying on the grass, lazy, little Peter beside her, hearing the shrieks of the other children, Katy's own Peter and sweet Rosannah, and Maria's Elizabeth and baby Rosena . . . Rosena Rosannah, Rosannah Rosena . . .

In May, the backbreaking toil of clearing the land for crops began to catch up with her Peter, the drudgery of trudging behind the oxen, the daily monotony of felling trees and dragging out the stumps, the toil of trying to clear enough land in enough time to plant enough crops to have enough food . . . The Lieutenant Governor's hemp seed went unused, and so did the tobacco plants, and the mulberry roots. Instead, potatoes went in, and cabbages, but not enough, and they'd used up most of the £10 in gold they'd been given to build their house, and there wasn't going to be enough. It was why they were on their way to Charlestown, after all.

Just then Heinrich Adolph returned with the innkeeper. Or rather, he was swept in ahead of her, like a log pushed to shore by an irresistible tide, for she was a very large lady, shaped somewhat like a turkey, with great wattles and a dress like a sail in a brisk breeze and a voice that would have been suited to hog-calling, had there been hogs in Charlestown. Mrs. Eager, as she announced herself, proclaimed that she ran a clean house, unlike some she could mention, and she didn't truckle with the Scots or the Irish, low people from high country as she called them, but of course you, dearhearts, are newly arrived and foreign to boot, you wouldn't know about the kind of people that ran wild like the Indians in the Back Country, back meaning back from civilization of course . . . Only about a third of this registered with Anna, who could by now understand English clearly enough but not when it all came jumbled together like a spring freshet. She did notice that all the while the mouth was moving, the eyes were not. They were assessing, taking in everything, and Anna, stained and travel-weary, felt Mrs. Eager's disdain like a hot breeze, and she tugged awkwardly at her neckline, trying to separate cloth from skin, as the innkeeper burbled on.

"We're here to see the Lieutenant Governor," Peter said in response to a query.

"Ho! The Lieutenant Governor! But will he see you, I wonder?"

With that, she led the way upstairs, to what she called their "chamblers."

Anna, following behind, stared. There must be twelve petticoats on the woman! And look at those striped stockings!

"Thank you, m'dear," the preacher told Katy insincerely. "You're too kind."

Privately, Katy agreed with the literal meaning of his words. She hadn't taken to this English High Church import, with his unsuitable black clothing and reedy voice, always on the edge of a whine. He was sitting sprawled on the grass, his back against an old oak near the blacksmith shop of Ninety Six, about halfway to the tavern, from which hoarse shouts and the occasional scream would issue. He had finished his labors hours previously, and she had thought to bring him some refreshment, a nip of spirit and a piece of pickled pork, which he insisted on referring to, mysteriously, as "brawn" and which he declined, with an ostentatious shudder that annoyed her no end.

At least he had said thank you.

He looks like a boiled red cabbage!

He looked, indeed, as if he were melting under his woolen jacket and tight neckcloth, his florid face moist from the high humidity.

She would have liked him better if he'd preached something uplifting, a sermon to the divine grace that rewards toil, for instance, something about the gifts that devotion would yield. Instead, he'd chosen as his theme "The cleansing of these Augean stables," by which he apparently meant the entire Back Country. That of which it should be cleansed, he made clear, was sin and licentiousness.

He had stood on the steps of the trading post and sent his tenor ricocheting among the group of small buildings, for an hour, an hour and a half, two hours, endlessly. He'd been careful to except present company, those devout who had come to hear him preach, from his harangue about the vileness and corruption of Carolinians in general, but still . . . *The whole country is in a state of debauchery, dissoluteness and corruption!*

Well! Thank you for those encouraging and uplifting words!

Katy looked about her. Her compatriots, and most of the other people in the substantial crowd—why, there must be better than four hundred!—were rapt, here and there nodding at the preacher's squeaky denunciations. They actually agreed with him!

It was not so surprising, Katy thought. They all missed the reassuring presence of the organized church and the soothing words of a man like Gustav Wachsel. They had no preacher of their own yet, in this new world. There were two or three itinerants in the Back Country, and a few small chapels. But there was not a real church or a real minister anywhere, at least not settled in one place. And the itinerants rarely ventured across the Broad River, preferring to spend their time further east, where, God knows, they had work enough. There were sufficient souls there who had never benefited from a sermon, even one as denunciatory as this. One of these wandering soul-savers, Charles Woodmason, later confided his own thoughts to his journal. "Lamentable," he wrote, "is the situation of these people, beyond the power of words to describe—thro' want of ministers to marry and thro' licentiousness, many hundreds live in concubinage—swapping their wives as cattle, and living in a state of nature, more irregularly and unchastely than the Indians—how would the polite people of London stare, to see the females (many very pretty) come to service in their shifts and a short petitcoat only, barefooted and bare legged—without cap or handkerchiefs—dressed only in their hair, quite in a state of nature for nakedness counted as nothing—as they sleep all together in common in one room and dress openly without ceremony. The men appear in frocks or shirts and long trousers—no shoes or stockings."

Lamentable? This preacher had also used the word in his sermon. But lamentable, Katy thought, was not the proper word. Lamentable was when you were abandoned, penniless and starving, in a strange capital, or locked in the hold of a blackened ship, or dying of ugly and terrifying diseases. Lamentable didn't describe the present. They were in difficulty, yes, and scratching a living from the red soil of Carolina was proving unexpectedly onerous (they hadn't realized when Stumpel had spoken grandiloquently of the great forests of the New World that they'd have to laboriously pull up that very forest just to make their fields). But, no, it wasn't so bad here.

She went back to the wagon that had brought them to Ninety Six. Little Rosannah was sleeping in the back. She felt heavy, sluggish from the heat.

I'm pregnant again!

She didn't know for sure, but she *knew.*

She thought of their neighbors, the English, or the Scots and Irish as they called themselves, and they filled her with unease. They were so hard to understand. They were so very violent! The preachers were surely exaggerating, but it was true many of them seemed filled with anger. She had heard that most had drifted down from Virginia and the northern colonies only because there was no law in the Back Country of the Carolinas. Ninety Six had been declared a Judicial District only a few months earlier, and the intention was to set up courts of justice somewhere in the area, and sometime after that, an office empowered to probate wills, handle administration and land deeds, and hold courts of equity for the division of estates. So far that was all talk—they had heard a magistrate might be coming, but he'd not yet arrived—and transgressions simply went unreported and unpunished. No wonder there were hard men here, predatory men. Like most of her neighbors, Katy had heard stories of things that happened at isolated farms, especially to women, killings or worse, worse than the Indians, much worse . . .

She'd seen no evidence of it for herself.

And yet she still wished the preacher could be more . . . joyous.

In Charlestown, the town bells rang at eight to signify that the govern-ment of the town was open for business and that petitioners could peti-tion, plaintiffs plaint. Peter Strum and his son would go to the small, square building where the Registrar of Deeds was located to make the platts they were carrying official; Anna's husband would go with her brother to request an audience with the Lieutenant Governor.

Anna, left to her own devices, wandered about the town.

She hadn't slept much the night before. The air had been so sultry it felt like breathing hot, wet flannel, and they were kept awake anyway by laugh-ter and shouts from the tavern below. She and Peter had gone down at around midnight to take a draft of something, which turned out to be raw cane spirits that kept her up much of the rest of the night. The tavern had been busy with drovers and sailors. It was presided over by Mrs. Eager, poised for trouble, gimlet-eyed, in a gown showing so much shoulder and sloping pigeon-breast that it appeared a heavy shrug would precipitate it to the ground. Which, no doubt, was why the men paid so promptly and so well.

Huh! What a chest! Damn things so large they'd tip her over if she weren't careful, like sails too full of wind.

And when did the woman sleep? Well, apparently it was in the morn-ing, for there was no sign of their hostess as she left the inn.

At around midday, Anna bought a piece of bread and a slice of cheese from one of the German shops—odd how German had begun to seem out of place here, more awkward on the tongue than it should—and went to the churchyard to rest, her back against a sprawling oak. The food had cost her enough, but she'd been appalled by some of the prices she'd heard in the shops along Broad Street.

The Strums joined her in the churchyard an hour or so later, clutching a thick sheaf of duly notarized parchment that made their sojourn in the Back Country legal. Heinrich sat next to her, his back against the same tree, folding and unfolding the papers. His own platt showed his hundred and fifty acres on Horsepen Creek. His father had three hundred on Cuf-feetown Creek, fifty more than his entitlement. A hundred for himself and fifty for his wife, fifty each for Jacob and Barbara. Where did the other fifty come from? Who was going to challenge it? Sickly Anne got her own hundred, and so did Eva, the seventeen-year-old around whose austere beauty the men were already accumulating. Six hundred and fifty acres for the family altogether.

Heinrich leaned back against the tree. Anna glanced at him quickly. There was a small pulse beating in his throat. His black hair was lying tight against his skull, his black eyes were closed. His long face was in repose. She could feel his shoulder touching hers, faintly, and she could smell him, heat on skin, leather, new sweat. She got up quickly, moved away. His father was sitting against another oak, his white head bowed, staring at the ground. He was paying no attention. She stood at the edge of a family's burial plot, staring across the wooden markers to the tangle of creeper and magnolia, and beyond that to the cemetery fence and beyond that . . . up the peninsula, up to the Back Country and then the Indian lands and the mountains, and after that, who knew? Her heart was beating, beating. First she thought, *Why does he do that to me?* And then she thought, *One day we'll own all this . . . not me, but us . . . it'll be ours . . .* She felt fiercely rooted to the landscape. And then she thought, in some surprise, *I'm not European any more! How fast it happened!*

Katy sat in her wagon with her husband, feeling light-headed. There was a jug of spirits on the boards between them, given them by Juliana Zange before they had left for Ninety Six. Juliana had said, "You'll need it after the preacher is done," and they had. The jug was half empty, and Abraham was close to comatose, hardly fit for anything, awake but snoring. She felt the world wheel about her, the wagon, the sermon, her neighbors, wheeling about on the axis of her pregnancy-to-be, her house, the farms, her neighbors, the Indians, the outlaws, the British Regulars in Charlestown, the grand ladies of the Charlestown salons, the planters, the slaves, the forests and the rocks, wheeling, wheeling . . . She pulled herself together. The preacher had gone, riding off to his next wrestling bout with sin. Who would miss him? No Wachsel he.

He'd refused their food and drink and dragged himself onto his horse, and, stiff as a stick, had ridden off.

He'd been disgusted because about half the congregation became drunk before they left for home.

What did he expect?

They'd been here for six months.

Six months!

For six months they'd toiled. The young people in their springtime, harnessed like oxen and put to dragging stumps from the ground, hauling rocks from the fields, building fences, hoeing weeds, working, working, working. And now . . .

She saw Eva Strum sitting under an oak, looking flushed and happy. Sitting with her was the blacksmith, or rather the blacksmith's son, Daniel Michler, a strapping and powerful young man who'd been drawn to her, who couldn't leave her alone, who was staring at her, snared by her bare feet and bare legs and the thin, white shift that clung to her, the blue tracery of veins under the white skin . . . The thin shifts that had so disturbed the preacher and sent him off into paroxysms of worry about the fate of their immortal souls. God help us! The soul would look after itself. All this was perfectly fine, Katy thought, holding her head to keep it from spinning. They lived for months in these isolated places, how else were they to meet, and court, and perhaps marry, if it weren't for these occasional forays to the fort at Ninety Six? She only wished the preacher had understood this, and had suppressed his sour fretting about their spiritual degradation. Because afterward, they wanted to give thanks in more earthy ways, with great feasting and roasting of hogs—the community was poor but it could afford a few hogs, shot in the woods!

She pushed Abraham onto his back. He toppled unprotestingly— indeed, he was quite unconscious—and came to rest with a heavy thud. She laid her head in his lap. Before she drifted off, she heard shouts from the tavern, and a faint tendril of worry intruded itself. This place was so violent, there were so many hard men here . . . She brushed it aside, clinging to comfortable imaginings of the bodies coupling in the dark about her. It made her feel . . . fertile. And with that she fell asleep.

It was almost evening when Peter and her brother returned. Peter was looking black, and Anna sighed. It had not gone well then.

They'd arrived at the Lieutenant Governor's mansion at a few minutes before eight. They'd expected to be the only ones there, but already a jam of carriages was waiting outside, stretching round the corner and halfway up the block. Thirty or forty people were milling about on the stairs and inside the vestibule. None of them paid the Ninety Sixers any attention.

"We stood there for a while and waited," her brother said. "No one did anything or went anywhere, so we asked 'em what was up. No one said anything, they didn't understand us. Though Peter's English is not so bad now."

"Didn't want to understand," Peter said.

Heinrich gave him a sideways look. "Yes, that's true. It's said Charlestown people don't like our kind." He paused. "Any case, when nothing happened for an hour, we pushed through a doorway and into another room. We knocked first," he amplified.

Peter Dorst took up the story. "There were clerks at desks in the room, and at the end, a fellow in some kind of uniform standing at a taller desk, like a schoolmaster. They were busy with papers, scribbling away."

The head clerk, or whoever he was, barked at them. "Who are you? What is it you want?"

"We're from Ninety Six, and . . ."

"Ninety Six, is it?" the clerk said, surprised. "We're always wanting news of Ninety Six. And what do you want?"

"To see Sir Bull," said Peter, getting the name confused.

A clerk tittered. "And why should Sir Bull see you?"

"On behalf of the community," said Peter, the rehearsed phrasing overriding his thick accent. "We're here to petition the authorities for help. Money and food in our community have given out. We're much afraid the settlement will have to be abandoned unless aid is provided."

"Money and food is it?" the clerk said. "Well, if that's it, you'll have to wait outside with the rest of them."

"Until when?"

"Until we call you," the clerk said, impatiently.

"How can you call us if you don't know who we are?"

The clerk lost his temper. "Out, out!" he said. "Wait out there! When you hear Ninety Six called, you can come in, not before."

Anna stared at her husband. "How long did you have to wait?"

"Four hours," he said, looking even blacker.

He fell silent. He was still smarting from the condescending looks the

Lieutenant Governor's staff had bestowed on him (though his brother-in-law, he thought, had missed them entirely). It was that infuriating blend of disdain and pity that irritated so. *We're English, here by right, and you're not . . .*

"At last, we were summoned into yet another room where yet another paper-handler told us that Governor Bull could do nothing for us."

Anna stirred. "Did you see him, at the end?"

Peter shook his head. "I said, 'Is that what he said?' And he said, 'My words might as well be the Governor's words, because they're the only words you'll get.' Then he pulled from a desk a heap of money, and put it in a chamois bag, and gave it to me.

" 'There,' he said. 'There's £30 to defray expenses for your fruitless trip.' "

Peter smacked his hand on the wall. "He just handed it to me, like I was a lackey! And what's worse, I took it."

"Thirty pounds! That's not very much," said Anna, thinking of the prices she'd seen during the day.

"We'll leave at first light," Peter said without answering her, and strode off into the dusk.

"Wait!" she said, but very faintly. Wait for what? *Let's stay in town and buy fine things for our mansion at fine shops? With £30?* She knew the money wasn't for them. She knew Peter would fold the linen bag into his shirt. It would be a little seed, that bag, a seed of resentment, and after a while it would grow into a fortune of accusation and anger. She felt it, too, after all. Charlestown didn't care about them, about the Back Country, any more than it cared about the Indians. They were there for Charlestown's use, that's all.

"At first light!" she called, acquiescing, and watched him recede into the dusk. Heinrich Strum was staring at her. But she couldn't read his expression.

Once again they passed Christian Beckman's grave without stopping and without comment. They camped that night in a glade in a forest of lofty pines. Heinrich Strum shot a deer and butchered it, and they ate venison and fresh sauerkraut bought the previous night from a Herr Schneyer in Charlestown, and their beds smelled of pine and crushed moss, and later when the fire went out, Anna and Peter made love, hard, Peter grunting when his time came, Heinrich lying no more than a few yards distant, Anna thinking of him lying there, rigid, and then her hunger overtook her, and Heinrich and Peter and the haughtiness of Charlestown fled from her mind, for a while.

The following day the Merk boys, Conrad and Lorentz, came over to the Frietzes' place to help Abraham finish a fence, and when they had gone, he took a piece of ash and carved a likeness of Katy and gave it to her, as a gift.

I have two lives, Anna thought. *Wife and mother, colonist. And Stumpel's girl, wild child.*

Katy knew it would be a boy. In her mind she named him Charles, with the English Ch.

They arrived home after six days' hard riding, weary, whipsawn and weatherbeaten, and the news of their failure and Bull's refusal spread rapidly through their community. There was some disappointment, for many had hoped for another miracle, the second coming of a Wachsel. There was also resignation. The winter would be bad, but no one would starve. There was food. There were deer everywhere, and many a poor shot had developed a taste for porcupine. By next spring the fields would be better ready for the crops. Peter, Abraham, Heinrich . . . they all had a few acres cleared, maybe enough. So did Balthazar Merk and Adam Bauer, and the Zimmermanns.

Katy learned that young Eva Strum, strong-willed Eva, determined Eva, had cleared three acres of her own land, with the help of her burly blacksmith from Ninety Six. When she heard that she knew the colony would be all right.

Five

Sitting there on the bench, listening to the drowsiness, Anna felt some distant echo of the old angers that had so shaken her in Charlestown. *They were so gullible, my sister and her husband. They never saw the sneers behind the grand words of their patrons. They could always see through the lies, but never through the hypocrisy. And then, when we quarreled, she would accuse me of arrogance!* Katy was sniffing, a dry, irritating sniff. *The gullible are always wounded when you point out their folly.*

August 1768
Dutch Fork, South Carolina

Katy sat on the backboard of the wagon and listened as the itinerant preacher tried to make himself heard over the clatter of a passing cart and the shrieks of the children playing behind the tavern. He was going on as all these preachers did, in what she thought was an increasingly shrill and desperate way, about the evils of licentiousness and the necessity of avoiding sin, and the congregation was as rapt as ever. But the congregation was much smaller these days, only about a hundred people squatting in the grass or leaning against their transports.

Well, the fever's carried so many of us off, she thought. *What a few years it's been!*

Of course, it was more than that. More than the fever had carried them off, and more than the fever was keeping them away. There'd been the meeting last night, for one thing, held by the men calling themselves Regulators. Abraham had gone, and Heinrich and others. They'd roused themselves to a pitch of excitement, and afterward had gotten drunk as expected, and this morning were nursing hangovers here and there, but mostly there.

The preacher knew about all that, of course. He was keenly aware of these Regulators. He'd been sharp against them in the past, though his opinion had lately changed. But it was the fact of their meeting on a Saturday that seemed to exercise him most, and the Sunday morning hangovers only made his denunciations all the sharper.

She listened as the phrases tripped out.

Clattering together like leaves in an autumn breeze. Blather.

That wasn't the only reason the congregation was so small. It was that the good Reverend had his competitors, the Presbyterian preachers and charismatic New Light Baptists who'd drifted down from Virginia with the Scottish immigrants. Oh yes, the charismatics had found fertile soil in Carolina for their mischief. And why not? They preached Salvation, and Redemption, and the Triumph of the Righteous, and the Smiting of the Evil-doers.

Why not, indeed? It has been a terrible few years.

They had gotten through the winter of '65, somehow, despite Bull, despite everything. They had looked for some relief in 1766, with more fields cleared and an early start, but it was not to be so easy. The spring arrived hot and sultry, the hottest year since the colony was founded, and then in March it began to rain and it hardly stopped until August, more rain in a few months than in the previous ten years, so they said, until the whole country seemed rotten with steamy damp, everything was sodden, the fields were mud and muck and the crops that hadn't washed away had rotted in the earth. There was fever everywhere, in the town, in the parishes, in the Back Country.

In August, the rains stopped, but then it grew exceedingly hot and dry. The mud in the fields turned to iron, the roads to burning steel. What plantings had survived the rain were now desiccated. The sickness seemed to sweep through the community like a gale, a fever that felled adults as well as children, bringing with it panic and heartbreak. Few families escaped. Many died. Many others abandoned their new homesteads and departed, some for the relative civilization of Orangeburg, a few just to the Dutch Fork, one or two all the way to Charlestown.

That winter, the weather turned savage, with bitter frosts and piercing cold. The following spring, it rained again. The creeks were full of water and almost impassable, bridges were carried away, the roads became muck again and carts sank to their axles and horses to their withers and travelers rode for miles up to their skirts in mud and water, exhausting their mounts.

The summer came, passed. It was all fever, sickness, hard work, exhaustion.

And so it went. Hard rains, the streams in flood, fords impassable, bridges not yet built, boats often carried away, horses terrified, men drowned. Then exceeding cold, great storms. Snow. Many perished from cold. Spring again. April. Greenery nowhere to be seen. Not a blade of grass or leaf on the trees. Some wheat and barley were coming in, but hundreds had not a mouthful of meat. The people boiling apples, peaches and greens from the trees for food.

Green peaches for food!

But they'd come through it, again. They sent the children into the woods to gather sodden mushrooms, the green peaches, whatever of last year's acorns they could find, the greens of dandelions, cowslips . . . They made tea from the cowslips, broth from burdock roots enriched with turkey blood. One of the boys had found a turkey flapping on the ground with a leg broken in some unknown accident and had dragged it home. They bled it directly into the broth, brushing away the feathers, then put it into a pot to boil. It weighed nearly thirty pounds, drawn, and fed the family for nearly two weeks. They ate the meat and the wattle and the crop and the dead, staring eyeballs, and when they were done, they boiled up the feet with the bones for soup. Katy prodded at the little foot bones lying in the bottom of her bowl. They looked like baby's fingers, pointing at her accusingly, but she picked away at the knuckles of gelatinous flesh, and it kept her going for another twelve hours or so. That was how it was

done. They measured life a day at a time, prayed a lot and planted whatever they could whenever they could.

The preacher was still going on about those "villainous wretches," the
New Lights. Katy listened with only half an ear. She had attended one of
their preachings, once, in a public meeting house the other side of the
Broad River. She'd gone with Abraham and a number of others, but it had
made her uneasy, and she'd never gone again. Their preacher was one of
those charismatics, shrieking and jumping about and slapping his head for
Jesus, as though to beat the Devil out of his brain, and when he'd gotten
his flock properly worked up so they, too, were swaying and calling on the
Lord, he commanded them to show their love for Jesus by stripping off
their clothing, which they did, standing and swaying and hauling off their
clothes, piles of clothing dropping to their feet, growing bundles of cloth,
until they were right down to the netherest of nether garments, and if the
preacher had demanded they strip those off, too, they would gladly have
shucked off their shifts and gone home stark naked, still praising their
Lord. She had been frightened at the deep passions the charismatic had
uncovered; they seemed to her part of the convulsive waves of lawlessness
sweeping through their little community.

It's in the air, she thought, *like an evil wind.*

By "it" she meant, or so she supposed, this, whatever it was, this . . .
contempt for rules of any kind. Down in Charlestown, they said, the legislature had been debating the matter for months and had become "con-
vinc'd that the Num'rous Troops of Banditti and Freebooters and
Unsettled Profligate Persons of both Sexes originally sprung from the
Great Number of Orphans and Neglected Children scatter'd over these
Back Countries who live expos'd in a State of Nature and were obliged
almost to associate with Villains and Vagabonds for Subsistence . . ." All
very well; if so, it was their fault for not laying out the Back Country into
parishes and making provisions for the imposition of law and order.

But it was more even than that. It wasn't just that parents were careless
of their children when they were poor, but the children themselves seemed
vagrant by nature, and there were swarms of neglected orphans who hung
around the settled areas, vagabond children with fluid and tenuous links to

those adults who made their way in the world by thievery, "to the great increase," as Charles Woodmason later put it in his journal, "of all manner of Vice and Wickedness."

Some of Katy's neighbors, the Bauers, the Merks and the Rupperts, had already encountered gangs of these "wild orphans" and felt themselves lucky not to have suffered more than some trifling thefts.

The previous year, Reverend Woodmason had written, on behalf of a delegation of Back Country farmers, a strong remonstrance to the authorities at Charleston to pay attention.

"Behold," he wrote, "on every one of these rivers, what number of Idle, profligate, audacious Vagabonds! Lewd, impudent, abandon'd prostitutes, gamblers, Gamesters of all Sorts—Horse thieves, cattle stealers, Hog stealers—branders and Markers, Hunters going naked as Indians. Women hardly more so . . . very pernicious in propagating Vice, Beggary and theft—still more pernicious when united in gangs and combinations, broke every prison, whipp'd in every province—and now set down here as Birds of Prey to live on the Industrious and Painstaking. Speak O Ye Charles Towne Gentry . . . can you suffer poor helpless pretty boys—beautiful, unguarded, promising young girls for want of timely care and instruction to be united with a crew of Profligate Wretches from whom they must unavoidably learn Idleness, Lewdness, Theft, Rapine violence, and it may be, Murder?"

Early in 1768, he went at it again, this time including a backhanded swipe at the wretched Palatine community: "There are rather more Bastards, more Mullatoes born than before [the arrival of the New Lights Baptists]. Nor out of 100 Young Women that I marry in a Year have I seen or is there seen, Six but what are with Child? And this as Common with the Germans on other side the River . . ."

Indeed, the Carolina Back Country had become the most lawless place in the Thirteen Colonies. Peace had broken out in Europe in 1763 and thousands of demobbed soldiers on both sides of the Atlantic, by now "rendered unfit for peace," ended up plundering villagers and farmers. A good many of these, along with vagrants, escapees, criminals and adventurers of all kinds from Pennsylvania to Georgia, sought refuge in the Back Country, where there were no sheriffs, no militia, no courts nearer than Charlestown, no effective law enforcement at all. By the end of 1766, matters were bad enough that the authorities in Charlestown began issuing a few ineffectual orders to suppress the growing number of gangs of horse thieves, and to bring about what they mildly called "a reformation of manners," none of which helped very much. The robbers only grew bolder. Charlestown's heart, clearly, wasn't in trying to stop them. Though the countryside was fast filling with settlers, the Assembly refused to lay out new parishes; they were creatures of the town and the planters, and had little interest in diluting their influence by authorizing new voters.

Virtually every day, cattle were stolen or destroyed, cowpens broken up, horses carried off, families stripped and turned naked into the woods, stores broken open and rifled (several traders were ruined), private houses burned or plundered or people tortured in the Indian manner. Everyone knew of married women who had been attacked and raped, or virgins forcibly deflowered. "Vile and Impudent fellows," Charles Woodmason recounted later, "would come to a Planters House, and tye him—lye with his Wife before his Face, Ravish Virgins, before eyes of their parents, a dozen fellows in succession . . . At one house they ty'd the Midwife to the Bed Post, and left the Poor Woman helpless, who, providentially was happily deliver'd, the fright effecting it. They carried off about twenty of the finest Girls in the country into the Woods with them and kept them for many Months, as their Concubines in Common among them till they grew past Shame and never could be brought back to a Life of Virtue when regained by their Friends."

Was it any wonder, then, that the settlers banded together into vigilante posses they called Regulators? In the absence of law, they would create a law of their own. They shot robbers, hanged horse thieves, left rapists pinned to trees with spikes, object lessons to their fellows. The countryside filled up with grim bands of horsemen, ominously silent, intent on retribution more than justice.

Katy had often argued with her sister and Peter about what she saw as their lack of respect for authority of any kind, without ever being quite able to explain what she meant. Not that she blamed them for the lawlessness and the savagery, not at all, but somehow she sensed it was all of a piece. It started with the ruleless children and the adult vagrants, but it also had to do with matters like Peter's hostility to Charlestown, and by extension to the King. Hostility for what? She didn't know. He seemed to want Charlestown's presence in the Back Country, but only if Charlestown did what it was told, if it was there to support and protect, and not to lay down rules. Peter always talked about the Frenchman, Voltaire, and Martin Luther in the same breath, which she thought almost blasphemous. Luther had taught men to look directly to God for their spiritual salvation, well, they all knew that, it was what they believed. Voltaire had translated Luther's thinking to the political realm, where somehow the corrupt hierarchy of the Mother Catholic Church became associated with petty local tyrannies and tax collectors. Now, in the meeting halls and the legislatures of the colonies, this personal connection with God had become the notion of liberty, a word they used like a magic potion, a word they said meant freedom from tyrannical government, but which seemed to mean a rejection of all rules and decency . . . But here Katy got lost. It seemed it had always to do with the rights of the Back Country, and never its obligations, unless it was the obligation of all to fight for their rights. It all sounded so high-minded, and when Anna talked of it, too, in her quick, emphatic way, it sounded so convincing . . . and in its way so thrilling. But Katy sensed that without obligations, liberty became licentiousness, and in any case, the New Lights preachers seemed in tune with the tone of the times, because . . .

What I want is tranquility, peace and quiet, predictability, security for my family.

Instead, there seemed only frustration and anger, everywhere.

All justified, Anna said, reasonable anger.

Katy couldn't explain to her sister why she thought the anger was part of the problem. Anna always seemed so sure of herself and her ideas.

Sometimes, when the six of them were together, she and Anna and their brother, with their spouses, they argued about what was happening. The four of them had quarreled with Peter and Anna; Anna was cold and disagreeable on those occasions, and apparently accused them of all kinds of crimes that none of them understood. What Katy remembered most were her angry eyes and her tight mouth, and she felt her sister becoming a stranger.

One morning in late April the arguing became more . . . personal.

The night before, she'd returned from a visit of several days to Maria's farm, where she had discovered most of the family ill from fever. Heinrich Adolph, sick as he was, she found staggering behind a plow. Maria was lying listlessly on the family's bed with a feverish newborn. Katherina and Elizabeth were both feverish, too. Only Rosena, the four-year-old, seemed well, perhaps because she spent most of her time in the woods with the dogs, coming in only for meals. Katy had brought with her a bag of barley and a brace of woodcock that her boy, Peter, had snared, and she made them into a stew with burdock and wild celery, building up a fire in the crude hearth and bustling about cheerfully—she had developed a theory that cheeriness was what benefited the sick most, and when she put her mind to it, she could out-cheerful a township full of optimists. There were no physicians, of course, in the Carolina Back Country, no medicines, no nurses, no caring for the sick. It was the fashion of the people here, someone told Katy, to abandon the sick, instead of visiting them, "so that a stranger who has no relatives or connections is in a most terrible situation," but she'd misunderstood, missing the reference to strangers and hearing only the word abandon. It was where the argument with Anna began.

"Even family members won't visit the sick," she reported to Anna. "They just leave them, to get well or die as they might."

"'Tis only robust common sense," Anna said, using a phrase newly popular in the colony.

"What is?"

"If you pay a visit to the sick, and after your return, your own household falls sick, have you done them then a good deed?"

"But Anna! If our brother and our brother's children are ill, must we prolong their suffering?"

"And if my Peter then falls ill and dies, have I done him a great service?"

It went badly after that, Katy accusing Anna of heartlessness, Anna accusing Katy of sentimentality, of being prepared to sacrifice her own beloved on the altar of duty, an accusation that left Katy spluttering with futile anger. She hadn't known Maria was ill. But if she had, it would have been her Christian duty to visit her, to keep her spirits from flagging and her body from wasting away. Anna had a more flinty view of duty, and maintained that loyalty was owed first of all to your husband and children. But loyalty was too deep a subject for Katy. Loyalty to whom? Loyalty to her children or loyalty to her brother? What if these loyalties conflicted?

Everything is so clear to her, cold, clear Anna!

She left soon afterward, still seething. On her way across the fields, she saw a crew of men working. Who were they? Where had Peter found them? She took comfort from this picture of work, as she took comfort from the growth in their small community. Anna still had only the one child, but she herself had born John earlier in the year, her seventh. Adam and Katherine Bauer had had Philip, a few months earlier. And there were two new Henry Zimmermanns, an infant born to Philip and Apolonia and another to Friedrich and Margaret. Even Balthazar Merk's wife, Elizabeth, had borne a child or two since coming to this place; though she seldom saw the Merks, young Conrad kept her up with the news. And Elizabeth Strum, Heinrich's Elizabeth, had a girl the previous year and was pregnant again.

The stories that began to be told around the fires at night were like the tales of Old Home, like the stories of Schinderhannes, fright stories to tell against the winter's black night. In these stories the Cherokee Indians, with their coppery skin and mysterious ways—*the human trophies hanging from their belts, the wild calls in the woods, their way of melting into the distance, like ghosts*—blended slowly into the more brutal reality of the newer villains, white men but hard men, with hard hungers and a contempt for farmers and their settled ways. At first, these were just . . . stories.

Then one day Peter Strum came to Katy's house to ask for help.

He rode up in the forenoon, exhausted. He was nearly seventy, but he looked a hundred.

He slipped from his horse and sat, weeping, on the rough boards of the cabin stairs, his head in his hands.

Katy remembered long afterward staring at the top of his head. He was hatless, his scalp visible through thin gray hair that looked soft as a baby's.

"Please come," he said. "Please come." His eyes looked haunted. "Please come. Elizabeth has been . . . killed."

Heinrich Strum had returned home from some errand to find his wife lying dead in the yard, naked and bleeding on the rough grass under a sycamore tree.

The first thing he saw was her white belly, tight as a drum from her pregnancy, gleaming obscenely in the sun.

She was still warm.

She had tried to run away, and they had caught her in the yard.

Whatever they did to her they did there in the open, on the grass.

She was bleeding between the legs, where they had abused her, and from the head, where they had struck her, and her fingers looked twisted and broken. Her mouth was distorted in a silent scream. Flies were feeding on her blood.

Heinrich focused his rage into a point of icy calm. *What if they were still here?* He fetched his weapon from his horse, and with it a long knife, and squatted on his heels next to the corpse of his wife, waiting. He fell into a reverie of revenge and pain, and was only roused from it by the whimperings of the child from within the cabin; the baby was too young to have interested even these animals, and they had left her alone in the wreckage of the cabin.

They had gone, taking their plunder with them.

Heinrich took the child to his father's house and returned with his brother Jacob, now sixteen, and his sister Eva's husband, Daniel Michler.

There they quartered the yard, looking for signs, and took inventory of everything that was missing. As expected, all the horses and the cattle were gone. The pig had been killed and left to rot. Little remained in the cabin; even the boards of the bed were splintered. The Bible was gone.

What manner of man would steal a Bible?

I'll kill them all, every one!

Jacob was a skillful tracker; his early fascination with the Indians had led him to spend time in their company, and he had learned much from traveling with them in the bush. Now he put these skills to use. There had been at least four horses, he said, maybe more.

"They tethered them there," he said, pointing to a copse at the rear of the house. "And came to the house on foot. See, here are the prints. Elizabeth must have heard them and ran from the door, here, trying for the woods. But they caught her little more than half way." He looked over to where she lay, covered with canvas brought from their father's, and shuddered.

Heinrich was staring at the footprints in the sand, as though he could learn who had made them.

I will, I will find them!

A short while later, Katy and Abraham arrived, and with them Maria and Heinrich. Philip Zimmermann came, and three or four of the Webers, Georg and Suzanne and Barbara, and some of the Henns from the next farm. In the evening, Anna and Peter Dorst came, bringing with them blankets and a small tub of pickled pork.

By nightfall, the house had filled with people. A bonfire had been lit in the yard, and men were repairing what damage they could. Anna and Katy saw to Elizabeth, washing her body and smoothing away the blood. They managed to close her eyes, but there was not very much they could do with her terrified expression. They dressed her in a borrowed shift and wrapped a shawl about her and laid her in the coffin some of the men had cobbled together from boards. No one said anything of the unborn baby. There was nothing to say.

They stayed there the night, sleeping in the cabin, in a row, like children.

Anna slept badly, the thought of Elizabeth's bruised body crowding her dreams. About every hour she awoke, and saw Heinrich still sitting upright by the door, motionless and silent. A few hours before dawn, she opened her eyes again, but he was no longer there. She slipped outside and found him in the moonlight by his gate, staring in the direction the thieves had gone; she knew he was willing them to return, willing them to feel his pain, willing them to fear what was to come, what he would do to them. She laid her hand on his shoulder. He said nothing, but his shoulder lifted a little, acknowledging her presence. For ten minutes or so she stood there, her hand on the rough fabric of his shirt, but he didn't stir or say anything, and after a while she went back inside, and lay down beside her husband.

A week after Elizabeth was killed, a passing band of marauders burned Adam Bauer's corn crop, for no apparent reason other than it was there. His neighbors joined together and followed the arsonists ten miles, where they came upon them, overpowered them and beat them raw and bloody. One died. They left him where he lay.

Almost the same day, a corpse was found hanging from a tree near Cuffeetown Creek. No one knew who it was. There was a sign around its neck: *Gotten what he given.*

Four days later, when Heinrich was alone on the farm, he had a visit from Nick Kiess, an emissary from the Regulators. Kiess was just a boy, but a strapping lad, already broad in the shoulders, powerful, contained, serious. He invited Heinrich to a meeting at the farm of Barnaby Pope, one of the Regulator chiefs.

"Why should I come?" Heinrich asked.

"Because of what has been done to you," the boy said. "We are the law in these parts."

"The law cannot help me," Heinrich said.

"An eye for an eye," the boy said, "a body for a body. We believe in revenge."

"I'll come," Heinrich said.

There were about thirty men at Pope's place. They sat in rows on the ground, like children listening to a schoolmaster, but these were not children. They were tough men, and heavily armed. They exuded the air of competence and inner stillness that Calhoun displayed to such an exaggerated degree.

Pope was a lanky, laconic individual after the manner of Patrick Calhoun, and so were his two main allies, Joseph Kirkland and Thomas Woodward. Pope was haranguing the assembly when Heinrich arrived.

"We're wearied out," he was saying, "with being exposed to the activities of these robbers. We're wearied out of having to live without laws or government, church or schools, without police established or justice present. We're wearied out with our property being insecure, with our friends and family being injured and killed, with our wives"—here he looked at Heinrich, who stared expressionlessly back—"our wives mutilated, ravished and killed."

Too many meaningless words, cheap tricks, Heinrich thought. *We know all this.*

He'd been told that the Regulators had sworn to harass all horse thieves and robbers, to punish thieves with whipping, to hang murderers and rapists, "to pursue," as he put it, quoting Pope, "the rogues, break up their gangs, burn the dwellings of those that harbor them and drive the miscreants out of the province."

It's all so obvious. Why does Pope waste our time with it? A windbag!

Families and neighbors, banding together to combat the predators, had begun to strike back only because they'd been driven beyond endurance. Heinrich knew that, as they all did. They'd been encouraged when, in August, Governor Montagu offered money for any bandit leader captured and taken to Charlestown jail. But Montagu's offer only made things worse. Gang leaders were captured, shipped to Charlestown, convicted— and released. Why? Nobody knew, but everybody knew—*by dint of money*. Money had changed hands. As Woodmason put it, laying the irony on thick, it was because "the Mildness of Legislation is so great and the Clemency of the Cheif [sic] has been carried to such Excess . . ." It fueled their disgust with the authorities in Charlestown.

For this we pay them taxes!

Continuing losses to thieving bands focused their resentments greatly.

After a while, the Regulators began to turn . . . political.

Heinrich was with a group of Regulators who caught up with a small band of fleeing horse thieves on the banks of the Broad River.

They caught them as the dawn was leaking into the sky, coming at them at a dead run from the dark forest like avenging demons, and he remembered afterward only the orange glare of their campfire, the early light gleaming on the river, silver on black like an oiled gun barrel, men rearing up in panic, horses squealing, the smell of churned earth, then his mount struck some- one, who went cartwheeling backward into a tree, shapeless and broken and very dead, and Heinrich felt a fierce exultation—*Maybe he was one! One of the animals who killed my Elizabeth!*—and in a few seconds it was over. Three of the thieves were killed, three more on their knees near the fire.

Two of Pope's men whipped them until they screamed, and then whipped them again until their screaming stopped and they lay face down in the mud, more dead than alive, their clothing in tatters, matted blood and ridges of flesh tangled with fabric and mud and grass, more like bro- ken animals than men. Heinrich took no pleasure from the sight, but felt no regret either.

A few weeks later. Another place, another band, another posse, another dawn. Heinrich Strum sat on his horse at the edge of the woods and watched. Somewhere in the blackness were his fellow Regulators.

Creeping about, he thought suddenly, *like a band of assassins.*

Then there was a faint flicker of red, and a pillar of golden flame at the corner of a barn, and within a minute this exploded into a great billow of reddish smoke as the flames leapt into the stored hay and burst through the roof. There was the shrill scream of a panicked horse and another sound, a kind of baying, that set his teeth on edge, the sound of a human mob with its blood-lust up.

He remained where he was, on the back of his mare.

Within a few minutes, the barn was fully alight, the glare casting a ruddy glow on the nearby cabin. He could see black shadows flitting about, then there was a crash as two of them tore down the door and went inside.

It looked like a tableau at a circus sideshow, tiny and far away. Except for the sounds, as mindless as the harsh croaking of a crow.

There were, he knew, about twenty of them. They had crept up on the house in the middle of the night; the intention was to seize its owner, Nathan Terrapin, and teach him not to harbor horse thieves or to have any dealings with them. Nathan wasn't a thief himself, but he was a trader in leather goods and harnesses, and horse thieves had often been seen coming and going from his premises. Harboring villains was as bad as being a villain yourself, and the only way to stop the chaos and the looting was to turn the countryside against thievery, and the only way to do that—or so said Regulator theory—was swift and certain punishment for the very slightest suspicion of collaboration.

They'd said all this to Heinrich, believing he'd agreed. He was taciturn even by the standards of men not known for their garrulity, he never spoke of his loss, but they could all see the tight, black knot of his anger.

Still, he thought, anger was one thing. It was entirely his own and entirely justified, coming as it did from the wellspring of his own hurt. This wild baying . . . that was another. He'd heard something like it once before, as a boy back in the Hunsrück, when he'd watched a grim procession of men set off from the village at night, torches smoking, heading for the home of some *demon* whose nature he had ill understood, and he'd heard how their silence turned to this same malignant baying once the house was burning and the *demon* had been dragged from it, stripped and thrown back into the flames.

It was this savage chorus that kept him where he was.

Two figures in white, apparently women, were thrust from the broken entranceway to the cabin, staggering, propelled violently from behind by the Regulators within. They were followed by three more, smaller, figures, children. The five of them stood uncertainly in the yard, clutching each other, looking about them in panic. Behind them by the barn a group had seized an escaping horse and thrown it over on its side, and one of them leapt on it and cut its throat, and as it died it gave off a horrid, choking scream, and then they turned their attention to the women and children, and danced about them, pushing and shoving, yelling, and tearing at their clothing.

A woman's panicked cry woke Heinrich from the semi-paralysis that the smoke and the fire and the mob's insane energy had caused him, and in it he heard an echo of Elizabeth's screaming, out there in the yard where she'd died. He slapped his heels to the mare and goaded her into a run. He pulled up a few yards from the taunting mob, but the mare was hard to control, spooked by the noise and the flames, and she reared dangerously. He fought to get her under control.

"Where's Nathan?" he shouted.

"Not here. Only his woman and his get," one of the men yelled back.

The mob was pawing the women, tearing at them. One was now naked, her body glowing redly in the glare of the fire, the other clutching torn remnants of clothing to her breast.

"Stop!" Heinrich yelled. "We have nothing against them!" When no one paid him any mind, he once again slapped the mare and drove her into the men, knocking them flying in a tangle of limbs and curses.

But they recovered swiftly. One of them grabbed his mare's bridle and hauled her aside with main strength; others grabbed Heinrich and pulled him from the saddle. He thumped heavily to the ground, jarring his shoulder and hip. Then a boot took him in the head, and the tumult faded into flashes of light that hurt like shards of glass, and he blacked out.

When he awoke, just after first light, the fire was dying out. There was no sign of the women. Both the barn and the house were gone; all the animals were dead, wantonly slaughtered, their entrails spilling to the grass, horses, sheep, a pig, fowl, all dead, all killed. Some of the men had gone; others rested on the grass, leaning against trees or lying prone, heads in their hands.

"Where are they?" Heinrich demanded.

No one answered.

"Where are they?" he said again, angrily. "Where are the women? What have you done with the women?"

There was a long silence. At length one of the men stirred. "Gone into the woods," he said sullenly.

"Are they hurt?"

"They're alive, ain't they?"

Heinrich said nothing. A picture came into his mind, his boot taking the man in the head, the head splitting, the blood . . . *I didn't come here to make war on women*, he would say. But he kept silent. He knew what they'd say. *Serve them right for harboring thieves.* And in truth, he was confused. Elizabeth's ugly and meaningless death rattled around in his head like a flea in a glass jar, and he wanted to hurt someone, he wanted someone to suffer as she had suffered, he wanted to look into their eyes as they died, to make them know why they were dying. Or so he thought. But he remembered the belly of the naked woman glowing red in the heat of the flames, and he heard her terrified whimpering, and he remembered the belly of his Elizabeth beside him all those many nights, and the same belly cold and white and so very dead in the yard in front of his house, a yard not so very different from this one, and he thought of the gang of men she had tried to flee, different yet not so very different from this one . . .

He sat in the yard for a while, then he retrieved his horse, mounted and rode away. The woods swallowed him, and after a while only the smoke remained, faint trace of their night's work, and then it, too, was gone, and he was alone with his thoughts.

Thievery, banditry, rapine and murder continued unabated. On the Regulators' part, whippings, hangings and, yes, lootings, burnings and rapine continued. They hanged horse thieves when they caught them. They whipped those they suspected of thievery. They whipped those they suspected of consorting with thieves. They whipped those suspected of being friends of those suspected of consorting with thieves. And then they whipped their families for good measure. Too often, they inadvertently whipped those who were as indignant about horse thieves as they were themselves.

Gradually, opinions split, and focused, and hardened.

The people looked to Charlestown for help, first for assistance against the bandits and, now, against the bandits' nemesis. For their part, the Regulators' suspicions and anger turned gradually from the criminals amongst them to the authorities who would do nothing for them. And, by extension, to those who would do nothing with them.

Suspicions and denunciations grew into raids. Raids grew into skirmishes, skirmishes into pitched battles by armed gangs.

Charlestown must help. We want law and order. These Regulators cannot be our government. Their actions are flagrant, their words seditious. We want courts, we want sheriffs, we want jails. We want the pious words of the legislature to be made actual. We want punishment for wrong-doers. We want justice.

So thought Katy and her husband Abraham. So thought Maria and Heinrich, and Adam Bauer and Balthazar Merk. They were weary of grief, turmoil, mayhem, disruption, violence, murder. They wanted the peace that law should bring.

Charlestown is the problem. Irresponsible, callous government. We can put a stop to the killing ourselves. We want assistance, not interference. We demand the resources we need!

So thought Anna and Peter Dorst, and with them Philip Zimmermann, Dieter Utz (newly arrived from Germany), Balthazar Merk's sons Johan the firebrand and Lorentz the passive, and Adam Bauer's future son-in-law, the Frenchman Jean Henri. They were a community, and could stop what needed stopping without assistance and the condescension of King and planter.

Heinrich Strum, haunted by dreams of violence, wanted peace and needed revenge, and the contradictions tormented him. For some months he withdrew to his farm.

A few people visited him there, his father and mother, his sister Eva and her husband, young Jacob. Anna and Peter came, once or twice, and Katy and Abraham, but seldom together. Young Nick Kiess, whose feelings for the older man veered between affection and awe, came often. Sometimes Nick would bring a younger brother. Once he brought his sister,

Catherine, a headstrong young woman of twenty, who laughed a lot and tried to tempt him into a mood less somber.

He resisted, but that night his dreams were worse than ever.

By the late summer of 1767, the inchoate and seemingly random violence began to take on a clearer pattern. The Regulators, finally, got the attention of Charlestown.

On October 5, Governor Montagu told an alarmed Council in the capital that "a considerable number of settlers" had assembled and "in a Rioting Manner" had gone up and down the country, burning the house of some persons who were reputed to harbor horse thieves, "and talk of Coming to Charles Town to make some Complaints."

This "considerable number" was considerable indeed; some fifteen hundred were involved, and had "signed a Paper to support one another in defiance of the Civil Magistrates and against the Laws of the Country." Such magistrates as there were, and such laws as existed.

Montagu ordered the rioters to disperse, and "enjoined all officers to keep the public peace," a sentiment as obvious as it was useless, for the fifteen hundred men made ever more threatening noises and ever more militant speeches. The Governor retaliated by forming a new militia company on the frontier, but within a week, one of its senior officers was dismissed as a leading Regulator.

"The situation of the Province makes it absolutely necessary that Courts of Justice should be established as speedily as possible," an Assembly committee notified London, and within four days, they reported in favor of a court system and a vagrancy act, and recommended dispatching two companies of soldiers to the Back Country for three months to help "Suppress and prevent Disturbances." A commission of peace was struck and, as a sop to Back Country militants, the Governor found it "necessary" to appoint leading Regulators as officers. The troops were commissioned as Rangers and began a three-month pursuit of the outlaw bands.

The Assembly had done its work, but the members were themselves playing a parallel political game with the Governor and the Crown. At issue was the limitation of power—either theirs or the Governor's. The Assembly supported the circular letters from Massachusetts and Virginia on the Townshend

Acts advocating a boycott of British goods, and set up the Non-Importation Association, a thinly disguised anti-British political movement.

Meanwhile, Montagu's agents continued to arrest Regulators for what he called "their illegal acts." Bull, the Lieutenant Governor, persuaded Montagu that these arrests were regarded as persecution, and convinced him to limit the number of convictions. This would have soothed the growing sectional conflict, but it came to naught. More warrants were issued, without the knowledge or consent of the Attorney General in Charlestown, and several more Regulators were convicted. The countryside boiled up once more, and petitions again circulated. Nearly five thousand people signed a declaration that they'd intercept and dispatch any officer attempting to serve a warrant; they were confident that their numbers were now sufficient to make defiance practical.

In June, a huge crowd gathered at the Congarees. By the time the rhetoric was over and the declamations finished, they had shifted the argument into open rebellion and had adopted a so-called Plan of Regulation, which authorized agents of the Regulators not only to purge evildoers, but denied the jurisdiction of the Charlestown court over "those parts of the province that ought to be by right out of it." Thereafter writs and warrants from Charlestown were to be served only where and against whom the Regulators thought proper.

A few weeks later, at Marr's Bluff in the eastern end of the province, a good long way from Cuffeetown Creek, some of the Provost Marshal's militia were attacked and killed, and others whipped. The news was in every household within days. All of South Carolina held its breath.

Because the Governor, Montagu, was on leave in London, Lieutenant Governor Bull was left to deal with this new emergency. He issued two proclamations. The first was uncompromising in tone, commanding all peace officers and loyal subjects to suppress all "Tumults and unlawful Assemblys," and insisting that all citizens who failed to help them would "answer at their peril for the Neglect thereof." This was proclaimed on

August 3; two days later, he hastily issued another, somewhat less inflammatory, which admitted the possibility that some Back Country people "concerned in the said Acts of Violence have unwarily been drawn in and were Provoked thereto by the Great and repeated Losses they have sustained." He also offered "his Majesty's most gracious Pardon" to all Regulators, except those involved in the Marr's Bluff affair, for acts and misdemeanors committed before the proclamation was issued.

Late in 1768, Andrew Williamson, Patrick Calhoun and others, among them Peter Dorst, went to Charlestown to present yet another petition on Back Country needs to the Assembly.

Near the capital they passed a small party headed by the Provost Marshal, who was, provocatively, off to Marr's Bluff armed with warrants for the arrest of the instigators of the incident there. When he arrived at his destination, he summoned five militia officers, demanding that they join him with twenty men each. Instead, they brought sixty each, and when they were told why they had been summoned they "absolutely refused to act."

Heinrich Strum had also read the petition, but wouldn't endorse it, sign it or go along with the others to present it. In his view, the struggle against lawlessness was deteriorating into squalid compromise, politicking, hypocrisy and posturing. He had wearied of the Back Country habit of punishing lawbreakers while whining about the imposition of lawful authority.

So he stayed on his farm, clearing more fields and working his garden, and by the act of staying aloof and by virtue of who he was, he increased his value to the Regulators and his stature among the community.

He was also, though he didn't know it, in the thoughts of a number of women: Katy, who thought of him with a sisterly affection; Anna, who thought of his strength and his skin and black hair and cold black eyes; and Catherine, Nick Kiess's sister, who, though she'd seen him but once, thought of him with . . . curiosity.

Six

It was obvious, Katy thought, *that Anna believed her innermost desires were secret. But they were not, not at all. We all knew why she rode down the Devil's Racetrack!* Katy's hip ached. She had been sitting still too long. *Somewhere in that time, I lost her. I knew her innermost desires, but I no longer knew her.*

November 1775
Ninety Six, South Carolina

A few days from her fortieth birthday in the spring of 1775, Anna and Peter Dorst went to a community gathering at a meeting house near Ninety Six. Not everyone was there, of course. There were friends, neighbors, preachers, politicians, militia leaders, but not everybody. Only "our" side, because everything seemed to be "sides" these parlous days. The Royal government in Charlestown had apparently collapsed, the Regulators had mutated into Whigs, Peter, though not exactly a man of eminence, was at least crony to cronies of William Henry Drayton, the Lieutenant Governor's rebel-rousing nephew, confidante of provincial leaders . . . oh, yes, "our side" was doing rather well.

And "their" side? Sides, for there were many. Anna was dismissive.

Neighbors or not, they didn't understand. New ways called for new think-ing, new thinking for new doings. Royal toadies! Huhnh!

Barnaby Pope was at the gathering, and the Watsons. Philip Zimmer-mann came, now a man of substance, with his women, wife Apolonia, daughters Adalalia and Anna, the girls as fresh as spring buttercups. There were others she was pleased to see. The elder Merk girl came, to the prob-able fury of her brother Conrad, who was already sniffing around that young hussy, Rosannah, Katy's girl, and she only fourteen. Maria had come, out of friendship, and because Maria was incapable of saying no, but she had prudently left her husband at home—Anna's brother was loyal to the old ways.

Her sister Katy was nowhere to be seen. She hadn't spoken to Katy for . . . how long had it been?

Years!

Well, she wasn't alone. Many families were splitting, their loyalties torn.

Not everyone has the stomach to do what needs doing.

Philip and Friedrich Zimmermann didn't talk to each other any more. The Merk family was at odds. The Dorns were squabbling, Loyalty and patri-otism at war around the family hearth. There was fractiousness among the Bauers. A couple of the Bauer daughters were there, along with their elder brother Karl, whom Anna mistrusted in any case. None of the Rupperts came; they were too linked to the Strums. Old man Henry Ruppert had been a neighbor to Peter Strum, and the boy, Friedrich, was affianced to one of the Strum brats, Barbara. None of the Strums were there, of course, though per-haps Jacob would have appeared if he hadn't been so afraid of his brother. Peter and Maria had both died the previous year, carried away together in one of the mysterious plagues that swept through their community—how weary they had been, how little resistance they would have given to the Reaper. It had depressed Anna at the time—*how little they were missed!* None of the Webers came either. Well, that wasn't surprising. Nor the Henns. Adam had married Georg Weber's sister, and Anna would likely marry Jacob Strum, if she could ever find him, running as he did with the Indians.

Heinrich Strum? Of course not!

Too busy breeding with the Kiess woman!

In truth, Heinrich was one of her great disappointments. She'd seen him often after Elizabeth's murder. He had seemed so sound! Nick Kiess hadn't needed any eloquence to get him to join the Regulators; he had brought to Regulator affairs a formidable force, an energy, his great will, but then he had gone sour, and had stayed away. Why? Just as the Regulators were sensing their purpose!

She had tried to argue with him, once, but her usual persuasiveness deserted her. It was like arguing with a mountain. He looked at her with those disturbing black eyes. "The Assembly in Charlestown cries for liberty," he said. "They echo the northern cry, refuse taxation without representation at Westminster."

"Yes," she said, "that's . . ."

"Yet the Assembly does the same to us," Heinrich said.

"It's not so . . ."

"It is. They arrange matters so we are not represented in their councils, yet they tax us in any case. It is hypocritical. Besides," he said, his face smiling while the eyes remained cool, "explain to me why I would be more free ruled by Peter Dorst and William Henry Drayton than by William Bull?"

She'd become angry then, but it was girlish anger, to her further fury, and she felt like a small child trying to punch an oak tree in a tantrum and feeling the tree's oaken indifference.

Soon after that he'd married again, Nick's sister Catherine, *the Kiess woman*. Why did that make her so angry?

She looked over the crowd. It was an unusually warm November day. One of the men was crudely carving a spit-roasted hog, using his hunting knife; the tables were laden with pies and whisky and potent elderberry wine.

No, she didn't miss Heinrich. Let him huddle in his cabin with his Catherine! Not for her the trap of the might-have-beens. Nostalgia was good only for skin rashes, tics about the eyes, a heart that thumped against its cage, images that burned—No! She was a woman of the now, the momentous present.

But what were those black eyes like when he reached for his woman? Was there a fire in him? *What was he like, in those intimate moments?*

Peter called her then, and she went up into the hall to listen to the speeches.

The world was a different place, even five years ago. All those wellsprings of passion had gathered into a torrent, but the torrent had not yet become a flood, and the flood hadn't yet flattened into that sinister, glass-smooth water-race that meant the great falls were imminent, a plunge into the raging maelstrom below.

Sometime back in 1769, William Bull had reported to the London Board of Trade that the Palatines "have surmounted the difficulties which naturally attend all new settlers, especially strangers to the climate and language. By their industry they now enjoy all such conveniences as are to be found with the humble state of life—comfortable houses, orchards, plenty of provisions, stocks of cattle, hogs, poultry, horses for labour. They now raise more than they can consume and consequently add to their capital. Some raise flour and some raise hemp. They are loyal and very useful and orderly members of the community."

Well! Anna, of course, never saw Bull's optimistic missive. If she had, she would have wondered in what colony the man had been living. Bull was a decent enough fellow, a person of some conscience, but even so . . . Comfortable houses, plenty of provisions, stocks of cattle . . . All true enough. And more—real glass for windows, pewter for drinking, chests of clothing. But loyal? And orderly?

She would have concluded that Bull was just trying to persuade his Royal masters that matters were less perilous for his "side" than they were. The orators in the Assemblies of the northern colonies kept politics there in more or less constant upheaval, and even in Charlestown, the Commons was using the Stamp Act (despite its repeal) and the ever-increasing taxation to shape the colony's debate. The tonnage of shipping leaving Charlestown was almost that of New York, Boston and Philadelphia combined, and the merchants of Carolina were making huge fortunes, but they, too, followed the political principles seeping down from Boston, or at least allowed themselves to be bullied into believing them. By the end of the summer of 1769, an assembly of merchants, planters and artisans formed the Non-Importation Association, rammed through the Commons by mobs of artisans standing threateningly outside. For the rest of the year, gangs of the Liberty Boys, as the artisan hooligans called themselves, kept dissent in line; even the most radical Whigs acknowledged that this was hardly a model of democratic debate.

Of course, the Back Country had its own arguments with Charlestown—arguments with the Commons as well as the Governor's Council. In truth, with the thievery, lawlessness, illness, isolation, the little community of German pioneers was more a victim of misfortune than bountiful luck. So many had died, so many had departed for the older and more prosperous German settlements in Newberry, Richland and Orangeburg counties. Who was left? She counted them up—only twenty-four families remained, out of the seventy-eight that had made their way up from Charlestown as immigrants. The Dorsts, the Strums, the Adolphs, Frietzes, Zimmermanns, Bauers, Merks, Schildnachts, Rupperts, Flicks and Zanges, the Zwillings. Who had left? So many!

The matter of the Regulators and Back Country unrest had finally come to a head about the time of Bull's missive.

There was an election early in the year. The Back Country was still not organized into parishes, and so Back Country folk could not vote in their home districts. Yet they could vote, if they wished. They certainly were not denied the opportunity, oh, not at all—they just had to get themselves to the polls down on the coast. It was a system that had worked well for Charlestown in the past. The Back Country was effectively disenfranchised, but the coast could safely maintain its high moral tone.

This time, however, the Back Country did indeed come down to vote. Here was a new sight! A thousand men in a cavalcade, galloping a hundred miles or more to the election site to cast their ballots, after which, to the great alarm of the authorities, several "country gentlemen" were elevated to office.

The oligarchs of the coast, not to be out-maneuvered, told these pesky voters "that their actions were rebellious . . . And the assembly was not of long duration, being dissolved post-haste . . ."

New elections were called.

The Governor, Montagu, aggravated the situation by bringing a Back

Country magistrate, Jonathan Gilbert, to a meeting of his Council. Gilbert, a tattle-tale-teller of great merit, told how a friend of his, one Musgrove, had been savagely whipped and driven from his home by Regulators, unfairly and unjustly, and how he himself had risked his life to escape to Charlestown to tell the tale. He was happy to put names to the Regulators in question, whereupon the Council promptly decommissioned those among them who were magistrates and militia officers. This cynical act of political manipulation, with its confusing mixture of truth, fiction and collusion, led to the inflated rhetoric of shock and dismay so usual in these circumstances, and persuaded the Council to put an end to Bull's policy of conciliation. By doing so, they brought the colony to the brink of civil war.

A bench warrant was issued for the arrest of twenty-five Regulators and was given for execution to one Joseph Coffell, a man in ill repute in the Back Country. Coffell claimed the rank of colonel, appointed Musgrove his major and enlisted men, many of whom were the thieves whose activities had prompted the Regulator movement in the first place. Not surprisingly, Coffell's "troops" did more than arrest a few Regulators; they plundered the homes of settlers as well.

It seemed transparently obvious to the Back Country what was going on—they would be drawn back to defend their homes just as the voting went on in Charlestown. It was a particularly crude method of disenfranchising them. It could not be tolerated.

On March 13, Musgrove wrote a panicked letter to Montagu, in which he said eight Regulators had been seized as they tried to rescue another of their own, named Bossard, but that their captors had been surrounded by other Regulators and were unable to take their prisoners to Charlestown. A few days later, eight of his men did make it to the capital, but the prisoners turned out to be, in Bull's words, "poor Germans," and though they were convicted, Bull speedily obtained a pardon for them.

Enough was enough. About five hundred settlers assembled on the Wateree River on March 18, and nearly the same number came from the Broad and Saluda rivers, ready to march on Coffell's camp.

Peter Dorst, who had narrowly missed being arrested himself, helped draft their manifesto, which was laced with the bracing rhetoric of liberty. "Every man of property" in the Back Country is a "Regulator at heart," the document said, and then, with a final flourish: "The right of the People is the supreme right."

There were four hundred, five hundred, six hundred men under arms, their very numbers swelling their hearts with pride and implacability, a sense of righteousness that filled them with joy.

Anna stayed behind at the farm. Her heart was filled with their endeavors, but also with some confusion.

If only we could speed up the engine of time, she thought. *So we could arrive instantly at where we're going, the great hoop of time rolling over the intervening years, all the heartbreak, all the disappointments, flattened under its great rim.*

Coffell himself had more than four hundred well-armed and resolute men.

Both sides resolved to fight it out and give no quarter.

There'll be blood spilled, but in what a cause! Our first true battle of this great war!

Anna felt herself to have a sense of the times, and word had come to Ninety Six that England was at full war with France, and that Louis had pulled Spain into the alliance (the Spanish wanted Gibraltar back, and some of the West Indian islands stolen by English pirates), and that Holland was teetering on the brink, fearful of its Batavian trade and willing to kick a mastiff already distracted by terriers.

A liberated America could be part of that grandest alliance!

But who were they fighting here, really? The King? The planters? Or some of their own? Wasn't it true that so many of those now baying for liberty, those most agitated about any exercise of Royal prerogatives, were the same men who arranged matters so the Back Country was without representation?

There were men loyal to the King riding to deal with Coffell too.

Heinrich Strum was there, she knew it, riding boot to boot with the rebellious leaders.

Yet he seemed unshakable in his cool contempt for rebellion.

Why? When he himself had been so savagely bereft, stripped of family and possessions?

Does he think the King really cares?

As the great crowd of Regulators spilled across the Broad River, three prominent planters rode to town to let the Governor know what was going on in his Back Dominions, that this little matter of Regulator unrest was threatening to tilt the province into full-blown war. The Governor scribbled a paper for them to take back up-country; in it, he revoked Coffell's warrants and ordered "all persons to disperse, to their homes, on pain of punishment."

This tiny but prominent cavalry of three returned in time to find the two parties by the Saluda River; both sides were drawing up in battle array, advancing to fire. Galloping between them, waving their paper, they proclaimed the Governor's orders, demanding that "all People [should return] to their Homes."

They reluctantly dispersed, both sides brandishing their weapons and hurling oaths like musket balls.

Worse than musket balls! Bullets only wound and kill; words fester for generations.

As the rogues drifted away, disappearing down the trails and into the woods, groups of Regulators peeled off in pursuit. They whipped some, stripped others of their clothes and possessions, which were confiscated or burned. Others of Coffell's men simply . . . disappeared.

What happened then? The years have been such a blur. But I think, for a while after Coffell, we were very much left alone. Katy and Maria and I . . . Heinrich . . . Peter in the councils of liberty . . . The great hoop of time traveling in its own ruts. Jacob Strum told me once, the Indians said the past was like a great bear, trampling on your heels, and would rend you limb from limb if you ever stopped. Well! The Indians thought the same of the future, it was said, and lived only in the everlasting present.

What is death but the sudden cessation of yesterdays?

Early in the new year, 1770, the Church of England's Society for the Propagation of the Gospel in Foreign Parts sent the Reverend Samuel Frederick Lucius to the Back Country as a missionary to the Church Established. He wasn't a Lutheran, but at least he did speak German. His reports back to Charlestown and London were carefully headed "Cuffee Town."

"I delivered a Sermon," he wrote, "to a numerous and attentive congregation on Easter Sunday. There are some two hundred families under my pastoral care who have been so long without the ordinances of religion that their children were growing up like savages." In his first month, he baptized forty children and thirty adults.

But it was stony soil for the Episcopal Church, and as a lure, the Reverend Lucius was no match for the charismatics.

Heightened emotions demand intensive solutions.

In the spring, two justices of the peace were appointed and a jail was built at Ninety Six. At last! Villains no longer had to be dragged off all the way to Charlestown, at great expense and inconvenience.

Bull also urged the Commons to establish schools at Camden, Ninety Six and New Bordeaux. The Commons thought this a splendid idea. But nothing was done.

A ferry was begun at Saluda Old Town, to cross the Saluda River. Charles Carson was vested with responsibility for maintaining it. Carson was a good man, a solid man. All the Carsons were good Whig stock.

Another ferry was established at Robert Cunningham's. The Cunninghams . . . Robert was well respected, but his brother, Bill . . . A Whig at first, later a notorious Tory. *Bloody Bill!*

All the ferrymen were politicals, in one way or another. It was how they got the assignments in the first place.

In April, an act of the provincial Council was adopted authorizing several roads to be built in the Back Country. Better roads than votes, in the Council's view; at least roads would give swift passage to militia when needed.

The Council also approved maintaining what was already there, the Martintown Road from Robert Goudy's at Ninety Six to the Ridge, and then to the road between Long Cane and Indian Head.

Anna had taken this road often, in the months after Elizabeth Strum's murder, tempted almost beyond enduring to comfort the black-eyed boy so bereft. Halfway along it, somewhere between Heinrich's farm and Ninety Six itself, lay a stretch called the Devil's Race Track, a stretch of blue mud impassable in wet weather, a mire as mucky as . . . as the tangle into which she'd gotten her emotions.

She herself thought Devil's Race Track an appropriate name in other ways.

It's the slippery slope the New Lights speak of!

A son, Henry, was born to Heinrich and Catherine Strum.

It was said Catherine gave birth without the saving presence of midwives, in the company only of her husband. And that she had laughed through the delivery and afterward, though you know how the stories grow.

Henry was baptized by the Reverend Lucius. Anna didn't attend.

In 1773 the Treaty of Augusta was signed, at the request of both the Cherokee and the Creek tribes. The Indians ceded more than two million tribal acres in Georgia to the provincial authorities, to relieve the seemingly hopeless Indian indebtedness to white traders.

Hardly anyone cared.

On November 2, 1773, at Charlestown, Jacob Strum married his Henn, Anna Elizabeth. (As the documents put it, "ANNA Alizabetha Henn(in) b:1752 at Bergen Birkenfeld Pfalz/Berschweiler in the principality of Salem nr Kirn d/o Johann Adam Henn & Anna Alizabeth Weber.")

She did it! Anna thought. The child got Jacob to Charlestown for the wedding! Now how is she to keep him there?

Ten months later, Anna Elizabetha Strum was born. Her christening witnesses—at Charlestown, of course—were Philip Zimmermann and Catherine, her father's brother's brand-new wife. Anna was not invited.

The father made it down to the capital from Indian country in time for the ceremony.

Anna's boy, Peter, was almost ten. For five years after his birth, there had been no more children and Anna, though she put a brave face on it, had felt she was . . . shriveling up. But then, in '70, the bung, as she had come to think of it, was finally knocked clear by Peter's battering, and the children came, one two three four . . . first the girl Magda, in '71, then Anna, and Rachel, and the baby, George, to whose name she gave an "e," in the American way.

And so it went.

The years rolled around. The trees stumbled into leaf. There was a great windstorm that stripped them off again; the trees swayed furiously in the wind, in unison, like an army on the march. In Boston, the fish got drunk on tea, and the First Continental Congress met in support. A raven hopped into Anna's chimney and she was warned not to light a fire, because ravens were evil omens. Paying no attention, she fired up a smoky thing of damp twigs and the raven, groggy from smoke, fell with a musty crash into the grate. She grabbed the sooty bird and tossed it into the yard, where the dogs got it. In Charlestown, the Commons called a meeting at the unprecedented hour of eight in the forenoon, secretly, without telling Bull in advance, knowing that Bull would still be snoozing, the last of the previous evening's canary wine making its sluggish way through his system. Somehow the Lieutenant Governor got word anyway, but by the time he'd dressed and issued the order proroguing the meeting and disbanding (not to say demolishing) the Assembly, it had already voted money to support Congress. Anna had a horrible dream, in which she lay on the floor inside her cabin with her ear to a small hole in the door, to hear if there was still life outside. Later in the year, a Grand Jury for the Ninety Six District condemned the attitude of the British government toward the colonies. But they were still getting it all mixed up. Cited as a primary grievance was the fact that magistrates for the district "were appointed at the behest of the Charles Town merchants," whose "motives & designs" were, of course, dishonorable. Among the people who signed were Andrew Williamson, Moses Kirkland, LeRoy Hammond, Patrick Calhoun and Robert Goudy. Of course, Peter was not consulted, but if he had been, he would have refused—what had the merchants to do with anything? This was a matter of colonialists against the King! Heinrich and his brood mare had another child. He stayed on his farm and did nothing, but people on both sides of the growing conflict wanted to know, *What will Heinrich do? What did Heinrich say?* until she wanted to scream. Why did his opinion seem to count for more the less he did?

On December 19, 1774, new elections were held, called not by any authority, not by Bull or his Royal masters, not even by the increasingly restive Commons Assembly (though members of it were involved), but called instead by the disaffected everywhere to choose members of a General Provincial Committee to consider the increasingly troubled state of relations between the province and the Crown. It was everywhere blandly denied, but the intention was to set up a parallel governing structure, to be there at the end, when the swelling chorus of dissent drowned out the whingeing of the Loyalists, when the cobwebs of Royalism were swept out by the cleansing air of . . . &c &c, as the saying went—the rhetoric was familiar enough.

The Back Country, for the purposes of this exercise, was divided into four electoral districts, each to supply ten Committee members. The nearest poll was at White Hall, home of Andrew Williamson.

Anna, shivering with excitement, waited outside as Peter cast his votes for, among others, LeRoy Hammond, Andrew Williamson, James Mayson, John Purves and Patrick Calhoun.

None of us, us Germans, really play much of a part in all this, Anna admitted to herself, in a fit of honesty. *We're honest soldiers, no more, among the great captains of the age. But this is not to say we're unimportant. Without the yeomen, there is no army . . .*

The newly elected Committee met in Charlestown in January the following year, 1775, and out of its ballooning verbiage and the consequent sound and the fury came a resolution declaring itself the Provincial Congress of South Carolina. Shortly afterward, this Congress created a smaller, more secretive body called the Council of Safety, which was meant to be the executive arm of the people's will, the sword arm of the revolution.

The Congress, this new tribune of the people, immediately declared itself for a total ban on trading with Britain. The Council of Safety was charged with the task of persuasion, which it undertook with gleeful zeal. Ships were driven from Charlestown harbor, chased across the bar and, in one case, scuttled. Warehouses of the recalcitrant were burned. The great convoys of deerskins coming down from Indian country began to pile up in the streets of Charlestown; the pipe was full, furs everywhere, alleys paved with 'em. One wagonload stopped on the Martintown Road on the way from Ninety Six to Augusta, its drovers simply abandoning it in the mud, forcing other traffic to edge cautiously around it. Within days, the skins and furs had gone, stripped away, but whether by Regulators and Congressites or Loyalists or Whigs or Tories, no one really knew.

The Council concerned itself greatly with the matter of loyalty; not everyone seemed to share its belief in the inevitable merits of the new way of doing things, which was intolerable—a free country cannot tolerate unfree people in its midst!

Take the case of Thomas Browne, a Scotsman and Indian trader living in Augusta, who was notorious in his contempt for "Whiggery," as he called it, or sedition, as he put it in his rasher moments. Ah! He had a talent for invective, though, and the revolutionary cause stung from the lashes of his tongue. Something had to be done, and it was.

He was seized and hauled down to Charlestown.

Oh! They gave him every chance!

He was taken before the Council, tried and sentenced. He refused to recant his political heresy, keeping up his string of insults and denunciations, despite the very laborious hints consisting of puncheons of tar by the door, and sacks of plucked turkey feathers, and the very explicit warnings of the Judge Advocate appointed for the trial.

So he was tarred and feathered and carted, dragged about Charlestown for all to see (and people flung mud and dung along with ridicule), but when he still stupidly refused to recant and take the Oath of Allegiance to the new government, the mob became angry. In a clearing by the city gates, they built a large fire and exposed his naked feet to it, to subdue, as they put it, "his stubborn spirit."

In vain. The torment just fired the coals of his resentment.

"A mistake, a great mistake," Peter said when he heard of it. "We should leave torture to Royal jailers. It doesn't fit with free men. All we have done is make a vindictive, implacable enemy where once we had an opponent; I fear he will take his revenge in blood."

So the Back Country slid further toward Civil War. Armed bands formed themselves into militia, and the militia into regiments. There were skirmishes and hostile flourishes everywhere. The German community, in particular, split. There were many, to be sure, who had come out for Congress—her own Peter, of course, and Philip Zimmermann had broken with his brother. But Anna admitted that many of them remained stubbornly loyal, unmoved by the rhetoric of independence. Her own sister, Katy, and her husband. The Adolphs and Strums . . . especially the Strums, especially *him*, Heinrich.

She knew the arguments these . . . these *Loyalists* used. She'd heard them so many times in Katy's house before she'd marched out, refusing to return. The government they were living under, so far away from the seat of Royal power, gave them in practice far greater freedom than they'd ever had in Germany. The Stamp Act had nothing to do with them—the government, the despised Charlestown, hadn't given them courts in which stamps could be used; nor were they engaged in the commerce that the stamps were supposed to regulate. As to tea, they didn't use it. And why should they join a war against taxation without representation in the Parliament in England, when first the Commons and then the people's own Congress refused them adequate representation? Did not this same Congress levy taxes—ever-increasing, punitive taxes? Hadn't they been tricked out of voting? Hadn't they been called rioters? Hadn't the Charlestown militia been turned out against them merely because they had tried to come down to town to vote? Had the British government and the generosity of its people—remember Wachsel and the coffee-house subscriptions!—not helped them to come here in the first place? Did they not hold their lands by grants of the King? Were they not ignored all along by both sides, and weren't they now, suddenly, being courted, not because of any desire on the part of Congress for natural justice but because Congress wanted money and men into whose arms they could press the liberating muskets?

Congress, hearing the faint heartbeats of these plaints, had sent a few German-speakers, among them Georg Wagner and Felix Lang, up from Charlestown to reason with them.

Anna could have told them that wouldn't work.

It just enabled them to express their resentment more eloquently.

Wagner and Lang duly returned to the coast, with Back Country grievances ringing in their ears.

The Governor, for his part, tried emissaries of his own. Same tired, old arguments: that British power was ultimately irresistible, blather and more blather, that the whole dispute was about a trifling tax on tea, that the "gentlemen on the sea coast were willing to involve the people of the back country in a quarrel that would deprive them of salt and other important necessaries, and that the expenses of an insignificant tax on tea was nothing as compared to the expenses of a war with the mother country," all of it blather and none of it necessary, because they were already inclined to believe most of it, the lies as well as the truths, the little lies as well as the great ones. Heinrich Strum and so many of the former Palatines had already thrown in their lot with the Tories under the Cunninghams, and the vocabulary of complaint was already far too familiar . . . Dishonorable, disreputable, rogues, villains, traitors, sedition, infamy . . . all the oh-so-familiar words, tacked together in long strings like sections of a henhouse.

The whole quarrel, in this view, looked like an effort to exchange one set of rogues for another. Just a struggle for political mastery, barren of principle.

It made Anna furious that Heinrich and Abraham and the others shared these views. And her sister.

Katy! Sister! Sister traitor!

She'd marched out of Katy's house, angry, refusing to listen any more to stupid arguing.

She hadn't thought much about that stormy departure. After all, it hadn't been the first. But she'd never gone back. She hadn't seen her sister since.

Maybe I never will. Until the fighting is done, and everything is settled, and then we will see . . .

On April 19, 1775, fighting broke out at Lexington and Concord, in Massachusetts. Both sides accused the other of being the aggressor. It was the first military actions of what was being called "the civil war."

In Charlestown, the Council of Safety declared Royal power obsolete, passed the Act of Association and demanded that all citizens swear fealty to the new secular power, in the name of the people and of God.

So full of grand phrases!

"We consider ourselves united, by all the ties of honor and religion, for the defense of our country against all enemies whatsoever; we are ready to march whenever or wherever the Congress should judge necessary, ready to sacrifice fate and fortune to maintain public liberty . . ." And so on and so on.

They raised more regiments.

And they did the one thing all governments do in such circumstances: they printed money and bills of credit.

It wasn't so easy, of course. They had "money" now, because they'd just printed it, but they had no stock of arms or munitions; they were without equipment, ships or experienced officers. And they were terrified of their slaves, so formidably numerous. "Accessible to seduction, by gifts and promises, they might be instigated to massacre their masters at the moment of their most unsuspecting security . . ."

Still, the day the news came of the affair at Lexington, they seized the arsenal and removed everything it contained, which wasn't much, distributing the ordnance to soldiers in Congressional pay.

Thomas Fletchall, the "Colonel" of a Back Country militia regiment and therefore deemed by Congress to have great influence on Back Country ways, was among those called upon, like Thomas Browne, to declare himself. Of course, this was no Browne to be hauled down to the capital for interrogation—not with a regiment at his back!—but Congress was running out of patience with pleases and may-we's, and peremptorily demanded he decide his loyalty and his fate.

Fletchall was no Thomas Browne in other ways too. The mere hint of tar would have sent him quivering to the confessional; his most sterling qualities were equivocation and evasion. He replied that he'd of course called his regiment together, and had duly read each company the Articles of the Provincial Association, otherwise known as the oath of fealty. However, not one company had signed it. Instead, they had devised an Association of their own, and it had been "very generally signed from the Broad to the Savannah Rivers."

So supported, he added, with entirely uncharacteristic bravado, that he was "concerned that I'm looked upon as an enemy to my country . . . I must emphatically declare that I utterly refuse to take up arms against my King . . ." Then he added, giving himself an escape hatch, ". . . until and unless it becomes my duty to do so."

On July 12, a large party of horsemen swept down the Martintown Road, past Heinrich Strum's farm, heading for the Savannah River. A few days later, another party, or perhaps the same party, swept back again, heading like a whirlwind for Ninety Six. Stragglers followed, and then more horsemen, other bands. Back and forth, like a sapling bullied by a gale.

The first party had been two troops of Congressional Rangers, under Captains John Caldwell and Moses Kirkland, with Major James Mayson in command. Among the riders was Bill Cunningham, the flamboyant younger brother of Tory stalwart Robert Cunningham, and cousin to Patrick.

They occupied Fort Charlotte on the Upper Savannah with no resistance. Taking possession of its stock of powder and lead, they then thundered back to Ninety Six, sending up clouds of dust as they clattered past the Strum farm.

Heinrich, his curiosity piqued, made his way to Ninety Six to see what was happening. There, on the common in front of the new courthouse, he found the Whig troops in disarray and their leaders at odds. Kirkland, rankled by slights both real and imaginary from the Provincial Congress, and loathing Mayson as an all-too-successful rival for military rank and influence, had secretly changed sides, and sent a message to Thomas Fletchall.

Come and get the powder and lead, the message said. I will see you're not opposed.

Fletchall declined. But Kirkland's ill-kept secret made its way to Major Joseph Robinson, who with Robert and Patrick Cunningham and two hundred quickly assembled cavalry from the Broad River, came to see what they could find.

Among other things, they found young Bill Cunningham, who shrugged his well-tailored shoulders and left without argument. Mayson had already departed with his men, leaving the turncoat Kirkland in charge.

The new arrivals had no trouble taking possession of the ammunition in question. Kirkland not only passed it over, but himself and his troops as well. He openly joined the Loyal muster, which now amounted to some fifteen hundred men. Among them were Richard Pearis, Thomas Browne, Kirkland and the two Cunninghams.

It also included a let's-see-what-we-shall-see Heinrich Strum and Conrad Merk.

As a small but not insignificant aftermath, the Congress ordered Bill Cunningham to Charlestown. He retorted that he'd go only to resign. His resignation was promptly and discourteously rejected. There was a brawl. Cunningham was clapped in irons and tried by a court-martial on a charge of mutiny. He was acquitted, freed and galloped off in a rage to Ninety Six.

Later that July, the Council of Safety resolved to send a delegation to the Back Country to attempt to conciliate the inhabitants. For this task, they chose a perversely unlikely duo, William Henry Drayton and William Tennant. Drayton, a firebrand orator, didn't have the word conciliation in his political vocabulary, and as for Parson Tennant . . . to him, moderation was as much an evil as the whiskey and unfettered fornication that played so prominent a role in his sermons. These two assembled a delegation and sent word that they'd address a mass gathering at the edge of the Piedmont.

Before they even reached the meeting point they learned that Moses Kirkland, "without lawful authority" (as though there were any), was assembling men and arms in the very district their meeting was to be held.

Rumors buffeted the Back Country in a hundred tornadoes of suspicion, innuendo and sometimes-accurate fact.

"They say Kirkland declared their meeting canceled, and it was," Abraham told Katy. "And that Drayton, to retaliate, declared that everyone following Kirkland and assembling in arms without authority shall be deemed public enemies to be suppressed by the sword."

Here was a sensation—conciliators uttering threats of war, persuaders resorting to weapons, loyalty to be imposed at sword point. Soon, everyone felt impelled to declare himself, for Congress or against it, for the King or against him.

"They say Drayton came to the Dutch Fork to see LeRoy Hammond and appealed to him for help in persuading us to sign the Pledge of Association," Abraham told her at another time. Not surprising. Hammond was, after all, a man of influence, being a merchant and promoter of the tobacco trade, greatly esteemed in the Back Country.

A day or so later: "They say Robert Cunningham and Browne from Georgia have confronted Drayton and Tennant up at King's Creek, where they were holding one of their meetings."

Heinrich Adolph had picked up other rumors. "They say the Governor is sending a Royal army, Regulars from England," he whispered to Maria one night. He kept to himself the other rumor he'd heard—that three thousand Cherokee warriors were expected to cross the frontier to join them in their struggle against the Provincial Congress. The Indian Nation was a dangerous beast to prod into wakefulness, he feared; no point in alarming his wife with the thought of its stirrings.

Dorst heard tales of the other side. "They say Tennant has raised three companies of volunteers along Long Canes," he told his wife one evening, as they took the cooling air on the stoop. "They're to serve under Andrew Pickens."

Anna had been listening too. "I heard Joseph Robinson and Moses Kirkland have been accused of tampering with the Indians," she said.

And so it went. As Drayton and Tennant moved back and forth across the Broad and Saluda rivers, they were here welcomed, there repudiated, though not always in equal proportion. It seemed that, for the most part, the Back Country remained suspicious of their motives, charging them with fomenting rebellion and, in Joseph Robinson's words, "to be Lords in these new states, lay the country off into manors, and have taxes paid to themselves."

Convinced that a show of force would be useful, Drayton, now at Ninety Six, called upon the local Congressional militia-leaders to deploy three hundred men each through the countryside between the Saluda and the Savannah.

The rumors returned.

Moses is going to the Governor for aid and ammunition.

Kirkland will carry our assurances of loyalty to the King.

Men back from Charlestown say the Governor is impressed with our constancy, and has sent Kirkland to Boston, to General Gage, asking for Royal troops to assist us.

True, but to no avail.

In September, the Royal Governor fled Charlestown on a British frigate.

The same month, Kirkland was captured off Delaware Bay by a "privateer," as Congressionally approved pirates were called. His papers, seized and returned via Philadelphia to Charlestown, created an uproar.

Drayton issued a circular throughout the Back Country warning that Kirkland's seditious schemes would be suppressed, and sent word to the Committee of Safety to close all the roads to the capital. He also dispatched a small group to seize the leaders of the Loyalists but, forewarned, they evaded capture.

Despite Drayton, or possibly because of him, Robert Cunningham was able to raise an army of twelve hundred men, who established a camp just north of the Saluda within a dozen or so miles of the fort at Ninety Six.

Drayton's ordered Colonel Richardson to attack Cunningham from the rear.

Drayton's ordered John Thomas to burn the homes of all those damned non-Associators.

I hear Drayton arranged to have his orders fall into Cunningham's hands.

Drayton's demanded a conference.

They're going to meet . . .

Suspicious that this conference was just a ruse to capture them, neither Cunningham nor Thomas Browne, who was with them, would agree to go. Thomas Fletchall, typically, didn't even consider it. Instead, they sent emissaries, to whom Drayton dictated his own terms, which he grandly called the Treaty of Ninety Six.

Naturally, the loyal Tories were dissatisfied with its terms and sent Browne to seek help. Unfortunately, he fell into the hands of the Whigs, and though he escaped, it was to Florida, not to the Back Country.

They say Cunningham has been captured.

Robert was arrested and they're sending him to the Provost in Charlestown.

Damned Whigs!

Williamson has called out his militia!

He's mustered five hundred men at Ninety Six!

Two thousand men have gathered under Joseph Robinson over the river!

On November 11 and 12, British ships of the line, still in the harbor, fired on Charlestown. There were no casualties.

On November 18, Robinson's men crossed the river.

War was coming.

There was what Colonel Williamson called "a warm engagement," followed by a brief siege and an honorable, more or less, capitulation by the outnumbered Whig forces.

Heinrich Strum, Daniel Michler, Friedrich and Christoph Ruppert, Peter Mehl, Conrad and Lorentz Merk, Georg Weber and Christian Zange were all there.

Philip Zimmermann was not present among the defenders, but his brother Friedrich was among the attackers.

Jacob Strum was in Charlestown with his wife.

Neither Heinrich Adolph nor Abraham Frietz was there.

Peter Dorst wasn't involved.

But Johan Merk, only fifteen, was in the fort, and was seen aiming a long rifle in the direction of his brothers' troop. He probably didn't fire, and in any case, neither of the other two Merks was hurt.

Adam Bauer remained on his farm; his son, Karl, watched from the woods.

Two of the Weber boys, Thomas and Henry, were there with their father.

Heinrich Strum killed one of the Whigs. Shot him with a long gun. Saw the puff of dust, the man fall down. No blood, or none that he could see. The dying man called out for a while, a high, plaintive sound like a sick sheep, and then he was silent. Heinrich felt nothing. It was what he was supposed to do. Afterward, he talked to an itinerant preacher, but the preacher had no words of wisdom, and Heinrich went home to his wife.

The first Battle of Ninety Six, a very small act of war. Nobody won. A few died. Others were crippled for life. One or two wasted away and perished months later. Only their families noticed.

Everybody lost, a little.

Seven

Anna stood up, moved a few yards away, stretching. *Damn the woman, she's asking too many questions. Let it come slowly! We've been forty years, we can take a little longer. It was around this time, wasn't it, that Peter captured the Strum boy? Captured him, and threw him in jail. This wasn't any longer a family quarrel. It was warfare.*

But sometimes, we couldn't see the difference.

January 1776
Great Cane Brake, South Carolina

Early one morning, Catherine Kiess, or Strum as she now was, appeared at Katy's house. She had been walking half the night, and was chilled to the marrow, but as she thawed out in front of the fire, Katy thought, *She's chilled from more than the cold. She looks as though the wind has been making too much noise in her dreams, ghosts rattling the shutters.*

"What is it?" she asked.

Catherine shook her head, huddling closer to the fire, rubbing her hands.

How beautiful she is! Katy thought. *She's a young girl still, but more beautiful than I ever was. Strong hands, though, capable. Heinrich is a lucky young man.*

"What is it?" she asked again.

Catherine lifted her head. "Heinrich's gone," she said.

"Gone? What do you mean, gone?"

Gone could mean anything. Gone to the Indian Nation. Gone to the Long Canes. Gone to Charlestown. Gone to heaven. Gone to perdition.

"Tell me! In what way, gone?"

The man couldn't have just left her! It would be insane!

Catherine got some sense of her meaning, and sat up suddenly. "No," she said. "Yes. You know, there are soldiers everywhere?"

Of course Katy knew it. Every few miles, some rising-sap young upstart who could gather fifty troublemakers took to calling himself a colonel, and joined up with one side or the other. Mostly Associators, now. Parading his soldiers about the country, harassing citizens. She'd heard that a patrol under one of these upstart colonels had struck at Fair Forest, where they surprised a bodyguard of King's Men, captured poor old Thomas Fletchall. Hauled him out from his hideout in a hollow sycamore tree, so they said. Hustled him into the prisoner compound at Evan McLauren's, now converted to the Whig cause. Unkindly, they called him a fat, old coward. Well! He was a commander of the King's Men, and had every right to be afraid. Some of those Associators would just as soon shoot as talk, and no reason not to practice a little tarring and feathering first . . .

But more recently, after the events at Ninety Six, it had become more serious. There were real armies about now, with real leaders, more harassment than ever.

"Well," said Catherine, "Heinrich had heard that Colonel Richardson's men were looking for him . . . "

"Heard from whom?"

"Oh, from friends," Catherine said vaguely.

Everyone in the Back Country knew of Richardson. Colonel Richard Richardson, in the name of the Council of Safety & the Common Weal & the People Assembled in Congress, in all these names and more, had been gathering strength and scourging the country from the Broad to the Saluda, hunting down the Loyalist leaders.

"They captured Richard Pearis, you know," Catherine said.

Katy knew of Pearis. An Irishman. Came to America, to Virginia, as a child and later moved to Ninety Six and the Cherokees, where he'd set himself up as a trader, taken an Indian wife (wives, more likely) and, through some finagling, got hold of a large tract of Indian land. They said he held as much as twelve square miles in the upper Saluda.

Fletchall, Pearis, others—cut them out and round them up like so many obstinate cattle and send them to . . . some Whig butcher shop somewhere?

Richardson wrote to the Council of Safety that some of his prisoners were "of the first magnitude." Pearis and the others he sent down to Charlestown under escort while he continued on to the Enoree River, where he made his camp, and there the Council, well pleased with his work, sent him even more reinforcements. Congressional troops came in from both North and South Carolina, and in the middle of December, Colonel Stephen Bull from Beaufort and Captain LeRoy Hammond arrived from Augusta with Georgians, while Colonel Williamson added the support of his regiment from Ninety Six.

With his army now numbering some five thousand, the greatest ever seen in the Back Country, Richardson moved on up the Enoree and encamped around Hollingsworth's Mill. His mere presence, this brooding, threatening presence on the Enoree, intimidated many of the Loyalists, and captain after captain brought his King's Men in to Hollingsworth's to pledge fealty to the Congress.

Those who kneeled, hypocritically or no, he treated well, on the advice of Council, allowing them to return home with their arms, only demanding they sign an affidavit that would forfeit all their property should this newly minted Rebel return to the King.

Oh yes, everyone knew Richardson in the Back Country.

The previous morning, Catherine said, Heinrich had gathered together his weapons and a pack, and had prepared to ride.

"They're coming," he'd said, "coming for me. I have to go."

"He just rode away?"

"Held me until my back near cracked, and whispered that he was leaving the farm in the best possible hands, then he rode away, not even looking back . . ." She turned to Katy. "What will I do if he never comes back?"

"Heinrich is the kind who always returns," Katy said, thinking of the younger Strum's steady strength.

"Yes," said Catherine. "Yes, I suppose he is."

They had, indeed, come later that day, as Heinrich had predicted, about a hundred of them, guns at the ready, a hard-looking, violent band, under the nominal command of one Colonel Thomson. Near the back, and trying to be invisible, was her little brother Nick. *Only a boy, but a man in his own heart!* Catherine stood in the doorway, tall and upright, trying not to show her panic. At a gesture from Thomson, men dismounted and fanned out across the homestead, into the barn and the woodshed. Two came toward her, but she refused to move, and after a few seconds they went round the house to the back door. She heard them crashing about inside, and then they emerged, shrugging their "nos" to Thomson.

The commander leaned forward in his saddle, studying her. "And where do you think he is, this husband of yours?" he asked.

Catherine took the offensive. She pointed at her brother. "I see you're letting brothers make war on their sisters now? Is this Congressional policy?"

"As to that," Thomson said equably, "we're not making anyone do anything that goes against his nature. And this is not war. We're rounding up a nest of traitors, is all."

"My husband was a Regulator, as was Nick," she retorted. "And when armed bands invaded farms, the Regulators hunted them down and punished them with whipping. God willing, that will happen to you."

There was muttering from some of the men. Before Thomson could reply, Nick yelled, "He turned against us, Kat! When we needed him, he turned against us!"

"As to that," she said, mimicking Thomson, "as to that, it's a matter of dispute whose spines are crooked."

Thomson lost patience. "Count yourself lucky we're gentlemen," he said, and pulled his horse around, urging his men into a gallop.

None of them looked around. Not even Nick.

Katy heard all this with a shudder. Catherine had been lucky, *and so have I!* Nobody was yet looking for Abraham, because he was a pacific man, but she knew if they asked him to take the Oath of Association, he would refuse. He was a slow man, but strong in fiber she deemed, if as yet untested. She hoped he would never be put to that test.

After an hour or so, Catherine got up to go.

"I must return," she said, in answer to Katy's suggestion she stay until word was received of Heinrich. "The children are with my sister, but the farm needs me. I am," she said proudly, "a capable farmer."

Katy saw her to her horse.

"We'll prevail," she said, comfortingly if meaninglessly.

"We'll endure," Catherine said. "We've always been good at that."

Heinrich rode slowly, using Indian trails and trackless woods to make his way across country. It wasn't difficult. Like all his fellows, he knew the countryside intimately, having hunted it for a decade or more, and he had no need of highways.

Best to stay off traveled routes, in any case. Too many spies now. Too much chance of running into the militia, or some of Richardson's troops.

Even so, a band of armed men did pass him.

Impossible to tell whose side they were on, but probably not his. They wore no uniforms, carried no colors. Most of the Germans were Loyal, but Loyalists would be keeping a low profile now.

He was one lone horseman, and had heard them coming, slipping out of their way and into deeper woods, tethering his mount in a small depression fifty yards on. He watched as they rode past swiftly, in close file, swords in scabbards; they looked as though they had urgent business elsewhere.

Easy to ambush, he thought. Not looking to left or right. No outriders, no scouts. Too much confidence.

He was better at it than they were, he thought. It filled him with gloom.

I didn't set out to be a soldier!

Catherine and his children, family, the farm, to make his way and be left alone, it was all he wanted. But the country was filling with soldiers as inevitably as the tide fills a small harbor, and there would be war. Surely the Loyalists would win, in the end. They had the greatest empire in the world to fight for them. And this was their home; they were Americans, they'd be fighting for their own place. They'd prevail, but it would be years . . . He wondered how long before he'd see Catherine again, whether she'd be safe. He thought of the women and children. No one would be safe in this war! He'd seen how the conflict had poisoned families. He'd seen how the sisters Katy and Anna, who'd once clung to each other in the hold of the black hole on the river Thames, were now at each other's throats, Abraham threatening to fight (more belligerent than he'd let on to his wife), Peter zealous in the other cause. Everywhere, families splitting—how could they say, in Charlestown, that this was America against the King? It would be family against family, sister against sister . . . No, there would be no safety for the women and children, not in this war.

He slept that night in the deep woods, without a fire, and the next day picked his way through the countryside toward the northwest, skirting farms and avoiding the ferries. He was looking for Patrick Cunningham and his followers, the last substantial Loyal force in the Back Country. Cunningham had retreated after the fracas at Ninety Six had come to naught. He had taken his men to Alexander Cameron's plantation in the Cherokee Nation, where they knew the Provincial Congress's army couldn't follow, and was now said to be encamped somewhere in the Great Cane Brake, preparing to regroup. Cunningham could use whatever help came his way. Heinrich liked Patrick—there was a man who wouldn't swear fealty to anyone just to save his skin, unlike his brother, the dandy Bill, who seemed to Heinrich a natural turncoat. Patrick struck him as an American of the best sort.

The following day he stopped at a farm he believed to be Loyal. The woman of the house swept out to the edge of the stoop and greeted him with a warning shot that gouged the earth disturbingly close to his horse, but when she learned who he was, she invited him in, fed him and offered him a bed for the night. Her man was already off somewhere, she said, likely with this Cunningham.

Heinrich accepted her meal and a jug of her whiskey, but declined the bed. He preferred the woods to the rankness and chaos of sharing his bed with children, and the house was overrun with them, of all ages, from babies to adults, more children, he thought, than one woman could possibly have borne, more whelps than a she-wolf, though it became clear after a while that some of them were not hers but her children's children. He tried not to think of who their sire might be.

After his meal, he sat for a while by the fire, letting pictures of his own home fill his thoughts. First Elizabeth, then Catherine, their children, the house now furnished with all the things they'd made themselves and properly chinked against the weather, the door tight-fitting, everything in working order and as comfortable as their plain life could afford them. He thought of Elizabeth, Catherine, Catherine, Elizabeth, the women in his world. He thought of Catherine, her warmth, the warmth of family, of house, of community. *Why are we turning against ourselves? In the name of what cold philosophy are families fighting each other?* Two hundred years hence, would small parcels of earth still be issuing declarations, demanding liberty? Would Carolina demand liberty from Boston, Ninety Six from Carolina, Cuffeetown Creek from Ninety-Six, free republics all, and for what, in the end? So men and women could find each other in the dark and, fumbling, cling to each other as they always had? He stared across the fire, where one of the daughters was feeding a baby, its stubby fingers spread out across her breast, mouth sucking greedily at her nipple. He stared at the breast and its delicate veining. But in his mind he heard the rattle of drums, a faint bugling, the ghostly thump of cannon. Too many men would rather fight for an abstract idea than for the warmth of the hearth, and that was the sad truth. He took this thought with him as he trudged outside to make up his bed in the hay.

He left at dawn, riding away from the sun. The woman had given him a skin of whiskey and a boiled fowl; he made the fowl last two days and the whiskey four, and by that time he'd found out from Cameron where Cunningham was to be found, and had headed back southeast.

Cunningham was deep in the canes, but Heinrich found him easily enough. Far too easily. Cameron had been criminally free with information, Heinrich thought. *How did he know who I was?* He'd asked several others along the way, and without fail they told him what they knew, which was considerable.

"Well and why not?" Cunningham asked, when Heinrich told him this. "We're not hiding. We're not a flock of ducks, waiting here in the reeds for the hunters."

But they were, Heinrich thought. For one thing, Richardson had thousands of men under arms, Cunningham less than three hundred. That alone made them ready for the plucking, unless they stayed on the wing. He was profoundly disturbed by the absence of sentries as he entered the camp, the apparent lack of readiness, their want of interest in his identity. Cunningham didn't know who he was, had never heard tell of him, they'd never met and dissimulation would have been child's play. Did he never think of spies?

"Why are you fighting?" Cunningham asked Heinrich that night, as they sat around the fire. "You men"—he meant the German immigrants—"are mostly Loyal, are you not? Why?"

Heinrich sat for a while before answering. Mostly Loyal? Yes. Of course, there were many who were not. He thought of Peter Dorst, of Philip Zimmermann, of Johan Merk and Nick Kiess, both still youngsters but already firebrands. The young ones you could understand, though his brother Jacob was the same age as Nick and Jacob was Loyal, wasn't he? It was always hard to tell with Jacob; there was a secretive side to him that Heinrich mistrusted. Philip Zimmermann puzzled him. He was a mature man, sagacious, calm in spirit, not a man vulnerable to the blandishments of orators, a man of community spirit—hadn't he been christening witness to Heinrich's second daughter, and to Jacob's first? Zimmermann believed every man had a right to take part in his own governance. All very well. Who could argue with that? Heinrich, too, had heard the speeches. Representation was the essence of that belief. But to the stage of killing others? And if Zimmermann never gained his representation in the Parliament in London—how was his life diminished? Why was that worth so much animosity?

For him, he knew, it was a simpler matter. They pushed him, he pushed back. The British King had given him his land, had settled him on it and was then more remarkable for his absence than for his governance—wasn't it the very absence of lawful authority that had led to the formation of the Regulators? Now along came the Whigs and demanded he revolt, and if he didn't, his property would be forfeit, and his life, or at least his liberty, at risk. They would force him to be free, or at least free of something they detested. Heinrich didn't think this insistence on conformity a very sound basis for the formation of a republic. They called him a King's Man, and he supposed he was. But it wasn't how he thought of himself. He believed himself to be an American, as they were.

How to explain this to Cunningham?

"I'm freer here than I ever was before," he said at last. "Parliament is too far away to understand us properly, but also too far to affect us much. Bull helped us. He was a good man. If there are problems, men of good will can solve them. So when a Rebel comes by with a gun to my head and says I must sign an oath of allegiance, I must say no."

"Good, good!" said Cunningham. "Many of us have suffered the stupidities of colonial rule. Of course Parliament and its ministers don't understand us. How could they? They're not Americans as we are! Why, many of us respect the intentions of the Rebels, and believe as they do that we should have a say in governing ourselves. But we believe in persuasion, not treason, in talking, not ranting, in argument, not weapons."

It wasn't, in the end, a conversation that went anywhere. What they believed, what they didn't believe, no longer mattered. Their enemies were in the grip of their orators, and now they were being hunted, and that was all that mattered. To fight when one had to fight, to stay alive, to think of home . . .

He took his bedroll into the canes and lay down, wrapping himself in his blanket. The dampness of the ground seeped into his bones. He put his hands between his thighs to keep them warm. At home, there'd be a fire going. Catherine would get up in the morning, stoke the embers, the children would yawn and stretch, she would go out into the yard to feed the animals, out through their American door into their sunny American yard to feed their American animals . . . She was soft and pliant, but he'd seen her splitting wood, whipcord strong . . . He wondered whether he would ever see her again.

Richardson stayed where he was for another week. His job was almost done. The Back Country was peaceful. Not pacified—he was too experienced a soldier to believe that sullenly swearing an oath changed a man's loyalty—but there seemed little danger that violence would flare. Only one thing remained to be done before he could disband his army and send the militia home. Patrick Cunningham and his men would have to be rooted out and dealt with. This last nest of unrepentant King's Men, this last armed band, this last determined aggressor, this last foe, would have to be defanged. He knew where they were. Somewhere in the Great Cane Brake.

On December 21, he called for volunteers. Some thirteen hundred troops, both Rangers and militiamen, responded. One of them, a militiaman of no particular eminence or renown, was Peter Dorst. Colonel Thomson was newly back from his patrols. Richardson put him in command and sent him after Cunningham.

The army set off at dusk.

It wasn't hard to find where Cunningham was camped.

"Following a night march of 25 miles, [we] struck Cunningham's camp at break of day."

So said Thomson's regimental report the following week. Easy to write, not so easy to do, as Dorst's aching bones and screaming nerves told him so eloquently.

Dorst's troop was in the van. His troop leader had learned the use of scouts from the Rangers, who had learned their tricks from the Indians (until a Ranger, even on horseback, was as fleet and silent as a visitor from the netherworld), but no matter how silent, a soldier was never certain that the enemy were not more silent yet. The scouts reported no activity. That could be a good sign, or a very bad one. Each time they passed through a defile, or crossed a creek, or threaded a ravine, every man in the vanguard could picture Cunningham's soldiers lying in wait, dug in behind redoubts of rock and heavy timbers, ready to lay down a withering cross-fire, the musket balls whistling through the leaves, the heavy thud as a ball hit flesh . . .

A few hours before dawn, the convoy was halted by a returning scout. He'd heard horses, smelled the smell of a dying fire. They'd found Cunningham.

"The main body will wait here," Thomson said. "The enemy is but half a mile hence, to the north. You," he said to Dorst's troop, "circle round to the west. There's a rise there, you won't be seen. You," he said to Hammond, leader of another troop, "circle round to the east. Careful there. Not as much cover."

"And then?" the troop leaders asked.

"And then we wait. At daybreak I'll attack from the south with the main body of men. It should be enough. With luck, we'll have surprise on our side and they won't be prepared. But some will escape, take to their horses and flee. That's for you to contain. No one should escape, mind!"

"Should we not attack from the west?" Peter ventured.

"No! Too much confusion. You're the net in which our fleeing fish will be caught."

"Prisoners?"

"Prisoners. But kill if resistance."

Relieved and disappointed, Peter's troop crept in a looping circle, first a little south of west, then west, then north, until they judged they were parallel to the Cunningham encampment. They dug in at the edge of the rise.

"When they come, they'll come fast," their leader said. "In a panic. And they'll come through the cane one at a time. They won't have time to group."

And then they waited. It was quiet enough that some small forest thing stirred in the leaves a few feet from Peter, a field mouse or a chipmunk. Well! It had enemies of its own, no doubt, and didn't worry about being pounced on by a human warrior.

He settled into his cover, listening to the silence, to the blood pumping in his temples. The minutes seeped away, the future drifting into the past. There was nothing to do but wait. His knee hurt where it pressed into a root. Wasn't it getting light? When would Thomson act? Why wait until they . . .

That's when he heard the first whump! of the shooting.

Instantly, he was on his knees.

There were hoarse shouts, more shots, the chilling female scream of a horse in pain, more shots, silence.

Then the shooting started again.

Suddenly out of the blackness came two horses, running fast, riders bent low over their necks, moving so fast they were almost gone before they were seen.

One of his men fired, missing, the bullet tearing only leaves. But the muzzle flash, going off as it did without warning, caused one of the horses to rear, lose its footing and topple, throwing its rider. Several men pounced on him. The other horse, going like a fiend, leapt by only feet from Peter's head, and was gone before any of his men could aim.

Heinrich came awake at the first shot, rolling from his blankets further into the reeds. Fast as he was, Cunningham was faster. The leader was already on his feet and had taken in the situation in a glance. There were Whig soldiers everywhere! There seemed to be a solid wall of them! A blur of bodies, horses, the glint of metal, an army crashing through the cane like a thousand-legged demon. A gun went off, the bullet taking one of Cunningham's men square in the chest, lifting him like a rag doll; he died soundless.

"Flee, men, flee! Save yourselves!" Cunningham yelled.

But Heinrich was already on the move, running fast, bent low, changing direction often, dodging trees. A Whig loomed up, but Heinrich's knife took him in the throat and he gurgled once, then subsided. Heinrich hurdled his body and dashed for the horses tethered in a clearing some fifty yards away.

Cunningham passed him before he got there. The leader hadn't even paused to don his breeches, and his long, bare legs flashed like the hindquarters of a deer as he sped past. Heinrich, prudently, had slept fully clothed.

They each leapt astride a bareback horse—no time for saddles, no time for anything, time only to get shot. Cunningham clung to his mount like a giant spider, clapping his bare heels into the beast's flanks, urging him on. Heinrich did the same.

"Make for Cameron's!" Cunningham yelled as their horses dashed for freedom. "We'll regroup there!"

Heinrich had no time for reply, even had he thought of one. Regroup! The man was mad! This was a disaster, his troop was finished, the war was over, Cunningham was a fugitive and he was thinking of regrouping . . . He clung to the horse's mane, the twenty-foot canes whipping at him. Cunningham, beside him, was riding hard, but he looked comfortable, as if this were just a friendly race, with the prize of a barrel of beer and a mess of pickled pork hocks at the end. Heinrich was just trying desperately to keep from being thrown when a musket went off no more than a few yards in front of him, the ball whistling past, the muzzle-flash blinding. Cunningham's mount paid no attention but leaped through the flash, diving into the dark like a swallow into a barn, and was gone. Heinrich's mount reared, stumbled, reared again and Heinrich toppled to the side, pushing himself off to avoid being trampled. He landed heavily, bruising his shoulder. His head banged onto the ground, and everything went black.

When he awoke, his head throbbed and his bones ached, but he seemed otherwise unhurt. He had been stripped, propped roughly against a rock, his hands bound. The sun was well up. Whig soldiers were still prowling around the clearing where Cunningham's troop had bivouacked, sorting guns, ammunition, baggage and stores into piles to be carted away by wagon.

Heinrich looked around. He and a dozen other prisoners were being guarded by a troop of Rangers. He could see Peter Dorst bustling about in the middle distance. Dorst was paying him no attention, whether because he'd not seen him or because of unease it was impossible to say.

Ten yards away, in another knot of prisoners, he saw two familiar figures, Christoph Ruppert and Christoph's brother, Friedrich, his own brother-in-law. Christoph was about his age, Friedrich a good thirteen years younger. They were neighbors.

He called over, "Christoph! Christoph!"

Christoph turned his head. Heinrich, arms tied, waggled his head. This made it throb terribly, and he stopped.

"Ich wußte nicht, daß Ihr hier seid!" he called.

"Wir waren mit Patrick in Ninety Six," Christoph called back. *"Waren bei Ihm die ganze Zeit. Konnten nicht heimgehen. Die haben unsere Hauser beobachtet."*

"Ich konnte dich letzte Nacht nicht sehen?"

"Wir sahen dich kommen . . ."

A Ranger stood, and interposed himself between Heinrich and Christoph. "Enough!" he said. "What's that you're saying?"

"I'm asking my friend how he is," Heinrich said.

"That Hessian you're yellin'?"

"We're Americans," Heinrich said, his face tightening.

"Get your feathers down, son," the Ranger said. "Just askin'. Whyn't ya talkin' English, then?"

"The King's English, I suppose?" Heinrich said.

"Call it what ya will," the Ranger said, refusing to be goaded.

"What happened here?" Heinrich asked, giving it up.

"We cleaned up," the Ranger said. "A dry American cloth to a damp Royal waterspill, and soaked it up clean."

"How many dead?"

"Only six, I b'lieve," the Ranger said. "At last count. A hunderd thirty captive, like you. The rest scattered into the canes, with neither food nor clothing nor guns nor horses. They'll not be in there long, I reckon."

"More than two hundred got away?" Heinrich started to laugh. "You let more than half get away?"

"You would have done differently, I s'pose?"

"I would. I'd have taken them all."

"Who are you?" asked the Ranger, suddenly curious.

"Heinrich Strum, of Cuffeetown Creek."

"Never heard of you."

Heinrich said nothing more. Two hundred escaped! Clearly, Thomson wasn't going to risk his men on blind forays into the long canes. It was too easy to hide in there, too easy to mount an ambush, too hard to move at anything but single file. Maybe Cunningham had been right after all. Maybe they would regroup.

He looked over at Christoph and Friedrich. What would happen to them all? Would Richardson offer them parole, as he had to other bands? Could they go home again, with their homes being watched? Would they be harassed, tormented, liable to arrest, the target of looters? Young Friedrich, married to Barbara, the youngest Strum sister, they with their first baby, though she was only a baby herself. A quiet young man, Friedrich, deferring always to his older brother. Imprisonment would be hard on him. Christoph? Heinrich liked Christoph Ruppert. A good man, shrewd and capable, a survivor.

And me? This Ranger might not know me, but others do. Anna chatterer sees to that! What's for me? A bullet in the neck, Catherine a widow, a doe in the woods, to be hunted by criminals?

By mid-morning, the operation was effectively over, and Thomson set his thirteen hundred troops and their prisoners marching back toward Hollingsworth's Mill on the Enoree, where the main body of Richardson's troops would be waiting. They moved slowly, since the prisoners perforce had to walk, and had to bivouac along the way, on the banks of an unnamed creek. They were united with Richardson's army early the following morning.

After the congratulations were done, the prisoners interrogated, the troops victualed, the horses watered and fed, the army prepared to move out.

But just then it started to rain. Richardson decided to stay encamped until the rain was done.

By noon it had become a downpour. It was still raining at sundown, a torrential rain, sheets of water. The creeks flooded in hours, rising ten feet or more above their accustomed levels. The Enoree itself threatened to engulf the Mill. The millrace turned black and threatening. The river filled with debris swept from the countryside—sodden logs, dead animals, badgers, snakes, deer, legs broken, upside down in the water, racing past in the deadly black. After sundown, the temperature dropped and the rain turned to snow.

It snowed the rest of the night. By morning there was more than a foot on the ground, by noon almost two feet.

Richardson released the volunteers who had made his army such a formidable force, leaving them to find their way home as best they could. With his own regiment and the prisoners, he turned toward the Congarees.

Heinrich marched with the Rupperts and Christian Zange, who had been taken still wrapped in his blankets; his naked legs were blue from the piercing cold. With them were several other neighbors in the Londonborough settlement, Adam Fralich and Henry Siteman among them. The other Germans who had been at Ninety Six were nowhere to be seen, Daniel Michler, Peter Mehl, the Merk boys, Georg Weber and his sons. Presumably they had scattered to their homes after the fracas there. Or maybe they'd been taken elsewhere and no one knew it.

Heinrich recognized only Dorst among their captors. The other Rebels in his community weren't there. Nick Kiess was nowhere to be seen, for which he was thankful. Nor was Philip Zimmermann.

Before they had gone more than a mile, Richardson released Christian Zange, gave him a horse and sent him on his way. "Because of advanced age," as his report later put it; he'd been afraid the man would die—he looked much older and frailer than his fifty-two years.

Army and prisoners alike had been unprepared for the weather. All were lightly clad, without raincoats or wraps. Richardson had them cut blankets into strips to warm their feet, but this was worse than useless; the snow soon got inside their boots, and the blanket stockings became sodden and frozen. They marched in the snow, not once setting foot on dry earth. At night, they had to shovel it away with their hands and make their beds on pine boughs laid on the soggy ground. Their bedding was sodden and wouldn't dry no matter how hot the fire at night. They were cold, hungry, miserable. None of the others gave even a thought to escaping, only to surviving.

It lasted seven days; even to the victors, this march felt like punishment. They reached the Congarees on New Year's Day.

Then the snow melted, the weather relenting only when they no longer needed relief.

This was taken as an evil omen.

But an omen of what?

Christoph Ruppert thought it presaged a long and bitter war. God would not grant easy victory. The world in which they were living, this pond in which they were minnows, this America, would be seized in a cruel hoarfrost; charity, generosity, kindness would be branches frozen and cracked by the cold of pinched souls, meanness, deviltry . . .

Heinrich didn't believe in omens. He believed men made their own fate.

But he didn't disagree with Ruppert. There would be no laughter in Carolina. Not this year, nor for many years to come.

For that, the Snow Campaign might stand as a metaphor, if not an omen.

Richardson had triumphed in the Back Country. Only Patrick Cunningham was still at large, with his henchmen Robinson and Evan McLauren. He had no doubt they'd be taken soon enough. Where could they go?

He disbanded the remains of his army. The prisoners he sent in a boat to Nelson's Ferry, under the command and guard of Captain Thomas Sumter.

Sumter borrowed a flatboat from one of the ferrymen, herded the disconsolate King's Men aboard and, though the weather had relented somewhat, began a still-wretched, cold, windswept, miserable voyage down the Congaree-Santee. At Nelson's Ferry he hauled the boat ashore, landed his prisoners and sent them shambling off to Charlestown, where they were thrown into the Provost to await judgment and sentencing by the Council of Safety.

Heinrich was never tried. He was taken directly to a prison ship on the Cooper River off Charlestown.

He never knew why, or by whose malice.

Though he suspected.

In the middle of January, Georg Weber, uncle to Jacob Strum's wife and neighbor to the senior Strums, died at sixty-four.

They said he died of a broken heart. His son Thomas was captured, Henry had fled, Georg was in hiding and Friedrich, well, he was blind. His daughters Suzanne and Barbara were partisans of the other side. The family was rent by dissension and acrimony. His wife Katherina had become a ghost, too distraught to speak to anyone, afraid of everyone.

But he could have just died of exhaustion.

A reward was offered for the capture of Patrick Cunningham, King's Agent, and in early March one Major Jonathan Downs turned up in Charlestown with Cunningham in tow. He and several others had been taken as they passed through on their way to the Cherokee Nation. The Congressional triumph seemed complete.

The prison ships were moored just inside the bar. They were vessels no longer fit for venturing beyond the harbor or even for warehousing valuable cargo. Their only possible uses were for firewood or as a home for rats and prisoner scum. Killers were sent there, and lunatics, human animals with rat eyes and rat minds and rat instincts.

The jailers were generally men that the army couldn't tolerate on land. Cruelty was their main virtue. Pain was their mistress and their obsession.

The ships stank. They were overcrowded. They were freezing cold, for none dared make a fire. They were overrun with vermin.

An official report a year or two later called the prison ships " . . . a brief epitome, or condensed edition, of hell." They were modeled after the ships that existed on the river Thames, in London, by which means the gentry solved the problem of the existence of the Rabble.

Most prisoners eventually escaped by the blessed relief of death.

A few endured. An even smaller number were reprieved.

Heinrich was among them.

He was being exchanged for prisoners taken by the King's Loyalists, he was told.

Would he give his parole not to take up arms against the Congress?

He would swear to anything to get out of prison.

He had spent five months in hell. And when he came out, haggard and ill, he was not the same. They had made an opponent into an enemy. Rebellion was no longer a misguided thing, an ill choice among many, a consequence of grievance to be forgiven. It had become a coral snake, gaudy and deadly, and its practitioners *things* to be stamped out.

Was false swearing dishonorable? He no longer cared. Honor was not a thing to be accorded to the seditious. It was all right to lie to the treacherous. It was fine to deceive traitors.

Civil wars were ever thus.

Katy hugged her husband as if she could squeeze the restlessness out of him. So many families in disarray, torn or shattering. *The Zimmermann brothers, Philip and Friedrich, well, they say they ride off merely at the sight of each other. Proud Balthazar Merk, with his wife Elizabetha Katerina, trying to remain aloof while their children squabble—Susannah Margaretha a Tory, her husband a Whig; Lorentz drifting in the same direction, while Johan has run off altogether, who knows where, but they say he's gone to Charlestown. The other daughters—Rosina Gabel, Elizabetha Dorris and Anna Maria Mehl—all with the Tories, especially Peter Mehl, a zealot, that young man . . . And then there's Conrad, who's so besotted with our Rosannah. They say he was in the fighting at Ninety Six. And Maria, dear Maria Adolph and her good, solid husband, steadfast, and their children too (but heaven knows what will happen to Rosena, the wild child); the Strums Loyal too, Heinrich locked in a Congressional prison ship, Eva and her husband Daniel active in the cause . . . Ah, and the Bauers . . . the mysterious Karl coming and going from the Indian territories, the girl Susannah taken up with a Whig, Alizabetha and her future husband quarreling in the public roads; as full of argument as her father, that girl is—and how old Adam loves to argue!*

And Anna . . .

Oh God, Anna!

Why?

A frost has settled into my sister that no summer heat will disperse . . . She's so cold that her bones must seize up. Her poor children!

She hugged Abraham again. He was up before dawn every day and into the fields, working like an ox until sundown, coming home exhausted, falling asleep, all to avoid thinking about what was happening. He focused his mind on the six inches behind the plow, watching the red earth turning, curling back like a pelt peeled from a carcass, trying not to listen to the clamor in his head. But she knew him too well; one of these days his restlessness would overcome him, and he would take his gun and go off to join the chaos.

Until then . . . She put her face to his warm shoulder, feeling his strength, and tried to give steadiness back.

It was all she could do.

Eight

Anna sat down again, at the precise distance from her sister as before, as though she had measured it, which in a way she had. *We lived those years on two separate continents, Katy and I. I was in America. I don't know where she was. She and her stupid, stupid husband.* She remembered the English she had met. Even those on her side had something . . . *soupy* . . . about them, a built-in obsequiousness. How could you be loyal to people like that?

September 1777
Charlestown, South Carolina

At the end of a sweltering June day in 1776, Catherine Strum cantered into Charlestown, her face flushed from the heat, her hair unbound, streaming out behind her, her hands burned brown as tea by the sun.

She'd been riding hard for several days.

She'd come to fetch her husband home.

Several times in the past months she'd made the arduous trek from the Back Country to the coast, each time leaving her children with family or with dear, compliant, ever-helpful Maria. She no longer had any compunction about leaving them or the farm. The farm would run itself, and those parts that wouldn't would be looked after one way or the other. And as for the children . . . she was going to bring their father home.

Each time she'd attempt to visit the Governor, Rutledge. She'd wait in the ante-rooms with the crowd of supplicants, sitting upright and haughty, refusing to be bowed, refusing to be moved until she was given a hearing. In the end, for she was more stubborn than they, someone always did.

Eventually the young scribes and secretaries who infested the Governor's mansion, well-brought-up young plantation dandies most of them, felt sympathy for this striking young woman with the black hair and the haunted eyes, and carried her message to the inner chamber, where the Governor wrestled with ever-growing mounds of documents.

Her determined embassy probably wasn't decisive in shifting Mr. Rutledge's mind, for he had weightier matters on his agenda than reuniting a family, no matter how soulful and beautiful the young wife. His dispatch boxes were filled with news from the North, and his mind's eye was set more upon the movement of armed men than the movement of one family, no matter how . . . Well, he had somehow to bring peace to the Back Country; certainly Richardson's pacification program hadn't done so. For some time he had been pondering his advisers' notion of paroling the captured Loyalist leaders and sending them home. Surely such a gesture would not be misconstrued. Perhaps they wouldn't resent him as much. And after Catherine's third visit, he sent instructions to the capital's jailers to carry to their prisoners his offer of parole. They were to take an oath of neutrality; they would swear not to bear arms against Congressional forces; they were to return to their occupations and livelihoods, so as to restore the commerce of the province to its accustomed level of activity . . . And on and on . . . All it really meant was, they could all go home, if they wished.

A few stayed imprisoned. One or two because they were either mad or men of high principle, or both, and refused to give their word not to take up arms once more. And some because they'd been convicted of treason, and the Governor needed scraps to throw to the Draytonian dogs growling for Loyalist blood.

Heinrich Strum would have sworn to anything to get off the hell where he had spent the last endless months.

Two sailors rowed him to shore and left him, shivering in the pale dawn, on the quay.

By some chance of fate, it was the same quayside where he had first set foot on American soil, only twelve years earlier.

Catherine came to him then, her heart on her sleeve, her heart in her mouth, her heart pounding in its cage of bone and flesh.

He looked forlorn and fragile standing there alone on the quay, dressed in his tattered pantaloons, his feet bare on the bleached timbers, his hair tangled and unkempt, unshaven. When she approached, she could see his body was covered with welts and bruises and sores; there were sores on his face and neck, and one of his ears was swollen and torn.

From closer she could see that what she had mistaken for fragility was something else entirely; his was not a body wasted to skin and bone, but toughened to sinew and leather. As she stood with her hands on his shoulders, looking up into his face, she could see there not the panicked look of illness that she had feared but a deep look of calm and tranquillity. Only later was she to realize that the tranquillity was really implacability.

She had brought him clothing, and he wasted no time, stripping naked on the quay and tossing his prison-worn garb carelessly into the sea—let the crabs tear at it! The muscles of his legs stood out in relief, like gullies in an erosion plain.

He looks like a deer, all bone and tendon and coiled tension, ready to bolt for the woods!

He stood there naked, his arms at his sides, letting her look at him, then he put his hands on her shoulders in turn, and smiled, and she laughed, a joyous laughter, and made him get dressed.

She took him back up to town, to her rented room on Broad Street, where she washed him and dried him. Then she took him to bed. After that she took him to a tavern, where they sat in a corner and drank German-style lager. Then she took him to bed again, where she demanded him and surrounded him and exhausted him. And after that she took him home.

Rutledge's release of the Loyalists captured in the Snow Campaign brought peace to the Back Country, if peace is defined as the absence of armies on the march. But it was a peace filled with menace and anger.

Richard Pearis, who spent five months on a prison ship before taking the oath, returned to his farm only to find it destroyed, plundered of livestock and possessions, his family dispossessed, scattered to relatives. He tried to rebuild, but was constantly harassed by taunting Whig bands, everything he repaired, broken again, everything he acquired, stolen. After some months, he was forced to flee back to Charlestown.

Some who returned to their homes were simply scooped up once more, captured and taken back to the coast. Some were locked in impromptu "jails." Others were beaten, a few killed. Still others, to evade capture, took to the woods. William Rittenhouse, a Strum neighbor, hid in the forest near his home. It was said of another that, "in a starving condition, at hazard of his life, [he] would meet his distressed and overgrieving wife who brought him bits of victuals and spent some of the solitary hours, chiefly in tears, in the dark and dismal night; no safety was there in the daylight for husband to see his wife."

Many Tories succumbed to their neighbors' harassments and agreed to do non-combat service for the Rebel militia, trenching, driving wagons, camp duties, whatever was needed save the pulling of a trigger.

Others went further. Lorentz Merk, who was then twenty-five and who had fought for the Loyalists at the skirmish at Ninety Six, was, in the words of his neighbor Nicholas Cruhm, "not so good a Loyalist," as he allowed himself to be drafted into the Patriot militia and served, as far as anyone knew, diligently enough.

For a while, they left Heinrich Strum alone. He stayed on his farm. He listened gravely to his children. He loved his wife, keeping in his mind a souvenir, her black hair tangled on the pillow. He plowed his fields. He listened to the buzzing of the wasps and kept his weapons clean.

In Boston, General Howe had sat on his hands too long and on March 17, 1766, he was forced to abandon the city to the besieging Rebels, he and the Governor fleeing in a small boat, like petty smugglers on the run. Oh, there was a spectacle! The mighty army of England had shamefully languished behind the walls of the city, not daring to show itself, and instead of re-establishing Royal authority were forced to fly from their posts, take to the boats, abandoning a continent sinking under the weight of popular discontent.

Anna was gleeful. What news! The overladen cart, filled with the spoils of state, was toppling their way!

A month or so after Boston fell, a visitor from England passed through Ninety Six. He was a member of Parliament, in opposition to the ministerial party, and he was touring the provinces to gather what intelligence he could, "since the ministers will say whatever shameful lies come into their heads." He had been to the north, had talked to Arnold and Washington, had passed through Virginia and was now on his way to Georgia. He was an unkempt little man, untidy, his wig shedding, his skin greasy as a roasting hog; it made Anna squirm to look at him. But he had news of Europe, which he imparted to a packed meeting outside the tavern.

Anna, despite her distaste, was interested in his views of the old continent's affairs. How the French were re-arming, equipping ships and accumulating naval munitions; how, with the tacit approval of the Royal court, French ports sent armaments to America. How French officers were in conference in Boston with General Washington, and how they were afterwards admitted to an audience of the Congress. Clearly, the French were simply waiting for a declaration that the Americans accepted England no longer, then they would declare themselves, and once more the great enmity between Britain and France would come into the open. What a help this would be to the American cause! No doubt, the little emissary said, if France declared, so would Spain. Not only because of the Family Compact, but because national interests coincided with those of France.

The British had stationed mighty ships of war on the American coasts. They were sending twenty-five thousand English troops and seventeen thousand Hessians. Add to this British Canada, the Loyalists and the Indians, and the British could field fifty-five thousand men at arms, a formidable number. The Rebels would have great need of the resources of France!

"However, you have no need to worry," the emissary said. "They will send against you numerous armies and formidable fleets. But you are at home, surrounded by friends, and abounding in things. The English are at an immense distance, having for enemies climate, winds and men. And how to subdue your troops? Impenetrable forests, inaccessible mountains will serve you in case of disaster as retreats and fortresses. The English will be under constant necessity to conquer or die, or to fly ignominiously to their ships. You have only to endure . . .You can vanquish them by dint of fatigue alone . . ."

Yes, Anna thought. This might be true in the north, she didn't know. She wished the man would take some time to learn the state of affairs here in the south. In the Carolinas, it was not so simple a matter as army against people. It was Carolinian against Carolinian.

What about Fletchall? What about Pearis? What about Cunningham? *These are not Englishmen, or Hessian mercenaries clanking about for gold. These are Americans! Even I know that!*

Misguided, occasionally villainous, always stubborn to the point of imbecility! What about my sister, and her husband?

What about Heinrich Strum? He's no soldier of an occupying power! Will we have to kill them all?

In March 1776, with a British fleet under William Campbell cruising about on the southern coastline, a new constitution was adopted for South Carolina. It provided for a provisional government "until such time as reconciliation with Britain be achieved." There was no mention of independence.

The Legislature got rid of Henry Drayton, or so they thought, by appointing him Chief Justice. This was a strategic error: his new platform only gave further prominence to even more firebrand speeches demanding full and complete independence from Britain. But Drayton was defanged, in the end, by his own error. Part of his strategy for independence was to create larger and larger forums for his own influence; he thus visited Savannah and suggested that Georgia merge with South Carolina—the capital, of course, to be Charlestown—and was promptly run out of town with a price on his head of a hundred pounds sterling.

Meanwhile, in the Back Country and in Loyalist pockets and homes all through the province, plans were afoot to restore peace, order and good government, by which it was meant sober and stable government that had no place in it for rabble-rousing Whigs. Some of these plans, hatched on isolated farms, amounted to little more than waylaying traveling Whigs and whaling the tar out of them. Others, usually developed in taverns, were grand schemes to involve England's natural allies, such as Catherine of Russia or the Tartary hordes, who could at least be depended on in battle, though the means to persuade them to join said battle seemed absent for the present.

Other schemes were more constitutional in their intent. The Loyalist Colonel Robert Cunningham, for instance, was a candidate for election to the House of Representatives for the District of Ninety Six. He got in, too, and took his place to the jeering of the Whig delegates, but the Cunninghams always were stubborn, and he stood his ground.

Heinrich Strum watched all this with a mixture of bemusement, contempt and apprehension. He attended one of Cunningham's election rallies at Mount Willing. The candidate wasn't there; instead he sent his brother Bill to look after his interests. This was a provocative gesture, for Bill Cunningham had a flamboyant personality with extreme and often violent views, and sending someone like that into a volatile crowd of Whigs and Tories was like dropping a match into a powder barrel. Sure enough, the afternoon deteriorated into a bloody brawl, and Bill, among others, was nearly beaten to death.

Heinrich had stayed near his horse on the periphery of the crowd, and when the fracas began, as he had expected it would, he quickly mounted and edged his horse away.

Nevertheless, he was spotted, and two Whigs galloped toward him.

He knew them both. Two farmers from Mine Creek, on the south fork of the Little Saluda.

Their faces were contorted, but whether from rage or effort he couldn't tell.

He sat up straight in the saddle and pulled out his gun. He leveled it at the oncoming horsemen.

They pulled up, staring at him.

He did nothing, but the gun didn't waver.

After a while, they turned their mounts and went back to the fighting. Heinrich watched them as they rode recklessly into the melee, knocking men flying, and then he turned and faded into the woods.

When he returned home that night, he found that Catherine, too, had been forced to employ her gun.

"There were three of them," she said, leaning on his chest at the entrance to their house. "I had warning. The dogs let me know they were coming. I went into the house. When they were close enough I told them to leave, but they just laughed. They said they wanted you. Then they told me what they would do to traitor women . . ."

Heinrich felt an icy rage welling up from a spring deep inside him. *They would dare!*

". . . So I fired, and nicked one of the horses, nearly throwing the rider. After that, they left. But not before doing some damage. Look, they trampled the henhouse."

"Who were they?"

"Hammond's men, I think, I don't know their names. No," she said hastily, seeing his look, "no Palatines."

Heinrich went out into the yard. Catherine had already made rudimentary repairs to the poultry shed, propping it up with lengths of unsawn spruce. The hens had been chased back to their nests. They clucked at him, unconcerned.

He went back to the house and sat on the steps, his head against her knee. So it had come to this. His very presence here was causing trouble. He had become a provocation in their eyes.

What to do?

"Were you afraid?" he asked.

"A little," she said. "But I did what I had to."

He touched her shoe. It was the right answer. No one could escape without fear. Some fear was necessary, to ensure alertness. As for himself . . . He was more afraid of his own coldness than of what LeRoy Hammond or Pickens or any of their Whig recruits would do. Once, in the Cherokee country, he had come across a camp where three men had been brutally murdered. They had been captured, stripped, beaten, then sat down on sharpened stakes, until the wood penetrated their bowels and guts and heart, and eventually came out their mouths, like great obscene tongues, and they had died in agony. He knew he would be capable of doing that to any man he caught who had killed Elizabeth. And if anyone harmed Catherine . . . He would find him, and he would enjoy his agony. It frightened him to know this about himself.

He tried to tell her some of this, later, but she didn't believe him, not really.

That summer, a small British fleet attacked Charlestown, and two days later there was an uprising in the Indian Nation. But the enterprise came, in the end, to naught.

The attack on Charlestown's Sullivan's Island fort was woefully inept. Instead of waiting for reinforcements that would have given him a substantial force, the British commander assailed the fort with only a small squadron. He lacked even surprise; the attack was so little a secret that the defenders had dug in, and George Mason, from the Back Country, even had time to collect a small company of men and march them down to the coast to assist in the capital's defense. He lost a leg there to a musket ball in the knee and the butchers' knives, but he survived (and, as Anna was to know years later, lived to be an old man before drowning in Red Bank Creek while under the influence of whiskey).

The attack, though it failed (repelled by Colonel William Moultrie's South Carolinians, in one of the first decisive Patriot victories of the Revolution), did set off an assault by seven hundred Cherokee under Chief Dragging-canoe on two forts in North Carolina. Both these failed, too, but they were followed by a series of raids by Cherokee, Creek and Choctaw on the frontier across the Carolinas and Virginia. Villages were destroyed, trading posts looted and burned. A trail of scalped bodies was left on isolated farms in a great arc from the Savannah well into Virginia. For the moment, Whig and Tory forces stopped harassing each other to focus on a more immediate threat. The other side might be hateful, but they weren't menacing, not like the Indians. The prospect of the Indian Nation suddenly boiling out of the endless forests was still enough to chill the settlers' blood. No one saw the Indians' desperation, only their cruelty and their mysterious otherness; everyone feared they would spread across the land like a brown stain, infecting farmland, village and town alike.

General Andrew Williamson was instructed to punish the instigators and put a stop to the troubles. Many men from Ninety Six, both Whig and Tory, rode with him. Bill Cunningham recruited his own contingent. Karl Bauer went along. The Ruppert brothers, Friedrich and Christoph, rode with Neely Carghill. Two Weber boys were there. So were both Zimmermanns, the Whig and the Tory, though not side by side. Peter Dorst went. So did his wife's sister's husband, Abraham Frietz.

Jacob Strum found business in Charlestown.

Heinrich Strum stayed on his farm. He had no quarrel with the Indians. No Indian had killed his wife. It wasn't Indians who had threatened Catherine. In his view, the Indians were just reacting, as men should, to having their land stolen, reacting to the indignity of being told by strangers on which side of the great river they could live.

He knew he, too, was about to be driven off his land. For Catherine's sake and the future of his children, he would have to accept it.

But not yet.

His quarrel was with the lawless forces of Congress. Congress wanted to overthrow one government and substitute another with equally flyblown ideas, of equal rapacity, of equal violence, corruption and stupidity, and to this end they turned men against each other, brother against brother, and sent bands of criminals to terrorize innocent women.

He hoped the Indians would kill a few, before it was over.

It would make his task that much easier.

The overwhelming success of Williamson's punitive action was later enshrined in dozens of local legends. LeRoy Hammond, for example, one of Williamson's troop leaders, made sure his own tale was told: "The officer who was ordered to lead the advance hesitated and evaded the duty. The men themselves shrank from the advance. Hammond volunteered to lead, and the movement was executed with gallantry and success and Hammond received a promotion."

He wasn't the only one. "In the War against the Cherokees Michael Watson rendered very efficient service at Little River, when the division was in some confusion, by collecting a chosen band and charging the Indians, driving them back and so saving the division."

Many a grandfather, family stories say, saved his division, or troop, or company, usually single-handedly, by urging his men, through acts of personal gallantry, to the duty they were shirking

It seemed after a while there were so many gallants that there must have been no one left to be gallant for.

Williamson went on to burn all the Cherokee lower towns, and after several weeks was able to disband his army.

Of the Indian laments, around their fires late at night, scattered in the deep woods, the stories are silent. Gallant or not, they lost or died. And their power faded into history's long twilight.

After that, nothing much happened in Ninety Six, at least not for a year. Oh, there was news of this and that. The Continental Congress stopped shilly-shallying and issued its Declaration of Independence in Philadelphia on July 4, which was followed by a similar one in Charlestown in August. A month later, Robert Goudy, of Goudy's Store at Ninety Six, died, and left a substantial inventory of such things as boxes of gold buttons and panes of window glass, as well as dozens of promissory notes. The new "American" navy captured New Providence in the Bahamas, but a little later, most of the American fleet on the Great Lakes was destroyed by the British. Washington crossed the Delaware. Benjamin Cook snared the right to operate a ferry over the Saluda River south of Island Ford, enabling him to charge rates of 15 shillings for a cart and horses, 25 shillings for a wagon and horses. He was told that "all state officers, all ministers of the gospel, all persons on Sunday going or returning from divine worship, or persons going to or from militia muster as well as troops and free Indians were to be carried free." The following May, 1777, the Indian wars were formally ended by the Treaty of De Witt's Corner. And on September 25, the British took Philadelphia. Otherwise, the year was quiet.

Quiet, quiet, but in the stillness and the silence emotions roiled, reverberating like the ringing of a great, demented bell. Armies stayed in their barracks or packed into ships that patrolled the coasts, but the countryside suffered from the small knife-cuts and wounds of a thousand acts of petty cruelty. Dogs were killed, children abducted, cornfields burned, men were hunted.

Twice in the spring, armed men came looking for Heinrich Strum. Both times he escaped, but the second time they smashed all the furniture and roughed up Catherine. A week later he ambushed two of them, shot one through the neck and left the other tied to a tree, for the wolves or whatever else wanted him. None of Catherine's family would any longer associate with her.

They came a third time, while Heinrich and Catherine were in the woods with the children retrieving a calf, and he watched in helpless rage as they circled his house, yelling and yelping like hounds. He knew then that he'd have to go, to get away until this thing, this civil war, was settled one way or the other, until the armies came out from their lairs and the cannons cauterized the country's wounds.

Many Loyal men had already migrated to Florida. Alexander Cameron had joined a Loyalist leader, John Stuart, in Pensacola, where they organized a regiment called the West Florida Loyalists. Both Cameron and Richard Pearis brought followers down from Ninety Six. Others had stopped at St. Augustine in East Florida. Thomas Browne recruited a regiment of mounted militia from among them, and named it the Florida Rangers, placing himself under the command of Brigadier General Augustine Prevost. The South Carolina Royalists were formed there in 1778.

Still, Heinrich stayed, spending his days in the fields or the woods, warily watching for riders, and the nights in the arms of his wife.

But in late August he could wait no longer.

Catherine held him for a long while, then sent him on his way. She refused to cry. There were children to look after and a farm to run, so much to do.

It was only later, in the dark of the empty marriage bed, that her control broke, and she wept tears of desolation and fear.

By that time Heinrich had crossed into Georgia, and was on his way to St. Augustine.

Nine

For the first time, Katy and Anna looked at each other, looked away. It was hard to say who dropped her gaze first. *Probably me*, Katy thought. *But in a way, those are the years easiest to talk about. Oath-takers and oath-breakers! Only men would govern their lives that way. Women would have more sense. Even Anna. Women do what they must.*

December 1778
Cuffeetown Creek, South Carolina

An oath-breaker came by, walking, for they had stolen his horse. His arms and chest and neck were cut by the whip, as Katy could see when she took him down to the well to wash, and he laughed, somewhat hysterically, as he told her the blood sloshed around in his boots as he strode along. It felt greasy, he said, like walking in mud.

Well, maybe he wasn't an oath-breaker but a non-oath-taker, which to the Rebels amounted to the same thing. It gave them the right to tickle him with the rawhide they'd been wont to use on oxen—how much more pleasant to whip the softer skin of traitors!

How did loyalty get to be treachery? They are twisting the meaning of words!

She told him to stay, for he'd surely die if he left.

He refused.

He propped his old musket against the well box as he washed. Its muzzle was clogged with mud and grass. If he struck a flint the damn thing would bite his head off.

He wanted to get to Pensacola, in the Floridas, where he'd heard Stuart and Cameron had holed up. He talked of Pensacola as if it were Paradise Lost; if only he could reach Stuart, everything would be fine.

He wouldn't say his name. He looked like a Siteman from further up Hard Labour Creek, but you could never tell with the Sitemans, there were that many. It didn't really matter who he was. Hadn't young Henry Bauer gone off in similar straits not long ago, on his way to Savannah, he said, but was never heard from again? Of course, he could have drowned in a river somewhere, for he never could swim. Or it could be the blood in his boots had risen to drown him . . . Or maybe he was sitting tied to a tree somewhere, watching in surprise as his guts spilled onto the grass through the new hole someone had made—oh, they had learned a thing or two from the Cherokees, these Back Country folk! Or maybe he'd just become disgusted with the whole thing, changed his name to Butler or Bull, and was living the grand life in Charlestown. Who knew these days? Maybe he was writing a newspaper in Charlestown extolling the virtues of Congress . . . Half the city seemed to be scribbling news these days, and the other half quarreling with them. That would be like the Bauers. Quarrelsome, but essentially good-natured. Always knew where you stood with them. It was a good part of their charm. Old Adam was stubborn but Loyal, or rather stubborn *and* Loyal, but his house was an unlicensed tavern for Whig volunteers nevertheless. He never turned anyone away. Never would.

Well, Katy fed this unknown soldier and he slouched off, grinning, and that was the last anyone saw of him, too.

That damned oath!

The South Carolina government, a grand collection of miscreants, had decreed that all inhabitants (or citizens of the republic, as they declared) must swear an Oath of Abjuration, which was not exactly an Oath of Allegiance to this brand-new United American States, but not exactly not either. One of the Charlestown sheets that had been circulating in the Back Country explained that the oath had been modeled after a similar declaration by the Dutch in 1500-something-something, when they'd thrown off the yoke of foreign domination, in that case Philip of Spain. In this case it meant, or so the sheet said, the abjuration of loyalty to the British monarch, his colonial arms and his Hessian henchmen, who were no better than the Hun, the Golden Horde re-invented for use in the Americas. This oath was not uniformly enforced in the Back Country, but nor did it need to be. What it did was mark non participants for plunder, and that was surely its purpose. Hah!

They had drawn up their list of such "non participants," a long list of Tories, known Tories, denounced-as-Tories, suspicioned-to-be-Tories and has-shown-hostility-so-must-be-Tories. Several of these were whipped. Many were imprisoned for a few months to improve their temper. A few, here and there, died. Many more went to the woods, where they lived like animals, provisioned where possible by their families. There were men flying about the countryside, everywhere.

That list had made its way around to the Frietz farm, in due time. Abraham was on it, so was Peter. Not Katy. Not Rosannah, who was as hot as a musket's muzzle for the Royal cause. No woman was on that list.

Should Abraham sign this oath? And her beloved sons?

They'd talked about it, of course. Everyone in the Back Country had been talking about it. It was a prime reason why there was this long, melancholy procession of men slipping away from their farms and going to Florida, that illusory refuge.

Some had signed, some had refused. Heinrich Strum would never have signed a document of that sort. But then Heinrich might never have been offered the opportunity—too many Whigs wanted to see that stiff-necked, stubborn, inflexible, *honest* man punished. They'd argued about it, and Katy had won as usual, twisting Abraham around in her philosophical knitting until he didn't know which thread was which—was it dishonorable to lie to dishonorable men? She herself would have signed anything put before her with a clear conscience and no intention whatever of obeying. Any woman would. Except perhaps her sister.

"All you'll do," she'd argued, "is give them a reason to steal your horses or drive you from your farm. And for what? So you can tell your grandchildren you'd been driven into the woods to live like an animal, so you could maintain your side of an argument by then long forgotten? By which time the King would be back in the saddle, or Great Britain a faded memory, and no one will any longer care . . . "

Abraham listened. Peter listened too, though he spluttered something about bowing to tyranny, hers or the Whigs', she wasn't sure. Her daughters, she knew, understood. The younger boys, Charles and John, were too callow to care, though she knew they found Peter's defiance exciting.

So Abraham had laboriously spelled out his name. Peter refused. He had disappeared and was living in the woods, skittish as a doe with a new fawn. He'd built himself a shelter from spruce boughs and deadfall logs, but someone had found it and trampled it into the mud when he wasn't there, and after that he lived only in his blankets and on what food she was able to get to him. Someone was spying, trying to catch him. She saw, in the distance, horsemen passing by, and occasionally there'd be a lone figure standing by the gate, watching. It couldn't go on, of course; soon he'd slip away altogether, looking for companions in Florida, maybe John Stuart, or maybe he'd follow Heinrich . . .

Like so many others.

The countryside was bleeding men.

The taverns and waystations were so full, the travelers slept four to a bed, toe to head, head to toe, and the whores had no place to ply their trade, unless on the floor. Men passed through, stealing chickens or begging. They swam or waded across creeks to avoid the "taxers" who waited at the ferries, Rebel vigilantes who would make them sign away their property, or whip them, or both. Every now and then one would just disappear, or be found pinned to a tree by a widow-maker ax; perhaps this was what happened to the Bauer boy, after all.

And sometimes they went in larger numbers, doing their own taxing as they went. George Dawkins, from Broad River, who had been imprisoned for three weeks on suspicion of being "friendly to Great Britain," fled to Florida with no fewer than five hundred others. George Long took another large group from Long Canes. James Wright, just released from prison, gathered an army of three thousand and led them down to Pensacola.

Who had it harder, those who left or those who stayed?

Some of those who stayed, Katy thought.

Catherine Strum, for one. Eva Michler, her sister-in-law, told Katy about her.

They hated her because she was beautiful and stubborn and she ran the farm by herself with the children and she was married to the traitor, Heinrich.

One day last month, she had walked across Horsepen Creek and through the Rambougs' land and the Weisers' land and across Cuffeetown Creek to the Michlers' farm, and asked Eva if she would mind taking three of the children, "for a while, until the trouble is over." She looked haggard and her clothing was torn and there were bruises on her face, but she refused to say what had happened, only that she had already left Eve and Henry, along with the three-year-old, John, with the other Strum sister, Barbara Ruppert, who lived just on past the Michlers. Eve was eleven, almost grown up, she could help. Catherine had with her three solemn children in tow, the middle three, Elizabeth, Maria and Fredrick. The baby, Peter, she kept with her. She and Heinrich's first born, the fourteen-year-old Anna, would run the farm on their own. Anna was capable. She was like her ma, Elizabeth. Stubborn. Just as solid, just as stubborn.

It was such a good farm, too, and she ran it like any man, better than most. She and Heinrich had acquired a hundred and seventy-five acres of land, had built a good house, as fine as any in the settlement. There were two orchards, and they had cleared about twenty-five or thirty acres for crops. There were two horses, a wagon and gear, and twenty head of cattle, ten sheep, tools and furniture, including a mirror for which they had paid half a year's income.

One of the children told Eva later that "some men had come and hit ma, and she fell down, and then they gone away."

Katy felt a great upsurge of anger and bitter hatred at this news. She loved Catherine like a daughter; had done so ever since Catherine had confided in her when Heinrich had "gone away" to Patrick Cunningham; Katy admired her resolve and her competence and her steadiness of nerve, loved her beauty and her kindness.

To hit such a person!

Seventeen of their twenty cows had been stolen by Rebel bands, Eva was told.

No, I beg your pardon. Taxed.

A week later, Katy had heard, another group of men, or the same, had burned the Strum cornfield. Late at night they'd appeared at the farm, hooded, their heads covered with sacks with holes cut through for the eyes, and shouted threats at the two women inside. Fire was their weapon. Fire, and terror.

What manner of man would do that?

Late one afternoon, Alizabetha Bauer rode into the camp of a group of forty Loyalists who were, to use their own word, "withdrawing" to join Colonel Alexander Campbell, who was somewhere near Augusta. Her appearance astonished the sentries, for the camp was half a mile off the Martintown Road, and they'd been keeping an uncomfortable silence, cold-camping as the army called it—no fires, horses silenced, equipment at the ready. No one was supposed to be able to tell they were there. She saw their astonishment and grinned, her jaunty beak of a Bauer nose pointing like a retriever. She was one of Adam's children, a wild child as so many of the young ones were, brown as a berry like Maria's daughter Rosena, another of her kind. They both rode the countryside Indian fashion, without saddles, Alizabetha scandalizing the church-goers by hiking up her skirts and petticoats and clutching the horse between her strong, brown, bare thighs. She could teach them a thing or two about woodcraft. And she only fourteen! She hadn't seen Rosena for some time now. That one preferred to run with the Dorst children. Rebels all!

One of the men caught the bridle and she slid off the horse in a flash of flesh, and along with it confusion, theirs, and amusement, hers.

"You'll not want to take the ferry, up ahead there," she said. "You'll want to take the long way around, old Martin's farm way."

She had no saddle, but strapped to the horse's haunches were two bags tied with rope, full of provisions, cut cabbage or *kohl slaai*, as they called it, calf's foot jelly, dried meat of indeterminate origin. One of the men poked through it suspiciously.

"And why would we want to do that?" a graybeard said. She guessed he was what passed for a leader.

"Well, you could go on," she said, grinning, pausing to scratch at a scab on her elbow. "You could go on. You could get half way acrost, an' they'd open up, those men hidden in the reeds on this side, near thirty of 'em." She mimed taking aim, then being hit by a bullet, staggering about the clearing in an exaggerated way.

The leader gaped at her.

"Then, as those what lived got to shore, more guns from t'other side, more than forty of 'em there. Bang! Over you go! Back to t' crick!"

"And how do we know you're telling true? This isn't some Whig trick?"

"I'm Adam Bauer's girl."

"That doesn't help none," the leader said, recovering some of his dignity. He'd had a few drinks at Adam's place himself, time to time.

"Well, go see yrself," she said, unmoved.

Two men volunteered to do just that.

"When the road takes that big bend to the right," she said, "you be careful there. They're bedded down in the reeds beyond that, to the left." Then she went over to sit beneath a tree, humming quietly to herself, smoothing her skirts over her knees. Her horse grazed peacefully nearby. She could have been on an idle summer picnic for all the care the two of them showed.

The leader shook his head. These children!

An hour or so later the scouts returned, slipping into camp in what they imagined was silence, though she'd heard them coming ten minutes back.

"True," was all they said.

"Good!" she said, springing to her feet. "Then I'm gone. More work to do."

"What are you?" the leader said, amused. "Joan of Arc?"

Aliza the wood nymph, more like it!

She said nothing, but flashed him that dazzling, full-beaked grin and disappeared into the woods.

A month earlier, she'd been snared by a Whig patrol near Stevens Creek. Her saddlebags then, too, had been stuffed with provisions. They knew she was taking food to Tories hiding in the woods.

She hadn't grinned, then. They beat her a little, roughed her up to see if she would talk, but she maintained a stony silence and said nothing. After a while they trussed her like a chicken and took her back to the lockup at Ninety Six.

"What is this?" the jailer said, disgusted. "Prisoner of war? Only remnant of a regiment? She's a child!"

"She's a damned spy," the patrol captain said surlily.

"Ay! And dangerous as a hellcat!" the jailer said sarcastically, untying her. She winked at him.

"We'll see if being locked up in here will loosen her tongue," the captain said.

"On what charge?"

"What do you care?"

"What's the charge?"

"Suspicion of spying, suspicion of carrying provisions to Tories in hiding."

"Suspicion of bad thinking?"

"Yeah, that too," the captain said, missing the barb.

They kept the child in jail for fifteen days, but then released her for want of evidence.

She'd said nothing in all this time. But she had eaten well, and was irrepressibly cheerful, delighting the guards and agitating her would-be interrogators no end.

After that, she spied more determinedly for the British and their Loyal allies. Of this, she told her father nothing. Not that he was a bad man, he wasn't. But he loved to tell a good story, and out it would all come, he couldn't help himself. She told only her brother Karl. He was as circumspect as she was, she believed. He had many friends among the Whigs, and seemed to move easily about the countryside despite patrols, but then he had just as many friends among the Tories. And the Indians for that matter. Wasn't he rather like an Indian himself? Somewhere deep inside him was a great core of silence, like a cool pond in the summer woods. So easy to plunge in! She trusted him. He'd not tell.

The only other person she trusted was Catherine Strum. She'd visited the Strum farm after their cornfield had been burned, and had gone back often since. They never said very much to each other, but they were companionable together. Alizabetha was in awe of the older woman's unyielding strength. She told her this once, as they sat on the steps of the Strum house, Alizabetha's head against Catherine's knee. But Catherine had just smiled, sadly, and rumpled her hair. "I don't want to be strong," she said. "I just want my man back."

Katy watched the men slip away, one by one. *The countryside*, she thought, *is just holding its breath*.

Anna watched the men slip away, too, but with fury. *One day Florida will be one of the United States. No refuge then!*

Christian Zange, who was fifty-four, left Juliana and the baby with her sister, and one midnight rode away with three of his sons. Three of his three adult sons, since the fourth, Johan Peter, was already dead, caught by a Rebel band and hanged from a tree, where his grieving mother had found him and cut him down. Christian had been in jail once already, and had been captured during the Snow Campaign, but they'd let him go because of his "advanced age." He'd sold his land to Balthazar Merk in 1776, but had stayed on the farm to work it, resentfully making it prosper for his new landlord. He'd refused to sign the oath when the enforcers came by, and reprisals had followed sure as the dawn follows the black heart of night. More hooded men. Beatings. Animals driven into a barn, which was then set on fire, the thin, rasping shrieks of the terrified pigs carrying for miles across the flatlands. Confiscations, with the whip or without it, harassment, intimidation—how that oath focused the rage! By the beginning of the summer, Christian knew he had no choice. Capitulate, or leave. And there was some doubt that capitulation would any longer be tolerated.

After sundown, he slept one more time in the arms of his wife, and then he rose, dressed, packed his saddlebags, checked his weapons and left his house. Juliana's sorrow and fear pierced his heart, but he just hugged her and then shook her gently in inarticulate love, and then he rode away, not looking back, Johan, Jacob and the youngster, Christian, at his side.

By morning, they were at the Savannah River.

They were almost across, their horses' hooves clattering on the stones of Georgia, when a scouting party came up behind them on the Carolina shore. The scouts yelled and brandished their weapons, angry to see Tories escaping. They loosed off a volley, more in demonstration of anger than with any real thought of hitting anything, for the distance was great enough to test the most skilled marksman aiming at a stationary target. But by some horrible mischance, a stray bullet chunked into young Christian's neck, sending a geyser of blood over his horse and tearing away half his throat.

They did what they could to staunch the wound, but it was too grievous, and he died in his father's blood-stained arms ten minutes later.

He died without a word, for blood had choked his throat.

Christian thought he'd have been trying to call his mother, but he couldn't be sure. That's what he would tell Juliana, if he ever saw her again.

The boy was just eighteen years old.

Eighteen!

He looked back at the sun, whence had come the killer bullet. It shone blandly, as it always did. He howled once, a queer, twisting, whining howl echoing across the reedy river, dying into a kind of whimper, and a sob, and then he was quiet. He never cried again.

A week or so later, he and his two sons joined the South Carolina Royalists as volunteers, to serve under Colonel Robinson and Major McLauren, at their pleasure and disposal. The regiment was based in Florida, within growling distance of Savannah.

Conrad Merk had seen his name on the list, too, along with his father's. But so far they had left him alone. Perhaps they were as confused by the Merks as some of the Merks were. Conrad seldom visited his parents any more, although their four hundred acres were just behind his own farm on Hard Labour Creek. The last time he'd been there, his young brother Johan had gone into a long, Whiggish tirade, a gale of revolutionary platitudes, and had subsequently left home to join a Rebel militia along the Dutch Fork. His father was sixty, and just snarled when anyone asked him his political sympathies.

Both his sisters Susannah and Anna had gone off, married some fanatical politicos, one of 'em a Whig and the other a Tory, and could hardly bear to speak to each other. Elizabetha was just sixteen, but had already married William Dorris next door; she was a sweet child whose soul had been captured by some charismatic, and she was now more interested in man's immortal prospects than in Royal versus Republican politics. Young Jacob was a pliable lad and would do whatever his father told him, if old Balthazar ever got it figgered. Rosina? No one ever knew what Rosina thought.

Damn it, we're like a nest of weasels! Tearing at each other all the time.

And Lorentz . . . He'd been in the Patriot militia now two years. Or was it three? Conrad held no grudges. Lorentz was a large, easy-going man, very hard to hate. He was like a Bauer, Conrad thought, the words tumbling out of him in a torrent of laughter and tall tales, like Adam Bauer but without old Adam's irascibility, retaining only the garrulousness and charm. The last time they'd been together was a few months ago at Ninety Six, outside Goudy's. Lorentz had been with two cheerful whores, and he'd produced a flagon of badly made rum and they'd gone into the woods and gotten drunk together, at first outrageous drunk, then maudlin drunk and finally, before they lay down to sleep it off, solemn drunk. Conrad had warned his brother about his militia duties. "It's not just parading and braggadocio," he said.

"It won't come to that," Lorentz said. "People will come to their senses."

"That's real," Conrad said, pointing at his brother's gun. "Real bullets that kill and maim. Who will you shoot with that thing?"

Lorentz looked distressed.

"Me? Your father? What will happen if you're ordered to Augusta, and inside is my Rosannah's father? Will you shoot him too?"

"It won't come to that," Lorentz said stubbornly. "I won't shoot anybody."

Conrad dropped it. Won't shoot anybody! If he didn't shoot when told, he himself would be shot in the back of the neck as a traitor. It was the way it worked. There was a fuzziness to his brother's good humor that was profoundly irritating.

Not for the first time, he wondered, *If we had known in Jacobsweiler that this new land would rend our family in this way, that it would order my brother to kill me, would we have come? Surely not!* He looked over at Lorentz, now sleeping with his mouth open, and beyond him at the two whores, lying side by side on the grass. They, too, were asleep. Their breasts rose and fell as they dreamed. They looked sweet and girlish in the afternoon sunlight. *How appearances deceive!* Or did they? Was that what they were like, under their bluster and rudeness and licentiousness?

He had himself been fined after the Ninety Six fracas, fined for what? For constancy? Conrad was a Loyalist, but resented Johan's accusation that he was some agent of a foreign power, some tyrannical colonizer. He had no animus against the British, true enough, priggish as so many of them were. But he felt himself a lover not of foreign rule but of peace, order and good government. Men were governed, whether from London or Philadelphia, and what did it matter the location of the governors? Government's task was to keep the highways free of thieves and rogues, and if they did it in a red uniform or a green, what matter? Accompanied by a red ensign or another piece of bunting, what matter? His pigs would make bacon, whether or not their proprietor had sworn allegiance to this or that fashionable cause.

Nothing was worth this killing, nothing.

But he felt himself drawn in, and no help for it. By now, the mere act of not killing was a treachery.

More would die, soon.

He had his own land, and a willing Rosannah, as she had proved many times. Her family were profoundly Loyal, no doubting it. He liked Abraham's solidity, his ox-like constancy, and Katy's chirpy edginess—her judgments about people were close to his own, Conrad thought, wary, sardonic, not very trusting.

He wanted to farm his land, raise his children, be governed by whoever would govern, if they'd let him be.

It didn't sound so bad. *Why can't they see that?*

Daniel Michler got into a brawl outside the blacksmith's shop in Ninety Six. He was a big man, and he bloodied the two of them more than they bloodied him, but still he lost, in the end, as Eva could have told him he would. Lost, in the sense that it was an unwinnable battle: ideology can be overcome with neither logic nor fists. And she did tell him, when he arrived back at the farm on Cuffeetown Creek, brimming with resentment and ready for a large dose of sympathy, which he didn't get.

"Fighting with them only stiffens their resolve," she said as she swabbed his face.

"Well, I argued with them first . . . "

"Arguing with them only stiffens their resolve, too," she said. "You can't talk them into it and you can't beat them out of it, so just leave them alone."

"They called me un-American!" he said indignantly. "Why, my grandfather was born in Virginia! And I knew one of 'em and he first came to these shores as a young man!"

She sighed, leaned on his shoulder. What did it matter where anyone was born? None of it had anything to do with anything. These men would argue about anything! Why couldn't they see that? They prattled on about liberty, but didn't know the first thing about it, on either side. They would shoot people to force them to be free! She thought of her brother Heinrich, now gone to Florida, leaving Catherine alone and bereft. How free was he? She thought of Anna Dorst, in the jail of her own emotions. No freedom there! She thought her children, little Daniel and Eve, Peter and Jacob, and the baby, William. Why couldn't they be as free to choose their governors as they were free to choose their preachers?

She dressed her husband's bruises with a poultice she'd learned from her brother Jacob, who had learned it from some Cherokee wise man, then she folded him in clean linen and put him to bed.

But she knew he wouldn't be there long. Wouldn't be on the farm long, or in the Carolinas. He'd leave, in a day or so, or a week or so, for Florida. He, too, had heard the call, and he could no more help himself than could the migrating birds when their time was come.

Time to soldier on!

We give birth and they go to war. It's the natural order of things.

A week later he was gone indeed, riding off sturdily, not worrying about the going, only about the path. He would go to St. Augustine, he said, to find the South Carolina Royalists there.

I'm thirty years old, I have five children, I have two hundred acres, I have a husband who has ridden off to war, perhaps to get shot, perhaps never to return.

Her chest felt squeezed, constricted. She clutched the children to her, held them, staring after him until he was gone.

To get shot!

Heart stilled, eyes closed, the door finally shut.

Somewhere in the mud of some strange country.

She fed the children and fetched in the eggs and saw to the cows and repaired a gate, swinging the hammer with great energy, fed the children again, fetched in some firewood, hoed the garden a little, did the washing, fed the horses and the pigs and went to bed. She would do that, and more, every day.

She would survive.

Barbara Strum Ruppert watched her husband ride away from her with his brother and their father, and what she mostly felt was anger. A little man on a little horse, and a big man on a big, rangy mare called, for no particular reason, Tommy, and the father in the middle, neither one thing nor the other. The little man was her husband, Friedrich. His brother Christoph had come and fetched him away to war. And he had gone, just like that, with not so much as a by-your-leave or an if-you-please.

I'm nineteen years old and a war widow, with a baby! And he rides off, without looking back!

Both brothers had been locked up for a while by the Rebels after the uproar at Ninety Six. Both were let out the same day. Both went home, Friedrich to his new young wife and Christoph to his Margaret.

The father, Heinrich, was a sarcastic old widower who lived alone, but she'd always liked Christoph. He seemed like such a solid man, heart of oak, courteous, respectful, reserved.

He had no right.

And for what? It was not like the Indians, fighting for their homes. They had a cause worth killing for!

Jacob had told her stories about the Indians. Once he'd been traveling with a small group of shooters and had come across some Rangers butchering the corpse of an Indian, for some mysterious purpose of their own. They were hunkered down in the grass, slicing away with huge knives; underneath the skin, Jacob said, it looked like horsemeat, all tendon and stringy muscle.

Jacob had been with a band of Creek once, who'd caught a few stray Iroquois escaped from some errant French raiders, lost in the woods. Kept them alive for months, tortured them to death one at a time, whenever their dreams went sour, or they needed an omen, or just for sport. They'd do the same for the Rangers, if they caught any. Or maybe not. Caught a Ranger once, but didn't kill him. Stripped him and painted him blue and made him marry a girl of theirs, a girl left alone after her man fell into a river and was drowned. He stayed with them, too. Never went home to his own family.

Of course, Jacob had been trying to shock her. And did he really know? He hadn't been in the Indian wars!

My man has gone away to war!

Yes, the war with the Indians was a war she could understand. Each scalp they took was one less invader to trample their cornfields, steal their goods, rape their women. But here were neighbors, brothers, sisters, sons and daughters, marching in great bands up and down the country, distinguishable only by the colors they carried and the learned slogans they spouted, and for what? Because armies in Philadelphia and London were doing the same? Because great ships prowled the coasts, drowning any who stood in their way? She had heard stories of the privateers from Jacob's wife, the Henn woman. Indians didn't look so bad after hearing about them. And pray, for what? Back of it all was a grand idea, or so they said, whatever side they were on, a grand idea that was the dawning of a new age.

A new age?

It's taking away my man!

To St. Augustine in the Floridas, Christoph had said, to join the Dragoons of the South Carolina Royalists.

As if she cared. What would the Dragoons do for her little daughter? Would the Dragoons care if they knew she was pregnant again?

Friedrich rode away, and he never even knew.

Nicholas Cruhm joined George Dawkins on his way to Florida, too. He'd paid a fine to stay out of the Rebel militia, but that was not the end of it, as he'd hoped. He had a two-hundred-acre farm on Sleepy Creek, lived in a small house he'd made himself, owned a little stock, went to hear a sermon whenever there was a sermon to hear . . . All in all, a very modest life. But there were persistent rumors in Ninety Six that the Cruhms had had great wealth in Germany, and had brought part of it with them, sewn into a sack, or hidden in a canvas, or disguised as this or that—the stories veered from improbable to impossible.

One July day when he was away, a militia band caught his wife on her way to Ninety Six, put a gun to her head and demanded she surrender the money. When she denied its existence, they beat her on the breasts and broke her nose, then dragged her home and put the gun to her head again.

Give it up, or die. A simple choice.

They beat her a little more, to loosen her tongue.

When she stopped screaming, she took them inside and led them to a flour cask. At the bottom, under twenty pounds of corn flour, was a leather folder containing nine English pounds. It was all they had, a decade of saving. They dumped the flour in the room, covering everything with fine white dust, took the money and left.

When Nick came home, she had cleaned up the flour. But she took off her shift and showed him her breasts, which were bruised blue, battered and broken.

He left for Florida when her body had healed. Her mind would only heal when they were all dead, he reckoned.

In May, France formally declared her alliance with Britain's American colonies and thereby declared war on her old enemy.

A month later, defying all expectations, Colonel Robert Cunningham, who'd already gotten himself elected to the House of Representatives, was elected to the State Senate.

The same month, Colonel LeRoy Hammond and a few others were appointed commissioners "to conciliate the Indian Nations." It was like setting a python to conciliate the chickens.

By November, Heinrich Strum had become a sergeant under Captain Faight Reisinger in the South Carolina Royalists. Reisinger, who had brought five hundred Loyalists with him from Dutch Fork, served in turn under Major John Coffin and Augustine Prevost.

There were two troops of rifle Dragoons and four companies of infantry. Their strength: six hundred and sixty. Serving with and under Heinrich were the three Rupperts, Friedrich and Christoph with their father Heinrich in the Royal Dragoons; Nick Cruhm; Peter Mehl; Peter, Jacob and Johan Zange; Georg Schildnacht Sr. and Jr.; and Georg Weber, who served under Dawkins' South Carolina Volunteers and with Thomas Reisinger.

At Augusta and nearby Hudson's Ferry were, among others, Jacob Strum's brother-in-law, Nicolas Henn; Katy and Anna's brother (and Maria's husband) Heinrich Adolph; Karl Bauer; Katy's son Peter Frietz;

Thomas Schildnacht; Henry Weber; and Friedrich Zimmermann with his sons Henry and Jacob.

Daniel Michler was still on his way to Florida.

Adam Bauer stayed home.

Katy's Abraham stayed home, but his leash was straining.

Conrad Merk hadn't left for war. Yet. His father Balthazar had no intention of going, if he could help it.

Jacob Strum just needed a small push.

In November, Loyalist property was formally confiscated by the State. It was all legal.

The same month, November, a British fleet sailed from New York, heading south.

The British and their Loyalist allies in East Florida, and the Congressional forces in Charlestown, were each preparing to invade the other. The Patriot General Robert Howe, commanding the Southern Department, had moved his headquarters from Charlestown to Savannah in the spring. In April, Rutledge ordered three hundred men from Colonel Stephen Bull's command to rendezvous at Purrysburg on the Savannah River. The South Carolina troops then crossed into Georgia to join the Georgians, and together they crossed the St. Mary's River, but they were beaten by the British. Illness took a heavy toll. The Georgia and South Carolina commanders, Colonels Elbert and Williamson, refused to take orders from the unpopular General Howe, and the expedition dissolved into chaos.

In December, the British attacked Savannah.

Anna heard the news with a sullen resentment. She assumed Katy would be delighted.

But Katy was merely afraid.

Ten

I was more confused than you think, sister, Anna thought. *I suppose that was part of our problem. I always wanted to be sure of what I was sure of. But what they did to Heinrich and his poor wife . . . You can't win a country by waging war on young children!*

August 1779
Cuffeetown Creek, South Carolina

Anna Dorst was at home when her brother Heinrich Adolph left his family and rode off to war. He hadn't told her he was going and he hadn't said farewell. Nor was this so surprising. They hadn't spoken for several years; though they lived no more than ten miles apart, the gulf that now separated them seemed utterly unbridgeable. If it weren't for Maria, for whom friendship transcended everything, she'd not even have known he was alive.

She daydreamed often of how such a conversation might have gone.

"Farewell!" she'd say. "Keep your powder dry!"

"Why have you turned against us?" he'd say.

"I? I turned, brother? Nay! I'm an American, living in the present.

Americans are like the Indians, they have no past, they live in the great labyrinths of their forest in the everlasting present, the dreams of the present the great engine of the future . . . Nay, 'tis you who've turned. Back to the old ways, the ways of tyranny, of mad kings and perpetual jails, the old country with its goblins, priest-ridden, hag-ridden . . ."

How eloquent she would be!

He would be passionate, angry. "We were near six hundred when we left, six hundred neighbors and comrades. We've been dying ever since. We died in London. We died on the voyage. We died of snake-bite, drowning, exhaustion, starvation, we died of fever, we died from the arrow whistling out of the dark, we died of rape and murder. Whole families are gone, vanished, dead. Every week we are fewer. Less than a hundred, now. Let's stop the killing!"

She would be persuasive, irresistible. "It's such a small step to take," she'd say, "such a small step! But what large consequences! Just accept that all men have the right and the duty to govern their own lives. Who could resist such an idea? It's a natural law! Such a clear path! A straight road! With a view all the way to the future! It all flows from there . . ."

"You're right," he'd say. "Nothing is worth the killing. And it *is* a noble idea. Perhaps it's worth a little temporary dislocation . . ." And he'd lay down his arms and come into the house, where they'd have a celebratory roast and a jug of whiskey . . .

She knew, of course, that it would never have gone like that.

Instead, he'd have accused her of treachery. "Look what your people have done!" he'd shout furiously. "Houses burned, women raped and beaten, children abducted, maimed, horses stolen, men hanged . . ."

She'd have accused him of treachery, too. Of letting men plunder and pillage, of encouraging looting, and for what? For some foreign king!

And he'd have ridden away.

She trembled when she thought of it. It made her so angry! She knew much of her community had turned against her for what she believed. Well, there were others who felt as she did! Half the Zimmermann family, for one thing. Some of the Merks. Most of the Kiesses and Dorns and Knaabs. A few Bauers. But most of her people, who had suffered so much to get to this new land, had frozen her out. The men ignored her, the women turned their backs on her, the children taunted her.

It's not right! It's so unfair!

She'd watched the men drift away to Georgia or the Floridas, one by one, in groups, in a flood. First Heinrich Strum.

The bastard!

Then the others, all of them. And now Heinrich her brother.

Peter Frietz, her nephew, gone, his brothers Charles and even John on the brink, Abraham and Katy living in an armed camp, ready to shoot at whatever passed.

My own sister!

Peter, who had his own, if somewhat unofficial, militia troop now, was seldom home. He told her stories of how it was, out there in the world. The easy-to-confiscate property had already been seized, horses for the cavalry, forage, victuals for the men, guns, powder . . . But the Royalists had become better prepared. They had turned every farmhouse into a small fortress. They kept inside at night with the shutters closed, even in the hottest weather. Great beams reinforced the doors, the chinking in the log walls had been thickened. The people were wary, experienced, watchful. Surprise was now infrequent, small sieges necessary, though they were seldom worthwhile since there was little left to take. Nothing left to give, except punishment.

It was women who held these forts. Look at the Strums, he said. Eva, Barbara, Heinrich's Catherine. Peter spoke of them with admiration, which made her angrier. They're yeoman and soldier, all at once, he'd say. Farmer, mother, guardian, defender . . . very admirable . . . and she'd turn away.

The women might be everything he said, but when she met them in the village, they showed her their backs, spurned her advances. When Heinrich had gone and she'd heard Catherine needed a temporary home for her children, she had offered.

She'd met her at the trading post at Ninety Six.

"I'll look after them for you," she said. "They'll be safe with me."

Catherine stood there, her hands at her sides, her face empty of every emotion.

How beautiful she is! As beautiful as a childhood story!

"Whenever you wish," Anna said. "Whichever you wish."

Catherine looked right through her. She might as well have been a dust devil, as insubstantial as dandelion seeds, or fine sand wrapped in a breeze. Anna flushed, and turned away.

Beautiful, but heartless, cold!

Many times at night she relived the scene, in all its humiliating detail—the unseeing eyes, the turned-away faces, the sense that the village had seen and judged and rejected her.

But she was right. She clung to that.

She felt them coming before she saw them. Something in the pressure in the air, like distant thunder, and in the stillness of the leaves, something in the woods . . . The Indians would have been able to explain it. Maybe she'd learned something from Heinrich.

She was in the yard. The baby was inside, and the eldest, Anna, at the pump with a tub of wash.

She straightened, listening. She heard nothing. But she knew. She motioned to Anna. "Inside, out the back, to the woods and stay there," she said. "There's trouble coming."

"Not this time, Ma. I'll stay to help."

"You will not."

"I'm big enough to help," Anna said. "I won't panic, and you know I'm a good shot."

Catherine stared at her. She was Heinrich's child, all right. A strapping girl, mature at fourteen, with big, competent, red-knuckled hands. The same black hair as her father. "You're old enough for them not to stop until they have you," she said grimly. "But so be it. Inside."

She walked back to the house with the girl, fetched down the guns from the wall. There were two of them, ready as always. The long rifle that Heinrich had used for deer. The short one he'd used for boar. She didn't know their caliber, but she knew which bullets were which and how to use them. She was a very good shot. She took the long gun for herself, gave the short one to the girl.

"At least put on some clothes," she said, staring out the doorway.

"I'll be upstairs," Anna said.

Peter, who had just turned three, was playing in the corner. Catherine motioned him to go with Anna, and he went without a word.

The previous time they had come, Catherine had offered no resistance. The guns had been hidden in their box under the porch. She'd been afraid they'd steal them, and so she put them away. She'd not make that mistake again. They had come and beaten her, and then they'd . . . but she blanked the thought. There was no use dwelling on it, though her body still felt bruised, and her spirit had dimmed from its customary brightness into a sort of perpetual gray. There was anger mixed up with the gray, too, anger and something more . . . primitive. She'd not let it happen again.

She saw the dust from the Martintown Road, and for a moment hoped they'd pass on by. Perhaps they were bent on some mischief by the Savannah River, or maybe they were chasing some hapless Loyalist.

But no more than ten minutes later, the first horsemen appeared at the gate.

"They're at the back too, Ma," Anna called.

Her heart froze. The back? Why there, too? This wasn't a casual raiding party!

"Just as well I dint go to the woods, Ma," Anna said, cheerfully enough. "They'd have me by now."

She didn't reply. There was not much to be said.

"Stay inside," she said after a while, and stepped through the doorway onto the porch. She held her gun ready.

"What do you want?" she demanded as the horsemen lined up fifty yards distant. "I got nothing for you to take but the food for my children. You already got it all. Is that what you want, to take food from babes?"

"All disloyal property is confiscated," one of the men said, pulling a paper from his boot. "That means farms, land, build'ns too . . ."

"And you're to drive women and children into the woods?"

"I care not where you go," the man said.

"And when I'm gone you'll put my land and my house in your saddlebags and ride off, I suppose?" she demanded sarcastically. "How is land confiscated? Where do you put it when you've got it?"

"Enough talkin'!" He spurred his horse forward. She lifted her gun.

"Stop!"

He paused, then kept coming. She pulled the trigger. The butt slammed into her shoulder, but she'd been braced for it and held her ground.

She'd been aiming low, hoping for a leg wound. Instead, the bullet took the horse in the neck, and it went down, pitching its rider into the dirt.

Inside, the child wailed, drowning the screech of the horse and the panicked yells of the men.

The other riders scattered.

There was another shot from the back, a heavy rifle going off with a roar. Someone back there yelled, too.

"Don't worry, Ma," Anna called. "Jus' wanted to let 'em know I'm here!" She was in the loft. From there, two small windows commanded the front, where the chicken sheds were, and another the back, where there was no cover at all. The farmyard had been designed that way. They had cleared every bush that could shelter a skulker.

Someone fired from the chicken shed. The bullet whined past her, pinged a hinge and lost itself in the wood. She ducked back into the house, slammed the door.

Her heart was racing, but she was steady.

There was a barrage of shots, but none of the bullets made it inside. Upstairs, the rifle went off again, and a man yelled in pain.

"Anna!" she screamed. "Stay away from the windows!"

"Don't worry, Ma, I know how it works," Anna called back.

She did, too. It made Catherine sad to know how much she knew. She was too young for this!

For a while, there was silence. Then she saw one of the invaders light a torch, and stand up. He was going to fire the house! She squeezed off a shot, missed. He hurled the torch, but it went no more than fifteen yards and sputtered out in the middle of the yard. His comrades jeered.

Suddenly the back door smashed open. She whirled, saw two men in the opening.

For a heartbeat, she stood there, in indecision. What to do? Shoot one, the other gets her. Surrender, she was lost . . .

She fired. The bullet took the man in the head, and he exploded. Bad shot. Risky. Aim for the heart! The other yelled, leapt backward and disappeared, too surprised and frightened to take advantage of her need to reload. She cautiously pushed the door closed and shoved a chest in front of it.

There were so many of them!

But she felt savagely elated. *One less!*

Then she waited.

Her husband was at that moment on a Georgia beach, eating alligator steak and drinking Madeira wine. Of course, in Florida one got used to extraordinary things, but, he reflected, these were extraordinary vittles even by Florida standards, and especially for a lad from the Hunsrück or a farmer from the backest of the Back Country.

Matters had gone badly.

They had set out with Prevost from St. Augustine four days previous, in answer to a summons from the Commander-in-Chief Sir Henry Clinton.

The British government had decided that Loyalist control of Georgia and South Carolina was essential. General Clinton was directed to capture Savannah and, as soon as troops were available, Charlestown. Loyalist exiles in London had been pushing for a winter campaign in the south; in the summer, the troops would face malaria, debilitating heat, atrocious weather and spoiled provisions. On the other hand, no civilized army could campaign in the savage northern winters, so he had troops to spare. He had, he believed, more than enough men to seize Savannah, move up river to Augusta and then capture Rebel strongholds in South Carolina before they'd be needed for the spring campaign back in the north.

It sounded so easy!

Clinton placed Mad Archy Campbell in command of thirty-five hundred troops, the best of the American Loyalists: George Turnbull and his New York Volunteers; John Harris Cruger with two battalions of Oliver DeLancey's Brigade of New York; Isaac Allen and his battalion of Skinner's Brigade of New Jersey; John Hamilton's Loyal Regiment of North Carolina Volunteers; and two battalions of Hessians. There were also to be a few scattered companies of Loyalists from South Carolina, placed under Colonel Alexander Innes.

As easy as going to a regimental ball, surely!

They set sail from New York November 27.

The plan was for Campbell to hit Savannah from the ocean, while Augustine Prevost's Florida volunteers attacked from the land.

Prevost split his corps into two. The first, which included Heinrich Strum and the other South Carolinians, would make its way up the coast. The other, a corps under his brother, Lieutenant Colonel James Mark Prevost, was to join up with a Loyalist regiment commanded by Colonel Daniel McGirth. Thomas Browne, now a colonel with the Rangers, would be there too, with a company of Indian warriors.

All in all, it was a formidable army, if not altogether an implacable one. But that was when things started going wrong.

In what had seemed a sensible move, since they had control of the oceans and the hurricane season was largely past, Prevost decided to send their provisions by boat. He set up an elaborate series of rendezvous locations in coves up the coast. Too elaborate by half: the boats missed the first one and then the second.

The first night, they were reduced to hacking oysters from the rocks with their military swords, which gave them a hearty meal but also dysentery, and they spent the next day hunched in rows behind the dunes with their breeches and boots slung around their necks. The third day, they fed off a beached porpoise, which was filling but disgusting, and the fourth day they killed a couple of alligators, acceptable enough eating made even finer by the discovery of a barrel of Madeira wine in a nearby wreck.

As a result of all these mishaps, and despite the wine, the soldiers were in a foul mood, and the following day they pulverized the unfortunate town of Sunbury, which in any case was hardly defended, the Patriot army having hastened to Savannah. They captured forty pieces of cannon, a quantity of ammunition and two hundred and twelve prisoners, but reached Savannah too late to participate in its capture. It was all over by the time they got there. It had been a rout.

Prevost was irritated at having missed the action. Heinrich, by contrast, was delighted. He was already soldier enough to know that a battle missed is a battle survived. He was in no hurry to face the guns of the enemy.

From all accounts, the taking of Savannah had been an inglorious affair.

The defending Congressional armies were in disarray. The commanding general, Robert Howe, had annoyed Georgians by casually usurping their right to command the fight for their own lands; not that he didn't have the authority, but he did it so clumsily that he made many of them mutinous. Many officers simply deserted to look after their properties and families directly; when the officers left, the men just drifted away. It was made worse by the fact that most of Georgia's veteran troops were far inland, on the frontier, patrolling against Indians. The troops that did remain were short of munitions.

In the end, Campbell's troops were able to attack Howe from the rear, having been led through a swamp by an escaped slave with an eye for the main chance. The battle itself was over in a few minutes. The Americans were routed, and fled. Howe was chased through Savannah, and with a small part of his little army escaped up river and into South Carolina. Five hundred and fifty men were either killed or captured; Howe lost all his artillery and baggage. The attackers had only seven killed and nineteen wounded, and captured forty-eight cannon, twenty-three mortars, the fort with its ammunitions and stores, the shipping in the river, a large quantity of provisions and—not the least of it—the capital of Georgia.

"I am the first officer," said Mad Archy, somewhat grandiosely, "to take a stripe and star from the Rebel flag of Congress."

There was only noise, and terror, and sweat, and a gash where a splinter had torn into her leg, and whirling visions, and the glaring sun, and silence, and noise, and barrels too hot to hold, bleeding fists wrapped in torn cloth, fire, and dying chickens flapping in the yard, and muzzle flashes, men sprinting, evil curses, silence, in the silence the whimpering of a little boy, thunder, exhaustion, a terrified heart, and bruises, a battered shoulder from the ram of the butt, the battering ram at the door, men yelling, a wink-brief image of Heinrich, his black hair, the smell of him, the feel of him, explosions, pain, and running men, boots and buckskin breeches, reloading, a man bleeding in the doorway, scarlet runner, a whirl of limbs and grimaces, men dying, falling corpses, river of bodies, a bright flash of petticoat and spinning flesh, a heart-piercing scream as they reached her precious Anna, her brave Anna, and bore down, tearing noise, silence, tearing pain, and at the end only a huge regret that filled her body and burst out of it and went spiraling down into the blackness until it just . . . stopped.

They found little Peter in the room with the broken bodies. Their mother's blood, which had smeared his face and arms, had caked and was flaking off.

Someone said it looked like peeling bark.

It was Peter Dorst's militia troop, on a routine patrol of the Londonborough settlements, who found the bodies. They had seen the smoke from the still-smoldering outbuildings and that the front door was lying, smashed into splinters, in the yard. There was hardly a board in the building that didn't have a bullet hole or two. It was a miracle the child was left unhurt.

"Why did they leave the baby?" Anna Dorst asked. Her heart was sick. This wasn't the way to win the future!

"P'raps even animals have their limits," Peter said. "P'raps there are things even they won't do."

"What did you do with him?"

"I left him with Maria. She'll take him in. Until his father returns."

"If . . ."

Yes, if. He sat silent, remembering the morning. These were not the acts of Congressional troops, not even Patriot militiamen. This was devil's work. Only devils would rape and kill a young girl and her mother in a room where a small child cowered. This had nothing to do with why they were fighting the war! He'd caught up the little boy and washed him at the pump outside, then wrapped him in some blood-spattered linen and placed him on his horse in front of him. He rode to Maria's farm, his arms around the child protectively, hugging him, not saying anything, not having anything to say. He'd spent no longer at Maria's than he needed; he hadn't much to say to her either, any more. Her Heinrich had gone off, foolishly, stupidly, to join some rag-tag army somewhere, and she was living the life of a widow, long before her time. He told her what had happened and left the child enfolded in her embrace. At least she had love to spare!

He looked over at his own children, standing wide-eyed, listening. His eldest, Peter, was already fifteen.

Almost old enough to go to war.

"What did you do at the farm?" Anna asked.

"My men cleaned up the yard some, re-hung a door, and I told them to nail a cockade to the front, where anyone passing would see it."

"Why?"

"A sign to other Patriots to leave it alone," Peter said. "Enough has been done. Enough is enough."

"To the Tories it would just be the mark of the Whigs," Anna said. "Criminals leaving their confession nailed to the front door . . ."

"I know," Peter said. "But Heinrich needs no mark to think thus. And I considered it my duty."

"What will you do if you find who did it? If they're . . . ours?"

"They're not ours, never could be. They'll hang, like the criminals they are. If it were Washington himself, I'd hang him for this."

Anna hadn't thought of Heinrich for some time, not without anger and a touch of malice. Now she thought of him with pity. Two wives, two deaths, two women, two murders. *That beautiful, beautiful woman! He'll go mad!* She remembered her humiliation by Catherine, and felt ashamed. Such a small thing, set against a killing! And when Heinrich returned? Could she help to overcome his grief and his rage? She looked over at her husband. He was staring gloomily at the fireplace, head in his hands, his rebellious queue dangling over his home-made militia uniform, black on green. He'd taken off his boots, and his stockings were torn where the leggings covered them. What of him? He was quick and decent, and would ride where he thought his duty told him. And for what? How could they ever live in a peaceful federation with the other states, when they couldn't even live in a peaceful federation with Charlestown, or even Dutch Fork? When in their own community they were killing each other with impunity?

How did poor Peter ever get to be a leader of men? Only because the Rangers disdained leadership, she supposed, and left it to those who would. The Rangers fought with cunning and natural caution; to Anna, the Ranger way of battle was a solitary figure up a tree, spyglass in hand, an ambush, a secret shot to the throat, the enemy gurgling to death by himself, somewhere in the lonely woods. They had learned this from dealing with the Indians for so many years, learned also from Indian yelling and impetuosity how to contrive to lose battles.

But *Peter can't win their war for them!*

Nor will the deaths of children and young girls.

I don't want my children to die in this war!

Clinton had told Archy Campbell to take Savannah and he had, leaving him without anything very much to do. He didn't have enough men to control South Carolina—not without the reinforcements Vice Admiral Mariott Arbuthnot was supposed to be bringing from England—but he could jab them a little, and remind them of the sharpness of the Royal sword. So he decided that taking Augusta would strengthen his position and give him a base from which to harass South Carolina.

Before he left, Campbell folded the companies of Loyalists brought down from New York into South Carolina Royalists, and included many of the former residents of Ninety Six who had come up with Prevost from Florida, or had come down from South Carolina. He also issued a proclamation aimed at winkling out Tory sympathizers and tipping wavering Whigs. The British military presence, he said, showed the Crown's determination to protect its loyal subjects in the southern provinces. He urged the residents of Savannah and all of Georgia to reaffirm their loyalty. And he added a promise and a threat: protection would be based upon future allegiance rather than on past disloyalties. Georgians were being given the opportunity to choose, but if they didn't choose right, their property was at risk.

Campbell set off in high spirits, leaving Alexander Innes in charge of Savannah. Heinrich Strum thought this a good appointment—Innes had been secretary to the Governor, Lord Campbell, and more recently, an aide to Clinton; he was astute, highly political, but a good officer nonetheless, respected by the men.

Christian Zange stayed in Savannah with Heinrich. The rest of the Palatines went with Campbell: Friedrich and Christoph Ruppert, Nick Cruhm, Peter Mehl, Christian's boys Jacob and Johan Zange, Georg Schildnacht Sr. and Jr.; and Georg Weber. They were joined in Augusta by Heinrich's brother-in-law Daniel Michler, Nicolas Henn, Katy and Anna's brother Heinrich Adolph, Katy's son Peter Frietz, Karl Bauer, Thomas Schildnacht and Friedrich Zimmermann with his sons Henry and Jacob.

As soon as Campbell left, Innes added a proclamation of his own, demanding that the inhabitants of the town and the adjacent country bring in their guns, ammunition and other military accoutrements and surrender them to a commissary. All citizens were to reveal where arms or military stores were hidden, on pain of severe punishment.

Innes sent Strum, among others, to seize what weapons he could and administer Campbell's oath. He was briefed personally by Major McLauren on the delicate matter of dealing with the populace, but he barely listened.

He would make up his own mind and do things in his own way. Collecting guns and ammunition was the easy part, even in the teeth of insults and resentment. But, for him, administering the oath was a different matter.

"Why?" asked Zange, as they rode together through the town. "You read it, they recite it, they sign it, you leave. Where's the problem?"

"I take oaths seriously," Heinrich replied.

"Then it should be easier," Zange said.

"No, an oath is a matter of honor. You don't swear an oath unless you sincerely hold what it says. We're telling these people to swear to what they don't believe."

"They don't have to sign, after all."

"And lose their property?"

"It's their fault for signing or not signing," Zange said stubbornly. "They chose the losing side, we didn't."

"No," Heinrich said. "It's our fault, for putting them in a way of having to swear falsely."

Campbell's Thousand, as he liked to call his force, took Augusta without firing a shot. Andrew Williamson's Patriot army, which included that still-reluctant recruit Lorentz Merk, retreated and crossed the river into South Carolina. Williamson, Rebel commander at the first battle of Ninety Six, was a familiar figure to the Palatines; his home, White Hall, was on Hard Labour Creek just upstream from the Bauers, Merks and Frietzes.

Heinrich, when he heard about Augusta's fall, wondered if he could go home, however temporarily.

Home!

He felt a sudden chill. *Is she all right?* And then he thought, *But I was right to leave. I had to leave. I had no choice . . .*

On February 7, Abraham Frietz's leash snapped and he, too, rode off to war.

Katy had seen it coming.

Young Charles went with him. That made her mad. He was just a boy!

Wasn't it enough that her other son, Peter, was with Strum somewhere on the coast? Well, at least John was still at home, so far.

It was Campbell's arrival at Augusta that tipped the balance, as it did for many other Loyal men who hadn't yet risked leaving their families and farms open to reprisal by slipping away to Florida.

For Abraham was far from alone. There were still plenty of Loyalists in the Back Country. Some were living nomadic lives on the frontiers, attaching themselves here to an Indian band, there to a predatory gang of robbers. Others were still hovering about in the nearby woods, terrified to come out, secretly fed by their families. Still others, like Abraham, either feigned acceptance of Patriot ways or simply kept their heads down behind the plow and refused to be drawn.

Campbell had been counting on considerable numbers of these men joining his army, and had sent out emissaries from Augusta with a mixed bag of threats and cajolements to encourage them to come forward, "prodigal with promises and presents," as a Whig chronicler put it, "exasperating minds already embittered by flaming pictures of the cruelties committed by the republicans."

One of his more successful agents, primarily because of his own elevated stature, was Colonel John Hamilton, a Scottish veteran of Culloden, a man of some fortune, respected by his troops and opponents alike.

Abraham had set off to join Hamilton. Instead, he fell in with one Colonel Boyd.

The mysterious, shadowy Colonel Boyd.

No one seemed to know who he really was. Some said he'd come from New York with Campbell, but others maintained he was an "exile from the southern provinces." Still others said he really came from Rayburn's Creek, from the Little River district east of the Saluda, where the Cunningham brothers held sway.

Who made him a colonel? No one knew that either. He claimed to have his commission from Clinton directly. Who was to say? Perhaps it was true.

In any case, Campbell had sent him to the Back Country to recruit Loyalists. He had started in North Carolina and had made a sweep along the frontier, and was even now passing through Ninety Six; his route to the river would take him through Long Canes. He had more than five hundred men with him, a formidable force. He was going to join Hamilton, and then they'd make their way to Augusta to swell Campbell's army.

Katy watched Abraham cinching on his saddle. His face was set in that stubborn look that so irritated her. Charles was already mounted, his rangy mare prancing about in the gateway. He had made his farewells, and Katy had successfully refrained from weeping.

"Why now?" she asked Abraham, not for the first time. "And why him?"

Abraham sighed. They'd been through this before! It was true, no one knew Boyd. He himself suspected the "Colonel" was one of the bandit chieftains left over from the Regulator days. For one thing, his notion of provisioning his men was to raze Whig farms and carry off their livestock, and he often seemed to turn from his march to burn a particularly Whig-gish stronghold—typical bandit maneuver. But what did it matter? If some of his men were more properly robbers than soldiers, others were good men and Loyal, and were eager to join the Royal army at Augusta, bring peace and order back to the province. Most of Boyd's South Carolina recruits came from Ninety Six District, and many were neighbors from Stevens Creek and its tributaries, especially Cuffeetown Creek. He'd already told Katy all this. It was their last best chance to secure the province once and for all, while there were regular soldiers to sustain them. He had to do his duty!

At the word duty, Katy had laughed, somewhat grimly. *He's just like the others after all. Loves the idea of glory, wants to ride off to do battle. Never once thinking of the bullet that destiny has named for him. Never once thinking of the women and children he leaves behind!*

She knew this was unkind. He *was* thinking of her, of them. It was that he made her play second fiddle to men in cockaded hats that really rankled.

And he's taking away my Charles!

Abraham turned to embrace her, but she held her body stiff to show her disapproval. Disappointed, he climbed into the saddle. She wanted to cry out, but it was too late.

Stubborn!

She watched as he waved farewell and cantered out of the yard to join his son. They'd be in the arms of this Boyd by sundown. And then what? Augusta. Savannah? Charlestown? New York?

Later that day, she drove the cart the ten miles to Maria's farm. She sat with Maria on the bench down by Cuffeetown Creek, and held her hand, staring at the sluggish water.

Two war widows, husbands still alive somewhere, left alone to survive. As survive we will.

Colonel Andrew Pickens of Long Canes wasn't going to let Boyd's passage go unchallenged (even if a Royal army was lurking about Augusta); he called out his militia regiment, and with it Peter Dorst's troop. Peter told Anna about it later, after he returned, words tumbling out of him as furiously as a flock of startled starlings, arms gesticulating, flushed with excitement. It was his first real battle, and like many survivors, he'd found it both terrifying and thrilling.

"The colonel sent us from Ninety Six under Cap'n Anderson to get ahead of the Boyd gang. Boyd was then at Long Canes, heading west, so we crossed the Savannah at the shoals and circled back to wait for him. Sure enough, at Cherokee Ford there they came, on rafts, so many of them, must have been six hundred, seven. We fired on them as their rafts got close to the Georgia bank, but it didn't do much good. The canes on the bank made it impossible to sight well. We couldn't stay and fight. They were too many. So as they landed, we took to the horses, crossed back across the Savannah and rejoined the colonel."

He'd nicked one, he knew, firing his carbine through the canes. Couldn't see it, but heard the yell.

Like shooting ducks from a blind.

Pickens, meanwhile, with the rest of his army of five hundred men, had made a sortie against Hamilton. He caught up with Hamilton's men at Fort Charlotte on the river, but they were too well dug in and Pickens didn't want to waste time and energy on a siege, no matter how fruitful it might prove. So he returned to Boyd.

"We came up with them on the 14th," Peter said. "They were encamped beside Kettle Creek, which flows that way, into Georgia's Broad River." He flung his arms out, gesturing in Georgia's direction. "Our scouts came on him first. He was in a fenced field, horses turned out to graze, men butchering beeves, doubtless stolen, everything in confusion. Didn't know we were there, didn't care, posted no sentries, perfect. We attacked."

He was astonished to see how furiously the Loyalists defended their camp, in vicious hand-to-hand fighting with bayonets and swords, perhaps because, as a Whig sympathizer wrote later, "the action was engaged with all the fury of civil rancor, and all the desperation inspired by the fear of those evils which the vanquished would have to suffer at the hands of the victors."

But they were finally driven back. And while they were retreating, Boyd fell, mortally wounded, three rifle balls in his body.

The remaining Loyalists backed across Kettle Creek and formed up as best they could on a small hill. Pickens pressed through the swamp, waded across the stream and began moving slowly up the hill toward them.

What to say to Anna? *I spent an hour in the charnel-house of Kettle Creek. Men's innards spilling into the grasses. Blood everywhere, blood and terrible wounds. And I came through!*

The obstinate Loyalists lasted a full hour before they were totally routed.

I saw there many men I knew, facing me, with guns and grimaces, hatred and fear. Neighbors! And then I saw . . .

But he was silent. He didn't tell Anna what he'd seen. Not among the seventy dead, not among the two hundred and fifty exhausted, bewildered, shocked captives, but among the still able-bodied fleeing into the woods—Abraham and Charles! His own brother-in-law and nephew!

Her brother-in-law too. Her nephew. I can't tell her that!

Seventy dead, near three hundred escaped, fled back into South Carolina, even North Carolina, to try to creep back into their communities, hoping they hadn't been missed . . . And two hundred and fifty captives.

It could have been two hundred and fifty-two!

He settled into a chair, stopped waving his hands around. "Pickens had known Boyd, and as soon as the battle ended, he went to see him. Boyd said he knew he was near death and asked for two Loyalists to be assigned to wait upon him until his end, and to bury his body. He handed Pickens a gold brooch and asked him to deliver it to his wife."

"What happened to the prisoners?" Anna asked.

"Marched in chains to Augusta a day or so later. They'll be tried in due time, and very likely hanged."

Weeks later, Andrew Pickens went to call on Boyd's widow, as promised. He took the brooch to her. The colonel, he said, had died like a man, honorably, in honorable battle.

"It's a lie," she said, turning on her heel. "No damned Rebel has killed my husband!"

Campbell had evacuated Augusta at the very hour Boyd was meeting his doom. He'd become alarmed at being so far away from his base at Savannah, in such an exposed position. He had no idea where Boyd was. Several of his scouting parties had been ambushed and destroyed, including a detachment of Browne's Rangers, and he heard rumors that the Patriots were massing for an action against him. He knew that Congress had sent Benjamin Lincoln down to the Carolinas to take charge of the southern campaign; Lincoln was encamped not very far away, at Black Swamp, and was rumored to have up to seven thousand men in camps in various parts of Georgia and Carolina. Campbell therefore called in his scouts and left precipitately, dropping rapidly down the river until he reached Hudson's Ferry, reassuringly close to his main forces at the coast.

For the Loyalists, his campaign had been a disaster. They had rallied as they'd been urged to, only to be abandoned. But by rallying, they had exposed themselves to the ever-vindictive eyes of their Whig neighbors. There was no longer any doubt where their sympathies lay, and they were marked for retaliation.

Abraham and Charles crept back to the farm under cover of dark. They had walked home; their horses hadn't escaped with them. They had made a difficult crossing of the river by swimming, and had kept to smaller paths since then, ducking into the woods whenever they heard someone coming. They were exhausted when they banged on their own door.

Katy met them on the threshold with a single pistol clutched in both hands.

She put it carefully on the floor, opened her arms and hugged them both.

No one needed to know they had come back, for no one had known they were gone.

Or so she hoped.

A week after the debacle at Kettle Creek, the South Carolina General Assembly passed a new and draconian law called An Act to Prevent Persons Withdrawing from the Defense of the State to Join its Enemies, which would give those who had already so joined forty days to return, surrender and recant or face the death penalty and the confiscation of whatever property earlier confiscation acts had left them. A special court was set up to try all persons "charged with Sedition, Insurrection or Rebellion against the State."

A hundred and fifty were so charged. Seventy were survivors of Kettle Creek, who had been marched down to Augusta in chains.

After interrogation there, they were marched back home to Ninety Six and kept under guard.

Twenty-two were sentenced to hang. Gallows were erected and graves dug, and the condemned were forced to sign their own death warrants.

Then, for security reasons, the Governor had them all marched to Orangeburg. Five of these were returned to Ninety Six and duly hanged. The others were released after signing an acknowledgment that they'd be hanged if they ever took up arms again.

"There should have been more," Peter told Anna. "These were not soldiers. Most of the condemned weren't even proper Loyalists. They just used the word as a convenience to cover their plunder. Most were infamous—more intent on booty than the honor and interest of their Royal masters. Boyd's gang stole everything they could. The hanged men had all committed great atrocities, for which they deserved to die. They were hanged for treason, not for murder or pillage, but they were also murderers and pillagers."

He still hadn't mentioned Abraham and Charles. He didn't know if they'd seen him at Kettle Creek. He didn't know if anyone else had seen them. He didn't know how Anna would react if he told her. He was going to hold his tongue.

Perhaps she'd be furious that I hadn't told her right away. Perhaps she'd be relieved that they got away. Perhaps she'd be angry. Would she have wanted them punished?

And then he thought, *What would I do if she wanted them dead?*

The Patriot army was having its problems. The regulars were all very well, but the militia were in a mutinous mood. They wanted to go home. Troops and officers alike were needed at their country plantations, if only to prevent their slaves from escaping. Or so they said, and it might have been true. It was also true they were simply weary of this endless marching about, the endless encampment, the endless fighting of an apparently endless enemy. They were free men, were they not? Took their own counsel, able to make their own decisions. So they simply disobeyed every order of which they did not approve, left their posts and guards whenever they pleased, and refused to submit to the articles of war, though in the presence of their enemies.

No sir! Articles of war be damned! Those are for paid mercenaries and Royal lackeys. Free men make up their own minds!

General Lincoln, still fresh from the disciplined north, was angry. He was facing an enemy whose veteran troops were superior to his, and this mutiny only made things worse. He turned over command of the militia to Moultrie, in the hope they'd more readily obey his orders. Moultrie was a local hero, after all. But it didn't help. ". . . they continue in their contumacy," Lincoln wrote.

By the middle of February, though militia enrollment was in theory substantial, the commanders despairingly acknowledged that their force was in "a discordant and disaffected condition, without organization or discipline." The authorities passed a severe militia law, imposing much heavier fines on those who either neglected to turn out or misbehaved or disobeyed orders. Unsurprisingly, the men drafted under this law were more mutinous than ever.

The tougher draft laws had their effect on the Back Country, too. On March 10, Jacob Strum was swept up and imprisoned at Ninety Six as a Tory sympathizer. On April 12, his wife Anna turned up at the jail to pay his fine.

She was given a receipt: "To John Strum his gaol fees 13 days and Turnkey, 50s sworn 3d April, 1779; £4 0s.0d."

Another reluctant soldier made. But for the moment, he went home to Cuffeetown Creek. He wouldn't join up. Not yet.

Lincoln's main army of about four thousand men was at Purrysburg. His plan was to join John Ashe of North Carolina, who had about fifteen hundred men camped at Briar Creek, only about forty miles from Savannah; Ashe was supposed to be a threatening and harassing presence there, capturing the attention of the Royalists while the various armies consolidated. Lincoln believed that with Ashe, he'd then have enough troops for the complete recovery of Georgia.

Prevost, getting wind of this through his Loyalist spies, decided to attack Ashe before this consolidation could be achieved.

Heinrich and Zange, with a troop of Royalist militia, went along on the expedition.

Their sweep turned into an easy canter, the canter into a gallop and they fell upon Ashe's camp before the Patriots had any suspicion they were there; the Georgian militia, who didn't want to be there in the first place, fled without firing a shot, many of them floundering in the nearby swamp or drowning in the river. Ashe's regular troops did what they could, but abandoned by their own militia and overwhelmed by numbers, they were routed. They lost seven pieces of artillery and almost all their arms and the whole of their ammunition and baggage. A hundred and fifty died in the battle and in the pursuit, twenty-seven officers and two hundred men were made prisoners and a much greater number perished in the river. Of those who escaped, only four hundred and fifty were able to join Lincoln. Prevost had only five privates and one officer killed, and ten privates wounded. The benefits of Pickens' already famous victory over Boyd had been lost. The Royal government was again in place.

A week later, the South Carolina Royalists were again slogging through the swamps of the Savannah delta.

Prevost had become restless. He saw Moultrie holding the Savannah River and thus the approaches to Charlestown with only a thousand men. So why not push him? He also needed supplies, and the southern Carolina lowlands would yield up rich booty. He was sure he could liberate the spirits of more Loyalists. And if he drew Lincoln from Augusta, so much the better; he could perhaps find an opportunity for a favorable battle . . .

So he pushed across the river. The militia, surprised and alarmed, gave way after only feeble resistance. Moultrie began falling back toward Charlestown, destroying bridges in a vain attempt to delay Prevost while his forces gradually diminished from desertion. On May 10, Prevost reached the Ashley River without effort or loss. Moultrie sent out the Polish Dragoons under his erratic but energetic ally, Count Pulaski, to stop him, but Pulaski was routed and his men fled. To his great surprise, therefore, Prevost found himself poised to take Charlestown.

There he waited. Did he want to take the town or not? He was far from certain. And where was Lincoln? Couldn't the man read signals? Hadn't Moultrie let him know? Why wasn't he coming?

He advanced a little further, to the city's perimeter, where the South Carolina Royalists leaned on their swords and waited. This hadn't been a battle! It was an afternoon stroll!

Heinrich sat on a rock, gazing toward the town. He couldn't make out the harbor, or the river, but those smudges there, on the distant horizon, would be the prison ships. He wondered who was on them.

Are they still killing each other for food? Do they still try to hang themselves, or fling themselves overboard to drown?

And then he thought, *The last time I was here, I made love with Catherine in a back room overlooking the garden. Who's in that room now?*

And, *I'll get back to see her, as soon as this damn thing's over.*

On May 11, Prevost, who had been wondering if nothing would ever bring Lincoln down from his perch at Augusta and had been mulling over whether taking Charlestown wasn't more trouble than it was worth, at last summoned Governor Rutledge and the fuming Moultrie to surrender. Moultrie was nominally in command, but the Governor and Council, hearing rumors that Prevost had nearly eight thousand men with him, decided that "parlies and capitulation" would be worthy subjects for discussion. To Prevost's demand, they countered with a weasely proposition full of compromises and concessions: "To propose neutrality, during the war between Great Britain and America and whether the state shall belong to

Great Britain or remain one of the United States to be determined by the treaty of peace between these two powers."

Rutledge tried to pass this off as a delaying tactic, but Moultrie, who was not fooled, was incensed. The words "shameful" and "disgraceful" were among his more moderate responses. One of his officers, Lieutenant Colonel John Laurens, was designated to carry the humiliating terms to Prevost, but he balked. Moultrie refused to discipline him. Another officer was finally found to carry the message. Prevost, still trying to delay, at first wouldn't accept it; he insisted on talking only to Moultrie himself. After dawdling as long as he dared, he sent his brother Mark to the negotiations. Prevost's message was curt: surrender as prisoners of war, sign paroles and await a prisoner exchange.

Moultrie's dudgeon rose even higher. "I am determined not to deliver you up as prisoners of war!" Moultrie exclaimed to Rutledge and his Council. "We will fight!"

The following day, Prevost intercepted a message to Moultrie and learned, to his relief, of Lincoln's approach. He pulled out that night and recrossed the Ashley.

For two weeks they camped at Ashley Ferry, opposite Charlestown, and then turned southwest to Johns Island.

No Lincoln.

Damn it! Where was the man?

Prevost stopped again at Stono Ferry and fortified the mainland side with three redoubts behind an abattis some seven hundred yards long. A bridge of boats led to it from the island.

Lincoln, who had finally made his tardy way to Charlestown, moved a detachment down to Stono on May 31, while Count Pulaski's American Legion danced about on the outskirts, reconnoitering the enemy position.

The stalemate continued until June 16, when Prevost, seeing no easy way of either provoking Lincoln into rashness or mounting a worthwhile sally, decamped to return to Savannah, leaving about nine hundred men under John Maitland. Lincoln's eventual attack on Maitland was mediocre, and the ensuing battle, while exceptionally bloody, was indecisive.

The South Carolina Royalists, with Sergeant Strum among them, went with Prevost; their fighting, such as it had been, was for the moment over. They island-hopped their way back, first to Port Royal, where they paused, and then to Savannah, carrying a rich haul in plunder from the lowland plantations.

They also brought thousands of slaves, who had joined the Royal forces in an utterly vain expectation of freedom.

An Italian chronicler, whose dispatches were full of "Woes!" and "Alacks!" was scathing: "The Royal troops were not satisfied with pillaging; they spared neither women, nor children, nor sick. Herein they had the negroes for spies and companions, who, being very numerous in all the places they traversed, flocked upon their route in the hope of obtaining liberty. To recommend themselves to the English, they put every thing to sack, and if their masters had concealed any valuable effects, they hastened to discover them to their insatiable spoilers.

"Whatever they could not carry off, they destroyed . . . Every where ruins and ashes. The very cattle, whatever was their utility, found no quarter with these barbarians. Vain would be the attempt to paint the brutal fury of this lawless soldiery, and especially of these exasperated and ferocious Africans. But the heaviest loss of which the planters of Carolina had to sustain, was of these very slaves. Upwards of four thousand were taken from them: some were carried to the English islands, others perished of hunger in the woods, or by a pestilential disease which broke out among them afterwards."

The Royal forces were in charge of the Georgian coast, and part of the Carolinian shoreline. But not much else. Certainly not the hearts of the Georgian planters.

Early in July, Nick Kiess learned of his sister's murder. He blamed Heinrich for her death. He'd left her alone at home, the coward, to fight in a cowardly war. It was his fault.

Heinrich himself had yet to be told.

Eleven

For a long while, the sisters sat, saying nothing. About certain things there was nothing to say. The death of a brother is one of these. Especially if it's the death of a brother that also makes a widow of a great good friend . . . *Indeed,* Katy thought, *if she says anything at all about it, that's the end.*

October 1779
Savannah, Georgia

Maria Elizabeth, sweet, gentle Maria Elizabeth, everyone's angel, wandered dazed about the battered, broken streets of Savannah, clutching her daughter's arm. She held on with a grip like a shackle, like a drowning woman, like the iron band that imprisons the heart when grief comes, but Katherina didn't complain. She understood her mother's pain.

They walked aimlessly. They had come from a field hospital set up in a tent near the town market, and found themselves down at the river embankment, amid scars from the bombardment. There, Maria stared northeast across the river, across the marshes where the French had lurked, and beyond them to Charlestown, somewhere up the coast.

The marshes, where the snipers had waited . . .

Where the cannons were . . .

The killers.

Then they walked back through town, past the Chief Justice's house where the General's family had been staying, now blackened from the fire, ruined when the roof fell in, the furniture broken. It had caught fire, so they said, when the enemy flung over the walls a sheep's carcass soaked in kerosene. They moved away from the town toward the abattis and the redoubt where . . . where . . . it had happened.

Where the war got him.

My God! They killed him! My husband!

A week ago a message had come. From a passing peddler who'd got it from a traveler who'd got it from some militiaman, name unknown. The peddler came to the farm and told it her. "A great victory has been won in Savannah," he said. "But your man lies mortal wounded in a hospital."

Her heart didn't beat again until she found him there, in the army field hospital in Savannah, and then it beat as if it would tear itself from her body, for she'd arrived too late, and he was dead, the stump of his poor leg festering and stinking until the fever took him away.

Katherina had come with her. She hardly remembered leaving, what she had done, where they had all gone, the children. Elizabeth would look after the farm and the Strum children would go to Eva or Anna Henn and Henry had ridden off somewhere and Rosena too, she had gone to the Dorsts, to stay with Anna, as if Anna could ever . . . But that hardly mattered now. They had thrown a bundle together and saddled their only remaining horse and ridden until the beast was staggering with weariness and pain, and then they drove him on all the harder. She didn't sleep until she reached Savannah, not that she remembered.

Too late.

Maria and Katherina stared down into the steep-sided fosse, trying to imagine what it had been like, the attacking Americans and French, the pounding hooves of horses, the crash of cannon and the crackle of musketry, the hoarse shouts of men, the screams of the wounded, the rivers of blood . . . But it was no use. There was only one wounded that mattered, and now he was gone.

They went back into town, back to the main guardhouse on the river, where a commissary had been set up.

They would have to find some place to stay, she supposed.

In the afternoon they met others from Ninety Six, others of their kind, and a while later they encountered Heinrich Strum down by the river. He, too, had been staring across the muddy water to the marshes beyond. He was battle-weary, his leggings and jacket stained, but his weapons shone and his gear was in good repair. He looked strong, invincible. She forced away the thought.

"Maria! What are you doing . . ." He caught himself. Of course! "When did you get here?"

She said nothing.

He took her by the arm, led her to one of the few benches not shattered by the cannonade, sat down with her. Katherina fluttered about like a bird with a broken wing, not knowing what to say.

After a while, he turned to look at Maria. "I saw it happen," he said. "It was during the main assault. Heinrich was on his feet, repelling the Dragoons scaling the abattis, when the shot hit him. He fell." He paused for a long moment. He had seen the shot. It had taken Heinrich Adolph in the knee and cut off his leg like a giant saw, and he'd toppled, the torn leg thumping into the ground, and he'd cried out, something incomprehensible, and then someone had reached him and bound up his stump, and when the assault was over, he was gone, carried away. Heinrich hadn't seen him again. "He died bravely," he said finally, knowing how foolish it would sound to the widow.

They sat quietly for a while on the bench, side by side, staring at the river. He stole a glance at her. She was sitting rigid, the veins prominent on her forehead, throbbing. Her hands were clenched. He'd upset her, of course, but it was better she knew . . .

But Maria was not thinking of her husband at that moment.

My God, my God, he doesn't know about his wife! He hasn't heard!

How can I tell him about his murdered wife?

She started to cry then, and Heinrich took her in his arms, soothing.

He lowered his face to her head, kissed her graying hair.

"Maria," he said, "Maria. So much killing, so much dying. But we all love you, Maria."

At that, she cried all the harder.

A month earlier, on September 1, Count Charles d'Estaing had abruptly appeared off the coast of Georgia with twenty-two French ships of the line and eight frigates. Two he sent to Charlestown, to let them know he was there, and the others showed up at Savannah, alarming Prevost and causing him to send urgent messages to Maitland at Port Royal and to his troops at Sunbury, demanding that they come in at once.

Why was d'Estaing there? His sovereign had ordered him home, but after the previous year's debacle at Rhode Island, when he had twice inexplicably abandoned Newport "in the teeth of victory," as a bemused American later wrote, d'Estaing considered it more honorable "to obey rather the generous impulses of my heart than the dictates of the ministry." It also had something to do, as he well knew, with the peevishness of the American Congress at France's less than stellar performance in the conflict thus far. If he could only win at Savannah and return Georgia to the Republicans, something would have been salvaged from the mess.

D'Estaing's arrival caught the British navy completely by surprise. Their ship *Experiment*, of fifty guns, was obliged to surrender; three frigates and five transports shared the same fate. A small squadron lying in Tybee Roads got away, sailing up the coast; those vessels at anchor in the Savannah were either moved up river or sunk to impede French progress.

Lincoln, exultant at the arrival of an unexpected ally, had set off immediately for Savannah with a substantial army. He arrived on September 16. The previous day, the French, having disembarked in a gale, appeared below the walls of Savannah. They were accompanied by the remains of Count Pulaski's American Legion, which had made a forced march to join them.

Prevost, meanwhile, was digging in, entirely literally. He called sailors off their ships to dig, he put the free blacks and slave refugees to digging, every available infantryman dug his heart and sinew out. The South Carolina Royalists were set to constructing an abattis around the town. Heinrich found himself shoulder to shoulder with Friedrich Ruppert and his son, Henry, and with Jacob's brother-in-law, Nick Henn. Nearby were Peter Mehl and Friedrich Zimmermann. Daniel Michler was there, too, and so were Nick Cruhm and Peter Frietz. Karl Bauer had been there earlier that day, but had taken a fever and had reported to the hospital set up near the market. Defenses went up at a furious rate. But Maitland had not yet made it back from Port Royal, and without him, all this defense was doomed. It was going to be a near thing.

D'Estaing imperiously summoned Prevost to surrender. In a letter filled with overheated bombast, he wrote, "I here command the same troops that have taken Hospital Hill, in Grenada, by storm. I owe it to my humanity to remind you of it, Sir, after which it cannot be imputed to me if I should not be able to restrain the fury of my soldiers, in the event of a fruitless resistance. Sir, I, Count d'Estaing, therefore summons his Excellency General Prevost to surrender himself to the arms of His Majesty the King of France."

To the King of France! To hand Savannah over to a foreign king, no matter what the alliance, was not at all what Lincoln had in mind. The letter irritated him no end, and turned General Moultrie purple with Partisan apoplexy.

Prevost, with one anxious eye on the digging that was still proceeding, stalled. He hinted that he might negotiate a capitulation. He replied courteously: "I hope your Excellency will have a better opinion of me and the British troops than to think either will surrender on general summons without any specific terms."

D'Estaing replied, complaining about Prevost's unrelenting entrenchment of his troops and insisting that his columns would continue their advance upon Savannah. To his letter he appended a postscript: "I apprize your Excellency that I have not been able to refuse the army of the United States uniting itself with that of the King. The junction will probably be affected this day. If I have not an answer therefore immediately, you must confer in future with General Lincoln and me."

Messages passed back and forth. The Americans became increasingly restless.

Prevost's defenses grew more and more formidable. He had quadrupled the number of cannon mounted on his works, had called in all regular and militia detachments and had thrown up thirteen redoubts in a semicircle south of the town.

Still no Maitland, and Prevost therefore asked for a twenty-four-hour truce. D'Estaing granted the delay.

Francis Marion smacked his head. "My God! Whoever heard of anything like this before? First allow the enemy to entrench, and then fight him!" Marion's aides had to restrain him; he almost assaulted Lincoln in his anger.

Finally, Maitland made it through. He brought his troops down through the islands of the coast by boat, by raft, by wading, by heavy slogging through dense fog and dank swamp, in the end unimpeded. It was the afternoon of September 17. Prevost, who had won his gamble, sent a terse message to d'Estaing: "The evening gun to be fired this evening at an hour before sundown shall be the signal for recommencing hostilities."

He had done what he could. His defenses were as complete as he could make them. His troops, some twenty-three hundred regulars, militia, sailors and volunteers, were deployed about the city. "As the enemy is now very near, an attack may be hourly expected," he said in his general orders on the evening of the 17th. D'Estaing, meanwhile, settled in for a siege. By September 22, he had isolated the city from the land side, and his warships completely controlled the riverfront. He had four thousand four hundred and fifty-six men under arms, the Americans two thousand one hundred and twenty-seven.

Still the attack did not come. For the next three weeks, the commanders contented themselves with skirmishing.

This is not to say that people didn't die, some of them bloodily and in great pain.

On Saturday, October 2, the ship *La Truite* and the galleys opened a heavy cannonade on the city.

It seemed to have little effect.

Indeed, in the scheme of things, it was an affair of only minor consequence.

Except that a piece of shrapnel hit Heinrich Ruppert in the chest and tore him to pieces. Both his sons were with him when he died. There was nothing they could have done to prevent it.

The two hundred men of Andrew Williamson's brigade from Ninety Six were on Lincoln's left, with Brigadier General Isaac Huger; they waited restlessly for the main bombardment to begin, the bombardment that should soften up the defenses sufficiently for an assault to take place.

Their role, along with that of Marion's 2nd Regiment of South Carolina, was as yet unclear. What was clear was that the main task would be to storm the abattis around the Spring Hill Redoubt, and punch a hole in the enemy's defenses there, allowing the cavalry to get inside the town.

One of Williamson's men was Philip Zimmermann.

He was aware that his brother Friedrich was among the defenders, and Friedrich's sons Henry and Jacob.

He didn't know Friedrich had been assigned, along with many units of the South Carolina Royalists, to the Spring Hill sector.

Peter Dorst was also with Williamson's brigade. Dorst had no brothers in the besieged city. But his wife did. And his wife's sister's son, Peter Frietz, was in there somewhere.

At least Katy's husband Abraham wasn't there.

Heinrich Strum was, though.

He tried to feel nothing but anticipation. But what he felt mostly was dread.

Lorentz Merk was there, too, laboring in the trenches. He kept his head down and his mouth shut and his heart in his throat.

They all just waited.

Finally the trenches were finished, as much as they could be, and the batteries armed.

A few minutes after midnight, Sunday, October 3, the bombardment began.

Two hours later it abruptly ceased, on the orders of a French commander, a M. de Noailles. It seemed dozens of misdirected bombs fell into the trenches that he himself commanded. He demanded an explanation.

An hour later he got it. A ship's steward had mistakenly sent the cannoneers a keg of rum instead of the keg of beer they had been expecting. They were all drunk.

At four a.m. the assault resumed, with what the French called "more vivacity than precision," the cannoneers still being under the influence of their rum. But it became steadily more violent as it became more precise. Thirty-seven more cannon and nine mortars were unleashed, and another sixteen cannon enfiladed from the ships. To increase the terror, the attackers launched burning carcasses into the town, which set two blocks on fire.

At eight a.m., the firing stopped. D'Estaing's left battery had been shaken to pieces by its own ferocity. Workmen repaired it in dense fog. At ten in the morning, firing resumed, and went on without surcease until well after midnight.

No more rum came from the navy.

The relentless bombardment went on for five days. A good deal of the town was destroyed.

On October 7, Lorentz Merk's work crew was assigned to build a new trench in advance of the left battery. They all knew the trench wasn't needed. Its purpose was to fool Prevost into believing they were not contemplating an assault, but were planning to push their approaches up to his defensive works.

Prevost wasn't at all taken in. He was as aware as d'Estaing that time was on his side. The French were moored offshore, without secure harbor, in a season of storms, in a place which, as English prisoners pointedly reminded them, "an English squadron had never dared to remain for eight hours in the most beautiful weather"; a British fleet could appear at any moment and attack while the sailors were attending to siege duties; his supplies were dwindling. He'd told the Americans at the start he could only stay eight to ten days; twenty had already passed, and the defenses seemed as impregnable as ever.

Prevost knew they'd have to take him by storm.

So he delayed once again.

Lincoln and d'Estaing had agreed to try to crack the defense around Savannah by driving British troops from the Spring Hill Redoubt, but they would first have to capture the flanking redoubt and silence its contiguous batteries. They would therefore feint left, punch right.

They gave the honor of leading the assault to the impetuous Pole, Count Pulaski, and his American Legion.

Lincoln's orders were clear: "The Light Troops who are to follow the cavalry will attempt to enter the redoubt on the left of the Spring Hill by escalade."

In deploying the main body of his troops, Lincoln posted Brigadier General Isaac Huger on his left, with three brigades of militiamen, among them Andrew Williamson's brigade from Ninety Six District. With Williamson went Philip Zimmermann, Peter Dorst—and Nick Kiess, with his sister's murder still preying on his mind.

Lincoln's careful strategy, to which d'Estaing had concurred, was ruined when at midnight, a sergeant major of the Charlestown Grenadiers deserted. He slipped into the besieged city, carrying with him the American plans. Forewarned, Prevost shifted his troops, consisting of the 60th Grenadiers, the 71st Regiment and part of the South Carolina Royalists, to meet the attack, massing his best around Spring Hill. He then assigned the corps to the command of Lieutenant Colonel John Maitland. The deserter had also told Prevost that Lincoln had dressed his vanguard in white shirts over their coats, and white cockades, so they would recognize each other in the confusion of battle; Prevost dressed his defenders the same way.

On the barricades at Spring Hill and its flanking Ebenezer Redoubt were, then, Philip Zimmermann's brother Friedrich, Heinrich Strum, Peter Mehl, the Zanges, Heinrich Adolph, the Rupperts, Nick Henn, Peter Frietz, the Schildnachts, the Webers and Daniel Michler.

The besieging troops were roused from their uneasy slumbers at three in the morning of October 9. The air was still sultry from the previous day's unseasonable heat. There was thick fog on the ground; the air was rank from the swamp and the nearby army latrines. A few minutes before five, a little late by Lincoln's careful timetable, Prevost's morning reveille bugle went off in the camp.

It was Pulaski's signal, and his legion broke into a thundering gallop, aiming straight up the hill to the base of the redoubt; their intention was to sweep past it on both sides, pierce through the town, wheel and take the redoubt from behind, throwing confusion and fear into the enemy's ranks. Pulaski knew perfectly well the effect charging cavalry had on nervous defenders; a mass of hostile horseflesh, bristling with weapons, always seemed like some great, malevolent intelligence rather than a group of fallible men on flesh-and-blood horses.

Behind Pulaski came Colonel Laurens' light troops, who threw themselves at the forts, and Colonel Marion and his 2nd Regiment, who moved against Spring Hill redoubt directly.

It might have gone well for the attackers had Pulaski not been hit, a shoulder wound and a terrible gash in the groin, hurling him to the ground. Seeing their chieftain fall, his legion faltered, wavered and were turned back.

The withering fire continued to pour out from the defending cannons.

Prevost's cannoneers had stuffed all kinds of junk into their guns— scrap iron, broken scissors, bits of wire, fragments of old plows, anything metal that would fit went blasting across the intervening space, whistling horribly, cutting to bloody pieces everything it came into contact with.

The legion fled.

Marion's men pressed on, but they were encountering fire so heavy it was like leaning into a gale of metal wind, and they had little chance. They made it to the fosse, began scaling the ramparts and managed to plant one of their regimental standards on the berm. But the parapet was too high and the defending fire too hot. Men fell, cut to pieces, into the ditch below.

"The Ditch was filled with Dead. In front, for fifty Yards, the Field was covered with the Slain. Many hung dead on the abattis, and for some hundred Yards without the Lines, the Plain was strewn with mangled bodies, killed by our Grape . . . Streams of blood rilled from the wrecks; lamentable cries arose on every side . . ."

So said one awed witness, one among many.

The Ditch was filled with Dead.

To the attackers, it was like wading through a swamp of blood and the fragments of their comrades. No one could have borne it. They backed down the rampart and began retreating. Later, some dispassion having returned, Moultrie recast the slaughter in the bloodless objectivity of the military historian: "Our troops remained before the line in this hot fire fifty-five minutes. [Then] the Generals, seeing no prospect of success, were constrained to order a retreat, after having 637 French and 457 Continentals killed and wounded."

Meanwhile d'Estaing was leading his own assault to the left. His troops had to pass through a deep morass, in which they became mired to their knees. At the far end of this was an abattis of tangled tree stumps and sharp trunks, itself swept by artillery fire.

"Double quick!" yelled the General. "*Vive le Roi!*" And he ordered his drummers to beat the charge.

The defenders fired their deadly cocktail of grapeshot and scrap iron here, too, cutting the assaulting platoons in half. At one point, the gunners stuffed five- and six-foot lengths of chain into the smoking barrels, and they went whirling over Heinrich's head toward the attackers like a flock of savage eagles. The column began to recoil, and d'Estaing, who had never been accused of cowardice, moved to the front to spur them on. He was followed by about three hundred Grenadiers; the rest of the column, entangled in the swamp, was mowed down by Prevost's gunners.

They fought their way to a position in the ditch that the English cannoneers couldn't reach.

There was a lull, and then the defenders came leaping over the barricade, bayonets ready.

Heinrich killed two attackers, then a third. Peter Mehl was by his side. A Grenadier's sword sliced his thigh, and he screamed.

Count d'Estaing was wounded twice, first by a musket ball in the arm and then by another through his thigh, but retained enough strength to mount a horse and lead the retreat.

Of the three hundred Grenadiers with him, a mere dozen survived.

Many units of the attacking militia never made it to the battle. They fled into the swamps.

The road to Augusta, a causeway across a waterlogged morass, was choked with fleeing soldiers. Prevost's cannons swept it relentlessly; soldiers and horses died in a steaming heap.

On the barricades, the thunder of the cannons died away.

Heinrich Strum sat on the ground, shaking, his head in his hands.

By eight in the morning, the attacking army, or what was left of it, was back in its camps.

A truce was proposed, and accepted, for the purpose of counting and burying the dead and seeing to the wounded.

The truce would last until four in the afternoon. Hostilities could be recommenced any time after that, though both sides knew the phrasing was a formality. No one had the stomach for yet more blood.

In that time, the bodies of seven hundred and sixty French soldiers were stacked upon the plain. With them were sixty-one officers, and three hundred and twelve Americans.

One thousand, one hundred and thirty-three dead.

Of the six hundred South Carolina patriots who had charged up Spring Hill, more than two hundred and fifty did not come down again. "I went with heavy heart on parade, to take a review of the sad remains of the battle," one of the Patriot captains, Peter Horry, wrote later. "The call of the roll completed the depression of my spirits. To every fourth or fifth name there was no answer—the gloomy silence which ensued told up where they were."

One of the names that never answered was a young boy from Ninety Six called Nick Kiess.

His body was never identified.

Heinrich had not even known he was there.

Did the ghost of Catherine care?

The defenders lost a hundred and fifteen men and a dozen women.

Almost all the losses came at the Spring Hill Redoubt, where the Palatines had been stationed.

Next to Heinrich Strum, Peter Mehl had his left arm and part of his chest shot away, and died in the mud.

It was there that a cannon shot took Heinrich Adolph in the knee, cutting off his leg; he toppled backward, the torn leg thumping into the ground.

Friedrich Zimmermann was bayoneted by a troop of Dragoons. Johan Zange died from a bullet in the heart. His brother Jacob was gut-shot and died in silence, trying to hold himself together. Their father escaped unharmed.

Daniel Michler had been wounded in the hand-to-hand fighting in the fosse. Heinrich had seen him fall. He had been dragged away, but whether he was alive or dead, he knew not.

Others made it through. The Ruppert brothers were still alive. So were Nick Henn and Peter Frietz. Georg Schildnacht Jr. had been wounded, but not seriously; his father thought he would live. Thomas Schildnacht made it. Zimmermann's two sons survived to bury their father. Both Georg and Henry Weber survived.

Karl Bauer had been in the hospital throughout the battle.

Lincoln, taking his loss philosophically, was ready to move on. On the 15th, he dismissed his militia and on the 18th, broke camp. His army crossed the Savannah and trudged back to Charlestown. D'Estaing, too, was eager to leave. His commanders were afraid a British fleet would appear off the coast before they had recovered, and they expressed growing alarm at the prospects of being overwhelmed by a hurricane. On October 10, the batteries were dismantled and the cannon moved back on board. The troops re-embarked at Causton's Bluff. On the 21st, a Frenchman noted: "Causton's Creek, and all Georgia, are evacuated."

Georgia returned to its status as a province of the British Empire. The Patriot militia vanished like smoke, dissipating into the Back Country. But the fire had not gone out. Dorst and Philip Zimmermann passed up the Georgia side of the Savannah on their way home, and everywhere they saw the rancor and bitterness of civil war. "The rage between Whig and Tory ran so high," Moultrie wrote later, "that what was called a Georgia Parole, and to be shot down, were synonymous."

They crossed the Savannah upriver from Augusta, and made their way toward Ninety Six along the Martintown Road. They met no armed bands. But every place, every cart, every horse, every man, every woman, bristled with weapons. Many farms were apparently abandoned, empty, chimneys smokeless and yards unweeded. At others, people simply retreated inside and refused to come out. No one greeted them as they passed. Everywhere fingers were held near triggers. Suspicion and hostility were universal. The countryside settled into a terrified silence, the quiet before the crack of doom.

Maria Elizabeth stayed in Savannah, not being able to face the bleakness of a home without her beloved Heinrich. She could be found most mornings by the river, staring into the middle distance, as if looking for a sign. When spoken to, she answered politely. But she wasn't really there.

Twelve

Anna stared at her battered shoes. There was a blade of grass stuck in one of the buckles. She reached down to pull it off. *Perhaps it's time to concede a little*, she thought. *It was about that time that we realized there were monsters on our side as well as theirs. Yes, the death of a brother is a terrible thing. But Maria's tears were more terrible than that.*

June 1780
Charlestown, South Carolina

On November 16, a man came to Katy Frietz's house. He was an agent of the Provisional Government, and he had come to take her land away from her.

Her heart sank. *Had they learned of Abraham's misadventure with Boyd? Had someone seen him go, seen him slip back, had someone slyly denounced him?*

He came with a list, he said, of denounced Tories, and by the decisions of the uhduhduhduhuh and the something something something that she couldn't catch, the People were entitled to . . . He went on in this vein, but she stopped listening.

She was angry.

And after a little more of his droning, she started to seethe, and then to yell at him, in a voice that anger squirreled upward toward a shriek.

"My brother not yet cold in his grave, his widow gone, his children scattered, my neighbor's wife murdered by a band of scoundrels while he's away, children treated like hogs and their mothers like cheap whores, rogues and speculators in charge in the towns, and you come to take my land . . ." That very morning, the storekeeper in Ninety Six had tried to charge her forty dollars for a pair of plain, ordinary shoes, whining as he did so that the paper money was worthless, due to massive counterfeiting by the British and the printing presses never stopping in Philadelphia, and that unless she could pay in specie . . . Hmmm? Specie! It made her furious, that to the Patriot zealots had been added the pretend Patriots, more patriotic than thou, with their shameless thirst for personal gain, their unbridled desire for riches, no matter how acquired or at whose expense. It was they who were behind these confiscations, she was sure, insatiable robbers plundering for their private estates . . .

She wished she had gone with Maria, she could have been with her now, could have visited the grave of poor Heinrich, such a long, bitter way from Oberstein . . .

The Confiscator, for so she thought of him, just waited.

When her kettle had finally run out of steam, he explained that Abraham was on the list, denounced by more than one person.

"He's never taken up arms!" she protested, hoping the lie would be believed.

"He hasn't defended his country either," the man retorted. "And in these days, that's enough."

"In that case," Katy said, "you must be confiscatin' half the country."

The agent of the state smiled agreeably. "Just about," he said.

"And who made up this list?"

"It's put about by Colonel John Purves," the man said, "of Tories reported to him. He has the authority of the state."

He unfolded a leather pouch, drew out a document. "Here are the names. D'ye want to see?" He laughed. "Or wish to add any?"

She peered at the list. It was all run together in one mass of scrawled writing, very hard to make out, with false starts and missteps, full of ands and buts and crossings-out and tryings-again. It was even longer than the lists that had gone about a year or so earlier, after the matter of the Oath of Abjuration. Same people on it, only more. Half the damn province! She followed with her finger.

"John Adams," she read. "Hry Adolph." Her hands started to shake. They killed him, now they were taking what little he had left . . . What was Maria to do? And the girl Elizabeth, who was bravely running the farm in her mother's absence? "John & Hugh Akins, Josiah Allen, Wm Ammonds, Elijah & John Bailey, Chambers & David Blakely, Adam & Charles Bowers . . ." Adam Bauer! What had he ever done to draw their enmity? "Fredk Buckalew, Wm Burdett, Abiah Carpenter, Bailey Cheney, John Jr & Thomas Clark, Benj Colson, Joel, John & Jonas Cornet, John Cotton, Ephriam, John Sr, John Jr, Joseph & Samuel Davis, Hector Dickey, Joseph Doolittle, John Flannaghan, John & Jonathan Folk, Adam Fralich, Abraham & Peter Fritz . . ."

There they were! *My husband and my son too! If they take our land, where will we go?* End up in some camp somewhere, distressed refugees, again, in Whitechapel-Across-The-Sea . . .

And then she thought, *What if Anna had something to do with this? Could Peter have heard something? Could she hate us that much?*

My little sister!

Oh Anna, where have you gone!

She read it through without stopping. They were all there, the vanished and the stubborn, the fighters and the evaders, the active and the poor, weak cowards . . . Nick Henn! Dan Michler! She'd heard smallpox or some other fever had taken one or two of their children, and three of Heinrich Strum's little ones, too, but she didn't know who, or if it were really true. As though Heinrich hadn't suffered enough! Conrad Merk, yes, but Lorentz? That poor, sweet boy, taken to Savannah by the Rebels, used as a draft animal, now they were to take his land too . . . Jacob Strum . . . What had he ever done, except get himself stupidly locked up, for nothing? Well, at least that silly girl was standing by him. The Rupperts, the Shavers, the Sitemans, the Schildnachts . . . Barnet Snell . . . Wasn't his boy in the Patriot militia, all hot and fired up to do some confiscatin' of his own? Oh yes, they were all there.

Abraham was in the woods, hunting, a fortunate accident of timing. If he was here, reading this list . . . She was afraid that someday Abraham's own volcano would erupt, that he'd do some uncontrollable violence to someone important. She had seen him quivering with tension whenever anyone came by, friend or foe; he was just waiting for an opportunity. She was becoming afraid for him. His great solidity was wonderful in times of peace; but granite when it explodes is worse than sand, and would do more damage to those around him.

But most of all, damage to us!

In a while, the Confiscator left, having nailed to a post a piece of paper declaring the house to be forfeit and the property of the people of South Carolina and their Congress. He told her to leave the paper alone, on pain of imprisonment. Then he rode off. She tore the paper down immediately. She wasn't going to leave it there for Abraham to see. If they came to take the land, they'd take it. But maybe they wouldn't. Heinrich Adolph's death hadn't, after all, been for nothing, for no purpose. It had been for a cause. At least they had won a famous victory. Now they owned Georgia, could they not soon also own Charlestown? And if they owned Charlestown, could they not also own all the Carolinas? She had heard Abraham say that he'd heard someone say that—What was it again?— that more had died in "confiscatings" than in pitched battle between armies. They needed the presence of an army here in the Back Country. And mayhap they would get one . . . She went inside, tossed the paper onto the cooking fire.

The same day, Peter Dorst came back to Anna. And instead of welcoming him, taking off his boots, soothing his feet in mustard water, taking him to bed, she had quarreled with him. It made her angry, though mostly with herself. Why not treat him like a returning hero?

But it was so unfair! Peter had spent another month away from home. He was always away from home, on some self-inflicted duty or another, with this or that group of militia, or army, or collection of men. And never getting paid for it! Why? Because he had never formally joined the militia, signing a six-month term, or a one-year term, or whatever they demanded, getting onto the mustering rolls.

He must properly join, get on a list, receive his due . . .

"I'll go where I'm needed," he declared, over and over.

Where he's needed! He's needed at home! With his wife and his children!

"A Congress with justice in its heart should pay its men and compensate them for their efforts, for the time away from their legitimate occupations," she said.

He agreed. In a well-run country, this would happen. "But we're besieged by enemies! A man must do what he should, without seeking recompense."

And what about your son? Will he go away to war, too?

That was when she'd brought up the speculators, the profiteers, the evil men who seemed in danger of swamping their cause in the hypocritical use of the noble language of patriotism. And why was Congress sitting on its heels, waiting for the French, or the Dutch, or the Spanish, to do their work for them? Hadn't Peter himself said that the militias in the north had largely disbanded, gone home, that the enthusiasm for the cause seemed to have waned in due proportion as foreign promises were received? Why were they able to get away with this? Because of noble blockheads like Peter, who took the salvation of their cause on themselves . . .

Well, it went on in that vein for some time, moving neither forward nor backward, until they went to bed, angry and depressed. Huh! He'd get over it, and perhaps it would have a salutary effect. Perhaps if the fighting went on, he would at last see that he had other duties than to his country . . .

For my sake, if for nothing else.

Sir Henry Clinton, the British commander in New York, had been mulling over the same thoughts, albeit on a somewhat grander scale and with a somewhat different perspective. The demoralization in the American ranks had been obvious for some time, not just in the desertions from the militias, but in the reluctance of any one United State to go to the aid of the others. The American economy was in a mess, with depreciation of paper money the norm, speculators everywhere . . . The Americans' own writings were filled with dismayed reports of how private interest was everywhere carrying the day against public virtue. Nobody would any longer enlist without exorbitant bounty, nobody would contract to supply the armies, or to supply the contractors themselves, without enormous profits first lodged in their hands. Everywhere people demanded scandalous payments, illicit perquisites. *There is no halting place on the road to corruption,* or so Clinton comforted himself. The Americans were tearing at each other even in Congress, and had been ever since Silas Deane had come back from France with d'Estaing's squadron. It had even been suggested in Congress that the supreme command of the American armies should be turned over to some scoundrelly European general, perhaps Prince Ferdinand or the Marshal de Broglie . . . What self-respecting country could consider that? Why, then, not take a substantial army to the south, in this quiescent season in the north, in the midst of all this Congressional squabbling, and take back the southern provinces, hit them hard, thrash the bounders, teach 'em a lesson or two?

He also wanted to get in a good punch before the court of Madrid took a hand. Clinton was well aware, as all Britain was, of the hatred Spain had for what it considered British arrogance. The Spanish wanted Gibraltar back, and Jamaica as well, and seemed determined to conquer the Floridas, which appeared to them to be essential to the command of the Gulf of Mexico, *Spain's own pond* . . . Spain had been wavering, perhaps uncertain of the contagious effect one liberated colony might have on others, were her soldiers to get close enough to catch whatever it was that caused it. But France was pushing, and the family compact would probably hold, and Spain would soon enter the war. Yes, best get on with it.

So on the day after Christmas, Clinton departed from New York for Savannah with a formidable army of eighty-seven hundred men, conveyed in an equally formidable armada under Admiral Arbuthnot, finally arrived from England with a fresh expeditionary force. There were twelve hundred horses in the transports, to be used by the even more formidable Colonel Banastre Tarleton, whose reputation for ruthless efficiency (as well as efficient ruthlessness) preceded him.

Clinton's intention: the conquest of the southern provinces.

Benjamin Lincoln, the loser of Savannah, got wind of Clinton's plans through Congressional spies in New York. Not that Clinton had kept the thing a secret. On the contrary, he had told everyone who would listen, hoping they would indeed carry messages of the formidable force he was sending—that would tip the wind from their blustering sails, make them fear for their miserable hides! Lincoln reacted precisely as Clinton predicted, by pulling his troops into a defensive perimeter. He had learned, he believed, from his enemy Prevost that towns can be successfully defended;

but he had failed to learn the much more important lesson from Washington's campaigns in New York and Philadelphia—that the best way to sustain the Revolution was to keep his armies intact, and not to get too bogged down defending any one place, no matter how apparently important. He shifted his five thousand Continentals into Charlestown and began the tedious but necessary work of repairing its mediocre defenses.

Lincoln also recalled Lieutenant Colonel Francis Marion from Sheldon, which was near Savannah. But Marion did not come. He had jumped from a second-storey window to avoid what he called "incessant toasting" at an impromptu officers' mess, and had broken his ankle.

Before the armada arrived, smallpox made its dreaded appearance in Charlestown, and there were one or two deaths. Quarantine was strict, immediate sterilization by fire the intention, but the Back Country militias, getting word of the epidemic, refused to come to the town's aid.

Peter Dorst stayed home. Honor was one thing. The pox altogether another.

Early in January, Anna and Peter went to Ninety Six to fetch a bag of salt and to sell a bushel or two of seed. There was a man on the porch of the tavern, ranting to a small but attentive crowd. He was arguing for the immediate hanging of anyone caught harboring Loyal sympathies, and most particularly any able-bodied man not eager to join the Rebel militias. That such people lived, he said, certainly attested to the magnanimity of the American people, but that magnanimity was a dreadful mistake. Tories were criminals, monsters, slaves or hirelings of foreign tyrants; they fouled whatever they touched. They were thieves and robbers; no man's property was safe from them, no woman's virtue.

Looking at the orator, Anna felt a sudden chill. His lips weren't foaming, his eyes weren't wild. He looked . . . normal. She had seen him before; he had a farm somewhere near the Broad River, a wife, children. These were her allies!

We are being asked to murder our neighbors!

In the audience were four children, all younger than ten. One of them was carrying a gun longer than he was.

And my eldest daughter already nine. Poor Magda! What sort of life are we making for her?

Off the New Jersey coast, Clinton's armada was scattered by a savage winter gale, a north wind that howled through the rigging and froze the spray instantly on the decks. The soldiers spent most of their time sleeping huddled together, or chopping great blocks of ice from the masts and rigging to prevent the vessel foundering. The ammonia-drenched straw froze under the horses every night and had to be chipped away. Even so, every time the vessel lurched, another horse slipped. Sometimes a leg broke and the animal fell, whinnying shrilly, and had to be clubbed to death, dragged to the gunwales and thrown overboard. Of the twelve hundred horses that began the voyage, fewer than forty survived, and the men, hearing their commander's thunderous silence, knew that even hell was nothing compared to what Tarleton was cooking up for someone else, somewhere else . . .

Late in January, the scattered and battered ships made their way into balmier waters. Clinton knew he'd have to postpone his assault, and put into Savannah for repairs. On February 1, the armada arrived off Tybee Island and the weary men went ashore. Tarleton took himself off toward Beaufort, in the Carolina direction, intent on remounting his Dragoons on any "marsh tackie" he could rustle.

For the next couple of weeks, Tarleton amused himself by confiscating what he could from Rebel households. His men would descend on some hapless plantation and pick whatever they needed. At every farm he would play the same cruel joke. He would assemble the slaves in the forecourt, in the presence of the family, and announce that they were now free, free to leave, free to take what they wanted with them and, under British protection, free to own land of their own. Of course, it was all a trick, a ruse; he knew how much the farmers depended on the labor of their slaves, and how much they feared them, and he loved seeing the thunderous expressions of the family and the bewildered reactions of the Africans themselves. How few of them took him up on his offer! And why should they? One more white man, making promises he had no intention of keeping.

The day he'd reached Savannah, Clinton had sent runners into town to apprise the garrison of his intentions, and to let them know that Charlestown was the target of the new campaign. The message, as so many of Clinton's were to be, was filled with pompous bombast, references to scoundrels, rogues, duty, honor, &c, &c, sentence after sentence of pure wind, but its essential point was clear enough: *Be there. The reconquest of the South has begun!*

And so the defenders of Savannah went trudging up the coast, heading to the South Carolina capital.

Prevost himself stayed in Savannah; the command of the forces heading for Charlestown devolved to Brigadier General James Patterson. Under Patterson were Major Arthur McArthur and the first battalion of the 71st Regiment, Lieutenant Colonel Patrick Ferguson and his regiment of American Volunteers, and Colonel Alexander Innes and his regiment of South Carolina Royalists. With Patterson, too, went the engineer, Moncrieffe, who had so successfully designed the defenses against d'Estaing and Lincoln.

Under Innes was Captain Faight Reisinger's company, and under Reisinger was Master Sergeant Heinrich Strum and the other Palatines from Ninety Six, or at least those who had made it through the siege. With Heinrich rode Friedrich Ruppert, Nicholas Henn, Georg Schild-nacht Sr. and his son Thomas (Georg Jr. remained in a field hospital in Savannah), Georg and Henry Weber, and Henry Zimmermann. There were others who were unfit to travel and stayed in Savannah to heal: Jacob Zimmermann and Christian Zange were still suffering the after-effects of their wounds. No one knew where Dan Michler was; rumor had it he was wounded and a prisoner, but at least alive.

This mixed army moved up to Ebenezer, crossed the Savannah and began a slow, dawdling march toward Charlestown. As he marched Patterson extended aid and comfort to Loyalists—this was, after all, part of his purpose, to rouse the local Loyalists to their own defense—while he chased the Whig militia and ravaged their plantations.

These were the same plantations already ravaged by Tarleton's Dragoons, and Patterson found the population sullen and hostile.

It did them no good. Patterson's men, if not as aggressive as Tarleton's, were just as avaricious—and they weren't in as much of a hurry, so they stayed longer. On March 16, one of the adjutants wrote in a journal: "Remained at McPherson's plantation, living on the fat of the land. Soldiers every side of us roasting turkeys, fowls, pigs, etc., every night in great plenty." In another passage, he recounts the glee they all took at destruction, so satisfying a part of revenge: "[We set about] destroying rebel property, furniture, breaking windows etc., taking all their horned cattle, horses, mules, sheep, fowls, etc., and their negros to drive them."

Heinrich himself took no pleasure from these excursions. The frightened looks on the women's faces made him uneasy; fright and resentment reminded him too much of his own and his neighbors' emotions when the looters came. Once or twice he intervened, when the looting turned to bullying; the men he turned away always resented his interference, but the cold look on his face, and his watchfulness, inhibited them from saying anything.

Sometimes, wrapped in his blankets late at night, he would replay the incidents in his mind. What drives them? He once found young Henry Zimmermann behind a barn, savagely beating a young boy. Damn it, the lad couldn't have been more than ten! What had he done to deserve this anger? He had tried to run away, the most reasonable thing for him to have done, under the circumstances. And Henry Zimmermann such a decent lad himself . . . His whole family were decent. His uncle Philip, the Rebel commander, had a reputation as a gentleman who treated his enemies courteously and with dignity. Yet here was Henry . . . Afterward he'd sat the young soldier down and asked him directly, but Henry had only become confused and defensive, and in the end was unable to answer. What, after all, was the question? *What turns a man into an animal?* To say that war does, is no answer at all, Heinrich thought. But when three or four or more perfectly reasonable men get into a band together, and they have the power of death and destruction on their side, and a cause in which they believe, it's so easy to turn them from citizens into animals. In groups, men seemed impervious to the pain of others.

Heinrich could understand revenge; he well remembered the blinding rage that had almost consumed him after Elizabeth had been murdered. Since then, he had proved to himself and his masters that he could kill without compunction or any particular feeling. But he took no pleasure from it.

Lincoln, meanwhile, had sequestered his huge army inside Charlestown's walls, and had two French engineers supervise the erection of a system of fortifications across Charlestown Neck from the Ashley to the Cooper. He posted his Continentals and the Charlestown artillery in the center of these new works, placed the militia on his wings adjacent the rivers and emplaced his light artillery along the riverbanks to repel an attempted invasion by water. What fleet was at his disposal, eight frigates and a few smaller vessels, was pulled back from Fort Moultrie and sunk at the mouth of the Cooper River, in a futile attempt to impede invasion from the sea. He then waited, knowing how pitifully inadequate these defenses were, knowing that Arbuthnot's naval squadron was sealing off the harbor, knowing that he was trapped, forced to defeat the might of the British army in pitched battle just to escape. He wished profoundly that he'd never come.

Congress had promised him nine thousand men; they only sent nineteen hundred. The pox drove many inhabitants back to their estates in the hinterlands. The militias had disbanded and retired to their often remote habitations. The paper currency was so disdained by the local grandees that they simply refused to sell to the army the "necessaries of war." Congress had managed to dispatch a small flotilla of two frigates and a corvette, but these were soon scattered. Congress then exhorted the Carolinians to arm their slaves, a notion that was received with universal scorn and repugnance.

During a heavy rainstorm a week later, Arbuthnot sailed his warships past the fort on Sullivan's Island, entered Charlestown harbor and turned his cannon loose on the defenders.

The noose was tightening steadily.

On April 10, Clinton and Arbuthnot summoned Lincoln to surrender. Lincoln, despite his own forebodings and the bleating of the town's Social Register, replied that it was his duty and his inclination to defend it to the last extremity, which, as a matter of prudent fact, he had no intention of doing. But as a matter of precaution, he hustled Governor Rutledge with three members of his Council out of the capital, sneaking them out in a most undignified manner through the bog in a small, flat-bottomed boat, emerging at the last Rebel-held outpost, Monck's Corner, which was defended by Huger with about four hundred troops, including infantry units under Colonels Washington and Jamieson. Rutledge kept going—he wasn't going to risk being caught in a place like that—and indeed, within short order, Tarleton's cavalry was dispatched to brush the outpost aside. He took with him Ferguson's Sappers and units of Innes's South Carolina Royalists.

Heinrich Strum, along with Friedrich Ruppert and Nick Henn, were among them.

They struck at three in the morning, and caught the defenders off guard.

The Rebels had chosen a good site, to the right of the Cooper River at Biggins Bridge, a bridge accessible only by a causeway pushed through an otherwise impassable morass.

But when Tarleton's scouts cautiously advanced, they crossed the full length of the causeway without being spotted. The defenders had neglected to post sentries.

One of the scouts, an Irishman named Gilhooly, reported back to Tarleton.

"As easy as findin' mud in a bog," he said. "No one's lookin'. Disposition all wrong. Cavalry to the front, infantry to the rear. Shoot their own hosses in the arse, is all, if it comes to shootin'. We can do it, 'f we do it fast."

Tarleton, ever a man of impulse, at once signaled the attack. His cavalry thundered along the causeway and crossed the bridge at a dead run, routing the Americans.

By the time Heinrich's Royalists marched in a few minutes later, it was all over. The defenders were all dead or fled. General Huger and the colonels escaped by throwing themselves into the swamp and fleeing under cover of dark. Four hundred horses were captured, along with many carriages loaded with arms sent down from North Carolina, much clothing and other stores.

None of the attackers were injured.

Heinrich never fired a shot.

The victory at Monck's Corners was followed by much marching and counter-marching, much useless deploying and redeploying of troops, and the integration into the besieging force of reinforcements from New York, led by a young peer of the realm, Lord Rawdon, whose Irish Volunteers Clinton sent to serve under the man who would eventually take command of the southern war, Lord Cornwallis. Rawdon joined up with Cornwallis's other commanders, Colonel Nisbet Balfour and Colonel Turnbull, with the 23rd Regiment and the New York Volunteers respectively.

The noose around Charlestown tightened further.

At six in the next morning of May 4, Clinton sent an officer under a flag demanding the city's surrender. Lincoln requested a cessation of hostilities until eight, and then asked that the truce be extended until noon. Lincoln and the city authorities put together a proposal: they would surrender the town, provided not only that the citizens and the militias be free but that they should be permitted to sell their property and retire with the proceeds wherever they might see fit. Clinton's response was curt: he would promise not to pillage private property, but would promise nothing more.

Lincoln then asked that hostilities not be recommenced until four the next afternoon.

Clinton lost his patience and broke off negotiations. "Firing will (re)commence at 8 o'clock in the evening," he wrote, and was as good as his word, for he then "began a tremendous cannonade, with the throwing of carcasses and shells into the town, and an incessant fire of musketry all night." The firing continued "the next day, and very brisk all the next night." The fortifications were battered by the heavy artillery; bombs and more burning carcasses fell on the town, setting numerous fires; the Royalists, on the parallel closest to the town, the third, picked off whomever showed himself.

By the following evening, the defending fire had almost ceased; the artillery was broken and the gunners dead.

The city fathers, who had persuaded Lincoln to protect them in the first place, now clamored for capitulation, pleading with the General "not to expose to further destruction so rich, so important, a city."

Lincoln had no real choice.

He sent out a flag of truce. It was ignored and the firing continued. He sent out a second flag, which was accepted.

On May 12, he signed the capitulation.

Clinton wrote, laconically: "By this very important acquisition there fell into our hands seven generals and a multitude of other officers, belonging to 10 continental regiments and 3 battalions of artillery, which, with the militia and sailors doing duty in the siege, amounted to about 6,000 men in arms."

Some five hundred and twenty-five defenders were killed or wounded, and five thousand six hundred and eighty-three taken prisoner.

Congress "retired" Benjamin Lincoln, and he returned home a failure, though angry to the end. He was replaced by Horatio Gates.

Sir Henry Clinton, K.B., returned to New York, leaving Cornwallis in charge.

He had won the coast, but the southern provinces' civil government was still in the hands of the Rebels, and, as Cornwallis wrote to Governor Patrick Tonyn in East Florida, "considerable bodies of troops were [still] in arms against us on the Santee River and at Ninety Six." Before he left, Clinton ordered Cornwallis to drive these stubborn Rebel troops from the province and to take back the Back Country. The Rebels were to be taught that their chance had come, and had now irrevocably gone.

Heinrich Strum's unit went back to Savannah. There he again met the widow, Maria Elizabeth, and she finally told him what she had to, about his wife Catherine, and how she had died of hard usage and cruel sport, and then she held him while he wept, and her heart ached for him, and for herself, and for this cursed country into which they had tumbled, and for its scorekeeping, the piles of corpses on the unheeding, uncaring, compassionless scales of history, and she felt his heart thumping against her breast, and then she wept, too, out of emptiness and fear for the future.

They rode the first day in silence, using only those few words necessary for the division of trail chores. There was no need for words, no work that words could do. Each was preoccupied with his own thoughts.

They rode from Savannah through the bruised and battered land, past razed farm and burned field, past bog and morass, past gaunt and sullen farmers and frightened slaves.

Through the morass of human wickedness!

They passed a farm where the house was still standing, wide-eyed, its windows smashed and its doors torn from their hinges. There was no sign of people. The animal pens were empty.

Maria's thoughts were bitter. *We were afraid of the land, at first, of the wild animals, of the savages. How little we knew. Now we are only afraid of each other.*

She rode with her daughter Katherina trailing behind the brooding presence of Heinrich Strum. Behind them rode the soldiers who were still boys, Friedrich Ruppert and Peter Frietz.

Strum had said nothing since he had offered, two days earlier, to take them home. Home! It's not land that makes a home, she thought, but a family. She hadn't yet really thought of herself as a widow. Her children were her family now.

She was forty-two years old. Still young!

It was a week since she had told him his wife was dead.

Within hours he had returned to his unit, to tell them he was resigning his commission, leaving for the Back Country. He told them why, his voice steady. They helped him, as soldiers do, by saying nothing and doing all they could. Christoph Ruppert sent word to Innes, their commander, so he'd be prepared; Nick Cruhm and Georg Schildnacht found him supplies and horses, Christian Zange poured some rum into him, Georg Weber grumbled about the army and the lunacy of British quartermasters.

At one level, Heinrich heard all this and was grateful. They understood that he said nothing. They knew he was controlled because if he weren't controlled, he'd go mad, and they loved him, because he was a good soldier.

Innes, too, was compassionate. But he had a war to run.

"You'll have to find someone to take your place," he said, squinting at Strum, looking anxious, as though this would be a problem, with Royalists now pouring out of the woods everywhere in Georgia and along the Carolina coast, sympathizers or pretend sympathizers he knew not and cared less, so long as they fought where they were told to fight and didn't fade into the swamps like the American militia.

"Of course," Heinrich said, and it was as easy as Innes thought it would be. Within hours he had rounded up two men, Irish immigrants who were too new to have taken sides, but were grateful for army pay and army rations, and had a shrewd sense that things were going the British way.

"Two men for a sergeant," Heinrich said when he delivered them. "My duty is done."

He never remembered what Innes said then, or whether he replied at all. But he did remember his commander's steady gaze, and the way he had reached up to grip Heinrich by the shoulders, shaking him once, before letting him go.

That small shake. That was a comradely thing!

Ruppert and Frietz trailed along behind him. They, too, had won their discharges, and would accompany him to the Back Country. He offered to take Maria and the girl with him. They were capable of making their own way, he knew—hadn't they come to Savannah like a gale, not stopping for any hindrance? But it was better that women not travel alone, not in these violent times. And Maria needed to go back. There were her other children, the farm, her home . . .

Like mine. Gray, and dead. No more laughter.

He felt filled up with grief and anger.

Maria and the girl . . . She was twenty-one! She didn't look much younger than Catherine. He was almost overwhelmed by self-pity. How beautiful she had been! How warm the laughter! How resolute! Then his self-pity was swept aside by a chilly storm of rage. He knew that if he found them, any of them, anyone who had done this, he would hurt them as much as he could before they died. None of the codes of war for them, no honorable escapes. He would shoot them in the knees and make them crawl to their place of execution, which would be as long and as slow as he could devise . . .

That night, at their trail camp, the two young ones, Maria's Katherina and Katy's Peter, slept together, without explanation or apology, slept tightly wrapped in each other's arms, two golden-haired children taking comfort where they could, and instead of being envious, or having the self-pity return, Heinrich took some small comfort from it. He watched the two heads together on the blanket.

Life goes on. For some.

Then his bleak thoughts faded, and he slept.

On the second night, Maria came to him.

The day had passed, again, in silence.

They left early, and rode late, pushing themselves hard, as if by unspoken agreement they needed physical exhaustion to combat their grief. Even at noon, when they were forced to halt to rest and water the horses, Heinrich kept moving, striding into the pine barrens like a soldier on a forced march, his boots scuffing the sand, weary muscles dragging, keeping going, an hour, an hour and a half, forcing himself to keep moving, before returning to re-saddle the horses and move out. Move, because movement is life, and exhaustion makes it easier not to think.

They spoke rarely, Heinrich not at all.

In the early evening, he killed a turkey. He hung it by its feet from the saddle and rode on, its neck knocking against the horse's withers. He plucked and dressed it in camp that evening, spilling its insides into the sand where the fire would be. When his sharp knife split the skin of the gizzard and tipped out the stones, something bright caught his eye, shiny, amber in the evening sun. He picked it up, rubbed it between thumb and forefinger. It gleamed, deep fire, like an agate. Without thinking, he slipped it into a pocket and proceeded to build his fire over the pile of viscera.

They had made good time, forty, perhaps fifty miles.

Closer to . . . home.

After dark, and after the meal was done, he took his blankets a little way into the woods, spread them on pine boughs torn from a tree, removed his boots and lay down to sleep. The others did the same, scattering themselves at random around the axis of the fire, the two young ones huddled together as before.

Maria woke up abruptly in the middle of the night, her heart buzzing and her head thick with the coils of evil dreams, ghostly corpses, the thin mewing of distant horses, the faint clashing of spectral armies, hoarse shouts, screaming . . . She sat up. There was nothing. The woods were quiet. There was no wind, nothing stirred, the red eye of the embers her only reference point. It reminded her of a mask a Choctaw had once brought to the farm for Heinrich, a mask made of some red wood, rubbed carefully with bear grease until it gleamed, a single red stone in the center of what passed for its forehead, and on the top what was surely a Rebel cocked hat, complete with cockade. The Indian had squatted in the dirt outside the house, in the offering position, stuffing shreds of tobacco into the mask's mouth, as though it were hungry. Choctaw magic. Heinrich had . . . What had Heinrich done? Heinrich! Another overwhelming wave of grief washed over her, and she got up, smoothing her shift down over her body and moved over to the sleeping widower under the pines.

The woods smelled that peculiar pine smell of horse piss.

Nothing moved beyond the perimeter of black.

There was nothing out there but blackness.

Inside, and out.

She remembered what the preacher, Woodmason, had said, about the black hearts of men.

"Woe!" he'd cried. He'd been talking about the rot in men's souls.

How little he knew!

She looked down at the sleeping Strum. The black-haired boy, a strong man now. Her heart went out to him, surprising her that she still had room in her heart for the grief of others.

Then her own need overwhelmed her, and she sank down onto the ground beside him. She touched his shoulder, lightly. He said nothing, but he stirred slightly, moving into her touch. Her hand moved from his shoulder to his neck, behind the ear where the black hair ended. It was warm, and shockingly smooth. One of his hands came up and she took it and pressed it to her breast, and then he rolled over and reached for her, pulling her down to him, pressing his mouth into her neck, holding her tightly, and after a while he began to weep, quietly, she only knew because his body quivered, like small earth tremors, and then he rolled onto her, there were tuggings and pullings aside, quick, impatient movements as they shifted clothing this way and that, and there he was, and as quickly as she could she took him, out of her need and her own native generosity of spirit.

In the morning she was still there, wrapped tightly around him, careless of appearance, his sweat damp on her skin, but it didn't matter, for when she got up to stir a new fire, Katherina appeared and squeezed her hand, her own daughter but a woman understanding a woman's need.

The following night, they spread their blankets together, and as soon as they had eaten they went there, and this time they were quite naked with each other, and he played with her breasts and she hugged him fiercely, and she didn't think of what it meant, if it meant anything at all.

A comfort, is all, for a woman and a man alone.

For the next two days their tangling grew more feverish, and they occasionally even stopped during the day, moving away from the others into the bush to push urgently at each other till she almost became ashamed of the overwhelming strength of her passion, but her daughter approved and the two boys trailed on behind, embarrassed but saying nothing, and so she gave in to it and let it take over her body. She knew it wouldn't last beyond the journey. She knew the journey was itself a self-contained world, and they would reach the edge of the world soon, and the natural rules of the world would end with it, and the other rules return, and she would be the Widow Adolph and he would once again be the Man Whose Wives Are Murdered.

On the morning of the last day, as she felt him spurt inside her, she felt it as a small warmth that penetrated her grief, and she was grateful for that.

And then she let him go.

At last they reached the familiar roads close to home, and sometime after noon, they turned off to his farm.

To what had been his farm.

There was no one there. The yard was tangled and overgrown, the chicken sheds still smashed, all the animals gone, the front door off its hinges but nailed in place.

He found the paper Peter Dorst had attached to the post. His mouth tightened as he read it, and he tore it down, crumpling it into a ball and hurling it away.

He went around the back and entered through the rear door. The others waited in front while he spent his hour at the place she died.

Then he came out. He didn't look at her.

But it was all right.

She knew they had helped each other.

Thirteen

What does it matter now? Men living in the woods like animals? First our side, then theirs . . .What does it matter? They're all long, long dead. Katy turned to look back up the slope, past the barn, to Maria's newly covered grave. *Maria forgave even her own brother. Can I do less?* And then she asked herself one more question: *Is it my right to forgive?*

August 1780
Ninety Six, South Carolina

When her own brother spurned her, Maria made herself numb. Deliberately numb, so she wouldn't feel anything. It was surprisingly easy to do, perhaps because it was so unsurprising that, for Peter, Cause would defeat Family, and that he'd be unable to escape the iron bands of his own imaginings. It made it no harder or easier that Anna stood behind him, signaling her disagreement over his shoulder with a semaphore of eyebrows and tics and shrugs and entreating glances.

Heinrich Strum had taken her home.

They'd left his place after an hour, left it to the rodents and pigeons that had taken up residence, and ridden down Scott's Ferry Road and across the Long Canes to avoid passing the Kiess farm. The two boys had already left for their own homes, and there were just the three of them, but the starkness and bleakness of Heinrich's house had changed the way they traveled together; the comfort of the road was already a thing of the past, and she and Katherina rode stirrup to stirrup, with Heinrich a dozen paces ahead. No one said anything.

They passed a cavalcade of militia who looked at them curiously. Heinrich acted as though he didn't see them.

They had a prisoner with them, his hands roped behind his back, lashed to his own saddle. Which side was which? She couldn't tell.

The boots are the same, and the leggings, the jerkins and the hats. Only the colors are different, and I can't remember which is which. The rotten stench is the same, in any case.

They turned off along Cuffeetown Creek and into the Adolph property. The house lay up a gentle slope to the right, and there were clothes spread out to dry on the grass on the creek banks; someone had been doing laundry, a mundane and reassuring sign.

Elizabeth met them at the door, a tall and homely girl, dressed all in white. She took them inside. The floor was newly scrubbed, everything in its place. Henry was at the table, eating, showing no sign of fright or nervousness.

It looked so . . . normal. She started to cry, then. She hugged her daughter as Katherina, breaking into tears herself, tried to describe what had happened to their father.

When the sniffles subsided, Maria asked, "Where's Rosena?"

"In the woods somewhere," Elizabeth said, somewhat shortly. "She's not home much. And she never helps."

Maria sighed. It was so like her. She was a wild child, indeed, seventeen now but still as wild as a deer. "Isn't it dangerous?" she asked.

"Huh! No man would want her!" Elizabeth said, with sudden malice.

Maria gave her a sharp look. "It's not what I meant," she said.

Elizabeth's mouth set in a stubborn pout. Maria let it go, though she didn't agree. Rosena had the sleek good looks of a hunting cat, and men would want her all right. If they could catch her. And even then, they'd have to be careful not to get badly mauled.

They ate a hurried meal and Heinrich rode off. He would go to his sisters Eva and Barbara and retrieve his children. He said good-bye courteously, as though they were strangers. He didn't touch her, not even her hand, but just looked at her, then bowed his head briefly. She understood.

Before nightfall, she rode to her brother's house. He wasn't there when she arrived and Anna took her in, greeting her with hugs, feeding her a bowl of broth and letting her talk. Anna's three girls clustered around; the smallest boy, George, was playing with a rag horse in the corner.

But when Peter came home, striding through the door looking as busy as he always did, he saw her and pulled up short.

"What are you doing here?" he demanded coldly.

Anna got up and went over to the window. She stood there with her arms crossed over her breasts, staring at her husband.

Maria said nothing. She pushed her bowl aside and stood up.

"What are you doing here?" Peter demanded again. "Why did you come?"

"Peter!" Anna said. "She's your *sister*!"

"I can't afford to have her here," Peter said, "sister or no." He didn't look at Anna as he spoke, but stared at Maria.

"But . . ."

Maria held up a hand. "No," she said, speaking to Anna but staring at her brother. "I'll go. Thank you, dear, for your warmth. It's good to see there is some warmth among the expediencies of war."

Peter's mouth tightened. "I'm sorry for your loss," he said, "but you must see, I . . ."

She waved him to silence. "I do see," she said. "My loss is the death of a good man, the father to my children. He is now an absence where God had made a presence. And you . . . You're worried about what you can afford." She turned away to Anna, hugged her quickly and walked out the door before her brother could reply. What could he say, in any case? She had expressed what he really felt. She knew it wasn't coldness on his part, but anxiety. She understood better than he knew. He had to protect his own, his wife and his children, in the murderousness of the times. It was what the times called for. Why should she be surprised? It was why she had clung to Strum—a rock in the murderous swirl of wartime emotion! She felt nothing for him. He was a rock, that's all. She didn't feel at all confused, only depressed, weary and sad. Numb. She wanted to be numb.

She was walking toward her horse, tethered beside the barn, when Rosena came around the corner. The girl pulled up short.

"Mother?"

"Hello child."

"Are you going home now?"

"Yes."

"I'll go with you, if you like."

"All right."

"But I won't stay."

"All right."

"I live here now."

"It's all right."

They stared at each other.

"Mother, I'm sorry."

"I know."

"Did you . . . see him?"

"No. No. He was . . . gone."

Rosena fetched the horses, then, and helped her mother into the saddle. They rode back in silence, but without tension. Maria knew there was no malice in her daughter, that she had tried, had done her best. Besides, she thought, I don't feel anything, I can't feel anything now.

Only once during the ride did she allow herself some emotion. She leaned over and took her daughter's hand, squeezing it. Rosena left her hand in her mother's. She didn't withdraw, but there was no returning squeeze. Her fingers lay there, passively. After a while, Maria took back her own.

Numb, she thought. *I'm quite numb.*

A week later, Heinrich Strum sat with his boots off and his feet in Stevens Creek, brooding. His horse was tethered a dozen yards away, in a small copse, within easy reach of grazing. They were both hidden from any path.

He was brooding, but also wary, aware. They could kill him, but they wouldn't surprise him. Whoever they were.

He'd gone back to the house twice, but hadn't stayed. It was too close to the road, too easy to be seen. He knew they'd be hunting him if they knew he was there, and they'd know soon enough—there were spies everywhere these days, their hearts black from avarice or green with envy or red with the patriotic fire of Cause. The devil take them. And anyway . . . The silence in the house felt as raw and wounding as an Indian scalping knife.

My wife is dead, my children scattered I know not where, some of them dead from disease or wounded in spirit and body.

He felt weary in his bones.

What were my family are now ghosts, haunting the attics, rats gnawing their bones, ghostly laughter echoing into the future, consumed by the malice of those that killed them, my father and mother, dead, my sister, dead, two wives, dead, children dead, comrades dead, their skulls picked clean by worms, earth uncaring, eyes made of clouds, milk white . . . He shook his head, shaking out the circling ghosts. *Death by sword and musket would be easier than this!*

Katy had sent him food, but he hadn't gone there. Why bring disaster down on their heads? Even Peter, her son, was wise enough not to stay at home and had found his own patch of woods, where he lived like Heinrich, like an animal, roasting hares over careful small fires of birch bark and cones, keeping his weapons polished, trying not to think how long he might be there.

Will this thing ever end?

He had gone to his sister Barbara Ruppert, who had taken in Eve and Henry, with the four-year-old, John.

Barbara was in tears, almost at the end of her tether. She was only twenty-one, with two babies of her own and her husband Friedrich gone to war, and running the farm was almost too much for her. She had tried her best to look after the children, but the two eldest were headstrong like their father and wouldn't take instruction from a girl only a few years older than they.

And the baby? "Gone," Barbara said tearfully. "Gone . . . Carried off . . . Died in his sleep . . . Hadn't even been ill. The other two? Gone to town, gone somewhere, they'll be back . . ."

"Where are they?" Heinrich demanded.

"I don't know!" she said in despair. "Somewhere, they wouldn't tell me."

He had done his best to comfort her. It wasn't her fault. She hadn't asked to take them in. But they were family, and children! Eve was thirteen! Henry only nine!

Afterward he rode to the Michlers to find the other three. Big Dan Michler met him at the door, the first time Heinrich had seen him since Savannah. He'd been wounded there and fallen to the enemy, but they had released him because of his illness and sent him home. He walked with a heavy limp.

Michler offered him a pipe and took him down to the barn.

"Three of your children're gone," he said bluntly, "carried off by the fever before I came back. Alongside one of ours. Only the baby, Peter, is still alive. Others of ours are sick, too, though they live. They're in the house. Best you stay away, for now."

"And Eva?"

"Eva's healthy," Dan said. "She's a strong woman. She will survive anything."

In a while he rode away to his lair in the woods. There he sat with his head on his knees, for a long while. He felt too weary even for grief.

Toward the end of the day, Rosannah came by with part of a ham from her mother Katy. He knew she was coming because she sang while she rode, to alert him, a sweet, clear voice, a ballad from the old country, a nonsense rhyme of boys and girls and country flowers, as out of place in this sultry woods as she was in this war-torn land. Her voice was high and girlish, filled with teasing. She was twenty years old, and married to Conrad Merk, but she looked twelve. It gave her clear passage through the countryside, she said, with a shrewdness that seemed oddly out of place in that girlish voice. This was the way the refugees in the woods were fed, from the hands of young girls and children. For Peter and Heinrich, as for the other wary animals scattered through these woods, it was either Rosannah or the Bauer girl, treating the patrols with ridicule and riding unmolested, at least so far, and if you didn't count the debacle of the Bauer girl's imprisonment, which just made them all look foolish.

Heinrich cut into the ham with his knife, threw the rind to the dog that loped behind the girl.

"What news?" he asked.

She laughed. "Why, sir," she said with mock solemnity, "you ask me for news? Why, sir, I know nothing! It is my protection and my safety!"

He snorted. "I'm not some Rebel, blinded by the shrug of a delicate shoulder," he said.

She sank to the grass. "They do say the Lord Cornwallis is coming this way," she said. "Or a part of his army."

Heinrich sat up quickly. "How true is it?" he demanded.

But she didn't know. She went on to talk of the cavalry leader, Banastre Tarleton. "The Rebels are calling him Bloody Tarleton," she said.

This didn't surprise Heinrich, who had seen Tarleton at Charlestown and on the march from Savannah. There was a commander who had the loyalty of his men! But he had the gleam of the fanatic in his eye, and bloody was a word that went well with his surly, angry visage. Much more than with the boy, Cunningham, whom they were already beginning to call Bloody Bill. Bill was impetuous and reckless, and his men could fight with ferocity when cornered, but he was essentially guileless. Tarleton, now, that was a different matter. If Tarleton was coming this way, the Whigs would be in for an unpleasant surprise. For the first time in a week, Heinrich felt his spirits lifting.

She also told him there were rumors the Loyalist militias would reform. They had disbanded under the Whig resurgence, when the men were harassed and punished, along with their families. "My father is talking of joining," she said. "And so is Conrad. They all are. They feel their time is coming."

"You tell them I'll come too, when the coming is right," Heinrich said. "There's nothing for me here. Ambushing Whigs in the forest won't win wars."

"I will, I'll tell them," she said, looking at him sharply. In truth, she was a little afraid of him. They all were. They knew his pain, but they did not know what he'd do with it. "He's as unpredictable as a pan flash," her father had said. She didn't think this was so. She thought him entirely predictable. But she'd also seen the coldness in his eyes, and she thought they were right to be afraid of him, not for his unpredictability, but for what he almost certainly would do when he could.

As they talked, he'd been shaving flakes from the ham bone with his knife, and as she stood up to go, he suddenly drove the bone, as sharp as a knife itself, into the ground beside him, thrusting it home with a wrenching violence, as though he were tearing open the chest of an enemy.

She left him there, staring at the knob of the joint protruding from the ground, bits of flesh and gristle still clinging to it, and she shuddered.

She'd let Conrad fetch him in, when the time came.

Clinton had laid out a simple strategy for Cornwallis and his other commanders: first scour the countryside, then garrison strategic towns and hold
the country by raising Loyal militias, which would be supported by regulars
when necessary. These Loyalists could hold the district and, indeed, South
Carolina and Georgia, from their headquarters at Ninety Six. He was confident that his will would be done, and was determined to keep pushing, to
strike before his own people cooled or the enemy took breath.

He laid out three expeditions, one to the Savannah River and Georgia, a second to Ninety Six and a third, under Cornwallis himself, to clear
the country between the Cooper and the Santee of a Republican army
under Colonel Buford, which had been stubbornly holding out and was
now retreating, more or less intact, toward North Carolina.

The purpose of the first two was largely to bring the Loyalists out of
hiding. Clinton got what he wanted and perhaps more: Loyalists not only
flocked to join or rejoin the militias but dragged with them wagonloads of
prisoners, Whigs, Rebels, Patriots, Friends of Liberty, call them what you
would, so many that most had to be sent home with a warning, for lack of
place to store them.

On May 18, Cornwallis broke camp and set his army of British regulars, Hessians, provincials and Loyalist militia marching toward the Santee River. He crossed at Lenud's Ferry, swept the two banks of the Cooper
and made himself master of Georgetown.

Meanwhile, Colonel Buford retreated in a series of forced marches to
join another American army, rumored to be marching southward from
Philadelphia. It seemed certain that he would escape unpunished.

But Cornwallis sent Tarleton and his British Legion in pursuit, to see
what they could do.

Late in the afternoon of May 28, Tarleton reached Camden, his trail
marked by pillaging, burning and killing. Here he learned that Buford and
his Virginians were only a day ahead, dawdling along the road to Salisbury. He redoubled his already heroic pace, and after a forced march of a
hundred and five miles in fifty-four hours, he caught up with the Virginians as they were moving through the settlement known as the Waxhaws.

Tarleton demanded immediate surrender. Buford refused. Tarleton
immediately charged and Buford's inexperienced troops started to fall

back. Many of them simply gave up, but Tarleton's veterans killed them anyway. Hardly anyone escaped. Buford himself was one of the lucky ones; he managed to flee toward Salisbury.

In his battle report Tarleton wrote, "I have cut 170 off'rs and men to pieces."

The reduction, or restoration, of Ninety Six (depending on your perspective) was entrusted to Lieutenant Colonel Nisbet Balfour, commandant of the 23rd or Welsh Fusiliers Regiment and senior field commander under Cornwallis. Balfour was to move up the old Cherokee Path, destroy the South Carolina militia still in arms under Brigadier General Andrew Williamson and take possession of the strategic village of Ninety Six.

To protect Balfour's rear, Thomas Browne's Florida Rangers and about five hundred Creek and Cherokee Indians moved up to garrison Augusta. With Browne went Moses Kirkland, Richard Pearis and Evan McLauren. Georg Weber was with McLauren.

On May 26, Balfour marched from Charlestown. Beside him marched Patrick Ferguson and his Loyal American Volunteers.

Cornwallis, for his part, reached Camden on the first of June and set up his headquarters there, including an armory which would be used to hand out weapons to Loyalists. He also decreed military rule.

From there, he began deploying trusted commanders and their troops into strategic positions. Alexander Innes and his South Carolina Royalists he sent to Friday's Ferry with orders to cooperate with Balfour in his drive against Ninety Six. With Innes were troopers Christoph Ruppert, Nicholas Cruhm, the Schildnachts and Christian Zange.

A spy came to Innes one night at Friday's Ferry. "Williamson is there and in arms, but with a small force, who are all threatening to leave him."

4

The next day, another spy: "Williamson is still in arms, with Colonel Pickens, but they mean not to continue in a body, but in small parties in the Back Country, so they can't be caught."

And a third: "Williamson's in a panic, likely to surrender."

Williamson was, indeed, in a panic. He had suddenly realized that far from being the dominant force in the country as he had fondly supposed, with the British confined to a narrow strip along the coast, his little force was alone in the struggle. The village of Ninety Six against the planet's most formidable army, the might of the British Empire!

The General Assembly, after all, had fled; the state judiciary had disbanded; Governor Rutledge had traveled to Philadelphia to beg help from the Continental Congress; and Charlestown had become the operational base of the British army. Suddenly Williamson found himself the highest constitutional authority in South Carolina.

He could continue the fight or he could surrender.

Instead of deciding, he called a council of war and threw the question before his colonels. Predictably, the reaction was mixed. Some were for fighting, arguing that the militia could retreat to the Blue Ridge and from there continue harassing the British and the Loyalists. Others argued the militia should remain intact and march northward to meet the Continentals rumored to be coming down from Philadelphia. But a majority felt their position to be hopeless and voted to surrender.

On June 5, Williamson drafted a letter to Innes, asking for terms.

But matters were not so simple. Before Williamson's courier could reach Innes at Friday's Ferry, Browne had marched his Florida Rangers across the Savannah. In a swift move, he confronted LeRoy Hammond and his militia, offered them moderate terms and Hammond surrendered. Then, using the leverage of Hammond as prisoner and the momentum of victory, he rather grandly sent Pearis to demand the surrender of General Williamson and all the Patriot militia from Ninety Six District.

It didn't take them long to block out a rough draft of a treaty. After a preamble calling for a cessation of hostilities, Pearis laid out four conditions for surrender: the Whig militia at White Hall and Ninety Six would have to surrender their arms and disband; the arms of all private persons would have to be deposited with one person appointed to receive them; all public stores and property would have to be left under the care of a custodian at Ninety Six; the Whig leaders would have to publish the terms of the treaty throughout the district so that all inhabitants should return their loyalty to their sovereign.

Williamson read the document to the militiamen in his brigade and then put it to them to accept or reject the terms. All but one field officer and four or five captains voted to accept. "It was proposed and carried that a flag should be sent to Capt. Pearis to inform him of their determination and to settle the time, place and manner of surrender."

"Why surrender?" Peter Dorst demanded, waving his arms up and down, his voice shrill from frustration. "Why is it necessary? There's an army coming down from Philadelphia! There's a whole continent to retreat into! We could . . ."

"Why tell me?" Anna asked reasonably. "I'm not a general."

"Williamson, Pickens, they're . . ."

"I thought Pickens was a sound man, a hero, a man of parts?"

"He is! But . . ."

Anna put down the basket of laundry she was carrying, began placidly to fold the garments into a chest. "Stop spluttering," she told Peter. "Tell me what happened. Don't harangue. You're not a preacher."

Peter fell into a chair, stretched his legs out in front, crossing his boots. He sighed wearily.

"General Williamson came down from Ninety Six to Pickens' camp. Only five miles from here, at Six Mile Creek. Pickens and his regiment were already in the saddle, drawn up in formation. We were with them, my men and I . . ."

"Why? You're not part of Pickens' regiment."

"They're the last army there is. In any case," he said impatiently, "that doesn't matter. Williamson comes down, reads the terms of capitulation, commends us on our valor, offers us a retreat toward the Continental army, said to be coming down from the north. He asks for a show of hands."

He looked disgusted. "A show of hands! This is a general's job!"

"So what happened?"

"James McCall and Liddle, Moses Liddle, both captains and three of my militiamen were the only men who opted for retreat. I did, too."

"No one else?"

"No one!"

"And then?"

"Pickens dismissed the muster."

"And you all went home? This just happened?"

"No! It was three days ago! McCall and Liddle argued and exhorted for three days. Oh, they were grand, eloquent! They swayed some people, but not enough. In the end—they voted to surrender, too."

"Even the captains?"

"What could they do? A captain can't fight without his men, or a general without his army."

"You too?"

Peter scowled. "Me too."

On June 10, John Bowie, Richard Rapley, James Moore and George Whitefield signed the treaty of capitulation "in the name of the people on the south side of the Saluda River." Williamson, along with Major Mayson, Colonel Pickens and LeRoy Hammond, took what is known as British protection, and became paroled prisoners, like the soldiers and garrisons in Charlestown.

Abraham Frietz, seeing his chance finally come, rode into Ninety Six to offer his no doubt limited services to whatever militia commander he could find. Instead of joy and celebration, however, he found there only argument and acrimony.

Richard Pearis had marched his triumphant Loyalists into Ninety Six. But within days the place was in an uproar.

Pearis didn't seem to understand the need for revenge.

Thomas Browne, his own commander, had been tarred and feathered, and here he was, handing out paroles as though this were a parlor game!

Williamson's surrender had brought the Loyalists pouring into town. They were jubilant, but ripe for revenge. They remembered the lootings and the burnings. They remembered the corpses pinned to trees, women raped and children beaten. They remembered the arrogance of the Sons of Liberty, their infuriating assumptions of moral superiority, even while they were stealing the property of widows. They remembered the Snow Campaign, the humiliating trials before the General Assembly, Drayton's contemptuous offer of "two thousand pounds for the scoundrel Moses Kirkland, dead or alive." They wanted punishment. They wanted the jails bulging with prisoners. They wanted hangings. Hadn't the Whigs taken it on themselves to judge a man's worth here on earth, and to put themselves in the place of God, judging life or death? *Our turn!*

But Pearis wouldn't have it. He accepted paroles as if they weren't devalued coin; the protection of his soldiers was offered to those who gave their words not to fight again, to preserve their new-found loyalty to the King.

It was a travesty.

Robert Cunningham, who remembered his confinement incommunicado in Charlestown jail, was one of the most indignant. He galloped off to lay a complaint with the British army itself; he wished Lord Cornwallis to know that the Loyalists around Ninety Six were enraged. His message to his Lordship: "Richard Pearis is a scoundrel."

On the day the capitulation was signed at Ninety Six, Williamson's courier, with the offer to surrender in his pouch, finally arrived at Friday's Ferry. Innes's army, with its cadre of battle-hardened Palatine soldiers, was spread out in organized disarray along the banks of the river. It had the look of a regiment that expected no resistance, but that could, in any event, spring into action at a moment's notice.

Innes received the courier graciously, and offered him much the same terms that Pearis had already in fact imposed in Ninety Six, the same terms that Clinton had given the soldiers and inhabitants of Charlestown. The militia would have to surrender their arms, sign their paroles and disband. Both they and the private citizens would have to await the final punishment to be meted out upon the conclusion of the war.

The courier agreed to the terms.

A few days later, Balfour's force reached the Congarees and joined Innes and his regiment at Friday's Ferry. The two commanders agreed to coordinate their sweep toward Ninety Six. Innes would go up the Broad River and then turn up the Enoree, Balfour would move up the Saluda. "Innes will halt near the Enoree and await my arrival at Ninety Six," Balfour wrote Cornwallis.

Innes marched his Royalists up the Broad River as planned. But halting at the Enoree and waiting proved somewhat more difficult. The Palatines with him, Christoph Ruppert, Nicholas Cruhm, the Schildnachts, and Christian Zange, were close to home, and they began begging for leave to visit their families. It wasn't as though Innes needed them. The countryside seemed quiet. There were no armed bands in the neighborhood that anyone knew about. "I rather think the whole regiment will disperse," Innes wrote to Balfour, wryly. But after a heart-to-heart with the indignant Robert Cunningham, who filled him in on Pearis's doings, he began to sense that Ninety Six was about to deteriorate into a series of private squabbles and reprisals, and saw the need for some authority there. He added: "I find it absolutely necessary some officer should be at Ninety Six as soon as possible." Who should it be? Who was the proper commanding officer for the highly strategic post to be established at Ninety Six? Innes suggested someone he knew well, had seen in action—Lieutenant Colonel John Harris Cruger, commandant of the first battalion of DeLancey's Brigade, who was "an officer of much tact and resourcefulness."

Meanwhile, he insisted, his men should remain with him. Home would have to wait until they were securely in command of Ninety Six. The men grumbled, but acquiesced.

On the 16th, after several forced marches, the Royalists reached Williamson's house, White Hall, where everything was quiet. The Whigs of Ninety Six had stacked their arms and ridden home. Everyone seemed in a holiday mood.

Williamson himself was resigned, and received everyone graciously. Indeed, he went further. Balfour later told Cornwallis: "Williamson has decided to work on the 'Civil' side . . . [Useful because] he knows everybody and can keep things quiet . . . The people here are, of all mankind, the least to be depended upon." Colonel Cruger, when he in turn appeared at Ninety Six, made the same judgment: "Gen'l Williamson has just come in—he becomes more & more what we would wish."

What Cruger would wish was not, of course, what the Whigs of Ninety Six would wish. To Philip Zimmermann, among others, Williamson's act of submission was, in the end, forgivable, but his subsequent behavior was a serious disappointment, lacking dignity as it did. It seemed craven. A little later, Williamson's friend John Bowie was invited to dine at White Hall, and was astonished to find that the other guests were British officers in full uniform. Decent capitulation was one thing. But to entertain at dinner, as guests of honor, British commanders! It was treachery to the living and dishonor to the dead.

Williamson's influence drained away, and his utility to Cruger diminished.

On June 20, a senseless deadline set three weeks earlier by General Clinton in Charlestown came and went.

It was senseless because it caused unnecessary bitterness and was at the same time completely ineffective.

On June 3, just a few days before he embarked for New York, Clinton had suddenly issued a proclamation releasing all persons from their paroles and requiring that they declare their allegiance to the Crown by June 20 or be considered enemies.

His proclamation, filled with his usual bombast and empty rhetoric, "re-established in all the rights and duties of British subjects." To make sure his intentions were clear, he spelled out these duties in some detail: "Every man must take an active part in support of the Royal government; and in the suppression of that anarchy which had prevailed but for too long." He required "all persons to be in readiness with their arms at a moment's warning; those who had families, to form a militia for home defense; but those who had none, to serve with the royal forces for any six months of the ensuing twelve, in which they might be called upon to assist in driving their rebel oppressors, and all the miseries of war, far from the province."

Sir Henry justified his proclamation as a "prudent measure for ferreting out inveterate rebels" in order to provide Loyalists with the opportunity of detecting and chasing from among them such dangerous neighbors.

In practice, as his own commanders acknowledged, what he accomplished was to once again set citizen against citizen, have brother take up arms against brother.

As though they needed any encouragement!

Congress later called his actions "odious."

His own commanders privately agreed.

Odious. And utterly ineffective.

Worse. Counter-productive.

When they came to take his guns away from him, and to steal his horses and his grain, Peter Dorst ground his teeth, but said nothing.

Anna, on the other hand, said plenty.

She virtually drove them away with her bitter, bitter tongue.

And so the Dorsts made a moderate contribution of provisions, and an immoderate contribution to the rhetoric of the moment.

On June 22, Patrick Ferguson's corps crossed the Saluda River, ferrying the men and baggage in a scow, and fording the horses, and continued their march the six miles to Ninety Six, where they halted.

Ferguson had been charged with re-organizing the Loyalist militias and reviving the old Loyalist regiments. This, despite the fact that John Harris Cruger, the new commander of Ninety Six District, had a low opinion of militias, considering them unreliable and too easily distracted. This dismal opinion was entirely confirmed, in his opinion, when a raiding party of no more than forty or fifty Rebels made its way into the Long Canes area and, in Cruger's view, "frightened the whole of [Richard King's] regiment," whose "pusillanimous behavior" he found unconscionable.

Nevertheless, Ferguson issued a proclamation ordering the Loyalist militias to "hold their old formations" and urging "the captains, as soon as chosen, [to] prepare the returns of their companys and bring them to [the officer commanding] at Ninety Six."

The following Saturday, July 8, the field officers of the Loyalist militia in the district, and many of their militiamen, trooped into Ninety Six.

Ferguson, who was well liked and respected for his personal bravery, greeted them, chatting and offering them the hospitality of the British army.

By noon he had begun realigning the old Loyalist regiments. He formed the men into companies, each company containing from fifty to a hundred men, usually from a single community or from adjacent communities. Wherever possible, he formed these companies into battalions, each battalion containing from six to twelve companies, and then formed the battalions into regiments.

The men elected their own commanders and in most cases, unsurprisingly, rallied around the officers of the old Loyalist establishment.

Ferguson raised, in the end, seven militias. One, unnamed, was raised by Moses Kirkland. The others were from Fair Forest, Long Canes, Dutch Fork, Little River (Saluda), Upper Saluda and Stevens Creek.

Serving in the Little River regiment under Thomas Pearson as Colonel were Karl Bauer, Georg Weber and his sons Johan, Philip and Henry, Christoph Ruppert, Adam Fralich, Reuben Lively, Henry Siteman and others. Lorentz Merk, freed from his snare with the Rebel militia, also joined up.

The Stevens Creek regiment consisted of four hundred men drawn from Stevens Creek and its branches, including Hard Labour and Cuffeetown, many of whom had been involved since 1775 and exiled to Florida. The men elected John Cotton their colonel. With Cotton came Friedrich Ruppert, Abraham Frietz, Peter Frietz, Conrad Merk, Johannes Zwilling and many others, including William Rittenhouse and Barnet Snell.

And with them came Heinrich Strum. Once more a private.

Cornwallis, meanwhile, was keeping a sharp eye on Thomas Browne at Augusta. He was worried that Browne had refused to disperse his corps of five hundred Creek and Cherokee soldiers. He knew perfectly well that nothing would stir up the American hornet's nest like an attack by Indians. "I beg you will explain to Col. Browne that I wish to keep the Indians in good humor," he wrote to Balfour, "but on no account whatever to bring them forward or employ them." His growing irritation, compounded by Cruger's less than glowing reports, had also begun to influence his attitude toward the Loyalist militias and the regiments of Provincials. Among those whose reputation was dipping sharply, in Cornwallis's views, was the commander of the regiment of North Carolina, Lieutenant Colonel John Hamilton, "who is one of the most obstinate blockheads I ever met with." And of Ferguson he noted in a missive to Balfour, "Entre Nous, I am afraid of his getting to the frontier of North Carolina and playing us some cursed trick."

Militiamen treated with disdain began resentfully to live up to their reputations. Many turned in disgust to the Rebels, buying protection with information.

It was relaxing, as one whose coat had been turned confided to his diary, "to be safe to go to sleep without danger of having our throats cut before morning."

On July 20, Philip Zimmermann and his sons held a gathering at the Zimmermann house. All the former Rebel militia commanders from the area were invited. So were others, like Peter Dorst and his wife Anna, who brought their eldest boy, who was already sixteen, a clever lad, and quieter than his father. Under cover of drinking and carousing, a morale-boosting council of war was to be held.

Johan Merk was there, the fiery young man. Rosena Adolph showed up, uninvited.

As it turned out, there was more carousal than counsel.

There were too many spies, for one thing.

But Zimmermann did manage to get one message across: the current state of affairs would not last. It was a setback. Congress would rally. There were armies on the way. Courage, courage!

A week later, the remnant southern army of about nine hundred Maryland and Delaware Continentals, marching south from Hollinsworth Farm, North Carolina, was joined en route by twenty-one hundred North Carolina and Virginia militiamen. All units were desperately short of provisions—the men were issued molasses in place of rum and the officers used wig powder to thicken their soup—but an army was an army. And there was a new general on his way.

So the rumors said.

Fourteen

Men riding to war. This side, that side, our side, their side, no one knew who was winning. If anyone was. Anna remembered a painter who had visited Ninety Six once, and shown them a heroic canvas of their men at war. But all she had seen were the bayonets; he had captured the shining steel without the corrosive rusting of dried blood—the glory without the pain. *What those things were used for! For a while, we were afraid there'd be no one left.* For the first time, she felt a faint stirring of affection for the dried-up old crone that was her sister. How she had endured!

May 1781
Ninety Six, South Carolina

Perhaps, thought Heinrich, as he plodded wearily home after yet another fruitless battle with a will o' the wisp Patriot militia band, it would have been different had Clinton not stupidly revoked the paroles of honorable men; had he not issued his unprecedented proclamation to turn disarmed combatants into combatants for the other side.

Most of them would have stayed at home, weary of war, overly impressed with the power of English arms. But if they were going to have to fight anyway, to shoot or be shot anyway, might as well fight for home as for foreigner.

So while the army under the Baron de Kalb and General Horatio Gates made its difficult way southward to join the Carolina Continentals, subsisting on what fish it could catch or cattle it could steal (and trying not to use any more of the wig powder than it absolutely had to), the militias under Thomas Sumter swelled, and the war grew sharper and angrier.

In many cases there were just not enough weapons to go around; sometimes up to a third of the soldiers had no muskets at all, but were forced to wait anxiously in reserve until the death of a comrade yielded one up. That was true on both sides.

It didn't prevent them killing each other in small, purposeless battles. Though no less ferocious for all that.

Heinrich killed, when he needed to, and retreated, where he had to, and waited for purpose to emerge from the dizzying swirl of action. Any war's outcome, he knew, is the sum of many senseless actions.

For himself, he was always too weary now to hate.

Purposeless skirmishes: at Rocky Mountain, Lancaster County. At the Old Iron Works, Second Cedar Springs. At Musgrove's Mills, Laurens County. At Long Canes, at Hammonds store, at Williams Plantation, Newberry County. Dozens wounded. Dozens maimed. Dozens killed. A battalion of Royalist militia under Colonel Lisle defected and joined Sumter.

One of Rawdon's patrols came upon a Tory house recently visited by a Rebel party. It had been stripped of everything that could be carried off; the woman of the house was left standing miserably in the doorway in her shift, her husband vanished, her four children stripped stark naked.

Heinrich's militia troop came upon three Loyalists hanging from a gatepost. Pinned to the chest of one of them with a rusty bayonet was a message from the hangmen. "Done to them what they done to others," it said.

Sumter offered pardons to Tories who enlisted with him, but Rawdon threatened death to those who continued to resist; thereafter several persons "were inhumanly murdered, tho' unarmed & remaining peaceably at their own houses."

Sumter, for his part, listed a dozen Whigs falsely accused and condemned.

Sumter's men captured a British supply train, taking seven militiamen prisoner. All seven were shot after they surrendered.

A week later, unarmed civilians "taking sides with neither contending party" were killed in their homes.

Sumter attacked one of Cornwallis's outposts at Rocky Mount. He was repulsed. A short time afterward, his men assaulted another post at Hanging Rock and overwhelmed it. All the defenders were killed. A day later, he came across a small party of Loyalists and Regulars newly come down from North Carolina to join the fray. They got no further. All died.

Another troop of Loyalists, surprised on the banks of the Enoree, were taken and cut in pieces.

A convoy of sick soldiers, under escort on their way to Charlestown, were betrayed by their militia captains, who mutinied and joined the Rebels.

And so it went.

Peter Dorst told Anna the story of Michael Watson, a neighbor of a man he knew. It was typical of the stories that circulated in the Back Country, always told admiringly.

It seemed a band of marauding Tories assaulted Watson's house one night while he was in bed. He seized his gun, ran from a door at the rear and escaped to the woods, about fifty yards away.

Then he started yelling: "Here they are! Come on, boys! Charge!" Firing his gun, he yelped and yelled and made such an infernal racket that the Tories were frightened and fled.

Another time Watson's house was surrounded in daylight. He leaped out a window and hared for the woods. He escaped unhurt, though his clothes had several bullet holes in them.

For herself, Anna doubted the story. Those bullet holes were an awfully nice touch.

Men are such braggarts!

But not long afterward, three hundred Tories descended for real on Watson's plantation when he was not at home. They burned every building in the place, killed every hog and cow, and all the poultry, and either destroyed or carried away all the provisions.

So many stories!

She could feel them taking shape in the landscape around her.

How heroic our men!

James Ryan, for instance. Peter knew of him. He had been imprisoned at Ninety Six and then in Charlestown, but had escaped and made his way through the woods to the home of Colonel Thomas Taylor, an old friend. At the Congaree he was joined by three others, also escapees from Royal prisons. Since two of the party couldn't swim, they made a raft and Ryan towed them over. Taylor loaned Ryan a horse to help him on his way. Near the Edisto, he was stopped by a Tory patrol. He told them he was Rambo.

Anna snorted. Ramboug! She knew him. Lars Ramboug, or Lawrence Rambo, was a Swede who'd come to Ninety Six via Delaware long before the Revolution and settled on Horsepen Creek, across from Heinrich Strum. A well-known Tory in the neighborhood. Stupid to pick on Ramboug. Everyone knew the amiable Swede, Tory or no. The Tories searched Ryan's saddlebags and found his commission.

Then the story got confused. Holley, the Tory leader, seized Ryan's gun to shoot him, but Ryan asked him to wait a moment and then appealed to his feelings as a Christian and a man.

Anna snorted again. A Christian and a man, indeed! In war, it was his Christian duty to kill the fellow, wasn't it? What idiocy!

In any case (Peter said impatiently), Holley yielded but hauled him off to a nearby Tory stronghold where he said he knew he'd be put to death. But the Tory captain, an old man, refused to kill him and sent him off. Holley and the others, not giving up entirely, followed him into the woods, and stripped him of his coat, hat, boots and horse.

When he got home, Ryan gathered a band of Patriots and returned to the Tory camp, whose location was, of course, no longer a secret. There was no one there but an old woman, the captain's wife. She begged Ryan not to injure her, but to give her some food. He immediately had a beef killed, cut up and salted away for her to live upon. Soon after, he fell in with the Tory party where he captured and killed Holley.

What kind of a tale was that? Bravery and cowardice, creeping about the countryside, old women, aging captains, bizarre gestures, salt beef . . . And what's the lesson for Holley's widow? That Christian charity will get you killed? Life was confusing enough without these moral ambiguities. Anna preferred the stories of the Towlses, a family who had settled twenty years earlier in Half Way Swamp country. There was a clan! Implacable! No Tories survived in those swamps. They didn't go in there any longer; even large, armed bands skirted Towlse country. Too many stories of strange rituals in the swamps at night.

Just stories. Stories to be told by the fire at night.

Underlying every story, like a discordant melody, was the jangling rattle of musketry.

Muskets. And the mewing of dying men.

What had happened? What had happened to Cornwallis's grand plan for holding the South for Loyal forces? The plan that had the British army in well-spaced cantonments, and a six-thousand-strong militia patrolling the countryside? The armies were immobile, the militias being nibbled to death. Gradually, little by little, the momentum swung to the other side. By August 1780, the route from Camden to Ninety Six was under the control of the Rebels. And from Camden to Charlestown was no longer so safe either. Gates' army was looming. Rawdon, in Camden, sent an alarmed message to Cornwallis, who was then in the capital.

Daniel Michler was now with Rawdon.

Waiting.

The six-thousand-man army of General Horatio Gates appeared abruptly on the right bank of Lynches Creek, just above Camden. Rawdon's anxious garrison of thirteen hundred men were dug in on the left bank.

"There ensued," wrote a historian of the battle, "very warm and frequent skirmishes, with balanced success."

Daniel Michler took a minor flesh wound but kept on fighting.

Peter Dorst, who was not there, was in despair. Such overwhelming superiority, and the General did nothing! If he hadn't wanted to mount a frontal assault, why not back up the creek, turn Rawdon's left flank, maybe even take Camden from the rear . . . But either he didn't see it, or was afraid to take it.

In any case, Rawdon retreated to the town, where he was joined by Cornwallis with a hastily assembled army of nine hundred men, including units of the South Carolina Royalists. Cornwallis took charge with some energy. He filled out decimated companies with the more robust casualties from field hospitals, remounted Tarleton's legion on fresh horses from the capital and redeployed his forces. He had only fifteen hundred regulars, the rest being Loyalist militia or refugees; he considered a hasty retreat to Charlestown, but it would have meant abandoning upward of eight hundred sick and wounded, with a vast quantity of valuable stores, to fall into the hands of the enemy.

"What happened next?" Anna asked.

"The man actually attacked!" Peter said, still incredulous. "With two thousand men, some of them invalids, he launched an attack on six thousand!"

"Where was Gates?"

"Not far away. Cornwallis's army left Camden in the dark and marched, in absolute silence, through the night. Well, and so did our people. Gates had quit his camp at ten, intent on surprising Cornwallis. Two armies marching toward each other under cover of dark, in dead silence, not knowing the plans of the other, not knowing that the enemy was doing the same . . ."

"So Gates wasn't just being cowardly?"

"Cowardly, no."

"And then?"

"Each side left their sick behind. Gates left his baggage, too, anything that would impede his march.

"At two in the morning, his advance guard ran into British regulars, a company of light infantry."

In the woods, in the dark, once again, shocking action, hearts filled with fear and valor, the blind rush of panic and pain. The rattle of fire and the screams of the wounded. The profound silence of the woods shattered by the hoarse shouts of officers, the grunting as a bayonet was rammed home, the hiss of breath as a sword slid into a heart, the sinister whistling of bullets.

And then both sides withdrew, into an even more shocking silence.

Dawn revealed nasty gaps in Gates' deployment, and he hurried to fill them. Cornwallis, seeing his confusion, launched his attack immediately.

The English right broke the American left; the Virginian Regulars fled into the forests. The Carolina militia, exposed, broke and ran, "like a Torrent," they said, "and bore all before them." Gates himself was caught up and swept off the field of battle. At that moment, Tarleton, seizing his opportunity, made a furious charge into the American center. De Kalb, wounded a dozen times, fell dying into the hands of the British. The rout became general, and Gates' proud army vanished like smoke into the woods. Only a hundred or so infantry survived as a unit; Tarleton pursued them for more than twenty miles, cutting them to pieces.

The battle had lasted less than an hour. The Americans left behind almost two thousand dead, wounded or prisoners. The loss included seventy officers, eight brass cannon, two thousand firearms and a roadway strewn with wagons, stores and baggage.

The British counted sixty-eight of their own men killed and two hundred and forty-five wounded.

"It was a disaster," Peter said despondently. "And it got worse. The only Patriot force left in South Carolina was Sumter's, a mere thousand men on the banks of the Wateree. He caught wind of the disaster and retreated toward North Carolina. Cornwallis sent Tarleton after him."

He groaned. *Bloody Tarleton!*

"He moved with astonishing speed, as he always does, and fell on Sumter's men on the banks of Fishing Creek. It wasn't a battle. It was a massacre. Tarleton took them completely by surprise. They were just lying there on the grass, not even near their weapons! Some of them were fishing!" He groaned again. *The motherless sons had been fishing!*

Some fled, but the others fell into Tarleton's hands. They were bound, then slaughtered. Tarleton's excuse: he couldn't take them prisoner because they were three times as numerous as he, so he had, perforce, to kill them, *tant pis.*

Indeed, Bloody Tarleton.

Horatio Gates, like Benjamin Lincoln before him, was fired by Congress and retired in disgrace.

Before the battle of Camden, Tarleton had complained bitterly of what he called Cornwallis's clemency to "traitors, renegades, evil-doers, &c, &c,"

by which he meant the Whigs, and urged his lordship to hang deserters and punish with imprisonment and confiscation anyone who had taken part in recent actions against the Royal forces. Clemency, he said, "renders friends less hearty and enemies more audacious."

Cornwallis, for his part, responded mildly. To poison springs, to massacre prisoners, to take into slavery all inhabitants of a country, might sometimes be useful, he said. "But civilized nations, and conquerors not entirely barbarous, have abstained from these horrible extremities."

Yet as Peter knew, the gibbets were busy. At many a crossroad, from many a gatepost, men hung, killed for their beliefs or their supposed beliefs. Or, sometimes, just for their boots.

The stories got told, as stories do. Stories, and rumor, and the most insubstantial gossip, collected by passers-by, the idly curious, spies, children, troopers, young women like the Bauer girl, riding alone and fearlessly in the woods. Everyone seemed to know where everyone was.

Katy heard this tale: After Camden, Cornwallis left for Charlotte, in North Carolina, leaving Tarleton more or less in charge. Tarleton came down with yellow fever, and was at death's door for two weeks. Still, he spent that two weeks on the march with his men, delivering his orders from a hammock strung across the frame of a wagon; he would not let his troops rest.

Anna, for her part, had heard that Heinrich Strum had been with Cruger at Ninety Six , and had made a forced march to a place called Seymour's House to rescue Thomas Browne from Georgian militiamen, but she didn't know for sure. She thought her nephew Peter Frietz was there, too, and maybe even his brother Charles . . .

She did know for sure about the hangings. Before he left for North Carolina, Cornwallis dispatched Patrick Ferguson to patrol the Back Country, and Peter had seen a copy of an intercepted order from one of Ferguson's captains, who was at that moment near Gilbert Town, on the approaches to the Blue Ridge Mountains. "We have now got a method that will soon put an end to the rebellion in a short time," he wrote, "by hanging every man that has taken protection and is found acting against us."

At about this time another force, unreckoned and unexpected, began to make its presence felt, at first through rumor, then through anecdote, spreading alarm and despondency among the Loyalist forces, who were not nearly so confident as Ferguson's captain had boasted. These were the Mountain Men, sometimes called Back Mountain Men or Back Water Men. They were Whigs, and they started to drift out of the hollows and folds and hidden valleys of the Blue Ridge Mountains where they lived their isolated and independent lives; one by one they came, then in small groups, families, clans. Everyone, even on the Whig side, treated them with the utmost caution; and though they were in truth no different from, say, the Palatines of Ninety Six in either their manners or their ferocity, everyone feared them, in the same way they feared the Cherokees, and behaved toward them as though they were a brewing typhoon, a force of nature, to be avoided or used, but not managed.

Ferguson, for his part, began to seriously worry. He already felt himself overextended; he'd heard stories of musters high up in the mountains, and the stories grew in the telling. There were said to be a thousand, two thousand of the Mountain Men, armed with long rifles and a lifetime of hunting skills, all of them ready to descend on his army. Ferguson implored Cornwallis to send him Banastre Tarleton, the only commander he considered brutal enough to do what had to be done, "crushing the Back Mountain men, who otherwise cannot be reached and beaten." Cornwallis refused. Tarleton was in no shape to fight, and in any case was needed closer to home.

Ferguson began a retreat. He feinted toward Ninety Six, but instead headed for Charlotte, where Cornwallis's army was still encamped. He started a rumor that a formidable force from Ninety Six was due to meet him, and he circulated a letter to the local Loyalists:

"Gentlemen

"Unless you wish to be cut up by an inundation of barbarians, who have begun by murdering an unarmed son before the aged father, and afterwards lopped off his arms, and who by their shocking cruelties and irregularities give the best proof of their cowardice and want of discipline: I say, if you wish to be pinioned, robbed, and murdered, and see your wives and daughters, in four days, abused by the dregs of mankind—in short, if you wish or deserve to live, and bear the name of men, grasp your arms in a moment and run to camp.

"The Back Water men have crossed the mountains, so that you know what you have to depend on. If you choose to be degraded forever and ever by a set of mongrels, say so at once, and let your women turn their backs on you, and look out for real men to protect them."

What he hoped this alarming missive would do was generate a rugged resistance and a determination to fight. What he got was either derision or fear. Many otherwise sturdy Loyalists took him at his word, but instead of staying to fight, they fled. The Mountain Men advanced steadily, growing (at least in rumor) ever more furious and ever more violent.

Even their own partisans feared them.

"They were . . . transported with fury," a Back Country account said later. "They descended into the plain in torrents, arming themselves with whatever chance threw within their reach. They foamed at the name of Ferguson; they conjured the chiefs they had given themselves, to lead them upon the track of this monster, that they might expiate the ravages and blood with which he had stained himself. Each of them carried, beside his arms, a wallet and a blanket. They slept on the naked earth, in the open air; the water of the rivulet slaked their thirst; they fed on the cattle they drew after them, or on the game they killed in the forests. Every where they demanded Ferguson with loud cries. At every stop they swore to exterminate him. At length they found him."

General Elijah Clarke and Sumter joined these formidable creatures a week after Ferguson's letter. Ferguson had by then set off to join Cornwallis, taking a route from Cherokee Ford north of King's Mountain, over the North Carolina border, and en route he implored his Lordship for help, even "3 or 400 good soldiers part dragoons would finish the business. Something must be done soon. This is their last push in this quarter and they are extremely desolate and awed."

Cornwallis was skeptical, especially of the awed part. He wrote to

Cruger at Ninety Six to stay put, with all his men. The new Congressional General, Nathaniel Greene, was about to join the Mountain Men-Clarke-Sumter forces, by now under the command of General Campbell. Don't risk Ninety Six, Cruger was told. "If anything in force marches your way, I will take care to be soon after them."

Cruger would remember that letter, and later, at the height of his own battle with Greene, pin his hopes on it.

The combined Whig forces caught up with Ferguson at King's Mountain on the afternoon of October 7. Ferguson had taken refuge near the summit, on the top of a long, narrow, sloping plateau, which he'd chosen as a spot he believed defensible against a substantial force. The Whigs advanced up a branch creek and a ravine between two knobs, moving silently, unseen and unheard, and infiltrated themselves around the open field near the summit, where Ferguson had camped. They took cover behind rocks, fallen logs and trees, and when they were all in place, opened a withering fire.

Ferguson blew his silver whistle and his men charged downhill, with fixed bayonets. The Mountain Men melted into the forest. Ferguson regrouped. So did the snipers. Their deadly fire resumed. Ferguson charged again. Again, there was no one there.

The Loyalist force was encircled; the long rifles of the attackers were knocking Ferguson's mounted volunteers from their saddles. He himself lost two horses. From behind their natural shields, the Mountain Men were cutting down everything that moved.

From his seat on a third horse, Ferguson watched the growing confusion and terror in his own ranks. He knew he would have to break out, try to get to level ground, where his bayonets would have some effect. Brandishing his sword, he called for a charge and started to cut his way down the mountain. Only four men followed him, the rest cowered behind their wagons. The snipers fired, and Ferguson fell; eight rifle bullets hit him, one bursting through his head.

After the surrender, the British Regulars were taken prisoner. Many captured Loyalist militiamen were hanged, in reprisal, it was said, for Patriots hanged at Camden, Ninety Six and Augusta.

Only twenty-eight of the attacking force died. Ferguson lost a hundred and nineteen killed, a hundred and twenty-three wounded and six hundred and sixty-four prisoners. Camden was revenged.

The new and once-again-private Heinrich Strum had almost made it to King's Mountain. He was nominally under Ferguson's command, but had been detached to stay with Cruger at Ninety Six. There, his company was led by Henry Rudolph, and they served in John Cotton's regiment, Stevens Creek Militia, Ninety Six Brigade, and were patrolling the region when Ferguson was killed. Adam Bauer was a private with Rudolph, too. With Adam was his son Karl, on the muster rolls as "Charles Bowers." The rolls also recorded "Privates Peter Fritts, Daniel Michlar."

None of them regretted missing King's Mountain.

They would see action enough, soon enough.

On January 17, 1781, Tarleton's column was almost destroyed at Cowpens. Of the thousand men with him, eleven were killed, sixty-one wounded and six hundred taken prisoner. The rest fled.

Tarleton lost more than his men, his horses and his baggage; he also lost his air of relentless invincibility. Until Cowpens, he had been the scourge of the Rebel militia and the terror of the inhabitants.

Bloody Tarleton!

After Cowpens, just another soldier, sometimes winning, sometimes losing.

Or so the diligent scribes of the Rebel propagandists put it about, hoping to "animate [their men] with fresh spirits," as the victorious Colonel Morgan put it.

Cornwallis, when he heard of the twin disasters of King's Mountain and Cowpens, abandoned Charlotte and began his retreat back into South Carolina. In mid-March, he drove Nathaniel Greene's army from Guilford Court House, but at such cost that he had to retire to the coast with his battered army. Strategically, he had no choice.

There was no one to help him.

The mightiest empire in the universe was in a retreat from which it would never recover.

In March, Peter Zange, son of Christian, was caught and hanged by the Rebels, for no discernible cause other than their simple irritation.

Early in May, Nisbet Balfour, now sequestered at Charlestown as commandant, reported gloomily to Clinton in New York that "the revolt is now universal. The royal militia is in such a state of mutiny that a part of it had to be disarmed. Whereas at the beginning of the war years it was believed that only about a third of the population supported the Revolution, the recent successes of the Americans have by now turned the tide of popular opinion."

On May 10, Rawdon decided to abandon Camden.

On May 11, Sumter defeated a substantial British force at Orangeburg.

On the 24th, General Greene, whose strategy was now to reduce the line of strongholds the Royal forces still held in the Back Country, invaded Ninety Six.

Cruger, the garrison commander, was as prepared as he could be. Even before Ferguson's debacle he'd been hearing rumors that the "Back Water Whigs" were concentrating for an attack on the fort. He'd then called in all his troops, and had been laying up supplies, especially Indian corn, seeing to his water and designing his defense of the village.

"I have palisaded the court house and the principal houses, in about one hundred yards square, with block house flankers," he reported to Cornwallis.

Other than that, he could only wait for relief.

Heinrich Strum, Abraham Frietz and his sons Peter and Charles were inside the stockade.

With them were Friedrich Ruppert and his brother Christoph, Adam Bauer, and Conrad Merk with his brother Lorentz, now firmly and once and for all in the Loyalist camp.

Katy and Anna could only wait at home, in an agony of suspense.

For all of them, this could be the decisive battle of this long, weary war.

Heinrich Strum crouched on the palisades of Ninety Six's Star Fort and watched as General Greene made a slow perimeter of the village, studying it intently through a spyglass. Heinrich hefted his long rifle. He could almost, almost, almost pick him off, with a lucky shot . . . But he did nothing. One should never shoot a general without orders.

Fifteen

Anna! Anna! Anna! What are we going to do? We thought battles and sieges mattered, and perhaps they did, then. She shifted on the bench. She could tell me the story of that siege, of her rage and frustration. I could tell her the same story, from where I watched, my heart pounding, in constant terror . . . But we won't be any the wiser. We were so full of emotion it crowded out all thought.

June 1781
Ninety Six, South Carolina

The morning that Greene's army crossed the Saluda at Island Ford, seven miles from Ninety Six, Loyalist families walked and drove and rode out of the woods and poured through the gates of the stockade around the village. All of them, young or old, slave or free, black or white, carried bundles, sacks of clothing, copper kettles, hoes and sickles; Heinrich saw one young child clutching an enormous family Bible. What passed for a village square between the courthouse and the barracks was jammed with people and wagons; if the heat had not been so oppressive, the faces so somber and the anticipation so fearful, it could easily have been a village fair.

But they had seen the vanguard of Greene's army, Colonel William

Washington's white-clad Dragoons, earlier that day; they knew the main army would not be far behind, and would cross by mid afternoon. They knew militias from Virginia and North Carolina were with Greene, and they knew what Rebel militias in the south did to Loyal civilians; the stockade, no matter how perilous, was preferred to waiting on their farms for punishment.

Cruger had only five hundred men under his command, two hundred from New York and the rest from South Carolina; only five hundred to face Greene's army of more than two thousand, and he needed every able body. But he had nevertheless given the Carolina militias a chance to leave before the battle was joined. He had no great fondness for militias, no high regard for their constancy, so if they wanted to leave, they were better gone. He called them into the village square and addressed them from the tavern porch. He knew that if the fort fell, the chances were they'd be hanged. He told them that.

Most of them refused to go. They loosed their horses, let them wander off into the distant woods and returned to the square.

Cruger stared at them with a contemplative, schoolmasterish air.

No one said anything. Heinrich stood with the rest of them. Beside him was Reuben Lively, of the Long Canes Regiment. Neely Carghill, from the Ridge, stood patiently with his men; they had been with Cruger since the spring. On the far side Heinrich caught sight of Conrad Merk, with his brother Lorentz. Abraham and Peter Frietz were standing on a patch of dusty red earth to one side, side by side, looking as sturdy as two oxen ready for the plow. Next to them was the youngster, Charles, barely sixteen. They were all there, the Loyalist Palatines, those who had survived this far. No one had left. There was nothing to say. Without Ninety Six, there was nothing. They understood that, too.

A messenger had come that morning from the Savannah River. Augusta had fallen. Browne was a prisoner, his chief officer shot, their troops in irons.

Cornwallis was somewhere in the north, no one in Ninety Six knew where. Rawdon was hugging the coast; no one in Ninety Six knew he had urged Cruger to retreat, because none of his messengers had gotten through.

There was no one else.

Clinton might as well have been on the moon.

In the Back Country, Ninety Six was all that was left.

Cruger waited. Still no one said anything.

After a while, he cleared his throat. "Well," he said, "we have a job to do," and turned into the tavern where he had set up his command headquarters.

Six messengers were briefed, and told to slip away separately to tell Rawdon what was happening, that they depended on him for relief. The messengers were to impress on his Lordship the need for urgent action. No one knew that Rawdon himself was on a knife edge of indecision.

Alizabetha Bauer, now nearly twenty-one and still brown as a berry (and an old married woman of three years who had already left her husband on account of his late-emerging Rebel sympathies), was at Colonel James Mayson's house, three miles from Ninety Six, when she heard the faint rumble of cannon.

She'd never heard cannon before, but she was wary and world-wise, and she knew it wasn't thunder. She was on her feet in an instant, head cocked, listening.

Mayson's three daughters gawked at her. "What is it?"

She motioned them to be silent. She held her breath, straining to hear. There! Another distant growl, so low, so deep it seemed to come from inside her head rather than from any external source. She imagined she could hear the howl of the ball, the shouts of men, the crackle of muskets . . . But there was nothing but that bone-rattling rumble.

The others began to chatter again. She left the room, went downstairs. How she despised them! Empty-headed, vain, ignorant . . . So why was she there? It wasn't as though she needed the work, cleaning up after empty-headed misses, being condescended to by the ladified lah-di-dahs that surrounded the military hierarchs. But Mayson's house attracted her, despite it all, and so, in their way, did the girls, with their foolish but joyful behavior. The house was always filled with singing and music and fine things, and since Colonel Cruger's wife had come to stay when the colonel had taken command of the fort, it was also filled with officers of his army, Dragoons mostly, hard young men with awkward manners, their tongues hanging out almost to their boots at the sight of all that giggling female flesh. She knew. She was wise in that way, too. She loved teasing them.

In the parlor, the older women were silent. Mrs. Cruger was even more war-wise and world-weary than Alizabetha, and she knew guns when she heard them.

There were no young men there. They were all at the fort, Alizabetha guessed. Women were not much on their minds now.

Her own young man, her once-upon-a-time husband, was where? Off riding somewhere, some Rebel band, one of Peter Dorst's creatures, no doubt. She'd married him after he took her for a tumble in the woods, and she'd become obsessed with him, wouldn't let him out of her sight, and even after they were married, until in the heat of an argument she humiliated him and he grew angry and slapped her. It was the first and last time he did that! She took a knife and threatened to cut him, and he knew she meant it, and after that their love-making was cooler. It lasted only months, that marriage. He turned out to be just another incorrigible Rebel after all, and when he tried to stop her riding to help her father and her father's friends hiding in the woods, she lost interest in him altogether. Jean Henri, French Protestant from New Bordeaux on the Savannah. She moved back into her father Adam's house. She was alone with her mother and father, then. Her brother Henry had disappeared years earlier. Karl was off with the militias, Angelica was gone, who knew where, Maria and Margaret had their own homes, having married Rebels of a non-zealot sort, and the fourteen-year-old Philip was sniping at Rebels from a hideout in the woods. And she herself . . . twenty-one and here she was, tidying up after folk she despised and envied. They were all so stupid! She had no trouble outwitting these dull and ponderous people, even those who passed for great soldiers, at least in their own estimation.

Colonel Mayson himself was a portly soul, but courteous nonetheless, and with an honorable history. It was he, along with the turncoat Moses Kirkland, who had commanded the troop of Rangers who had fired on Fort Charlotte July 12, 1775, the first overt rebellious act in South Carolina. But after the fall of Charlestown he had felt the American cause hopeless, had given his parole and retired to his estate, which he called Glasgow. Since that time, his home had been considered, unofficially, neutral ground, and his dinners (and his daughters) had drawn not only the officers of Cruger's garrison but prominent Rebels too. It was such a center of gaiety! She'd seen Philip Zimmermann there once. Even the great Colonel Pickens showed up one day, but only once, being clearly uncomfortable at the thought of dining with damned Tories, even in the presence of all these lovely young women . . . Of course, they didn't talk war business, not in such a setting, but then they all thought women stupid, and would say things in their presence that would have got them shot in other company. How wonderfully blind they were! As though there could be anything neutral in a civil war.

The rumble came again. This time the cannonade, by some trick of the wind, was clearly audible to them all. It pushed the colonel's wife into action.

Within minutes all the women in the house were bustling about, collecting their movable valuables, jewelry and money. Mrs. Cruger knew what to do. She set to sewing her guineas in belts, so that she could strap them about her waist under her clothing; she was a practical person and a soldier's wife, and moving on at short notice was a way of life. Perhaps her husband would, in his calculations of casualties, decide to abandon the fort, to fight a rearguard action down to the coast, and she must be ready to be swept along. Or, if he stayed, and lost . . . this would be Rebel territory. She had heard the stories. She would lose first her money, then her honor, then . . . maybe her life. It was the way things were.

Mayson's daughters, the silly things, were called down to help.

No one asked Alizabetha. They knew she was not the sewing kind.

She was at the window, listening.

Preparations for flight were almost complete when Alizabetha saw a troop of soldiers on the approach road. They were American Continentals, with the Rebel cockade in their hats. She knew their army was in control by the way they walked.

Half a dozen armed men, with a mounted corporal.

The corporal dismounted, marched up to the door. He raised his fist to knock just as Alizabetha twitched the door open. He stood there, fist raised, gawping at her foolishly. She smiled.

"Are you Mrs. Colonel Cruger?" he asked, and she started to laugh.

She recounted all this to Katy later, at the Frietz house. She liked Katy. She was old, true—must be almost fifty!—but she was funny and wise, by which Alizabetha meant she didn't believe everything she was told. And she could still laugh, although her husband and sons were gone, into the stockade with Cruger, there to do or die against General Greene's army.

The corporal finally got himself sorted out as to who was who, and when Mrs. Cruger came to the door, he drew himself up to his not very considerable height and said he had been sent as a guard to protect the colonel's family.

"You need have no apprehension," he said, as if reciting from a prepared text. "We will remain as long as necessary, and see to it that no harm comes to you or your family."

"Does my husband know?" she asked.

"Messages have been sent," the corporal said. "Colonel Cruger has expressed his appreciation."

Katy stared. "He expressed his appreciation," she mimicked. "As well he might. 'Tis better than tying her to a post in front of the stockade." She shook her head.

Alizabetha said nothing. What was there to say? They'd protect Mrs. Cruger, but try their damnedest to kill her husband.

And Katy's family too.

They were supposed to be grateful?

Mrs. Cruger had given the fellow two guineas, to his astonishment. What for? Appreciation? Or an investment against the future?

How little they knew of women!

Heinrich stood on the ramparts of Star Fort and stared up the Charlestown-Island Ford road, where Greene's men would first show themselves. To his left was the stockade that surrounded the village; across the pickets, and across the dozen or so squared-log houses, the Presbyterian church and the disreputable tavern, stood the village's proudly built, big, blocky, brick jail, overlooking a shallow ravine on the western side. Two-and-a-half storeys tall, walls sixteen inches thick, wrestled at such cost from the Assembly at Charlestown not a decade before. A small path beside it led to a gate punched through the stockade; a few hundred yards further it joined the other road that passed by Ninety Six, the road that led to Augusta in one direction and to Fort George and the Cherokee towns in the other; the two roads were less than a quarter of a mile apart. It was why Ninety Six had been built here in the first place.

Aside from a few scraps of garden, now badly trampled, there was hardly any vegetation. Not a single tree inside the stockade or, for a cleared mile, outside it; the trees had been ripped out so as not to interrupt the sight lines. Even the weeds grew sparsely in the barren red soil.

Also near the jail but hidden from Heinrich's view was the covered trench that led across the ravine to the third fort of the Ninety Six complex, a small stockaded farmhouse called the Holmes Redoubt, which protected the only water supply, a small spring that welled up between the two roads and flowed in a leisurely way along the ravine's floor.

That water supply was their most vulnerable point, he thought, though Cruger had argued Greene would attack the Star Fort, in which they were now standing. Star Fort was the only place from which he could command the whole town, Cruger said. And it was a perfect place to raise a log tower for snipers. Apparently he'd done so at Augusta, and from it had raked the fort with a deadly fire. He was not known as an imaginative commander, Cruger said. "What worked there, he'll try here."

Heinrich leaned on a notch cut into the log stockade, squinted up the road. There was still nothing to be seen except the distant drab gray wall of sweet gums and red oaks that separated the village from the Saluda. It was hot, dusty; everything wilted. He felt sticky where the belts and webbing of his gear pressed on his clothes; there were sweat stains in his armpits and down his back. There was not a breath of a breeze; the sun beat down like drums.

Somewhere out there is the enemy, come to ruin us.

He squinted again up the road. There was a distant figure on horseback, but no soldier. The figure quivered and shimmered in the heat, throwing up sluggish clouds of dust.

He turned and looked down the road toward Charlestown. Nothing stirred there. Charlestown! What a journey they had made to see it that first time! The Nahe, the Rhine, the Thames, the gray Atlantic, the Caribbean Reaches! He thought of Elizabeth, of his children, so many dead and scattered. Of his beloved Catherine. He felt very weary.

Waiting was a soldier's lot.

Perhaps it will all end here.

It will be no great thing, he thought. In a hundred years, two hundred, will anyone care?

Heinrich Strum was there, they'd say. *He died for a cause he believed in, once. Whatever it was.*

If they win, my children's children will hear the tale differently. The thieves will become sheriffs, the sheriffs, thieves, and everything will be backwards, loyalty become treachery and treachery fealty . . .

Our voices will be forgotten, only our deeds remembered, motiveless, random, mysterious.

There was no sound in the fort but the occasional bawling of an officer giving orders. In the village, there was a constant shuffling and clanking; Cruger had made sure every newcomer, every inhabitant of the village, was sent to the creek to fill every pan, dish, bowl, bucket and container with water. He had already set his sappers to digging a well, but there was no surety of finding water. This place was so dry!

"Hoard it like gold," Cruger had told them, an hour or so earlier. "Because we must hold out, we must, and we can do so by prudence, thrift, hard work, grit, endurance. Remember!" he'd said, his voice rising, "we're fighting not just for ourselves, but for our province, for all the Loyalists who have paid in so much pain, with so much blood, for so long, and are dependent on us. We will endure!"

It had been a rousing speech, but it had been received in silence. The assembled Loyalists had heard too many speeches over the years. But they did what they were told, and passed down to the spring in procession, shuffling back with their precious drops.

There was a grunt from Reuben Lively next to him, and he pulled his attention to the present. Lively pointed up the road. There was a white smudge, two smudges, a string of smudges, in front of the distant line of trees. Horsemen.

Someone shouted for Cruger.

"Colonel! Greene's army has come!"

Cruger looked up from his chair, in the lee of the stockade under a scrap of canvas. He had been studying a map.

"Well?" he said. "What of it? We knew they were coming. That's why we're here."

Before dawn the next day, as the darkness thinned into gray and the east flushed with pink, a mockingbird began to sing. It was perched on a spiky branch of the abattis that protected the ditch that surrounded the stockade that guarded the redoubt. The air, smoky with dozens of Rebel campfires, was very still and already sultry, and the mockingbird's treble rose into the air, and it seemed to some of them the sound of liquid gold; it caught in the throat if you listened to it right.

Others, knowing the provenance of the sweetness and its essential falseness, heard in it the sound of treachery, and willed it to stop.

At dawn, Heinrich ascended to the firestep and peered once more over the parapet. What a difference! There were Rebels everywhere. Their tents were pitched across all four of the roads that led to the outside world. There was marching and counter-marching, seemingly without purpose. A canteen had been set off to the right, and men were lining up to be fed, just outside the reach of a long rifle. With apparent disdain for their soldiers' safety, and in certain disdain of the defenders' sensibility, the latrine was equally close. More ominously, the mockingbird's song had been replaced by the sinister chip and scrape and clank of shovels being poked into stubborn earth. Not seventy paces away, on the opposite side of the Star Redoubt from the village—just where Cruger had forecast they'd be—two trenches had been gouged into the red earth. Heinrich could see shovelfuls of earth and stone being flung onto the two long banks of red earth that protected the trenches from the fort.

He could even hear the men's voices.

It was then he found Greene's beribboned bosom in his rifle's sights. How would the world have changed if he'd pulled the trigger?

In a while the white-hot Carolina sun came up and glared mercilessly down into the stockade. They were going to need all the water they could get, and soon.

The whole of Star Fort was lined with red- and green-clad troops, watching.

Those trenches were getting close. They would have to be stopped. They were full of digging men, but there seemed no reserves. Sappers, but no soldiers. The rest of Greene's army was about its business at the edge of the woods.

It was either insulting, or stupid, or both.

Cruger decided it was mostly stupid, and resolved to take advantage of it. He had some of the South Carolina Royalists, including Heinrich and the Frietzes, lay down a covering fire, and dispatched a small troop of thirty DeLancey's New Jersey Volunteers to clear them out.

They used bayonets mostly, against men armed only with shovels. More than a hundred Rebels died; it was a massacre, and Heinrich took no pleasure from it. He could see the rifle butts rising and falling as the men speared the sappers, easier than fish in a barrel. Only one attacker was wounded, slashed in the back with a shovel edge, severing his spine, dragged back in agony into the fort to die. So thorough was the massacre, and so quick, that Cruger had time to dispatch his own crew of sappers, mostly slaves and free blacks, to fill in the ditch, which they did before Greene's cavalry could gallop to the attack. They returned to the fort with heavy booty in shovels and pickaxes and iron trenching tools.

"Stupid," said Cruger, shaking his head. "Why trench there? Why not protect the diggers? Why not an impetuous assault on the redoubt that protects the water? If they took that, they could have us out of here in a week . . ."

"Well," someone said, "don't tell them."

"It's not over yet," Cruger said.

The next night, Greene's men dug another trench, much longer and much further away, five or six times further. They had learned to beware the defender's bite. It was now clear to Cruger that there'd be no general assault, only a long siege. Greene would run a second trench from the first, at an angle that would take it closer to the fort. Then they'd dig a third, parallel to the first, but much closer—much too close!—to Star Redoubt. From there, they could lay in a tunnel to mine the abattis.

He was afraid it would occur to Greene to dig yet another trench a third of the way around the stockade. From there, they'd be able to lob missiles in two directions into the fort, a crossfire of projectiles. And they'd threaten the water supply.

The defenders would have to dig protective trenches inside the fort for the civilians. And they'd have to accelerate the well-digging. Every able-bodied person not needed for the defense would have to dig.

For ten days, in the glaring heat, they dug. They pushed trenches six feet deep at right angles to each other across the village; there were hillocks of bitter red earth everywhere. And they dug down, for water. They went down twenty feet, and found nothing. They went down another ten feet, and it was as dry as when they began, the hard earth filled with rock and small stones that jarred the shoulders when the shovels struck. Cruger pushed them on. They went down another ten feet. Still nothing.

Every day the enemy trenches came closer. Every night raiding parties would go out, faces and bodies blackened with soot, to harass and deter them, but they inched closer anyway. All day, every day, lines of women and children and the ambulatory wounded shuffled down to the ravine where the spring was, filling the buckets and dishes with water; but it was hard to keep up with the water-loss caused by the incessant physical labor and the searing heat. They were all burned deep brown, their skins leathery, desiccated, rough as alligator.

On June 3, ten days after they opened their new trenches, the Rebels sent a messenger under a flag of truce with a to-whom-it-may-concern letter that pointedly didn't address the commanding officer by name. The letter, a fine mix of bragging, threat and insult, demanded only "instantaneous capitulation."

Among all its bluster, it contained one paragraph that worried Cruger, though he never shared his doubts with the men. Greene, talking of his Southern Army, recounted some of its "magnificent successes" in this way: "It has swept from the banks of the Congaree, the Wateree and the Santee all the armed invaders sent by your royal master to harry and enslave our suffering people. With invincible gallantry it has driven Rawdon's troops from Camden and from Orangeburg, and forced him to retreat to the sea-coast, whence he will never return. The brave Pickens, Lee and Sumter are even now demolishing the forts at Augusta; nothing can protect you from complete destruction."

Bluster aside, was Rawdon really pushed to the coast? Cruger didn't believe Rawdon would abandon him. But what did Rawdon know? Had any of the messengers gotten through?

And where in the name of sanity was Cornwallis? So much for promises of rescue!

He kept the letter to himself, but asked his officers the simple question: Surrender or no?

None of them would give up.

The digging went on.

Fifty feet. No water.

The following day, June 4, the Rebels finished their third trench, the second parallel, and brought artillery into it to lay down a covering fire while they built a gunner's tower. From the tower they'd be able to enfilade the town.

Cruger responded by raising his ramparts three feet with sandbags. Women and the wounded stitched bags from whatever they could find, tent canvas, scraps of linen, their own clothes, anything, and stuffed them with the plentiful earth from the well.

The enemy responded by firing arrows tipped with flax dipped in melted pitch, and set on fire. One landed on the roof of the courthouse, but DeLancey's men were able to put it out.

Cruger responded by using the captured trenching tools to strip the roofs from all the buildings in town.

Heinrich and Abraham crouched side by side on the tavern roof. It sloped away from Greene's tower, so they were safe from snipers, but cannonballs trundled overhead, shrieking like demons, and the air was thick with acrid smoke. They sweated and groaned as they drove their shovels under the shingles, levering them off and tossing them to the earth below, where they were stacked by whoever it was that was free to stack them—they couldn't see clearly enough.

From up there Heinrich could look beyond one of Greene's camps to the southern horizon. Beyond the horizon, somewhere, was the ridge, and beyond that the sands and swamps of the Low Country.

Somewhere there was Rawdon.

But where, damn and rot him, where?

One, only one, of Cruger's messengers had slipped through the Rebel cordon. But one was enough.

When he got to Charlestown on May 31, he found Rawdon had come down with malaria. The temporary commander of the British Army, Lieutenant Colonel Welbore Ellis Doyle, didn't think his command strong enough to relieve Ninety Six, and was inclined to do nothing.

Early in the morning of June 8, a great shout went up from the sentries on the south side of town. They had spotted troops moving out of the woods on the Augusta road.

It had to be Rawdon!

The people, blackened with soot and sweat, thin as rawhide, exhausted, boiled out of the trenches and poured toward the stockade on that part of town.

Rawdon had finally come! It was over! They had held off the enemy, four times greater than they in numbers, maybe five . . . They had won!

Heinrich, though caught up in the jubilation, nevertheless found time to wonder, *Why the Augusta road? Why that way?*

Cruger and his officers ascended the firestep and looked out over the parapet. He stood there for what seemed an hour. Finally someone called up to him, "Is it Rawdon, Colonel?"

Cruger stared for a while longer at the troops massing in the distance. A flag appeared at the head of the column as it formed up. It was too far away to make out what it was, but he didn't need a flag to know who they were. He could clearly see the smudge of white and blue above the dark horses. That meant Rebels. It had to be the Dragoons of Colonel Lee, the man they called Light Horse Harry, fresh from the victory of Augusta. And if Lee was there, Pickens, or Pickens' men, were sure to be present, too. This was no relief. These were reinforcements for the enemy. His job had suddenly become much harder.

"No," he said to the people staring at him from below. "It's not Rawdon. It's Rebel cavalry."

The jubilation faded. Heinrich could almost hear it going out, sizzling like a bucket of water on a morning campfire, leaving behind only the damp smoke of disappointment.

Half an hour later the first of Lee's legion came within gunshot of the defenders. They came marching straight up the Augusta road, apparently paying no attention to the defenders or to the possibility of hostile fire. Instead of veering around out of range, they came so close that individual soldiers could easily be recognized.

No one in the garrison fired. They stood as if frozen, gaping at the column passing before them

They couldn't fire.

Between the Dragoons and the fort marched a long, ragged line of prisoners, the garrison of Augusta, bound together and to the horses, stumbling occasionally, many of them bandaged and bloody, their green uniforms torn and ragged, others naked to the waist, brown as leather— Cherokees, Browne's Cherokee guards.

Their captors jeered as they went by.

Cruger and his officers circled the ramparts as Lee circled the town, keeping pace, watching, saying nothing. They watched as Lee's men, marching to the drums and fifes, swaggered up to Greene's main camp.

"You see how they insult prisoners," Cruger said afterward. "Let no man here suffer from any illusion. That's why we're defending this place so vigorously. That's what they'll do to us, if they can, and to the Loyal militia, worse . . . much worse."

The insult had not gone without notice in Greene's camp. If the defending garrison was enraged, many of the American officers were chagrined.

Philip Zimmermann, who was with Greene, was furious. Lee just shrugged. "What does it matter?" he asked.

"These are not criminals, they're prisoners of war," Zimmermann said. "They should be treated accordingly."

"Even the Cherokees?"

"Even so." He scowled. "But it's worse than that. You've stiffened the spines of the defenders with this display."

Lee shrugged again. "Now that we're here, they won't last long."

Full of pep and vigor from his successes against Browne, Lee soon convinced himself and his men that Greene was conducting the attack ineptly. This slow pushing toward Star Fort, the prospect of at some time laying a mine, sat ill with his impatience. He told Greene he wanted to take Holmes Redoubt and cut the defenders off from their water. "If you'd done that, it would be over by now," he said. "The spring must be taken!" He repeated the phrase again, giving it the feel of an incantation. "The spring must be taken!"

"How?" asked Greene reasonably. "How can this be done without a general assault, with unacceptable casualties?"

"I'll take the stockade and my guns will drive them from the water," Lee said, full of bombast.

He had Thadeus Kosciusko, Greene's Lithuanian-born engineer, lay down two small trenches facing the fortified village and the redoubt that protected the water. Then, under cover of a thunderstorm, he sent a platoon to set fire to the redoubt.

It wasn't, Heinrich reflected, a bad plan. If they'd managed to set their fire, Cruger would have had to open the gate for an expedition to put it out. Lee would have attacked with Dragoons, Cruger would have had to order up reinforcements and Greene could have attempted a general assault on the far side . . . But the storm came to naught, merely a great wall of threatening purple clouds, the constant flickering of sickly-green lightning and a series of deafening crashes. Cruger wasn't fooled at all, and when his sentries spotted the creeping figures at the Holmes Redoubt, with their buckets of pitch, they were easy enough to take out. He called up the sharpshooters from the local militia, men who were able, in the phrase of the country, to part a chipmunk from his tail at a hundred paces, and Lee's men died their useless deaths.

After which Greene returned to his patient siege.

Nevertheless, Lee's riflemen were now in a position to use his zigzag scar to pour fire into the ravine along whose gully the spring trickled. Four civilians were shot the next morning as they trailed down with their buckets and pans for the day's meager ration. Cruger held the others back, waiting for nightfall.

During the day they parceled out minute quantities of what precious water they had left; they waited and endured in the burning heat, sucking pebbles to fill their mouths with something other than dust, lips cracked open, tongues like thick, dry sponges, craving water.

Heinrich's skin felt like old parchment.

The well in the fort had reached sixty feet after more days of heroic digging. It was still dry.

After dark, Heinrich and the other men from Ninety Six district were told to report, with their buckets, to the water gate in the west stockade, whence the covered way led to the ravine and past it to the Holmes Redoubt.

Cruger had also rounded up every black man within the defenses, from Ninety Six or not. He lined everyone up together, and sorted them by color and shade. They would form a human chain in the dark down to the water; the blackest men would take the greatest risks, down by the spring, the lighter the shade, the closer to the fort. There weren't nearly enough blacks, so he had volunteers stripped naked and smeared with soot.

Heinrich looked around him. It could work! The blacks, stripped of their clothes, vanished in the dark, the wooden buckets seemingly passing of themselves through the gate in the fort, down the covered way and out through the break in the way where the spring was. The soot-blackened whites, though they smelled of wet embers, were similarly invisible.

He was stationed next to Katy's boy Charles just inside the covered way a few yards from the spring itself, but he could see nothing until the buckets mysteriously appeared in the hands of the men near him and water passed on, vanishing into the covered way to be carried into the fort.

Letting the water pass was agony, but they didn't dare stop. Nor was there any sound. No one stumbled, coughed or even whispered. They all knew the risks of discovery.

Still, he thought he could hear the faint sound of splashing.

He managed to lick his damp fingers once or twice as the exhausting trail of buckets came through and went back empty.

It was after midnight before he had his first real drink. His throat was so dry he swore the water was absorbed before it reached his stomach.

All night he stood there as the buckets passed slowly up the hill, disappeared into the insatiable fort and came back empty, vanishing again down to the ravine.

Just before black faded to the gray of dawn, Cruger called the water-passers back. They were exhausted, and flopped to the ground just inside the gate, panting, some of them asleep within seconds.

They'd do the same thing the following night, if they had to.

They'd do it until they didn't have to do it any more. Until they were discovered. Or until they were relieved.

It was the 12th of June.

Ten days earlier, a squadron of the British navy had arrived unexpectedly in Charlestown; with it were seventeen troop transports bearing three regiments of reinforcements from Ireland.

Rawdon, who had recuperated from his illness only a few days after Cruger's messenger had arrived with his tidings of gloom and urgent requests for assistance, now had sufficient force to attempt a relief of Ninety Six.

On June 5, he wrote to Cornwallis, who was somewhere in Virginia, having essentially abandoned the Carolinas: "Two days hence I shall march toward Ninety Six. If I am in time to save that post, it will be a very fortunate circumstance."

And then he went on, in a reflective mood: "I much doubt whether it will be advisable to maintain it."

He would rescue Cruger, if he could. But then he would abandon the Back Country as indefensible. He'd establish a new frontier along the Congaree-Santee line. And of the Loyal settlers in the Back Country? "By . . . transplanting our friends from the Back Country to the rich plantations within the [new] boundary, I think we may with few troops secure and command a tract which must in the end give law to the rest of the province."

On June 7, Rawdon wrote again: "I march this night."

June 14, afternoon. Another in the long, long series of searing days. In the hours after noon, hardly anyone stirred inside the fort, unless they had to. Only the essential sentries patrolled restlessly on the ramparts. Everyone else took what shelter they could in what meager shade they could find. The thudding of the artillery from the Rebel trenches didn't rouse them; they had been hearing the sound of cannon for so long that it hardly interested them any longer, and they were too tired and apathetic to be alarmed, even when a cannonball stirred up another puff of dry red dust somewhere close to them. It was so hot that they had discarded most of their clothing; the garments that were left felt as though they were pressing against the skin with hot irons.

But then there was a sudden shout from the south wall, an unexpected shout, and the unexpected always meant alarm. Most of the garrison tensed, but lay where they were. A few went over to see what had caused the noise.

What they saw caused more shouts, and a flurry of action.

A rider was coming, flogging his flagging horse, making a dash for the gates.

Harry Lee, from the vantage point of his trenches above the ravine, looking down on the fort, described it this way: "A countryman was seen riding along the lines south of the town, conversing familiarly with the officers and soldiers on duty. There was nothing in this to attract particular attention, as from the beginning of the siege friends in the country were in the habit of visiting camp, and were permitted to go wherever their curiosity led them. This man was one of these; but when he reached the great road leading to the town (in which quarter were only an embankment thrown up for the protection of our guards), he put spurs to his horse and rushed with full speed into town, receiving the ineffectual fire of the American sentinels and guards nearest him. The gate was opened, and he was received with loud expressions of joy."

When the sentries saw him coming, they opened fire on everything they could see at the Rebel line, to give him what protection they could, while others used huge mallets to lift the bars from the gate.

His mount almost staggered into the fort; its rider was caked with dust and his clothing stained black with sweat. He looked almost as exhausted as they. But he was waving a letter and demanding to be taken to Colonel Cruger.

Within minutes, his message was spreading. He had left Rawdon in Orangeburg that morning. Rawdon was coming, with enough troops and cavalry to lift the siege. Rawdon was coming! Help was on its way!

But when? Orangeburg was over a hundred miles away. Rawdon, the messenger said, had green troops with him, gun carriages, a supply train— he couldn't move more than twenty miles a day. Five days! Five more days of sniper fire, ruinous cannonballs, prostrating heat, choking dust, sleeplessness, toil, hunger and terrible thirst. Five more days of men broken and torn by enemy fire. Five more days of exhaustion.

And then Cruger told them, expect an assault. The enemy would have to try to take the fort before Rawdon arrived.

"A general assault will be good news," he said. "It will mean Rawdon is so close they are growing desperate."

Heinrich stared at him blankly. Good news? He heard the words, but they seemed meaningless.

He looked around at the gaunt faces, the hollow eyes, the leathery skin of the soldiers and civilians. They had been rationed to one small meal a day, and their stomachs were all growling from hunger. They all craved water. They craved quiet. They craved sleep.

But they would endure. For what other choice had they?

They knew what their neighbors would do to them if they gave up now.

Rawdon was coming. Heinrich clung to the thought.

By the time Rawdon reached Orangeburg, his march had already slowed to a crawl. The troops fresh from Ireland, in woolen uniforms acceptable for an Irish spring, were being pushed to march through semi-tropical heat that made even the natives ill; whole units simply . . . stopped. Fever got them, or heat prostration, or sunstroke, they didn't know what to call it, but fifty of them died.

Sumter's scouts, who were keeping pace with Rawdon's army, were too far away to see what was happening. They were baffled at Rawdon's slow pace. Sumter wrote to Greene: "A party of their horse was at Orangeburg yesterday, their foot a few miles back. Their movements are very singular, if Ninety Six should be their destination. Not only because they marched very slow, but detached parties, some of which it is likely are not to be called in, one of three hundred said to be gone to Nelson's Ferry."

Greene, equally puzzled by his adversary's pace, instructed Sumter to slow him down even further if possible. Nevertheless, Rawdon's snail-like advance continued.

By June 16, Sumter was at Martin's Ferry and Rawdon only twenty miles away, at Cedar Ponds. Sumter just watched, to Greene's irritation. He defended himself by reporting that his foot soldiers were "very troublesome, but I will push them hard." They were now only fifty miles from Ninety Six.

The following day Rawdon camped astride the Ridge, and the next day crawled along between two creeks that flowed northward into the Saluda River. Sumter attacked, was beaten off and his men dispersed. He didn't really mind; his heart hadn't been in the enterprise in the first place. He sent a note to Greene: "I am very sorry that the post at Ninety Six can't be reduced before the approach of the enemy. The raising of the siege is a disagreeable circumstance, but in my opinion it will not prove so disadvantageous as some may think. If you can avoid a defeat, they are in a fair way to lose more than they will gain by saving the garrison."

Greene contemplated his choices. He could attempt an all-out assault. He could turn his back on Ninety Six and attack Rawdon. Or he could simply retreat. An assault seemed his best strategy. He might lose a pitched battle with Rawdon, and a retreat might enable the Loyalists to take back the Back Country.

Pickens and Lee agreed, and so did their officers. The assault would take place the next morning.

The day before the assault, one of Greene's subalterns, David Rush, went to Sleepy Creek to visit Anna and Peter Dorst. He liked Anna, with her direct gaze and forthright manner, and he was always interested in the frequently sensible if overly detailed military advice offered by Peter, but neither was the reason he was there, and Anna was well aware of this. She fed him cakes and strong tea laced with corn whiskey and sent him down to the barn, where the wild child, Maria's Rosena, was so often to be found, if she wasn't in the woods, off on some errand of her own invention.

Ach, she was impossible! Impossible, incorrigible and a delight in every way. Ever since she had come to stay, after her mother had fled to the coast and come back in the company of *that man*, Anna's household had been infested with young men, all of them obsessed with the child. It was not so surprising, she thought. Rosena was slim and slight, brown as an Indian, with the large, expressive, slyly intelligent eyes of a colt; she had a disconcerting habit of standing too close to the young men she talked to, and liked to touch them, a hand on an arm, a shoulder, a quick brush to the cheek, her face only inches from theirs as they conversed, as though she was about to kiss them, which she wasn't . . . It dizzied them and made them confused, which Anna supposed was her purpose, if there was any.

She loved the child for all this activity.

But it was true that more things seemed to amuse her these days.

The Loyalists—Katy's people—were quiescent, even subservient, now that Greene's army was in the vicinity. There was one band, supposedly led by one Cunningham or other, still giving trouble, a marauding force who were well mounted and who split into small, mobile bands all over the Back Country to waylay recruits or supplies headed for the besiegers' camp. Every now and then horses would vanish, or a small building would be set on fire, or someone would be shot by hidden snipers from the woods. But mostly nothing much happened.

Greene encouraged his boys to come around to Peter Dorst's, Anna thought smugly. They could learn something about the countryside there, something of tactics in the Back Country, how the war was fought, for Peter had attained something of an eminence as a commander of men who knew what they were doing.

A commander! A satisfactory word!

Eminent enough that he spent the nights of the siege in his own bed, commuting to war every morning. General Greene didn't seem to mind.

Even the anxiety-inducing fact of her eldest son's picking up a rifle and doing his duty with the local militia couldn't dampen her mood.

It'll be over soon! He'll do his duty, learn a man's ways, survive! David disappeared into the barn and since he didn't re-emerge in the ten minutes Anna watched, she assumed Rosena was there.

It amused her to imagine what was happening. Rosena would stand far too close to him, her breath would be warm and sweet, and he would be dizzy with frantic desire. And then . . . But it was too hot for the slipping of flesh upon flesh, and Anna went inside for a small nip of whiskey herself.

That night Katy lay in bed, drenched in sweat, alone.

They are trying to kill my husband and my sons!

The previous day she had walked all the way to Colonel Mayson's house for news, taking a long, looping path to skirt the town and its besieging army, but the colonel's wife had refused to see her and wouldn't let her in the house. One of Mayson's daughters, taking some pity on her, had come out to say that Mrs. Cruger was refusing to eat, and had become gaunt and anxious, bereft of intelligence or news, not knowing whether her husband lived or died. One of the troopers, the girl said, had cruelly if unthinkingly told her of the ultimatum Greene had sent to her husband, and one sentence had caused her anguish: ". . . Unless you unconditionally surrender . . . you yourself, as commandant of the post of Ninety Six, will be held personally responsible for a fruitless resistance, and for the death of those who will die from sword, bullet and starvation . . . "

On the way home, Katy had taken a path much closer to Ninety Six, drawn by some forlorn wish to catch a glimpse, any glimpse, of Abraham and her sons.

They're in there, without water, with cannonballs raining on them . . . Maybe lying wounded . . . Maybe dead . . .

She heard the thunder of the artillery, but never got within sight of the fort. She was intercepted by a Rebel patrol and turned back, though not unkindly.

He was a countryman with pocked skin and lank hair, his leggings ragged, but he was polite. She thought she knew him, but couldn't recall his name. At the back of his troop she caught sight of Johan Merk, Balthazar's Rebel son, who managed to look both belligerent and sheepish when he saw she'd seen him.

She glared at him.

He is trying to kill my sons!

Well, and what of her other children?

This damned war!

Rosannah . . . Her Conrad Merk was down there somewhere, too, in Camden or Orangeburg, with some army somewhere. At least she knew where Rosannah was, at home with her own family, the most normal of them all. Young Charles . . . God, he was only fifteen! He was running with the Cunningham boys in the woods, the long gun in his hands, already a killer of men. And her baby John, a young man of thirteen, was at home but restless to go . . .

The damned war lasts another year, he'll be gone, she thought grimly.

At least the other girls were home. Kat, and Mary, and Anna. What a comfort!

She turned over. The pool of sweat was clammy on the linen.

How she missed her husband! His solidity, heft, strength, his broad back . . .

In the small hours, she finally cried herself to sleep.

In Savannah, Maria Elizabeth Adolph, deserted by her poor, wretched, murdered husband, rejected by her own brother, bereft, lay naked on her bed. She had left Ninety Six, left her farm, gone back to the coast, to where poor Heinrich had fallen. She knew no one there, but the place drew her anyway. Why not there? Where else was there? She had taken a room with a Loyalist widow. There was no man in the house, nor any man in her life. All the Heinrichs, gone. Heinrich her husband, dead defending a town nobody wanted. Heinrich her son, gone to the wars. Heinrich Strum, he who frightened so many people, he of the drowning eyes, was gone to the fort to be with Cruger, a soldier drawn to a soldier's commander. That Heinrich is the last man I'll ever have, she thought. I'm forty-three and the flesh puddles on the bed when I lie. Nobody wants me.

Gone. All gone.

Heinrich Strum was standing on the parapet of Star Redoubt, facing the attacking trenches and the attackers' sharpshooter's tower, when the general assault began. It was noon on June 18, and he had been there since dawn, waiting. There wasn't a soul in the fort or the village who didn't know the attack was coming.

And so it comes to an end, all the hunger, the thirst, the heat, the noise, the death and the dying, all to end. Rawdon is coming!

He was crouched behind a pile of sandbags spiked together at the top of the rampart. There were gaps in the piles, through which they could fire when necessary. There were two men at each gap, firing and reloading in turn. His companion was Peter Frietz.

All morning they had watched the Rebel muster. Their trenches were so close to the stockade that Heinrich could hear the clattering of metal on metal as the equipment was readied and the artillery moved into new positions.

It will only end with the sound of Rawdon's drums.

At noon sharp, General Greene's zero hour, every Rebel gun opened up at once.

The deep booming of the big guns and the endless yapping of the rifles were accompanied by a deafening cacophony of other sounds—the queer, twisted whistling of grapeshot passing overhead, the nerve-wracking growling of cannonballs, the spiteful whistle of rifle bullets. Cannon shot threw up clouds of red dust inside the ruined village, with its roofless buildings and great scar trenches; a great roiling cloud of acrid smoke passed overhead, obscuring the sun.

But we're beyond panic. We only wait.

It was obvious enough what the Rebels were up to. They would send Lee around to the west, to knock down the palisades there, take Fort Holmes and charge the village. Greene would send his other commander, Richard Campbell, to move up through the trenches, cut through the abattis of Star Fort, enter the big ditch and pull down the sandbags from the parapet.

Soon.

The word was passed down from Cruger and DeLancey: concentrate your shooting on the ends of the lateral trenches, pile up the bodies there, make it difficult for them to pass, make 'em panic. Make every shot count! And don't let 'em take down the sandbags!

Heinrich took a quick peek through the slot in the sandbags. Sound, and plenty of it. The rifle and musket fire was continuous. But no movement.

And then . . . Forty-five minutes after the cannonading began, Rebels boiled out of the trenches and swarmed into the ditch, where they made a furious assault on the abattis, hacking their way through the sharpened logs with axes and great mallets.

The bodies piled up in the ditch. Like ants, the men at the back used the corpses of their comrades as a ladder.

A few feet from Peter, a hook arced overhead on the end of a rope and thunked into a sandbag. Its point set, and whoever was on the other end began to pull. The bag teetered. Peter dropped his rifle, yanked the hook from the bag and threw it back over the parapet. There was a yell from below. A dozen more hooks appeared, some on ropes, some at the end of long poles. Bags were yanked away, tumbling into the ditch.

An order was shouted. Make 'em stop! All fire!

They all stood, rifles propped on the bags, firing into the seething mass of soldiers below. Rebel rifle and musket fire was continuous. A bullet took a man near Heinrich in the head, and he dropped, his gun clattering to the floor. A little further, another man was hit. He staggered backward, toppling to the earth below. Someone took his place immediately. Heinrich peered down after him. Dead men were lying in heaps there, sprawled at odd angles.

Outside, the piles of corpses grew.

On the other side of the fort, Lee's legion hacked their way through the abattis and stormed the Holmes Redoubt, only to find it empty; Cruger had abandoned it, and pulled his men back through the covered trench into the village. Lee turned his attention to the blockhouses there. For him, things seemed to be going well.

Of this, the defenders in Star Redoubt knew nothing.

They fired, and killed, and fired again.

The screaming, the noise of the explosions, was continuous.

And then . . . finally . . . the attack began to falter.

Cruger, who had been watching for just that, opened the sally port at the rear of Star Redoubt and sent two teams of thirty infantrymen swarming through the door. One turned right, the other left, and with their bayonets closed in on opposite flanks of the attackers, already exposed to the fire from above.

The Loyalists used their bayonets like pitchforks; blood ran, men screamed shrilly, the wounded fell or were trampled, the dying crawled into ditches, the line of Rebels wavered and was driven back.

Greene saw his men reeling, falling back, and knew it was over. Rawdon was too close. It had been worth the hazard, but it was definitely over. He had his bugler sound the retreat, the horn cutting easily through the cannonading and the crackle of musketry.

The Rebels pulled back, taking their wounded and dying with them.

The dead they left in the ditch.

Heinrich waited on the rampart as the Loyalist sally parties came back into the fort. He waited for the Rebels to regroup, start the attack again. He waited as Cruger's men stacked the wounded in rows and called the women to tend them. He waited, but there was nothing. The Rebels had had enough.

It's over.

Rawdon was on the Saluda. Sumter was a day away, and in any case his militia, seeing the lay of the land, was evaporating like a morning mist. Marion was somewhere, elsewhere, Greene didn't know where. He'd be caught between Cruger and Rawdon if he didn't pull back.

But he was philosophical. He might be the tactical loser, but he would be the strategic winner: Rawdon would never be able to hold the Back Country together, not any more. The Patriots could fade away into the countryside, and just wait. Time was with them.

Over, yes.

David Rush knew what was coming. He made a dash for Anna's house and headed straight for the barn, where she was waiting. He took her by the ears, like a puppy, and shook her gently. Then he kissed her.

"I'll be back," he said softly, and she smiled, a dazzling smile that he carried with him into Virginia.

That evening, Greene's orders were clear: "the Army will march at five o'clock, by the left, tomorrow morning."

On the ramparts, quiet fell.

Sixteen

The worst were the horsemen, were they not? They always seemed to arrive at a gallop, menacing, violent, filled with rage. They took what they wanted and left only blood, bruises, bitterness. She looked at Anna, found her staring back. *Well, sister, those were the most terrible times of all. It's when we just . . . gave up . . . I even watched him, the one you admired so much, fading like a ghost, till I could see the grinning skull behind the flesh. And where were you, sister?* But Anna still said nothing.

July 1781
Ninety Six, South Carolina

Once again, horsemen appeared abruptly from the woods at the end of the farm road, the narrow track that wound down the creek to join the common road that eventually made its meandering way to Ninety Six. They just seemed to materialize, like djinns, from the shimmering summer heat. One moment the road was empty, the next, there they were, two of them, assorted green tunics dull against the gray-green of the mossy oaks, sitting quietly on their horses, still and menacing, staring at the homestead.

John saw them first. He was thirteen, alert and anxious with his father and brothers gone, and he saw everything first. His face was still bruised from the beatings administered by the last horsemen who'd passed this way two days previously. Had they been Rebels? Who knew these days? No matter. John had seen them first, and had taken the butt end of a musket before they were gone.

Katy had made a poultice of peach leaves and corn meal and wrapped him in boiled mustard leaves till he looked like a shrub, and she laughed grimly. She didn't hate them for what they'd done. You don't hate a tornado; you only resent its evil passing.

The girls she'd sent out the back door to the woods, as she always did when strangers appeared, because strangers always made demands, taking what they could in the name of whatever cause was theirs. These days it didn't seem to matter whose side they were on, or said they were on. If they were Loyal and you refused them anything, your horse, your last crust, your bed, you were denounced as a Rebel and your house very likely put to the torch. If, on the other hand, they were Rebels, to refuse them anything needed for the Just Fight was treachery, and to burn your house down about your ears was righteousness. In either case, the girls had made themselves scarce. Young women, even the children, were best hidden; it seemed that hunger for a young girl overrode any cause or discipline or scruple. The dogs went with them, along the path at the back that wound through the bush to a deep clearing half a mile further. This was their larder now. There were hams up trees, strung from high branches; cabbages and turnips wrapped in cloths and stuffed into clefts and cavities; a milch goat tethered to an old cypress down by the creek; and a few hens in a rough-and-ready pen, a little deeper in the woods. There'd be no more chickens, only eggs, because Katy had killed the last rooster a month before. His idiotic boasting carried too far, the sure sound of betrayal.

The previous horsemen had also appeared silently from the forest. John had seen only two at first. Then two more, then a fifth. They rode up swiftly, their passage stirring the sluggish dust, and clattered to a stop in front of the house where Katy and John stood waiting. The horses were sweating and nervous. The men wore no uniforms, just baggy, brown linen pantaloons stuffed into hide boots and tunics nondescript from dirt and wear. Their leader was lean and unkempt, with whiskers that wrapped under his chin like the strap of a bonnet.

"Mistress Frietz," he said, his tone flat.

Katy said nothing.

"Heard your husband and your brats are in the fort at Ninety-Six," he said. "And with the Sons of Liberty baying at their door. What'll be the outcome, think you?"

Still she said nothing.

"Well, no matter," he said. "The master of the house won't need what he can't get at." He gave a short barking laugh, without humor, and jerked his thumb at two of his men. They dismounted and went into the house. Katy could hear them clomping about, and then they emerged, shaking their heads. The other two went round the back, with the same result.

The front door banged shut, and one of the men turned on it savagely and bashed at it with his musket. The panel shattered. He put the musket down and hauled on the top of the door, against its strap hinges. It tore away and he heaved it off the porch onto the yard, where it kicked up a wavelet of dust.

John gave a yell, and the man turned and hit him sharply on the cheek with the end of his musket, a sound solid and ugly, like a blunt ax into ironwood. The assailant turned to Katy, challenging her to do anything. She stayed rigid, staring at her son.

Then the leader barked his humorless laugh, spat in the boy's direction and they all mounted and galloped off.

Katy picked up her son and took him into the house. The whole episode had taken no more than fifteen minutes.

No, I don't hate them. I don't even know who they are. But I'd cut off their hands, if I could. Wrist on the chopping block, cut it off, fingers, thumb, bones, blood, tendon, sinew . . . All of them, the brayers after liberty and the zealots for the King, let them try to hold a musket with the bones of their forearms, the blood seeping into the earth!

She'd held the scene in her mind as she washed John's bruises.

I'd do it myself, and watch as their lives drained into the earth they despoil . . .

Now here they were again.

A third horseman, this one without his tunic, appeared from the woods and joined the other two. A fourth followed. She watched in apprehension.

She called John to her.

"Out to the woods," she said. "And stay there."

"I won't," he said, stubbornly.

"You must go and warn the girls not to come back to the house," said Katy. "They don't know there's danger. You have to tell them." She wanted him out of the way of another beating—he was just a boy!

John slipped into the house and out the back door as the horsemen applied the rein and urged their mounts into a canter. It seemed to take them hours to get any closer.

She went inside, and watched through a crack around the window opening as they approached. When the horsemen were a few hundred paces away, one of them flung up an arm and pushed his mount into a flat gallop. She flinched. He was yelling at the top of his considerable lungs, yelling something unintelligible that she couldn't make out, but then suddenly it didn't matter what it was because she recognized him, she knew the voice and the form and the gesture, it was her eldest, Peter, whom she hadn't seen for so many months.

"John," she screamed, "John, come back!"

She ran out to the yard just as the boy dismounted and flung himself into her arms, swinging her around joyously. Behind him was young Charles, grinning like an ape, and behind him came the others, at a more sedate pace.

Her husband, Abraham, his once-pudgy face gaunt, one of his ears mashed in some unknown fracas, but still her Abraham.

And at the rear, leaning on the saddle horn, composed and still, was Heinrich Strum. He looked old, much older than she remembered him. He was battle-hardened now, sharper, tougher, with little forgiveness to his expression. Only his eyes seemed the same, piercing, black, assessing. She paused to greet him and he nodded gravely. Heinrich would be good at this business of warfare, she thought, much better than Peter. Peter would rail and fret, and try for revenge, and his temper would lure him into traps. Heinrich would be cold, icy. He was a survivor. There'd be no traps for him.

At that moment, she thought she liked her son better.

On June 19, the Rebel army that surrounded Ninety Six struck their tents. At dawn they began to melt away, and throughout the day the cavalry, infantry and artillery units, together with baggage trains and supply wagons, made their way through a haze of red dust up the Island Ferry Road to the Saluda. Lord Rawdon's relief column was just a short distance away, and now that the siege and their latest assault had failed, they could wait no longer. By dusk, nothing remained except the red slashes in the earth where the rebels had dug in and the tower outside the stockade that their snipers had used, looking forlorn now, purposeless, abandoned.

That night, for the first time in two weeks, the beleaguered population of Ninety Six went down into the ravine unmolested, and there they drank their fill, squealing like children.

And the following day, when Cruger's patrols had found no sign of even a Rebel rear-guard, most of the local men in the fort wanted to go home. Among them were Conrad Merk, who had suffered a minor wound, Peter Frietz and his father, Friedrich Ruppert and the enigmatic Karl Bauer, who said he wanted to return to his family.

Only Heinrich Strum, whose home was a heap of ash and whose wife's grave-marker was already beginning to fade, made no move to leave. He stood with Captain DeLancey, whose volunteers had helped hold the fort, and just waited.

In any case, Cruger forbade them to go.

"You'll stay here until Rawdon comes," he said. "Here you're safe. He'll tell us what's to become of this garrison."

"But my family, my mother!" said Peter Frietz. "I must let them know we're safe!"

Cruger was adamant. "You'll wait for Rawdon," he said.

Later that night, Cruger's patrols returned. They had found a few head of cattle the Rebels had unaccountably overlooked, and the population of the fort feasted on water and roasted beef, and were deliriously drunk on both.

On the morning of June 21st, a smudge of scarlet and a haze of dust appeared at the far edge of the clearcut that separated Ninety Six from the forest. In a while the smudge resolved itself into scarlet tunics and drummers, and the whiffling of the fifes heralded the arrival of the column itself, and the gates to the village were flung open and the thin, dark, saturnine figure of Lord Rawdon entered, astride a black horse. The surviving defenders, dirty and weary, stood to attention, and behind his Lordship clattered the cavalry, and behind them marched two regiments in shabby green osnabrück coats, volunteers from New York and New Jersey under Heinrich's old commander, Coffin, and Heinrich saw his little brother Jacob and his sister Eva's Daniel, Daniel Michler, grinning broadly from under their tricorns.

Behind them were the woolly scarlet coats of the British Regulars, still marching with precision under packs that must have weighed a hundred pounds, in those dreadful uniforms, fit only for a misty Irish spring. There were nearly two thousand men all told, and they filled the plain that the attackers had so recently abandoned. It had taken them fourteen days to reach Ninety Six along the Charlestown Road; not a Rebel had they seen since a brief skirmish at Orangeburg, but the sun had taken as much toll as a regiment of Continentals.

After the huzzahs and the celebrations had been done, and after the supply wagons had drawn up across the village square by the old jail and had distributed sweet potatoes, chocolate and generous dollops of rum, Rawdon drew Cruger and the Loyalist leaders aside.

"As soon as my men are rested I'll be in pursuit of General Greene," he said. "And if it can be done, if he hasn't vanished like smoke in a stiff breeze, I'll catch him."

Despite the size of his army, Rawdon knew he was stretched perilously thin, and knew he had to hold Charlestown until relieved by Cornwallis or Clinton. Nothing he had seen on his march north made him change his mind about abandoning the Back Country and shifting his Loyalist allies to more protected land if he could. Charlestown was all he could be certain of. If, instead, he tried to garrison the whole frontier . . . Charlestown would inevitably fall.

Clearly, he had already decided. He would see if he could catch Greene, though nobody expected him to succeed. Afterward, he would march his troops back down toward the coast and leave the Back Country to its fate. That fate would depend on actions taken elsewhere. The Loyalists would have to choose. Stay, or leave. A seemingly simple choice, but each possibility fraught with anxiety.

Later in the day, as the sun started to veer toward the horizon, taking the steaming heat with it, Rawdon called into the square all the two hundred or so Loyalists who had been in the fort and what families they had with them. He sat on his horse and raised his voice. "I must give up

298 / Marq de Villiers & Sheila Hirtle

Ninety Six," he told his attentive audience. "Colonel Cruger agrees there's no other course. I and my men must go; we have duties elsewhere. But we'll not abandon you, nor forget the good service you have rendered your cause.

"If you choose to stay, and want to hold these works, this fort and this village, I'll leave a party here at Ninety Six to instruct you in military defence. You have good soldiers here, you have proven that, more than a match for any damned Rebel. On the other hand, if you had rather submit to a temporary exile, I'll provide a sufficient escort for your families and goods and send you safely within the British lines. I'll move all the Loyalists in this region out, and take them to the Low Country, where we can protect them, and they can live on the estates of absent Rebels." He looked at them for a while, silent. They shuffled nervously. "I leave you now, to talk it over among yourselves."

He dismissed them and returned to his command tent, set up in the blackened ruins of the former tavern, where Cruger had held his briefings. He looked at Cruger, who looked at John Coffin, standing quietly by, who looked at Heinrich Strum, at ease but alert, on duty outside the doorway. "I want to get the word to everyone in the country. Get your people and their friends, find out what they want to do."

Cruger already knew what they'd have to do. The Loyalists in the fort had listened to Rawdon, but he knew them. He had fought with them and had watched them closely. They were tough in the fibre, he had come to understand that, tough in the fibre and tough in the bone, and they had already shown they were prepared to defend their lives with tenacity and—he admitted to himself—with an appalling ferocity. They would want to stay, but in the end, they'd have to leave. He knew better than Rawdon that civil war still raged in the Back Country. The day Rawdon abandoned Star Fort would be a day of reckoning. Reprisals would be taken, blow for blow, hurt for hurt, death for death. Any man who had worn a King's uniform, no matter for how short a time or for what purpose, noble or base, would be marked. Cruger understood how it worked. Their families wouldn't be safe either. Nor would distant cousins, or friends, or any person some Rebel fancied they knew.

He looked at Strum, standing patiently by the doorway. A man like that would never be safe here again. The same could be said for the others he had watched and fought with. All of them, the Strums and the Frietzes and the Michlers and the Adolphs, the Bauers, the Merks and the Rupperts and all their brethren, the Zanges and the Webers; they would come to see that, for Loyalists, the thought of staying behind was senseless.

Cruger, an honest soldier, felt a sudden, frightening weariness. What could an army do if the whole population was at each other's throats? Defeat or victory in battle was one thing. Armies were disciplined, civilized things—had not his own wife been protected during the late siege by Rebel Continentals, protected by the enemy? But this savage, hidden saturation of hatred, in which women and children were combatants as well as victims, could not be countered by any military means. How many of these people had brothers, sisters, cousins, on the other side, family that they regarded with rage and contempt? Brother traitor! Sister traitor! The fury of personal betrayal drove them, pulled the nooses tighter, thrust the sword arm faster, made the burning brand a greater friend, a dreadful spiral of hatred.

"What do I think they'll do?" he echoed Rawdon, responding at last. "They'll give up everything and go."

"Well, I value your opinion, Colonel," Rawdon said. "But I won't have it said we chased 'em from their homes." He turned to Coffin. "Take as many fellows as you can, go out into the country and explain matters to 'em, find out what they want. If they want to go, tell 'em to report here as soon as possible. Tell 'em," he said, his eyes steady, "that houses'll be found for 'em, places abandoned by departing Whigs, until such time as this war is decided."

Coffin inclined his head, said nothing. He would do as instructed. But he didn't need to look again at Strum. He knew his men. He knew there was no choosing. They would leave their homes. Again.

In the morning, Rawdon took his British Regulars and set off after Greene, across the Saluda and to the Enoree. But Greene had faded into the woods, and Rawdon sent word to Cruger confirming his decision to abandon Ninety Six and instructing him to take his army and whomever might accompany them and go eastward, south of the Edisto, while he himself passed down just south of the Saluda. By June 29, Rawdon had turned toward Charlestown.

Those who rode out into the countryside found what they'd expected to find. It was June, well into the growing season, and the fields should have been in full flower, orderly, fruit on the trees and many crops ready for harvest. Instead, the land looked weary, leached, used up. Roads were eerily empty; orchards and fields were tangled and overgrown with weeds and wild shrubs. The countryside seemed lifeless and the farms deserted. Families were living in the woods, wild as field mice and twice as timid, but when they saw who it was—that it wasn't just one more band of predators—they didn't hesitate. They were ready to go. They were weary of war and of worry, weary of taking to the woods every time they saw more than two horsemen. They knew they'd have to seek some other refuge, though they knew not where. Among the planters and their kin? They doubted it. They'd known for years of the disdain felt by Charlestown and the lowlands for anyone from the Back Country, *for the crackers*, no matter how Loyal.

Katy and Abraham sat on the bare bed, she holding his hands pressed to her lap. Heinrich Strum was outside with her sons, tactfully out of earshot. Heinrich was propped against a tree, chewing a grass stalk, one long leg straight out in front of him, the other knee drawn up. Peter sat nearby with Charles. John was pacing restlessly in the yard. The girls sat in a neat row on the porch, quiet for once. Katy looked at Abraham. His unshaven face was lined, his body, once so firmly fleshed, looked crumpled and badly used.

He would try to persuade her to leave, she knew that, to tell her stories she already knew, of friends dead and dying, of stray bullets flying through windows to kill women at their cookpots, of children lost . . . But it wasn't necessary. She knew it was impossible to stay. She knew so much better than he the mood of the countryside. She had been living with it for years, so much more closely than he. For a moment, she felt a stab of bitterness. He was a man, with other men. They rode and fought together, a tightly knit band of brothers, with codes of honor and conduct. How little they knew of the real war of the Back Country, a war of treachery and secret atrocity! But as she felt it, she knew it was unfair. He had been at home long enough to know what he had to know. He'd never shirked his duty, had never wavered in his allegiance, and his loyalty had used up his life and here he was, a tired old man.

We're both old. I'm fifty-one, and already waiting for the red earth to thud down on my coffin!

She thought of Maria Elizabeth, her dear old friend, her brother's wife. A widow, her husband dead in the stinking charnelhouse of besieged Savannah. My brother Heinie, killed, and for what? To hold Savannah for a while, until the great men decide they've had enough. His widow trailed back home, only to be rejected, spurned, turned away, and by her own brother . . . Oh, brave Peter, to turn his Patriotic beliefs against a newly widowed sister! And young Henry, Maria's son? Gone, no one knew where, fighting, no one knew where, for whom, no one knew. Well, perhaps he was a prisoner or perhaps he was dead, no one knew that either but Henry, God himself and with luck, General Cornwallis. Doubly, triply alone was Maria: herself a refugee in Savannah, only her eldest child, Katherina, with her, and her youngest, Rosena, gone to live with the Dorsts. Only seventeen! A wild child, skittish as a deer, rejecting everything her poor, dead father stood for, lost and gone forever. Living with Anna . . . Anna! At whose house Rebel soldiers congregated, nests of traitors and robbers. How had it happened? And what happened to the middle child, Elizabeth? Gone! Missing. Who knew where?

"Of course we'll go," she said, in answer to the unspoken question.

"To Charlestown?"

"To wherever your Lord Rawdon permits," she said. She kissed his hands, put them back in her lap.

"They say there are houses there for the taking. Not in the town, but along the coast. Houses of Whigs long gone to the army, unable to return after the fall of Charlestown, good houses . . ." His voice trailed off, but not before she heard its plaintive note, its vain hope that wish be fact.

And so it continues, she thought. And after Charlestown falls again and the Whigs come back, thirsting for revenge? Off again, off again? Where to? The Islands? What is to prevent the French from taking the Islands, as the tired old English King withdraws to his tired old homeland? Where, then? Perhaps we'll end up in New Scotland after all. Stumpelberg! Dear God! She felt an immense weariness. Did they really have to start over? Again? She pressed Abraham's hand, but she said none of this. What use would it be, to complain? He had his own sorrows.

After a while, they stood up and he went outside. In a few minutes the men mounted and rode out. There were dozens, hundreds more settlers to instruct, to help, to persuade to abandon the homes they had come so far to find.

Within days the whole countryside was emptying, people squeezed like droplets from a wrung cloth, running in rivulets down to Ninety Six. From the remaining houses or barns on what used to be farms, from the cabins or sheds on isolated creeks, from the villages, from the churches and stores and meeting halls, they came. The roads filled up with carts and wheeled contrivances for baggage, often with men, and sometimes women, between the shafts in place of horses or oxen, because the horses had been stolen and the oxen long ago used up for food. Most everyone walked, women suckling infants, carrying babies, leading small children. They dragged behind them their pathetic piles of possessions, what little hadn't been broken for firewood or carried off by some marauding band. Heinrich sat on his horse numbly watching the bitter procession pass, the residue of a deadly civil war.

Well, and there were Rebel redoubts, to be sure, Whig villages, Patriotic hamlets, Rebel farms. Not everyone left. At many a gate they stood silent, watching the exodus, too uncertain of the future to feel any joy at the fall of their enemies. From Honea Path the Loyalists came, and Ware Shoals, from Hickory Tavern and Sleepy Creek, from Hard Labour Creek and Cuffeetown. And as they moved down and across the Saluda, roving bands of renegade Rebels hunted and cut them off, killing the men and dragging the women away, later to be used, killed and discarded. These were men themselves displaced by the ravages of war and by atrocities committed by the same Loyalists they now watched departing, Whigs whose own settlements had been burned and destroyed. True, they were joined by others, "those habitual plunderers who for so long had disgraced the American cause," as General Greene had said in one of his voluminous dispatches, bands of thieves and killers, people who would, in less lawless times, have been called outlaws, but many of them were as much victims as those they preyed on.

Cruger himself was not without his share of blame. After the siege was lifted, he let his regulars, joined by some of the South Carolinians including the Merks and Peter Frietz, exercise their evil temper on the Whig settlement called Long Canes. This destruction of peaceful homes only made matters worse; the word spread through the Patriotic farmsteads and hamlets that orders had been issued to lay the whole country waste. Smoking dwellings stimulated the thirst for vengeance, and they attacked the straggling columns all the more venomously.

And so more died, Whig and Loyalist both, out of fear and anger and because killing seemed the only thing left to do.

Peter Dorst told Anna he'd heard that General Greene had been horrified by the brutality of the civil war between the Whigs and the Loyalists in the Back Country. David Rush, to help ingratiate himself with Peter, had shown him a fragment of a dispatch Greene had sent back to General Washington just before departing hurriedly from Ninety Six. "I lament the confusion and inhumanity which takes place," wrote Greene, who was at heart a gentle man, a Quaker's son who had never wanted to be a soldier. (In truth, he seemed to spend as much time at his writing desk as at the front.) "I lament the daily scenes of the most horrid plundering and murder, which can only be accounted for by the great length to which personal animosities are carried, and the want of civil authority."

Personal! Anna thought when he recounted it to her in a tone half disdainful, half admiring. *Of course it's personal! None of this would have happened had they not become mired in treachery. If only we'd been united . . .* She thought of her sister, and a wave of sorrow tinged with anger washed over her. *Katy! Katy! It could have been so different! But we're entitled to our revenge for what has been done.*

There was a thunderstorm that afternoon. It sounded like a roll of drums which sounded like the rattle of muskets which sounded like the clatter of small pebbles on the lid of a coffin.

Adam Bauer had refused to leave his home. "No," he said, stubborn to the end, "no, I'll not be driven off. I'm a Loyal subject and not a Rebel, but I'm a citizen, too, and my land is my land." His wife, Katherine, pleaded with him, but he wouldn't listen, and in the end she clambered into the cart that Karl had waiting for her, and left without a backward look, feeling a widow before her time, an angry widow—that old fool! That afternoon, after Cruger's agents had departed, a band of Rebels came out of the woods and hauled old Adam from his house. They strung him to a tree and fed him water and apple mash to make him shit, and used him for sport, cutting him about the face with their swords until he bled like a pig and could no longer see with the blood streaming down his face, across his chest. They took what was left of his livestock, they burned what was left of his wheat and his feed crops, and then they returned and sat around the tree, drinking and taunting him. He spent the night strung up like a chicken, in pain, wondering what had happened to his family. Where were Katherine and young Karl? On their way to the coast, there to live in some grand mansion, some house stolen from someone else's neighbor? He felt bitter, and then he felt remorse for being bitter, and after that he felt nothing very much but great pain, and fear.

Rawdon had departed on the afternoon of Friday, June 29, leaving the remainder of his corps at Ninety Six under the command of the priggish Lieutenant Colonel Doyle, a haughty personage with an irritating braying laugh, which accompanied most of his more outrageous orders.

It was Doyle who told Cruger to break up the fort.

"Demolish it," he said. "Take it apart, piece by piece. Hehheh, heh heh heh! Nothing left, what, not at all, heh heh! Then you yourself take these wretched people down to Charlestown, heh!"

"Sir, I'd be better served by going . . ."

"No, not at all, we've promised his Lordship they will get there safely, and get there they will, you'll see to that! Hehheh hehheh!"

Early on the morning of July 10, the cortege abandoned Ninety Six and began its trudge down to the coast. Cruger, with his battalion of New Yorkers and New Jersey Volunteers intermingled with Carolina volunteers and the men of DeLancey's Brigade, led the van of the exodus. In the middle, the shepherds were to be Colonel King and his regiment, marching alongside the Loyalist families and their cattle, horses and loaded wagons. Doyle brought up the rear.

As they moved slowly toward the Little Saluda, a special detail began setting fire to everything that had remained after the wreckage of the siege. First the church, which went up like a pyre, then the tavern, the blacksmith shop and the few houses disappeared in flame and smoke. Three men peeled off and went into the jail, where they set fire to the rafters. The building flared fiercely for a few moments, and then it suddenly collapsed. A soft pall of black smoke and ash began falling gently over the mortally wounded village.

Within weeks, Heinrich thought, no one will remember what happened here. The cries of the wounded and the dying will fade, the blood will seep into the earth, the weeds will fill the hollows where we lay, burrowing into the ground, waiting for the ball that breaks the bone, the shattering pain . . . The ash will cover everything, the ash and the grass, and then a farmer will come, and his crops will know nothing of blood. The pain . . . the pain will be ours alone, will have left with us.

Cruger's unsoldierly thoughts were similar. There'd been enough groaning and lamentation, he thought, to overpopulate the fourth circle of Hell itself.

The procession wound down out of the hills into the Fall Zone, and from there stumbled into what seemed to consist mostly of burning sand, stunted, scrubby pines and sharp grasses that tore at the clothing. In the hills it had been hot, but at least the air was clean and the streams flowing; here, until the flat plain began to merge imperceptibly into the muck and swamp between Orangeburg and Charlestown, there was only the heat, which struck like a blow, and burned everything it touched; many of the emigrants had nothing on their feet except their own tough skin bound with rags, and Cruger had them travel as much by night as he could, despite his anxiety about the Rebels and his need for haste; he could only push them so far, so fast.

On the fourth night's march, two troops of Rebels under LeRoy and Samuel Hammond suddenly attacked from the rear, as much to their own surprise as to Doyle's, who had been capably bringing up that very rear. The Hammond troops had been at the siege at Ninety Six; they'd been sent west and northwest to protect Greene's flanks from Tory harassment when the General retreated, but after a while they turned again, and from the hills they moved south and east in the direction of the Congaree. It was in the lee of the hills that they stumbled on the retreating Doyle. A few shots were fired, but they mostly missed, for it was dark and the troops spooked by the unexpected combat. A couple of baggage wagons fell behind and were captured, and their troopers with them.

A few days later, when the refugee train was almost at Orangeburg, another Rebel force under one Captain Mike Watson attacked the convoy. Cruger was ready and the attack was beaten off, the attackers driven into the swamps, where Watson was killed. It was a small engagement, of no great consequence for the war, or even for the convoy. But it was catastrophic for a family other than Watson's, for a stray bullet took Georg Schildnacht Sr. in the throat while he was on patrol with his unit, and he died that night in the arms of his wife Katharina.

Late that evening, two horsemen emerged silently from the woods and asked for Karl Bauer. No one knew them and they refused to say who they were. They huddled with Bauer for twenty minutes or so, then slipped away and rode back into the forest. Not long afterward, another horse vanished into the woods. The two men had been Rebels, but they were Rebels who had little stomach for cruel play with helpless old men, and someone had told them where the convoy would be found, and they had come looking for Adam Bauer's son. And so Karl was going back to Ninety Six, through Rebel-held territory, to fetch his father, if he could.

Of this, his mother knew nothing. She stayed with the cart, and thought her bitter, angry thoughts.

Near Orangeburg, the convoy halted while Cruger's scouts probed the route to Dorchester and then Charlestown. The once-again "wretched Palatines" clung together near the middle of the immense cavalcade, exhausted, weak with the long effort, the meager rations, many of them drained with fever and illness. Barbara Ruppert, six months pregnant, looked deadly ill. Near her were the Strums, Heinrich and Jacob, Eva and her Daniel, the Frietzes, Juliana Zange with her own children and a gaggle of orphaned nephews and nieces, Conrad Merk and his sister Anna Maria Mehl, "drove off," as she said grimly, "by them Rebels without any thing, without any necessaries save the cloathing on our backs." And the other Merk sisters, Rosina Gable and Elizabetha Dorris. Lorentz Merk was there, riding mostly by himself, and some of the Bauers, including Alizabetha and the boy Philip, who had been named after the now-Rebel hero, Philip Zimmermann . . . Only Adam Bauer was missing, and because of him his son Karl.

Cruger, patrolling restlessly up and down the convoy, noticed that one of the carts had been dragged off the road to the side, where it sat like a marooned ship aground on a shoal. He sent a militiaman to find out why it had been cut out of the herd, in a manner of speaking, and after a while he came back, his face expressionless.

"Well?" asked Cruger.

"It's Georg Weber's wife Mary," the trooper said. "It's her wagon."

"Well?" asked Cruger again.

"Georg is in Charlestown with the South Carolina Royalists," the trooper said.

Cruger was patient, accustomed by now to the elliptical nature of Back Country storytelling.

"Well?" he said.

"Well, Georg is the only Weber left. His father died in '76. His mother is dead. Brother Thomas was killed in Royal service. Brother Henry is no one knows where, gone to the Indian Nation, they say. Brother Friedrich is blind, but he is with his sister Suzanne, who is with the Rebels in Ninety Six. She married a Rebel, see. And here is Mary, Georg's wife, with her children."

"But why is the cart cut out in the way it is?"

"Mary and Georg had twelve children. One is taken by a Rebel band.

Young John Georg is over yonder, with the Bauers. Another is here somewhere. Nine were in the wagon with their mother, and the fever took
them. Two have been buried. Seven remain."

"Ah!" said Cruger, finally understanding. "The fever! What fever?"

"Some say one thing, others another. They say one of the little bodies
was yellow but whether it signified yellow fever I couldn't say. It could be
just country fever again. There are others who have it."

Cruger rode away. Fever! There was an implacable enemy! A practical
man, he lumped all fevers in his mind together under his private label of
Swamp Fever. There was always more of it around these lowlands. There
was the smell of decay to the whole place . . .

The following day, before he urged the convoy onward once more,
Cruger checked with Heinrich on the fate of the remaining Weber children. One more had died before sundown, the youngest, and two more in
the night, and there were three small new graves in a raised place between
patches of scrub. The others were lying in a row on scraps of this and that,
a little like firewood waiting to be seasoned, but they were all alive and
the fever had broken and Mary Elizabeth Barbara Doul Weber was with
them, exhausted and frightened, but she would go on. Cruger shook his
head. Just six children out of twelve to take to her waiting husband! He
was a soldier and used to death, but the death of children depressed him
with its senselessness and cruelty.

Just outside Dorchester, Barbara Ruppert stumbled heavily and fell. This
time she found it impossible to get up. She had fallen before, several
times—she was six months pregnant and the road was rough and the pace
over-brisk for her and she had no place to ride.

Nevertheless, she had set out from Ninety Six in good spirits. She had
her husband with her, for one thing. Friedrich had returned from his regiment, just in time to find his home abandoned and his wife a refugee—in
time, indeed, to become a refugee with her. Her brothers were there, too,
not only Jacob Strum, but Heinrich, and her husband's brother Christoph.
And other family. Yes, she was surrounded by good people.

She had first fallen just a few days out of Ninety Six; something had broken inside her, and she had walked on in pain. After that, Friedrich carried

the youngest, Barbara, who was only three, and Uncle Christoph took the six-year-old, Catherine, and kept her with him. And then, coming down off the Piedmont, she had been forced to rest, until the convoy inexorably moved without her and she had hurried to catch up. Again, she fell.

And again, for the third time, or the fourth, she had lost count. It was a few days outside Dorchester in the swamp country. She stumbled over a log buried and half submerged, and cut her ankle, falling into the stagnant water, as warm as if it had come from a kettle. Her ankle bled copiously for a while, and after some hours it swelled up and turned an ugly blue. She walked on, there was nothing else to do. After a day, the fever and the swelling and the burning moved into her body and she cried, because she knew it would attack the unborn child and because she was afraid, but she still walked on. By the time they came in sight of Dorchester, she was feverish everywhere and could barely stand; Friedrich had abandoned the baby, Barbara, to Eva Michler's care and was supporting her, the two of them locked together in a way that would have been warming had she not felt so wretched, and then, just outside the town, she fell despite her husband's arm, and this time she couldn't get up.

Friedrich carried her to the side of the path as the convoy flowed on inexorably around them; the leviathan could not stop, it was too big, there were too many people, there was no way of making it stop even had there been anyone to demand it; and she cried as she saw her children and her friends and her sisters borne along in the crowd; and her husband sat on the grass with her as she shivered and cried, and after a while she stopped shivering and burned with the fever, but that too passed and she lay still, until all at once she shrieked, and the veins in her neck stood out like cords with the effort of her struggle, and then she came suddenly to the end of her life, and died in her husband's miserable arms. Friedrich sat there with his dead wife until Daniel Michler and Peter Frietz came back to look for him. The convoy had halted and Cruger was preparing to depart for duties elsewhere, and they had gone looking for Barbara and her man. At first, Friedrich refused to let her go, but then they helped him dig a shallow grave and find a marker, so he would know where it was in times to come, when the war was over and he could return to say his farewells and the proper prayers for the dead. And that night he sat on the ground, with his brother on one side and his daughters on the other, and he wept bitter tears for the child she had been, for the woman she had been, and the wife, and tears for the endless, endless struggle that had taken her from him. One more dead, among so many.

The van of the ragged cavalcade finally reached a point no more than twenty miles from British-held Charlestown; Cruger halted where the Eutaw Springs road branched off from the Charlestown road, and he himself stayed there for two days, urging the straggling Loyalists to hurry. But they were close enough to Charlestown that he had no further fear for their safety, and he felt free to leave them under the protection of their own mounted men.

He assembled a company of militiamen, Heinrich Strum among them. "You should be safe now," he said. "But continue to keep a sharp eye for Rebel bands."

"They're this close to Charlestown?" someone asked.

"There's nowhere they're not," said Cruger. "Now, it falls to you to protect the vulnerable. Doyle will go straight to Charlestown with messages from Rawdon. I have other duties. Look to your flanks and mind your rearguard!"

"I always do," Heinrich said to himself, and saluted as Cruger whirled his horse and took himself off. He looked after him with affection. If only the British employed more American soldiers like Cruger, he thought, we wouldn't be losing.

There was no peace in the Low Country either.

Georg Schildnacht, who had fought with Dawkins and survived Camden, took a furlough from his regiment and rode up from Charlestown to meet his mother and father, only to find his mother alone, grieving. Katharina, who was called Caty, was only forty-five, but she looked ninety.

"*Ich werde dorthin zurückgehen, nach Hause,*" she said.

"They'll kill you too," said Georg despairingly.

"So much the better," she said.

The Merk sisters, Rosina Gabel, Elizabetha Dorris and Anna Maria Mehl, with their various broods were assigned a house belonging to a Whig of the Low Country, now fighting with some Rebel band somewhere in the interior. There were a dozen other women with them, from several families; they were not to have the luxury of a home to themselves. Still, they were told they could consider it theirs until the war was over, for themselves and the others and the children. It was a long, low structure with a cool verandah and a row of sycamore trees leading to the gate.

But the gate was barred, and when one of them tried to force it, a musket ball whistled overhead. Three men appeared, all armed.

"We were told we could stay here," Rosina said.

"Well, you can't," one of the men replied.

"What about the children?" she asked, in anguish.

"Be gone or be dead," the man said without passion.

Eva and Daniel Michler were in a group assigned the farm of a local planter killed at Camden, and whose sons even now were mustering to meet Rawdon or whatever British they could find. It was a fine farm for a fine family; Daniel was well regarded by the quartermasters in Charlestown, and they had their sons, Peter, Daniel junior, Jacob and William with them. When they got there, they found the house a smoking ruin, the fields burned and the slaves fled into the swamps. All the animals had been slaughtered in their pens and the buildings razed; the air was thick with the smell of roasted meat. There was a corpse in the yard, turning black in the heat; flies were buzzing around the nostrils and boiling out of the open mouth.

The Frietzes were among a group who went to a mansion that looked down a stretch of the Ashley, as they had been instructed. The house had been looted and the furniture smashed. It seemed like a regiment of men had defecated on the floor of the front room, the one that looked across the lawn to the placid river flowing beyond. The stench brought on waves of sickening memories: the black hole of the Indiaman on the Thames, despairing nights on Whitechapel Common, the slums of London . . .

I can't stay here! It's filled with furious ghosts!

Katy felt an unreasoning terror, and refused to remain another hour, another minute.

Abraham agreed.

"We can't defend this place," he said. "Any passing band can see us, and we're helpless."

So the family straggled back to the cavalcade, which, despite the brusque orders of British regulars sent from Charlestown, was only inching toward the town. There they met up again with Rosannah and Conrad, trailing their children forlornly behind them, bedraggled little ducklings fit only for plucking. The Merks, too, had found their refuge a mockery; the house they had been assigned was filled with a desperate woman and a brood of children, seemingly dozens, orphans she had picked up along the way, and there was no room for more. Conrad, in a fit of spite, set fire to the barn on the way out, but didn't have the heart to drive out the squatting tenants and destroy the house. So they left it there, the low, solid home of a wealthy merchant, who was no doubt sitting out the war safely somewhere in Europe.

So it was all lies. Lies, treachery and deceit. There was nowhere to go. A few did wedge themselves into Whig houses, occupied or not; some the fevers took; some, like Caty Schildnacht, turned back home, choosing now to believe another lie, that they would be graciously received (and, indeed, some were; the Rebel Colonel Pickens, a gentleman to the core, protected them where he could, and persuaded others, by dint of heroic speechifying, to turn the other cheek). A lucky few found lodgings in town, mostly by agreeing to do menial work for the remaining gentlefolk of Charlestown, and some found, by chance, a place in one of the big houses requisitioned by the army. But most wound up, disconsolate, ill, hungry, in the shantytown that had been formed by their predecessors among the dispossessed, Loyalist refugees from the carnage of Camden. They called it—and why not?—Rawdontown, a name of betrayal.

Ah, but the noble Lord had seemed so sincere up there on his black horse! How his eyes had shone as he talked of rescue! Of winning the war and of coming home!

Rawdontown seemed almost a full city, perched like a sad beggar just outside the gates of Charlestown between the Cooper and Ashley rivers. The Charlestown gentry looked down on them, which surprised none of them, for Charlestown people didn't like anybody but themselves, not really. In particular, they despised anybody who wasn't High Church, and the Back Country people were mostly Lutherans and Baptists and New Lights and Presbyterians, and while Charlestown didn't mind them fighting on their behalf, when they weren't fighting, why, they should keep their distance. So Charlestown was the unpromised land, but there was nowhere else to go. The huts of Rawdontown, so-called, were made of rubbish and refuse—scraps of canvas, torn fish nets stuffed with canes, smashed barrels, broken wagons, driftwood, wrecked boats, sapling trunks, leaves, anything.

Here they lived in squalor and poverty, dependent on the parsimonious charity of the quartermasters. Here they ate, sometimes, and starved, sometimes, and died, often. Here they brooded, bending their minds to the Whigs they supposed were now enjoying peace and plenty on their farms in Old Ninety Six.

On *their* land.

Misery breeds anger, and anger breeds revenge. And so the cycle continued.

How many died on this terrible exodus from Ninety Six, and in the camps thereafter? No one knew. Maybe a hundred, maybe a thousand. Almost surely more like a thousand than a hundred. They died of fever and of hunger and at the hands of their enemies. Some of them even died at the hands of family, their own families, whose spirit had been sapped and who drowned their rage in rage, their grief in more rage. And some of them surely died from hearts that were just stretched too thin, stretched until they couldn't take the pain, not any more.

Katy thought of the dead. *The children and the mothers, the soldiers and their wives, the Rebels and those of us who still remember the bounty of the King. Well, we'll all be dead, in any case, soon enough.* She wondered if Anna ever thought of the dead, as she did.

They had been in Rawdontown a week when two horsemen arrived, their beasts lathery with sweat, snorting more from exhaustion than from spirit. Karl Bauer was on the lead horse, as lathery and leathery as his mount, exhausted but held together by grit and gristle. On the other horse, his head wrapped in filthy cloths, his jerkin torn and bloody, but grinning like a maniac and as bombastic as a British general on a parade ground, was old Adam, his father.

They dismounted and Adam's legs gave way, pitching him to the ground. He never stopped grinning, though, all the way down and afterward as he sat there, rubbing his hip where the hard ground had assaulted him.

Karl went to fetch his mother and she returned full of furious garrulity, clutching a sheet that an arrogant British paymaster had given her the week before, with its single, stark notation: "Charles Bowers, thought dead." *And what of Adam*, she thought now, staring at her man grinning up at her from the dust. *Adam Bowers, thought demented?* At first she wanted to kick her son and her husband, then just her husband, but then she leaned down to the ground where Adam was sitting and took him by the cheek, nipping his cheek in thumb and forefinger as if she were testing cloth, shaking him back and forth till he yelped. Then she fell on his shoulder and started to cry. Adam, the old fool, took her in his arms and they fell backward, toppling into the dust. His grin became a laugh, then, laughter at her and himself and at the great folly of his kind, and then he got up and went with her into a tent and was not seen again that night.

Seventeen

How can I tell her? How can one speak of the death of a child, even across the gulf of the years? As though it were one more death, among so many? For the first time, she swung her body on the bench so she was facing her sister. She stared at Anna's face. There was a mole on her cheek, with a bristly hair growing from it. Her mouth was pursed. Her skin was the color of parchment; it looked rough, but she knew it would have that startling softness of old age. *Well, we are old, after all.* She sighed, attracting Anna's attention. *It was after that death that I finally—and not before time!—learned to substitute endurance for hope.*

September 1782
James Island, South Carolina

Heinrich Strum had no difficulty insinuating himself into Charlestown. As a precaution, he had asked Jacob's wife, *the Henn woman* as he called her to himself, for some names he could use if he needed them. She had come down with the rest of them in the exodus, but she was, after all, a camp follower of Charlestown society, and shared some of Charlestown's disdain for the denizens of Ninety Six and the Back Country, her relatives

316 / *Marq de Villiers & Sheila Hirtle*

and in-laws among them. She was, he thought, a woman who needed very high candlepower to come to life, a woman who wilted in the flickering glow of cheap tallow. Still, she was somewhat in awe of her husband's big brother, whose stare intimidated her, and she readily poured out all and more of what he wanted. She certainly knew of Colonel Nisbet Balfour, the purple-faced pomposity whom Cornwallis, in the absence of Rawdon, had entrusted with the protection of the city. And she knew where he was to be found, in an old mansion overlooking the harbor and the low islands that bracketed it, and she knew enough of the social ciphers that would unlock access. All in all, she proved quite useful, and he resolved not to dislike her so much.

There were mounted sentries at the "Charlestown gates," as the two crumbling, tabby columns were laughably called. The sentries made little serious effort to stop him, not after he managed to mention Cruger, Rawdon and Nisbet Balfour all in one breath; his battle-stained tunic and butter-smooth, Cherokee knee-leggings, polished by months of horseback, bespoke his own history, and so did the hard look he gave them when they hesitated for even a few seconds.

Well, so I don't really know them. Or I know them only as an enlisted man knows his commanders. But these soft-bellied sentries are too stupid to under-stand that.

"I've fought with 'em," Heinrich said, ambiguously if accurately enough. "Rawdon and Cruger and Cunningham and Cotton, I've fought with 'em all. Cruger was the best . . ."

"Well, he ain't here. None of 'ems here 'ceptin' Balfour, an' it'd be well not to trouble his highness Balfour right now. He's troubling himself whether to hang Mr. Hayne or no. He'll hang for sartin, and then it is that the Whigs'll get mad for sure."

Heinrich spent most of the day in the hands of pen-pushers and secretaries, trying to find who had authority to loosen supplies to feed the newly arrived refugees from Ninety Six. For a man of his nature it was a particularly irritating day, and more than once he wanted to pick up some little army toady by his breeches and shake some needed permission or paper from him. At length, he had what he wanted, and progressed to the commissary stores opposite Government Wharf on the Cooper River, only to find that the insufferable Doyle had done his duty and had been there before him, and that a supply train was even then being diverted from its passage to Orangeburg to feed the new arrivals. So the poor folk from Ninety Six, those who had arrived in Rawdontown and were now waiting for some word from someone, anyone, as to what they might do or what might be done to them, would at least be fed. It was at the quartermaster's that he heard about Colonel Samuel Campbell and the militia out on James Island.

It was several more days before he would free himself from supervision duties to make his way again into town. The sentries were different this time, but they stood in his way as little as the earlier set had. "I'm on my way to see Colonel Campbell on James Island," he said curtly. "Let me pass." And they did.

From the quartermaster's he rode a supply boat to the island. Last time he'd been there was with Prevost and Maitland, pulling back from Savannah. *So many battles ago!*

Heinrich had heard good things about Campbell. An American born in North Carolina, he seemed to have an affinity for leading other Americans that the British regulars lacked, blinded as they were by their High Church snobbishness and an assumption about colonial intelligence that was entirely misleading. Campbell had been a merchant in Wilmington, and had been, as he put it, "adverse to Militia and Rebels before the Moore's Creek battle" in February 1776. He refused to serve against the British, but took the Oath of Allegiance and paid a sum to provide a substitute for himself. Early in 1781, however, he joined Colonel Craig at Wilmington and was appointed Captain of Militia. He was later bumped up to Colonel by General Leslie when Wilmington was evacuated, and was appointed to lead the James Island garrison.

That evening, Heinrich was summoned into Campbell's presence, and was interrogated by that incredulous soldier on the details of the events at Ninety Six, the superior ability of John Harris Cruger, the lofty certainties of Rawdon, the rotund courtesies of General Greene and the appalling events of the exodus.

"Are you reporting for duty, Strum?" asked Campbell.

"Sir."

"Are there any others like you?"

"Yes sir, many. From the Ninety Six Brigade, Stevens Creek militia."

"What in the devil is that?"

"Major Ferguson, Sir. Colonel John Cotton. Also Captain John Cotton and Captain Henry Rudolph. I was with Rudolph. My brother Jacob was with Captain Cotton."

"Were there others?"

"Many, all good men. Many, many, many hardy men, fighters all."

"Well," sighed Campbell, "we'll have need of 'em yet. I believe old Balfour will hang Colonel Hayne tomorrow, and all the Rebels in the country will redouble their violence. Ah well . . . We're loyal to the British. I only wish all the British were as loyal to us. Balfour merely harms our cause by his pig-headedness. Do you agree?" he asked sharply.

"I? I agree? I only care to go home," said Heinrich.

By the evening he was back at Rawdontown. He once again had duties to perform, and so did all the men he had sold to Campbell, though the nature of those duties was obscure; they had something to do with preserving James Island from some unspecified invasion, whether by French or Rebel vessels was unclear, and a further unspecified role in defending the town, should it ever need defending, though if it ever did, doubtless the war would be more or less lost. Maybe it was Balfour they were to defend it against. At least, though, they would get paid for their duties, and not be dependent on quartermaster arbitrariness or disdainful Charlestown charity. And he urged as many of the Palatine refugees as he could to make their way to James Island too. There they could camp in relative comfort until it was safe to go home. There'd be preachers there, and surgeons. Pedagogues. All the accouterments of civilization.

In the morning, he called a muster of the men from Ninety Six. Himself, now a captain, courtesy of Colonel Sam. The Rupperts, Friedrich and Christoph, Christoph a lieutenant. Adam Bauer and his son Karl. The Frietzes, Abraham and his sons. Lorentz and Conrad Merk. Georg Weber Jr. The Weber boys. Christian Zange and Johannes Zwilling. And with Cotton, more good men, Daniel Michler among them.

In the afternoon, they moved with their families, leaving behind the fever-ridden, stinking shantytown for the equally fever-ridden and sultry swamps of James Island, south of the Charlestown harbor.

Three more children died on the way, to be buried on the island later.

One of them was Katy's son Charles. He was sixteen.

She was numb, numb, numb.

She'd watched as the fever invaded him and shook him to pieces from the inside.

It pushed the sweat out through his pores. It pushed out the yellow bile, and the stink, everything putrid, until his skin took on a ghastly ocher sheen, and he died quivering and shaking, without saying a word or uttering a sound.

They buried him in the sandy soil of James Island, along with the two other children the fever had taken. She watched, stricken, as the pathetic boxes were lowered into the ground. Across from her were Peter and Nick and little Mary, young John being on duty this day. Heinrich Strum was there, too, come to help her bury her boy.

Strum's face was composed, his eyes steady. She couldn't tell what he was thinking. She studied him carefully. How could he get so used to death? He had only two children left, she knew. Six children, dead. Two wives, murdered. Father and mother, dead. Sister, dead. But Maria had told her about Heinrich, and the brief comfort they had given each other there in the deep woods, in their anguish. He was human, then.

As the soil chunked down on the small coffins, the other mothers started to howl, and Katy retreated into her numbness.

Strum felt . . . nothing. He had enfolded death. It felt . . . normal.

As the numbers swelled at the James Island garrison, Colonel John Hamilton, appointed by the High Command as an inspector of refugees, set up a system of militia quartermasters, intermediaries between the army and the refugees themselves. In their own good time, the quartermasters turned from their eternal squabbling and reluctantly began disgorging supplies. The refugees, only a few of whom were in the militias, were organized into groups; each group received tents and then, as their numbers swelled, boards, scantling, shingles and nails. Christoph Ruppert organized the Ninety Six refugees into work parties to construct more permanent shelters, huts and small cabins. The paymaster of militia provided cooking supplies, casks, cloth and clothing. As the numbers kept swelling, the Ninety

Six contingent was split between John's and James islands; then a few were billeted in Gadsden's house and another house on Church Street in Charlestown. Those few who could afford to rented better accommodation in town. A school was organized for the children. Classes began in November for fourteen boys and fourteen girls; by May, there were thirty-nine boys and twenty-one girls.

Daniel Michler was a member of the School Committee, a group of refugees who certified the work of the schoolmaster, John Bell, himself a refugee from Stevens Creek.

The quartermasters logged the numbers in their interminable books. A hundred and sixty-three refugees were buried at public expense from November 1781 to September 1782; deaths peaked at twenty-five per month from December to February, and thirty-two from mid-August to mid-September. One man from Ninety Six became insane. The James Island surgeon and his assistant spent almost £80 in the three months ending August 1782, which the quartermaster general considered an outrageously high sum.

Militia officers received 4s. 8d per day above the rank of captain, and 2s. 4d below that rank.

They endured. The children played and learned and survived where they could.

And they waited for the war to be over, at last.

In the spring of 1782, Barnet Snell, who was not a Palatine German but who had been a neighbor, died a peaceful death. He left a will disinheriting his son, Christopher, who had been fighting with the Rebel militia.

It didn't matter. It was a purely symbolic act, a thing of pointless peevishness, with its roots in disappointment and filicidal anger. The war had already disinherited Barnet, and he had nothing left to bequeath.

Someone counted them. In the little community of Ninety Six, the civil war had left a thousand and four hundred widows and orphans.

No one bothered to count the men whose wives were wounded in spirit or killed in body.

The war had left scars on Heinrich Strum's heart, where they couldn't be seen. No one counted those.

Once again, bands of ragged orphans roamed the Back Country around Ninety Six. Anna Dorst fed six of them one morning; the next, another five arrived. She caught them trying to steal a pig and took them up to the house for a meal.

Afterward they wanted to stay, and when she wouldn't let them, they snarled at her, threw stones at her children, stole what they could and ran into the woods.

Some of them were just *kinder*; small, inarticulate, wordless, wild as rabbits and just as wary.

She told Peter about them when he arrived home the next day. He'd been on a patrol with some of Pickens' men through the Long Canes country. He'd seen more of them there.

"I watched them eat," she said, still appalled at the memory. "Like animals, tearing at the food like starving dogs, snarling at each other, not saying a word . . ." In truth, it had been the unnatural silence that unnerved her most.

Her youngest daughter Rachel had tried to talk to them, but they paid her no attention. They might as well have been deaf.

Peter sank into a chair, pulled off his boots. He sighed. "It's like that everywhere," he said.

He'd been with Pickens' unit after General Greene had ordered them away from Ninety Six. When Rawdon and Cruger departed with their pathetic procession of Loyalists, the Rebels rode back to the village, only to find it demolished, the ruins still smoking. Pickens subsequently set up his headquarters in Andrew Williamson's confiscated home, and set his captains on patrols through the district to assess what needed to be done.

Their reports were dour. For six years there had been civil war in the district, and the countryside, like the village, was in ruins.

"Pickens sent someone to General Greene," Peter said "His report was that people were reduced to begging and want from the ravages of the enemy, and desperately needed food."

Destitution breeds dominance and subservience, he thought.

Greene's Quaker heart responded as soon as it could. He ordered immediate relief, and appointed a distribution agent.

"Pickens was told to collect and distribute food to both hungry Whigs and Loyalists," Peter said.

At this, Anna sat up. She was about to say something, but Peter interrupted.

"Pickens is a church elder," he said. "He will give food to the starving, whoever they are."

"But . . ."

He waved her to silence.

"Anna, Anna, it's over, they've gone. We have to repair our lives and our country. Pickens is a wise man. He demanded we observe justice and restore peace and civic order."

He fell silent, remembering Andrew Pickens' demeanor. He was an austere man, Pickens, a Presbyterian, and not given much to humor. But a great man, in some ways. He had called in his captains and argued forcefully for institutionalized forgetting, for the truncation of memory, which was easier than forgiveness. Not, of course, for the active villains—there was no forgiving Browne, or Cunningham, or Tarleton, or Dawkins. But the children, and the men and women who had fought because they felt they had to, but had fought with some sense of honor and scruple—these people must be forgiven, and to do that, their deeds must be forgotten.

Anna said nothing. There was a knot of memory in her that would take some unraveling, she thought. All very well for the General to say . . . Perhaps the General hadn't had sisters and brothers on the other side.

There was a long silence.

"Is it really . . . over?" Anna asked. "How can we know?" The Whigs had been in control of the Back County before, and the seemingly inexhaustible resources of the English Empire had once again welled up out of Europe and . . . back they came.

After a while, she had another thought.

"Will any of them . . . come back?" she asked.

"Them? Loyalists from here?"

"Yes."

"I think so. After a time. If they're sincere."

He paused.

"You mean, your sister?"

She did, but she wouldn't say so.

"Where else would they go?" Peter asked. "They have nowhere else to go."

In the corner of her heart, a tiny hammer started beating. She couldn't tell whether it was malice or longing. She wouldn't know for sure until Katy was in front of her. However long that took.

On July 15 at Quarter House, near Charlestown, a detachment of Whig raiders surprised George Dawkins' brigade. Fifty men were taken prisoner. Fritz Henn, Nick's younger brother, Jacob Strum and Georg Schildnacht Jr., who were there, escaped.

It was just one of dozens of small engagements, most of them unrecorded.

Not everything had gone smoothly for the Whigs. Late in July, a deserter came to James Island with stories of dissension and friction within the American militia, most of it having to do with General Thomas Sumter, the Gamecock, as his men had taken to calling him.

Greene had been unwise to put Sumter in charge of the American forces while his army rested; he turned out to be vainglorious, and therefore reckless with his men's lives. Sumter decided on his own that it would fall to him to drive the British into Charlestown, and launched a precipitous attack on a British army unit at Moncks Corner, driving it out and down the Cooper River toward the capital. Sumter followed. The British holed up at a plantation. Despite their entrenched position, Sumter attacked. He was driven back.

Harry Lee reported to Greene, disgustedly, that "Sumter was so enchanted with the splendor of victory that he would wade through torrents of blood to attain it."

His men, however, were less enthusiastic about the torrents of blood, since they had provided it, and grew mutinous. Lee took his own Dragoons to Greene, refusing to serve with Sumter; Marion simply disbanded his militia. The Gamecock gave up his command and returned to his family.

Greene then gave the command to Marion.

Jacob Strum had been with the Dawkins raiding party that had captured Isaac Hayne and brought him into town.

Hayne had been a colonel in a regiment that surrendered at the fall of Charlestown. He'd asked to be released on parole, and it was granted. But then Clinton had issued his notorious revocation of all paroles, and the garrison commander demanded that Hayne either become a British subject or be jailed. At this time, Hayne's wife and two children were ill with the pox, and he was needed at home. So he signed the paper, stipulating only that he was not to be ordered to take up arms against the Whigs. Some time later, the British demanded that, after all, he would have to fight for their side. He refused. A little later, after his wife died and he'd nursed his children to health, he considered that he was no longer bound by his oath. The other side wasn't—why should he be? So he raised a regiment of his own.

Hayne then did something that enraged Balfour. He made a daring raid to the very gates of Charlestown itself, and captured Andrew Williamson, who had taken refuge near the capital. Captured him and took him away in his nightclothes. It was too much.

"So they sent us to get 'im," Jacob told Heinrich. "And we got 'im."

Fraser's Dragoons caught up with Hayne's men and released Williamson. Hayne fled across the Edisto. Dawkins, with Daniel Michler and Jacob Strum attending, captured him a few miles further on. He was in uniform, bearing arms and in command of enemy troops, in clear violation of his parole.

If that parole were still in effect. Who knew, any longer?

Balfour thought it was. He threw Hayne into a cell and kept him there.

"They'll hang him for sure," Jacob said.

"Let me get it right," Heinrich said. "They hang a man for not adhering to a paper he had only signed so he could be with his sick wife and children? After his earlier parole had been revoked without reason anyway? A piece of paper set against the death of a wife?"

"That's it."

"Then they're mad," Heinrich said.

If it were Catherine, I'd sign my life away in blood if I had to. I'd sign the world away to be with her. He thought, for the first time in months, of his dead wife and how she had been left alone, on the farm, and how she'd died. *I'd have done anything to be with her. So would any man. And against that, a stickler for regulations! No wonder we're losing!*

Hayne was confined in a cell for three weeks. Then Balfour conferred with his commander, Rawdon, who was back in the capital, and issued a proclamation: "In consequence of the most express directions of Lord Cornwallis to us that all those found in arms after being at their own request received as subjects of King George, we, therefore, direct that Colonel Isaac Hayne be hanged by the neck until dead."

On August 4, he was taken out and hanged in the presence of a small crowd, including his thirteen-year-old son.

The reprisals started almost at once.

On August 30, a detachment of Fraser's Dragoons out for a sweep for slaves was ambushed by Marion at Parker's Ferry on the Edisto. Twenty men were killed in the first volley. Jacob Strum, shaken, fled into the woods, and made his way back to Charlestown.

On August 25, weary from malaria and discouraged after five fruitless years campaigning in America, Rawdon went home to England. He left the British and Loyalist armies clinging to the coast, with little prospect of improvement and little hope of reinforcements from England. The command devolved to Alexander Stewart.

Before Rawdon departed, he addressed his troops one more time.

"Lieutenant Colonel Stewart is an able, energetic and resourceful officer," he said. "Under him, I am confident that the Carolinas will once again be returned to their lawful governors, as will Virginia under Cornwallis. I leave you in good spirits."

No one believed him. And if he really was in good spirits, they weren't.

A few days later, Heinrich, with Thomas Pearson's regiment of the Little River militia, Ninety Six brigade, got orders to move out.

"Where are you going?" his brother asked.

"It doesn't really matter," Heinrich said wearily. "Stewart's going to make himself a hero, if it kills us all. You're not going?"

"Not so far. Who's with you?"

"Ruppert. Christoph, the lieutenant. Adam and Karl. Three Frietzes, even the boy, John. Peter's a sergeant, in authority over his father, see how he likes that! Lorentz and Conrad. Daniel and George Snell. Plenty of others—every Weber that still moves, Christian Zange. That's about it. Then there's Fritz Henn. He's with Coffin's Ninety Six Cavalry. So's Friedrich Ruppert, I think. The idea is, our lot's going to be back with Cruger."

The idea comforted him somewhat. Cruger was a man who merited loyalty. Stewart was an unknown quantity.

There would be a force of more than two thousand, in all, more than half the force in the Carolinas.

A few days later, this weary army took on Nathaniel Greene at Eutaw Springs, only thirty miles from where Green had been encamped for the summer. In the ensuing battle, both armies suffered dreadful casualties. Greene lost a hundred and thirty-nine killed, and another three hundred and seventy wounded. Pickens and many others were wounded. Stewart had eighty-two killed, more than three hundred wounded and two hundred and forty-seven taken prisoner. Stewart himself was wounded, and his lieutenant, Major Majoribanks, fatally so, dying on the march to Charlestown. All the Palatines from Ninety Six escaped injury.

Both sides, of course, claimed victory.

Sometimes a victory is a victory only in a General's memoirs.

It was the last battle of armies in South Carolina. A few days later, Stewart and Balfour pulled all British troops back to Charlestown, there to await the outcome of Cornwallis's campaign around Yorktown, Virginia. Greene moved his army down river and began posting his troops in strategic places. He sent Marion's Brigade to the Santee, sent Sumter, back on duty, to replace the wounded Pickens at Orangeburg. And to seal the southern approaches to Charlestown, he settled the American army in a camp at the Colleton County village of Round O.

The Rebels had decisively won the struggle for the Back Country. This time for good.

Katy tried not to think of the farm on Cuffeetown Creek, but it insinuated itself into her mind. Plump land, ripe and fecund, or so she remembered it. She recalled suddenly the tales of her childhood in the Hunsrück, the romantic saga of the princess in the tower, she of the golden hair . . . Golden fields of forty acres . . . Golden tassels of Indian corn, cabbages heading up, pigs as plump as pregnant matrons, eggs with yolks as yellow as the summer sun, her own skin burnished bronze . . . She forgot, or wouldn't remember, that their stump fences had been mostly ragged, that the fields had been frequently unplowed because their horses had been stolen, that the yard was choked with stringy weeds, that the cabin was small and the chimney smoked . . . It was, after all, their own land.

Now I beg for food from the flint-hearted army! I feed my husband and my children scraps, and I go hungry! I make clothing from sacks! I live in a shack, tacked together. Worse than a hen house!

At night they lay under sheets discarded by the army. She'd scrubbed and scrubbed and scrubbed, but some of them still had the faint, brownish tinge of old blood, and smelled to her of the wounded, of rot.

I want to go home!

It wasn't all bad. The scar of her son's death was fading. Most of the children were still with her. Rosannah and Conrad were nearby. And she did have Abraham.

At night, she pushed her face up against his broad back. He was sweaty and solid and smelled of maleness.

Every day he went away, and she never knew whether he'd return. They'd sally off here, raid there, attack somewhere else . . . The earth must be as deep in lead shot and bomb fragments as in blood . . .

If he didn't come back, I'd die. I couldn't go on without him.

Maria Elizabeth Adolph, who was now forty-three and prowling the wreckage of Savannah, knew in her bones that the war was over. She'd known it since Heinrich had fallen, really, she'd seen it on the faces, the shocked faces of British regulars who had been so contemptuous of American rabble, she'd seen it on the face of her brother and in the strange ambivalence of her good friend Anna.

She had come to terms with being a widow, now. How else? Nothing would bring him back. You became reconciled, or you died. No choice.

So why not go home? She, too, thought longingly of her home on Cuffeetown Creek, of the knoll on which their house stood, the barn on the gentle slope down to the creek, the old bench by the water and how they'd used to paddle there, when the children were young, afterward lying on the grass, watching the small things creep and move in the water . . . There were quiet moments, tranquil moments, moments when friends visited and bread was broken, Anna and Katy both came, and the Strums next door, Heinrich was with Elizabeth then . . . Heinrich . . . She didn't think much about him, not any more, that was a moment in time, a momentary thing, though sometimes he came to her in her dreams, his black hair sleek as an otter, and she would stir restlessly, waking her children. Except for Katy, she'd never told anyone about him, except Katherina, of course, who had been there, and who had wrapped herself with coltish eagerness and fervor around the Frietz boy, Peter . . .

Oh, she could go home, but what about the youngsters? What would Katherina do? The child was twenty-two, and should be married with children of her own. Who would want her, this left-over Loyalist, up there in the Back Country?

Well, she'd find some man soon enough. There were men to spare here, despite the stacked graves of the dead.

Perhaps they should all go back?

And her brother, what of him? *Peter,* she thought, *Peter! Will you still be so angry at war's end? Is it just the fear that makes you cruel?* But she knew Peter wasn't cruel, not really, only frightened, a small man doing his best.

She spent her days wandering the ruined streets, her nights in her shabby room, rented from another war widow, staring at the floor.

The bucket with our story in it is empty. The bucket leaked, and the story drained away. How are we to fill the bucket up again?

Heinrich Strum, who was now forty-one, never fought again, not in a real battle. Cruger's men went out on patrols, probing at Sumter's defenses, and so did Coffin. George Dawkins, with Jacob Strum in tow, still raided the few Whig plantations worth raiding. Militia commanders with only a tenuous relationship to the chain of command recruited volunteers among the bored and resentful refugees from Ninety Six, and a few of them went along on reprisal raids deep into the interior, one of the young Webers and, for a while, the younger Schildnacht. These commanders included the Iron Dragoon, Hezekiah Williams, and the cruel, charismatic, capricious Cunningham, Bloody Bill.

If Bill had been in charge of the war, Heinrich reflected, it would have been long over, the inhabitants dead, plantations in ruins, the land fit only for wolves. He was more like a warlord of the Golden Hordes than a soldier loyal to the British King. Oh, they'd have caught him, eventually, hung him up by the thumbs and reduced him to size, piece by piece, while he cursed them and their progeny.

But Heinrich didn't go on any of these actions, these petty raids. No one asked him, not even Bill Cunningham. And he didn't volunteer. He did his duty and he stayed at home.

He lived in a spartan hut with his two remaining children, the solemn Eve and Henry, a miniature copy of his father, with the same gleaming black hair, assessing eyes and pale skin; the boy had a self-contained and slightly melancholic air that persuaded the other children in the camp to leave him alone, and he spent many hours by himself.

Of Elizabeth and Catherine, he had nothing, no mementos, no possessions, not even a lock of hair.

Only a child from each of them. And his memories.

Heinrich's sister Eva lived in an adjoining hut with her husband Daniel Michler, now fully recovered from his wounds, and their five children.

Heinrich liked Eva and Daniel, Eva because she maintained her gaiety in the midst of tragedy (and because her farm had been prosperous and bountiful right to the end) and Daniel just because he was a decent man who had always done his best.

Their children have the best chance of all. There will be no bitterness in their lives.

Nearby were the Merks, Conrad with his wife Rosannah, Katy Frietz's daughter, and the amiable giant, Lorentz. They shared quarters with the Merk sister, Anna Maria Mehl, and her five offspring. Anna Maria was a woman of chilly disposition and very little heart, or so Heinrich believed.

But is it any wonder? She was at Savannah when her husband Peter was killed by a Rebel bullet; and behind the Rebels was her favorite brother, big Lorentz. If her husband had killed her brother, would she be as frost-bitten? How could you tell? War is always a matter of inches and what-ifs, the fate of battle turning on the slip of a trigger finger or an idle tongue, and the past is useless as a predictor of the future.

Balthazar, the patriarch, one of the few to move through the years unmolested by either Whig or Tory, had remained in the Back Country after the exodus. Perhaps his son Johan, the Rebel zealot, protected him, or perhaps it was merely his own acumen.

And Johan?

How does a man go against his family? What cause is big enough for that?

Heinrich thought of young Johan sometimes.

How he must have hated his brothers!

Jacob Strum, though he did his duty, lived in town, where his wife had managed to find two rooms in an army-requisitioned mansion. She would have it no other way.

He also passed many hours in the taverns of James Island. Sometimes he drank with his brother; sometimes the widow Isabella, a refugee from North Carolina, joined them.

Jacob admired Isabella. He admired her wit and her jollity and her enormous breasts.

But she had eyes for brother Heinrich.

I'll make him laugh some day, she told Jacob. *See if I don't.*

Friedrich Ruppert, twenty-six, lived in a shack with his two children, mourning his wife Barbara, Heinrich Strum's sister, who had died so cruelly on the exodus from Ninety Six. His older brother Christoph had a bunk in the regimental barracks, had been taken into the army's higher councils by Colonel Hamilton and was hardly ever seen.

The irrepressible Adam Bauer, who each morning spent an hour telling stories and doing tricks for the schoolchildren and keeping their parents amused, had started a small barter exchange on the fringes of the James Island commissary, and seemed to be prospering. His son Karl, who had so bravely rescued him from the Back Country, was with him. Angelica, Maria and Philip were running wild. Catherine and Margaret were missing. Catherine had married the Rebel militiaman William Parker and had stayed behind at Ninety Six. Margaret stayed, too, but no one knew where she was. Alizabetha had taken up with the soldier, John Dorres.

The rest of the refugees . . . got by. They lived in the same suspended time frame as the army.

They were just waiting.

For some resolution, anything.

For it to be over, at last.

In mid-September, bands of Cherokee marauders struck the outlying townships in Georgia, drawing off Pickens' militia to frontier duty. It was all Bill Cunningham needed. He called out his horsemen, saddled his favorite gelding, Ringtail, and set off for his old home on the Upper Saluda.

The army couldn't do the job? He would. Battles being lost? He'd bring his righteous indignation to the Back Country instead, would make the Rebels pay, wish they had never been born. He'd find the ringleaders, the high and the mighty, the damned Rebels, and hang them all. That'd put a stop to it . . .

A month later, one of the survivors of Bill's consequent foray, a man from Long Canes, walked into the tavern where Heinrich was sitting with the Frietzes and Isabella. At first he would say nothing of his venture. He just mumbled, shook his head and stared into his drink. But after a while the rum loosened his tongue, and it was like raising a sluice, the pent-up words came crowding through the breach, tumbling over each other so eagerly that they barely made sentences.

"He's mad, quite mad," the raider said, pulling on his rum. He shook his head. "Hatred calls him like no other emotion, like no one else I've ever seen. It's like a flame two feet in front of his nose, tugging at him, pulling him forward." He shifted in his chair, leaning into his memories. "You know the Cherokees will pull the beating heart from a man, wear it like a badge of honor, say it makes them brave?" He shuddered. "Bill will do that not for honor but for pain. He wants them all dead . . ."

Their band would sweep up to a plantation, he said, the home of someone Bill Cunningham knew to be an enemy. If they were there alone, they'd be dragged out and hanged, if they were lucky, or cut to pieces with swords if the fancy took Bill. "One of those he caught was Captain Edward Hampton. Caught him on his plantation near Earle's Ford. Shot him without warning. Once, Bill slashed a man, Dannett Abney, who was sick at the time and unable to make his escape, and slew him in his wife's arms. He bled to death in his own bed while Bill watched, cutting at him, the woman pleading and then shrieking like a devil from hell, and he just stood above her, a smile on his lips . . ." If the plantation was guarded, if there was a band of armed Whigs, they would surround it, fire arrows of lighted pitch to the buildings, force them out. "Bill would promise them anything. Oh, they would be well looked after, given their parole, treated honorably, he'd say anything, and after they surrendered he would hack them to pieces. No one survived these raids."

Two days later, he said, they had taken a small post commanded by Colonel Joseph Hayes and his regiment of Pickens' Brigade.

"Of course, Bill had sent a messenger saying if they would surrender their lives would be spared. They refused."

There was a brisk fight, but after Cunningham set the defenders' log building on fire, they surrendered.

"Among those captured were Captain Daniel Williams and his fourteen-year-old brother Joseph, sons of the late Brigadier General Williams. Bill had Hayes and Williams trussed like chickens and hanged on the pole of a fodder stack. The pole broke, so Bill hacked at them as they lay helpless on the ground.

"Then he turned on the fourteen-year-old, who had been bleating like a frightened sheep, 'Oh brother, what shall I tell mother?' and hacked him in his turn. 'You tell her nothing, you damned Rebel suckling!' he yelled as he cut him to pieces."

"How many died on this rampage of yours?"

"About fifteen hundred, as best we can figure."

When Pickens returned from the frontier, having once again laid waste to the Indian lands, Cunningham split his troops into several bands and dispersed. "One of these fled across the Blue Ridge and took refuge with the Cherokees . . ."

Isabella, who had fallen into an unaccustomed silence during the telling of the tale, spoke up. "I heard Bill's horse Ringtail died, and was buried with full military honors," she said.

The raider smiled grimly. "So I heard," he said.

"And I heard Bill bawled like a baby when the nag died," she said.

"I heard that, too."

"Put his arms around its neck, and held on tight, through the dying spasms?"

"Also that."

Heinrich stirred. "I can understand that," he said.

She arched her eyebrows. "You can?"

Yes, he thought. *He's not weeping for the horse. He's weeping for the might-have-beens. All those years, all that pain, all that killing, all that hope, all that valor, the whole cause, everything he ever fought for, now come to this, an oversized hole in the ground and a melancholy bugling for a dead horse, a great-hearted symbol of Loyalism everywhere, Loyalism toppling into its grave, covered forever with the red earth of Carolina. Who wouldn't weep?*

On September 28, the village of Yorktown, Virginia, was besieged by the Rebels, trapping the British army inside. Almost three weeks later, on October 19, Lord Cornwallis, the Glorious Empire's Supreme Commander in America, surrendered with his entire army of seven thousand men.

A day later, Heinrich Strum got married for the third time, to the widow Isabella.

And why not? He was weary beyond measure. But she did make him laugh.

Eighteen

There we were, in the country we had won. Like farmers after a great storm, wandering dazed through the ruined fields, hearing only the silence. She hadn't thought of the departed, then, not even of Katy. Why should she? There was desolation enough for everybody.

October 1782
James Island, South Carolina

Skirmishes, skirmishes, but nothing much more.

Katy watched them go out in the dusk, the scouting parties, the raiding parties, reconnoitering parties, they all called themselves different things. With their families secure behind the lines, the chance to plunder and harass the Rebels proved irresistible. Twenty to thirty men, sometimes more, heavily armed, each man with a rifle, a long rifle, a pistol, sword, knife in boot scabbard.

And no doubt also a stick to thump people with when their bullets run out. They're just looking for people to kill!

Her son Peter went out on one of these, to her fury. So did Heinrich Strum, despite his new wife. Katy kept her husband at home. Wasn't going to get him killed, not now, not for this . . .

These battles were all inconsequential and meaningless, except to the dead and the dying. The men went out, prevailed or lost, came back, some of them. But they knew it didn't mean anything.

In July, in preparation for the coming but as yet unannounced evacuation, the South Carolina militia groups were cut by sixty percent. Other units were dismissed during the summer with a quarter of back pay. Privates got 6 pence per day.

They remained in town as refugees or returned to their homes.

Their choice.

The army had done with them.

Bloody Bill Cunningham made one last raid into the Ninety Six District.

Why?

In the grand conflagration of the times, his raid was one last flaring of a dying ember, perhaps, an ember that throws out fierce white heat until it, too, flickers and dies. Or so it seemed afterward.

But Bill was just Bill. Barracks were too small to contain him.

Years before, he'd told his men he counted each death he caused and carried it around in his mind as a souvenir of war, in the same way the Cherokees carried a bag of enemy scalps, and for the same reasons—proof of prowess, anger, revenge, the psyche feeding on the rotting remnants. "I carry my bag in my head," he'd said, smiling his terrible smile. "Cherishing each and every one."

Three bags full, Bill!

But this time the Cunningham luck ran out, and William Butler caught up with him at Caradine's Ford, on the Saluda.

He had divided his command into small groups, as was his wont on the march—they could converge on the agreed target from different routes, and confound the enemy that way. So when Butler's Rangers found him, he had only twenty men with him.

Butler had learned Bill's general whereabouts through a piece of trickery that involved mimicking the voice of one of his men, thereby fooling Joseph Cunningham, Bill's cousin. They crossed the river at midnight, and next morning halted in a peach orchard near Bauknight's Ferry. The horses, unbridled but with their saddles left on, were feeding on peas from a canoe when one of the men spotted a gray mare that Cunningham was known to have stolen. It had escaped from his camp. Bill couldn't be far away, and the Rangers got their marching orders.

There were thirty of them, to Bill's twenty.

Butler dispatched John Corley with eight men, to attack from the rear; he himself advanced under cover of a hedge. The Tories were drying their blankets by the campfire; Cunningham himself was a little way off. Corley's furious assault was the first the Tories knew that an enemy was at hand.

Taken by surprise and attacked by superior numbers, Cunningham fled. There was no time for a saddle. He seized his holsters and leapt to his horse. Butler dashed in pursuit.

Cunningham was mounted on a celebrated mare called Silver Heels, while Butler himself rode Ranter. Because both men were superior horsemen, and because Butler carried only a saber and Cunningham only pistols that wouldn't fire because of the rain the night before (for he attempted repeatedly to fire them over his shoulder as he fled), the fate of the chase depended on the speed of the horses.

In the forest, Ranter held his own, but on the open trail Cunningham's thoroughbred pulled easily ahead, and he escaped, finally, by swimming the Saluda at Lorick's Ferry. He returned to Charlestown, but it was the end of his band. A month later, he caught a ship for Cuba, where he lived for a while, and died. The fate of Silver Heels was not recorded.

As with any fire where the last embers die, the blackness seemed much blacker after his going.

For the first few months of '82, Peter Dorst joined a band of militiamen to perform a duty he came to loathe, that of picking off the "tory outlyers." These were lonely families or groups of families still living in the wild, men, women and many children. They lived deep in the bush, only emerging to steal cattle, horses or grain and to inflict what casualties they could on lonely farms, isolated riders or, where possible, small-enough groups of Rebel soldiers. Sumter had assigned Peter's commander a couple of Catawba scouts to help track them down and flush them out.

He refused to allow his son to take part in this mopping up. There was already enough . . . ambiguity . . . in the boy's mind.

"People act as if they're vermin to be eradicated," he told Anna gloomily.

He was sitting on the floor in front of her chair, legs stretched out before him. He leaned back, resting his head on her belly. She stroked his temples.

Vermin! He remembered what sessions court judge Aedanus Burke had said about these pathetic remnants: "Small tory parties who live in swamps and make horrid incursions on the peaceable settlements are neither given nor receive quarter," he wrote. "They sally from their swamps & destroy our people in cold blood, and when taken are killed in their turn . . . With the swamps filled with loyalists, the rebels durst not sleep in their houses." And then, having set the tone, the judge deplored its consequences: "Because of the spirit of vengeance the British had excited in the breasts of our Citizens, the very females talk as familiarly of shedding blood & destroying the tories as the men do."

"Well, they do have to be stopped," Anna said reasonably.

Peter sighed.

"Yes. But Anna, you should see them . . . They're not what you think . . ."

Two days earlier, his trackers had spotted a thin trail in the woods, and had followed it to one of the outlyer camps. Three men, four women, a dozen children living at the edge of a bog. The children naked, their bellies swollen with hunger and disease, some of them listless, others feverish. Even the adults looked ragged, haunted by hunger and fear.

He tried to describe their camp to Anna, the squalor of it, the wretched poverty, the filth . . . It was worse than an animal's lair. And how apathetic they were! They made no attempt to defend themselves. When the Indian scouts slipped into camp and held them at gunpoint, they simply stared. Not that there was anything they could have done, but you would think they'd try, reach for a gun, flee, anything. They must have known what was coming. The militiamen rode in a few minutes later, and as they did so, one of the men moved, put his arm around his woman and his hand on the head of a child. That was just before they shot them.

It was that simple gesture that stayed with Peter afterward, a gesture of affection. He closed his eyes. His temples were throbbing. A *protective arm! Resignation to dying! An affirmation of love! There was no expression on their faces at all, but he put his arm around her and they accepted their fate together, that simple gesture a symbol of a lifetime together.* Peter had seen many men die, and many women and children, but when his men shot them, and they crumpled together, and the child just stood there, not even turning to see her parents dying but staring with those horrid, blank eyes at the shooters . . . His stomach lurched, and he was violently sick.

"You didn't kill the children too?" Anna asked, her mind on the same scene. She sat up suddenly.

"Anna!"

"Well, what happened to them?"

"There are others who would have killed them," Peter admitted. "I've heard stories . . . No, we rounded them up, gave them to the Indians."

Anna took her hands from his head. "The Indians? You *know* what they'll do to the little ones."

"They'll raise them, that's all. The Catawbas are a good people. They'll take them home to Georgia. Their camps are overflowing with children of all kinds. They don't mind if they're white. And what else were we to do? Should I have brought them here? There is nowhere for them."

"Your good Indians will abandon the sick ones in the forest, you know they will."

"We could have shot them," Peter said bitterly. "We could have killed them right there . . ."

That night they clung to each other, afraid to lose touch. They both knew why—the haunted eyes of orphaned children. *I had no choice,* Peter thought. But of course he'd had. He'd merely taken the best choice in baneful circumstances. Anna lay there for a long time. She was thinking of small ones wandering alone in the woods. They'd go down to the creek at last, when thirst drove them, and there lassitude would overcome them. They'd curl into a ball and just . . . wait. She found it impossible to imagine, to really feel what they would feel, or not feel . . . Their spirits would stay there in the woods where they died, knotted and tangled like a ball of yarn, stay there forever, and the woods would be a place of wailing, for those who could hear it. And just before she fell asleep, she had a last small thought. *It's the memories that are the real evil this war has caused. My grandchildren will still know them. How long before they fade?*

The previous fall, a few months after Rawdon's hasty retreat to the coast, Governor Rutledge crept cautiously back into the province and issued a proclamation, which Sumter's men nailed to courthouses and taverns all over the Back Country. It offered, somewhat grandly, "free pardon and oblivion for their offenses, for having borne arms with or [who] adhere to the enemy," to all persons, "if they would appear before a state militia brigade commander within thirty days and volunteer for six months service in the ranks." As a sop to hostile Back Country opinion, the proclamation added a rider. Certain classes of persons were excepted from this magnanimity, including those who had left the state in the American Period and who had ignored earlier offers of pardon, or who had chosen exile after refusing the Oath of Abjuration. He also tacked on another category: "Others who, since the fall of Charlestown, have subscribed to congratulatory addresses to British Commanders, held British civil or military commissions, or whose conduct has been otherwise so infamous that justice can not admit them to pardon."

The proclamation was widely ridiculed in Charlestown, but closely parsed to see who, if anyone, wouldn't be swept up in this widely cast, finely meshed net of exceptions.

As far as anyone knew, no one took the governor up on his kind offer. But it was an ill-kept secret that those who ridiculed it loudest were almost certainly those who at least *thought* of taking advantage of it. For a while, security at the town gates was doubled, not so much to discourage straying sheep, but to monitor movements; spies were said to be everywhere, and more than one unfortunate was whipped on scant evidence, sometimes just on suspicion of harboring Rebel thoughts—"if thought's in the heart, soon word's on the lip," or so the saying went.

None of this stopped the incessant grumbling about the inept way the British had been running the war. And none of it stopped the rumors of impending betrayal by the ministers in Westminster.

But as military activity gradually slackened in the spring of 1782, word filtered back to the beleaguered Charlestown and James Island garrisons that the outlyers were gradually giving up, and that some Loyalists in the hinterlands were taking the first tentative step toward reconciliation by doing as Rutledge had recommended, enlisting for a term in the state troops. At first, these reports were treated with suspicion, as though they had been manufactured by some devious Rebel scheme to persuade them all of the folly of persisting in their Loyalist ways; but after a while, too many people knew too many other people whose friends or relatives or, indeed, spouses, had followed the course.

Still no one in the garrisons left.

In March, a public notice was posted and published in the *Royal Gazette* that an agent was prepared to talk with "Refugees who are desirous of going to East Florida to settle there, agreeable to the encouragement contained in Governor Toyn's proclamation."

And a new flock of rumors took wing as that notice was parsed in its turn.

Were they going to abandon Charlestown?

Every passing mariner was pumped for information; every arriving officer was sucked dry of anything remotely resembling intelligence. Every ship from New York brought disquieting rumors. The Board of American Loyalists had demanded that Clinton reassure them of Britain's steadfastness, and he responded by declaring that "no garrison in which Loyalists are joined with the King's troops, should be surrendered on any terms which might discriminate between them."

The rumors shifted ground: *Why were they thinking of abandoning Charlestown?*

When Sir Guy Carleton, Clinton's replacement, reached New York from Britain, he was greeted with a rousing welcome whose theme was the undying unity of the British Empire. Carleton's reply was lukewarm.

Are they thinking of abandoning America?

The army command was silent. But while rumors flew and anxiety mounted, the High Command was devising its plans for the evacuation of all the southern garrisons. In May, a fleet of transports was dispatched from New York for the evacuation of Savannah.

All campaigning in South Carolina ceased. The last action of the South Carolina Royalists took place in August, when they attacked a small Rebel force. But the Rebels had been warned, and the Dragoons suffered considerable losses. George Dawkins was severely wounded. A little later, Hezekiah Williams, with a couple of the Weber boys along for the ride, made what was to be the last Loyalist incursion into the hinterlands, with mediocre results (no one killed, no one captured, a few horses "requisitioned"); then he resigned his commission and sailed for Florida.

In July, Savannah was abandoned. Agreement was reached between the British and American commanders for a peaceful transfer of authority; it permitted merchants who traded with Britain to remain in the town unmolested until they could dispose of their inventories; many a refugee family fled to Tybee Island at the mouth of the Savannah River, where most of them died of fever and starvation; others made their way to East Florida, overland; yet others hazarded the ocean and, in a crazy flotilla of tiny boats, sailed to Jamaica. On July 11, the rest of the Loyalists, along with the garrison, were shipped north.

The fleet arrived off the Bar of Charlestown on July 27, and lingered just long enough to offload the refugees and to take on Nisbet Balfour, John Harris Cruger and other officers, before resuming its voyage to New York.

Among the refugees put ashore were Maria Elizabeth Adolph and her daughter Katherina.

Katy took them into her hut, and they hugged each other and cried, cried less for the might-have-beens or for those-who've-gone than for the fact of friendship, which survived in this world of toil and trouble. Those were the best tears either of them had shed for a long, long time.

A week later there was a brief pause in the steady downward slide of public morale when it was learned that Admiral Rodney had thrashed the French fleet in the Islands; a group of Charlestown Loyalists put together a petition urging Leslie, the new garrison commander, to countermand the order to evacuate Georgia. Leslie, who had been commanded also to evacuate Charlestown but had been anxiously waiting for the "proper" moment to announce this, ignored their importuning, and the rumors began again.

After a while, stories circulated of the fleet's callousness in its treatment of the Savannah refugees. Women and children had literally to battle soldiers for a berth on board, it was said. Others piled their possessions precariously into small boats and rowed to the evacuation fleet, which refused to take them aboard, leaving them rocking perilously on the open sea. Many of those who fled to Tybee Island did so not because they wanted to stay in Georgia after the fall, but because they were too weak for the pushing and shoving dockside; Loyalist settlers battling each other for precious space, while the sailors lounged about and watched.

Maria Elizabeth confirmed that the rumors were substantially true. She and her daughter had themselves reached shipboard almost inadvertently; they had been caught up accidentally in a group of families led by four aggressive, burly militiamen who simply bulled their way up the gangplank; many of their meager possessions had been abandoned dockside.

Leslie gloomily watched the rumors spiraling out of control. Angry crowds began gathering in front of his house, and he was forced to employ soldiers to drive them away. Some of the soldiers mutinously refused; their own families were often involved. The militia, particularly, were becoming unreliable. Some of the troops that had been disbanded threatened to reform, this time to support their wives and children against the cavalier disregard of the British authorities. Loyalist leaders urged forthrightness.

At last, he could put off the announcement no longer.

On August 12, the *Royal Gazette* finally confirmed the rumors. Charlestown was to be abandoned. The *Gazette* blandly sought to "inform the inhabitants that a Convoy will be ordered, and every possible assistance given to convey to Augustine such of them, who, from the expected withdrawal of the King's troops from this town, may desire to remove with their families and effects to the Province of East-Florida." Those who wished to take advantage of this opportunity were asked to register at the office of the quartermaster general, and to designate the specific property they wished to take with them. An unstated but widely accepted reading of this phrase "specific property" included the large number of plundered slaves held by families in Charlestown; this hardly affected the refugees on James Island, whose worldly goods were so few that a small skiff would have sufficed.

Leslie's announcement added that "those wishing to go to other places," unspecified, were asked to register those intentions also.

And it encouraged "those inhabitants who prefer to make their peace with the State Government" to do so.

The State Government! The Rebels! The enemy! It really was all over.

Finally he ordered "all inhabitants, well affected to the American cause, to quit the town in twenty-four hours, under penalty of being considered spies."

This final clause, while sounding callous, was well received because its intentions were understood. Not just that it would give Leslie a good excuse to rid the town of spies, suspected spies, "suspected friends," layabouts, criminals, gamblers, wastrels and other useless mouths, though it would do that. It was also ingeniously calculated to help those who chose to return to their homes; it would give them a pretext for "casting themselves upon the mercy of their countrymen."

See! We were with you all along! It was all a mistake! They expelled us because our hearts were really in the right place!

No one would believe it, but they would pretend to out of a necessary and civil hypocrisy.

Politics!

On a sandy promontory near Fort Johnson, on the Charlestown harbor side of James Island, the remaining Palatines gathered late one afternoon, perhaps the last time they would all be together. It was near the end of August, high sickly season in Carolina, and although the sun was already lowering, the heat was still intense. They sat in the shade, under a copse of scruffy palmettos. To the northeast, the harbor and beyond it the smudge of Sullivan Island. Slightly more to the south, the Bar, where the fleet from Savannah had briefly lingered with its dire news. The smokes from the town were off to the left, made lurid by the sullen sun.

Who had called this meeting, this town-hall-in-the-open-air meeting of . . . survivors? No one seemed to know. The word went around . . . Ninety Six . . . Germans . . . friends . . . families . . . gather . . . And slowly they drifted together, in their need and their anxiety, and ended up here, once again staring over an ocean, a sniper's distance from the fort. Heinrich sat under a palm, his back against its trunk, his eyes closed. He had come to the meeting, but had little to say. He was too weary to make another decision now. Isabella, colorful as always, sat by him. Maria Elizabeth and Katy both sat nearby. Maria Elizabeth sat where she could watch him, see the vein in his temple gently throbbing, his black hair flecked with gray, his face toughened by years of hard campaigning.

For a while, no one said anything. No one really knew where to begin. They had come so far! Most of them from the Nahe . . . But not all. There was George Dawkins, hobbling from his wound. And a few others. And Daniel Michler, though of course he'd married a Nahe woman. So far . . . but so what? What story were they now to pour into their bucket?

Maria Elizabeth stood first. She stood a little way away from them, as if afraid; her round, moon face was set, and her rough hands were clenched at her sides.

"I'm going home," she said, "back to Ninety Six, and Katherina is coming with me . . ."

There was silence. No one said anything.

"Home," she said again. "I can't start over. My husband is gone and I'm too old to start over." She looked quickly at Heinrich, but he still had his eyes closed. "All I have is my children and my home, and those are here . . ."

This time everyone spoke at once, a hubbub of exclamations, and no one heard anything. She held up her hand.

"We've decided," she said. "Mrs. Schildnacht is going with me, and Georg's brother too. They agree. Ninety Six is all they have."

"Maria! Maria!" Katy said. "You have us, wherever we are! And how do you know you'll have a home to go back to?"

"My brother's there . . ."

"Peter!"

"He's my brother. And my children are there, little Rosena, she's to marry a Rebel captain, I hear, if he ever returns to her . . . No, my dear, I'm going home."

"Maria!" Katy looked stricken.

"Why can't we just stay here!" This was from Anna Strum, the Henn woman. "What can they do to us?"

Her husband held up his hand to stop her. "I'm not staying here the rest of my years," Jacob said. "Nor will I willingly go to jail again. No, we can't stay."

Anna looked petulant, but said nothing more.

Her brother, Fritz Henn, spoke up. "I'm going to Augustine with my unit," he said. "The Royalists haven't disbanded. Not yet. I'll go with Georg Schildnacht and with George here." He pointed at Dawkins, sprawled awkwardly on the ground, his wounded leg twisted under him. "George can't go back, can't stay here. Not after helping to capture Hayne . . . Any more than Heinrich can, for all kinds of reasons." He looked down at his sister's brother-in-law, whose eyes were now open, but Heinrich only stared back, expressionlessly.

"I suppose they've promised you a mansion in Augustine, just as they did in Rawdontown?" someone asked.

"They've promised me nothing," Fritz said.

"So why go?"

"The war's not over yet, and we'll see . . ."

There was a derisive chorus.

"And what's to prevent them abandoning Florida like they're abandoning the Carolinas?"

Fritz looked angry. "Maybe they'll abandon America. You want to go back to the Hunsrück? It's too late for that."

"And Georg?" someone asked, looking at Schildnacht.

Schildnacht answered for himself. "I'm going to Augustine," he said, "because it's not over yet."

Heinrich Strum climbed slowly to his feet. The others fell silent. He looked weary, but he spoke firmly.

"It will be hard to choose," he said. "But there are no wrong choices here. Choose what your heart tells you." He began to tick them off on his fingers.

"You can go home, as Maria is. Not all of us will be welcomed there as perhaps she will. You must make your own assessment. As for me . . . It's my memories that will keep me away, not the Rebels.

"You can go to Augustine with Fritz and Georg. But that's a decision that's not a decision. You will have to decide again, in a year or a month . . .

"You can go to the Islands. But they tell me you're only welcome there if you have money, and you need slaves to survive. None of us have ever had slaves.

"Perhaps you can go to England. But they don't really want you. And as for me . . . My recollections of England are not such as to draw me there.

"You can do something else—go west through the Cherokee lands into the nameless country beyond . . . Or go south to the Spanish lands, though you're not welcome there. Go to New York . . .

"Or you can do what I'm doing, and go to New Scotland, where Stumpel would have sent us . . ."

There was silence. "It's where I'm going," he repeated then. "The journey will have taken me more than twenty years. But I'm going. It's my destiny, I think, to die there."

For a while he stood there, hands at his sides, saying nothing more.

Like a rock! Katy thought. *How tired he looks, how worn, but there is something immovable about him still . . . They'll go with him.*

Maria said nothing. She remembered their fevered clinging, how vulnerable he was then, in his grief. *Well, and so was I, before I became a widow in my mind as well as my body. It was a reflex, like a fit of weeping, but no more . . .*

Heinrich waited, looking them over. *They'll come to see that these choices really aren't choices, that there's only one choice, and they'll take it in the end. Except, of course, for Maria, dear Maria, God be with her* . . .

He looked at his brother. Jacob would go for certain, and so would his wife, and she'd hope there'd be Society in Halifax . . . Adam Bauer and Katherine would go, of course, Adam would probably start a tavern or a store and prosper, and so would the amazing Alizabetha, and good luck to whatever man she set her sights on. Karl, too, and Philip and the others, they'd all go. Katy, of course, the sweet little bird, so tough in the fiber, and her ox of a husband, and all their children, including Rosannah and her husband Conrad, and the sons, Peter and John. Heinrich envied Peter, and his resilience . . . Conrad's sister, Peter Mehl's widow, now married to Conrad Schade . . . They'd go. The Rupperts, of course, Friedrich and his daughters, Barbara's kids . . . But Friedrich was sick and withdrawn, and might not last the year. Unlike his brother Christoph, who would be a leader wherever he ended up. The Zanges, the Webers, Lorentz Merk and his Molly, Nicholas Cruhm. And those neighbors and friends who were here who hadn't been Stumpel's Germans at all, but were now so close-knit that they could hardly be untangled: the Snells, Chambers Blakeley with his wife Catherine and their three children, Andrew Myers, Henry Siteman with his wife Barbara and their five children, Reuben Lively and wife, Mary, Thomas Thornton and Mary, who had been a Snell, and her sister Nancy, with her husband Adam Fralich and their brothers George, David and Daniel and their widowed mother . . .

Family, really, all of them.

He sank down next to Isabella, who was fanning herself with an old shingle. She smiled at him.

He knew people disliked her for her constant smiling, her unfailing good humor, her laughter in the face of pain. But they didn't know her as he did. She had lost a husband and all her children up there in North Carolina, and sometimes laughter in the pig's snout of fate was the only human response; she had something of the soldier in her, her own version of the Dragoon's credo, *never surrender* . . . Her good humor was her ammunition; it wasn't callousness, only tenacity. He laid his head on her shoulder in salute, a brief touch, and she looked at him curiously.

They'd get a berth going north, he would see to that, not for them the mad scramble of Savannah to get on board at all. And then, the voyage north. And then . . . But there his imagination failed him. What was it like there?

Can I really start over? And Isabella? And the children? He looked down at his wife, her plump cheeks flushed from the heat.

Please, no more war, no more.

Two days later a wagon and three horses left James Island and headed out across the Low Country on a bearing that would take them through Orangeburg to Ninety Six.

Maria had spent the last night in Katy's bed, Abraham banished to the barracks. They'd sat up and talked, and then cried for a while, then talked some more, remembering, a conversation they knew would stay in memory for many years. Just before dawn they'd fallen asleep, finally, and when Abraham came to fetch them in the morning they were wrapped blissfully about each other.

Katy held Maria's hand as she climbed into the wagon. "God be with you," she said.

"Katy," Maria said, "Katy . . . You'll always know where I am. When you can, if you can, come back."

"If I can, I will."

They stared at each other.

"Maria, will you see . . . Anna?"

"Surely, I will. She's married to my brother . . . My brother, despite everything . . ."

"If you see her . . ."

"Is there anything you want me to say?"

Katy shook her head, said nothing.

How can she be so calm? They killed her husband! I'd see my sister and I'd hear . . . nothing but the rattle of muskets and the ghostly blowing of bugles. Too much bile under the bridge, too many grievances, a mountain of complaint, piles of corpses, liberty born in grief and anger, liberty that would have been freely given, if only they'd all listened . . . Tell her to remember Heinrich Strum's murdered wife! But she didn't say it.

"No, there's nothing. Look after yourself, dear Maria."

The wagon disappeared up the road toward the Wappoo and beyond it the Ashley, and Katy went back indoors. The hut seemed very empty.

Then Rosannah and Conrad came to visit, and Mary came back from school, and she took solace in family.

Family fills up the holes. In the end, that's all there is.

By mid-August, the registration was, more or less, complete, the rolls bulging with refugees—besides its own soldiers, the British army was faced with more than eleven thousand people who needed evacuation from the Carolinas. Of these, more than forty-two hundred were Loyalists, twenty-five hundred of them women and children. The others were some seven thousand blacks, freemen and slaves, who had been caught up in a quarrel they had been told didn't concern them, but which, of course, concerned them utterly.

By the end of the month they had chosen their destinations, the principal ones being Florida and Jamaica. Many decided to follow the army, probably to New York, though the actual destination was still unknown. Others went to Britain. Those who chose Nova Scotia were overwhelmingly from the Ninety Six district, families who had taken refuge around the fort after the siege and had clung to British protection through Orangeburg, Dorchester and Charlestown. There were a hundred and sixty-three men, a hundred and thirty-three women and a hundred and twenty-one children. There was another group with them—with them but separate—fifty-three free blacks from the Back Country.

On September 6, a heavy firing off the Bar announced the arrival of Sir Samuel Hood with his evacuation fleet.

The actual embarkation and removal was to take another three months.

In mid-October, a convoy for East Florida cleared Charlestown. Among the passengers were Fritz Henn, Georg Schildnacht and George Dawkins, along with Patrick Cunningham and two hundred and forty other officers and men, fifty-two women and children, and thirty-one servants. The convoy waited eight days for an appropriate wind. The voyage took another three. Then they lay offshore for eight more before they could land.

Several vessels ran aground the Bar off St. Augustine in an unfavorable sea, and were broken up by the waves.

All were saved. But Fritz Henn lost everything in his already meager kit.

Leslie and Colonel Sam Campbell, knowing the chaos of the exodus from Savannah and fearing an even greater debacle in Charlestown in December, began shipping out heavy ordnance from Charlestown and Fort Johnson late in September. Two ships were requisitioned to take the Fort Johnson weapons to the port of Halifax, safely north of the conflict—the *Free Briton*, three hundred and ninety-eight tons, and the *John & Bella*, one hundred and ninety-one tons. The cannon were loaded onto barges on the beach and towed out to the ships lying in the road just offshore, where they were hoisted on board by crane.

With them went some five hundred men, women and children from James Island, making their way out to the ships in a pathetic flotilla of makeshift boats and rafts, old logs, tenders and whatever other flotation devices they could find. Some of them swam, though the ships were some distance out. Most took with them only what they could carry.

By this time, Campbell's garrison, so-called, had been reduced to a handful of men, including most of the remaining Loyal Palatines, including the Strums, the Rupperts, the Bauers, the Frietzes, the Merks, the Webers, the Cruhms and the Zanges. They crowded onto the *Free Briton*. With them were assorted spouses and children. Another James Island commander, Thomas Pearson, had a hundred and eighty-five men under his command. Among them was Jacob Strum.

Isabella clambered into the rowboat in a colorful flutter of petticoats. A few sailors cheered. Katy followed with a little more decorum.

Heinrich and Peter Frietz had "requisitioned" the little boat, by the simple expedient of threatening to murder anyone who got in their way. Heinrich sat in the stern, his back to the beach and to James Island. Isabella sat by him. He leaned back, letting weariness recapture him.

I've fought to keep my new country, and now I have to fight to leave her.

He closed his eyes, letting his hand rest on Isabella's soft shoulder.

Katy saw him. *My lords in parliament will never know how very much he has done!* she thought.

They rode at anchor three days, while the ships filled with other refugees and while they loaded and stored the ordnance.

Leslie had written the commandant at Halifax to expect them. They had been provided with some light clothing, he said, and the militiamen paid. "But as to other supplies and the necessaries of life, I trust these will be available for them at Halifax."

At high tide on October 20, the heavily laden ships turned into the gulf stream, and the vessels found the rhythm of the ocean swells.

Eva Michler, who as a girl had excitedly awakened her father when they crossed the Bar in the other direction, began to cry. Somewhere up there, in the Back Country they'd won and lost, were her father and her mother, two sisters, nieces and nephews uncounted, buried in the red soil of Cuffeetown Creek. Evermore, Americans.

Katy stood at the stern rail and watched Charlestown become a smudge, and the smudge slowly disappear.

She wasn't sure what she thought.

Is this a beginning, or an end?

Heinrich refused to watch. Nostalgia was for children. God, he was tired!

He wondered what Halifax was like. What Nova Scotia was like. New Scotland!

Stumpel, the bastard!

Nineteen

For a while, neither of them said anything. They were both wary and awkward, but even so . . . the air seemed . . . deflated of hostility. Dragonflies skittered on the creek. A dead leaf floated by, and they both watched it go, snagging here and there on twigs and stones, but finally working its way out of sight. Katy groped for words. There were so many of them! So many tumbling about in her head they couldn't seem to find a way out. *And so we came to the end. But what happens when you get to the end, and it doesn't stop? How to explain that? It's a new beginning, and beginnings are always perilous.*

January 1783
Halifax, Nova Scotia

Then they backed into the future. They stood in a knot on the aft deck, staring back at the invisible spot on the ocean where they knew Charlestown to be, although it had long vanished from sight.

So very, very many dreams, below the horizon!

Only Heinrich Strum stood in the bow, watching the gulls planing, waiting for the first chill air of a New England autumn day.

On the fourth day at sea, Friedrich Ruppert went below decks and never came back up. He died there among the lashed cannon and boxes of ordnance, among the bundled swords, piles of military uniforms, tuns of biscuit, all the stores of an army on the move.

He hadn't been really sick, that anyone knew.

He simply . . . stopped.

Perhaps he was thinking of the wife he had left behind in her shallow grave outside Dorchester; perhaps the sight of his two children was an unbearable reminder of what he had lost; perhaps the screams of men and the pain of women had knotted up his brain; perhaps the sight and sound and smell of armies simply sickened him. Perhaps it was none of those things.

Perhaps he just grew tired.

It's not an omen, not at all. Katy watched as Friedrich's body slid into the oily sea, and she chanted the prayers to the dead, an incantation against loneliness. The girls were dry-eyed and solemn by the railing. Eva Michler had offered to take them, but their Uncle Christoph's wife Margaret said she would take the eight-year-old, Catherine, with her when they went . . . when they went she knew not where; the other child, Barbara, five, Eva and Daniel would add to their own brood, one more child to five others, what difference did it make? The Michlers didn't know where they would end up either—*in some Stumpeltown somewhere.*

Katy stared at Eva, sensing her strength. *We should stay with her, wherever she goes, my Abraham and me.*

After two uneventful days at sea, they reached New York. They made their way up the harbor and moored in the East River near the southern tip of the island. There they stayed for ten days, immobile, while army officers came and went, huddled in the captain's quarters, and left, looking worried.

Katy asked Heinrich what was going on, and Heinrich asked Campbell and Campbell asked Colonel John Hamilton, who spent several days ashore.

Heinrich didn't like Hamilton much, but the man was well informed and had become something of a leader among the Loyalists since he had helped organize the militia in Ninety Six after the fall of Charlestown. He'd served briefly under Patrick Ferguson, but had missed the chaos at King's Mountain. He was captured without a struggle the day of the siege of Ninety Six and exchanged in Charlestown, where, of course, he had been named Inspector of Refugees.

Hamilton was forthcoming, even garrulous, on the subject of New York. The place was a mess, crowded with impoverished and desperate people, rife with politics, double-dealing, favoritism, betrayal, deception and perfidy. Since the signing of the preliminary peace in September, New York had become the center of Loyalist affairs, the spider in the web of British North America. Its fortunes, and the fortunes of everyone in all the provinces, now lay with Sir Guy Carleton, His Majesty's Supreme Commander in America. He was surrounded, almost smothered, by American Loyalist leaders, men to whom his decisions and the outcome of his negotiations meant almost certain banishment, bankruptcy and ruin. No wonder, Hamilton said, it was hard to get a word in edgewise.

"The place is overrun," he said. "You think Charlestown was bad, James Island a mess, Rawdontown a joke. You should see New York. They say more than fifty thousand refugees have struggled into the city and to the shores of Long Island, most of them fleeing their neighbors and their neighbors' vengeance. This is what loyalty has brought them! They remained loyal to the Crown at the cost of everything they have. But does it save them from the slights and insults of British generals? Not at all! And you should see how the German mercenaries treat them," he said, looking sharply at whatever Palatines were nearby, as though it were their fault. "Carleton's not so bad, I hear, if you can get to him—he seems determined, in any case, not to evacuate the city until some place has been found for all the refugees. But you don't want to be in that place! No sir! If people don't starve in there, I'd be mighty surprised."

Katy stared across the water to the smoky city beyond. Not very much was to be seen, mostly warehouses and the masts of shipping. Fifty thousand unhappy people! Fifty thousand five hundred, if you counted their little convoy. She tried to imagine the great, brooding continent beyond New York island. Did anyone yet know where it ended, how big it was, how far it went? She supposed fifty thousand would disappear if you dropped them in the middle of all that great wilderness, but it was still a great number, and there would be thousands and thousands of others living secretly among the Rebels, too timid to say anything, too afraid not to pretend. What a way to begin a new country, in suspicion and dread!

How can they ever possibly heal this place!

Back in Charlestown, things hadn't been going well for either side. Instead of taking a month, the evacuation had taken three, and by the time the last British vessel crossed the Bar and vanished over the horizon, the countryside was stripped bare of livestock and wildlife, and the waiting American armies were destitute. They'd been camped in the surrounding swamplands since the spring, suffering from disease and dysentery; there was scarcely an officer free from sickness, and as General Moultrie gloomily confided to his journal, "a dreadful return of the mortality that had prevailed."

And then there was politics. Politics! At the end of a long and bloody war, at the point of victory, the snobbishness of the wealthy merchants and the great planters—of *Society*, Charlestown's sickness—reasserted itself. There were parades in the capital, and grand speeches, and endless locutions in the Assembly on the greatness of the democratic ideal and how obvious and inevitable its victory had been all along, and Charlestown patted itself on its brocaded back and congratulated itself on the fortitude with which it had borne its occupation. But the provincial militias were not invited to the festivities. No, the partisans were thought too "ragged" to actually enter the city they had helped liberate; they were, in Moultrie's resentful words, "ungratefully disbanded in swamp and thicket, without pay or praise, naked, starving."

The common soldier, uninvited to the victory gavotte.

Given a few Congressional dollars and sent on home. Go on! Git!

They drifted away, living on frogs and alligators, away across the barrens, up the Santee and the Enoree, up to the Saluda, back to Long Canes and the frontier settlements. Along the way they passed the vacant farms of the absent Loyalists, and in episodes of fitful violence, some barns were burned and houses broken down, but more in rage against their own commanders than any animus against any persons. There was little desire any longer to confiscate the land itself. Land wasn't the point. Everyone had as much land as he needed. To work the land took energy and energy took food, and there wasn't enough food to go around.

There were beggars everywhere. Travelers were beset with them. Every tavern and store was surrounded; to get a drink, you had to brush them off like flies; to buy a pound of salt, you had to run the gauntlet in and run the gauntlet out, while their hands plucked at your clothing.

Now that the war was over, there were no Tories any more, and the name simply fell away. But that didn't mean there were no outlyer families left living in the woods, or groups of wild orphans, or horse and cattle thieves, criminals and murderers. A name was just a name, survival still necessary.

In late October, Philip Zimmermann called a meeting at Ninety Six. Several hundred people came, because Congress had sent a wagon train of emergency supplies to the district and the announcement of its arrival coincided with Zimmermann's summons.

"What was the meeting about?" Anna asked Peter when he returned.

"He wants us to build a church and new schools."

Anna looked skeptical. "Sheriff's office and a jail, more likely."

"I thought so, too, at first. So did most of the others. Many still do. But he convinced me."

Anna looked around at their cabin, at their meager possessions and at the row of guns in a rack by the door. "Convince me," she said.

He considered. How to summarize Zimmermann's eloquence? The man was so damn fluent! Could have been a preacher. "What he said was, if we who remain act and behave in as normal a way as possible, then we'll become as normal a society as possible. Or rather, he put it the other way around: We'll never be normal, he said, unless we act normal. It's like this. You can be angry, really furious, and in reaction you can sit at home and brood, or go out and harm the person who angered you. But if instead you act normal—you go out and plow a field—after a while your anger will probably fade, but even if it doesn't, you'll at least have food on the table as a consequence of your plowing, and no one will have been infected by your anger because they didn't know you harbored it because you were out in the fields, staring at the plow . . . It's like that with us, he said. If we build prisons and send posses into the woods, we will clean up the criminals, but what will happen to our children? Instead, we should hire teachers and preachers who never mention the dreadful events of war, and then at least the children will think normally, and their children, our children's children, will at last be able to celebrate our victory . . ."

Normal! Anna thought. *Will we ever be normal? We've won this great victory, and everything is the same. The same people will win, the same people will always lose. Someone has to build bridges and operate ferries, some one has to stand guard, preach to the people, teach our children, hang criminals, sell salt, brew beer . . . They did it before, they have to do it after. What, after all, have we gained?*

Does sending the soldiers home to England put food on our table?

Will my children eat better, live better, be better?

Are we better people because our neighbors have fled?

Why does victory taste so hollow?

For a long while, there was silence. Philip was right, of course. She bent to the pot, preparing the evening meal. Normal would come. After several hundred years, what they had gone through would just be another story, a tale to amuse the children, all its blood and anger, passion and fire, leached away. The tale of General George and his mighty Patriots would be told in schools across America, and the children would clap and giggle, and it would be just a story, as real or unreal as Hansel and Gretel . . .

She stared into the flames.

They would forget the pain.

Katy, sister, sister traitor, where are you now?

On November 26, the *Nova Scotia Gazette and Weekly Chronicle* carried a small, non-committal paragraph: "Since our last, arrived here a number of Transports from Charlestown, under Convoy of the Perseverance and Ceres Frigatas. We hear that these vessels have brought all the heavy Cannon and Ordnance Stores of the Garrison and that the final Evacuation was to take place in a few days after their departure. Between 4, and 5000 of the inhabitants have removed to Augustine, a number to New York, and about 300 have arrived here."

The new governor of the Nova Scotia colony, Parr, a small, vain, incompetent bureaucrat from an influential family, reported on their arrival in a letter to his master, the Right Honorable Thomas Townsend, one of His Majesty's principal Secretaries of State and the one under whose lofty purview Halifax and its doings might be said to roost. "Sir, I have the honor to inform you that, with the arrival of the heavy Ordinance from Charlestown in South Carolina, came five hundred and one

Refugees, men, women and Children; in consequence of directions from Sir Guy Carleton to Lieutenant General Leslie, who has sent them to the Care of Major General Paterson, commander of the Troops in the Province; with whom I have Concurr'd, as far as was in my power, to afford them a reception."

To a colleague, Parr was a trifle more anxious. "Those [refugees] from Charleston are in a much more miserable situation than those from New York, coming almost naked from the burning sands of South Carolina to the frozen coast of Nova Scotia destitute of almost every necessary of life."

If the burning sands were something of an exaggeration, so was the frozen coast of Nova Scotia. It wasn't frozen solid. Not yet. And they did have clothing, if not nearly enough.

Still, Parr was right, to a metaphorical point.

They sailed in past Sambro Light under the suspicious scrutiny of its keepers. Up the long channel, McNab's Island to the right, looming, rusty banks to the left. A naval frigate was moored there, watchfully. The banks, almost high enough to be called cliffs, were dusted with a thin coating of frost or snow, they couldn't tell which. The sky overhead was leaden, the wind chill, the air gray with smoke, the restless sea the color of lead.

Halifax harbor was like a broad, placid river between the hills, guarded from the ocean by a few heavily wooded islands, black spruce covered with lichens and seamoss. As they pushed up the channel, they saw the harbor was dotted with sails of every description and size.

After half an hour's steady progress, the town came into view on the left.

"It's so small!" Katy said, wondering. "Neat enough, but so small! Is that all there is?"

The town was laid out in regular blocks on a hill sloping down to the harbor. It was about a mile wide but only four blocks deep. The streets were gray, rock and gravel, a uniform fifty-five feet. There were a few stone houses, but most of the buildings were gray-painted wood with blue slate roofs.

"It looks fine from the sea, doesn't it?" said a corporal who had been there before. "All wood houses, a town of boards nailed together. A wood house, well made, is as good as stone, and warmer."

He shook his head. "Up close, though, not so fine. Except for the lodging houses and taverns, most of these places are just one storey high, only one room on the ground floor, dreadful crowded. The streets'll break your neck in the dark. The only real buildings are those there." He pointed. "At the top of the hill, the fort, the blockhouses, the magazines, the officers' quarters and the barracks. Somewhere the governor's house. Over there is the English church. There's also a German church. And a Catholic chapel."

"How many people, altogether?"

Colonel Campbell, who was standing nearby, shook his head and looked gloomy. "Including the soldiers, perhaps six thousand," he said. "But you see those buildings on the foreshore, warehouses, tanneries, breweries, distilleries and the like? Filled up now with refugees, I hear."

He straightened. "It must be difficult for them, you know. Where to put everyone? How to find enough stores? And this is just the vanguard! Maybe three hundred went directly to the Annapolis Valley, across the province, but Halifax has taken the majority. They're in every house that can be spared, in warehouses here on the waterfront, under canvas up there on Citadel Hill and at Point Pleasant, back where we passed, and in two of the churches, St. Paul's, I think, and Mather's."

He went on, but Katy wasn't listening. She had stopped at the words "under canvas." She said nothing, but stared across at the town as it drifted slowly by. Tents! Would they be made to live in tents? Again? Were they to go back to the London days, then? And in this cold!

Their vessel slid past the town toward a thicket of masts in what was called the King's Dockyard, a repair station for ships of war and the headquarters of His Majesty's navy. Tucked into a fold of the hillside was a squat, blinkered, stone building, jail for French prisoners. Otherwise there were just sheds, slipways, utilitarian entrepots, gantries and storehouses apparently scattered at random.

Katy, frozen, went below to warm up, and when she returned they were moored to a quayside between two ships of war, and two gangplanks had been lowered. A boat had taken a hawser end to the embankment, and they had been hauled smoothly in.

There was a reception committee, a dozen gloomy Hessians and a bustling little man on whom the ship's master pressed a bundle of papers, on which their names were supposed to be recorded. But the lists were far from complete, and the little man kept dropping pages, which didn't help.

He called them forward in family groups, checked them off and sent them across the gangplank.

"Strum, Heinrich, and three children?"

"Two children and a wife," Heinrich said.

"Wife? No mention here of a wife!"

"Well, there is, wife Isabella."

"All right, all right," the little man said, scribbling. "Pass."

They shuffled off the ship and waited on the quay.

"Strum, Jacob, wife and two children?"

"Yes."

"Go on, go on," he said impatiently, waving them forward.

"Ruppert, Christoph, Margaret, Friedrich, Barbara, children . . ."

Christoph was holding his niece Catherine by her hand. "My brother Friedrich and his wife Barbara didn't survive," he said. "I have one of the children."

"And the other?"

"With the Michlers."

"Ah yes, Michler, Daniel, Eva, five children . . ."

"Six," Eva said. "The Ruppert child, Barbara, is with us."

"Eh, yes, good," he said, scribbling. "Who's next? Bower, Adam, Catherine, Elizabeth and . . ."

"Alizabetha," Alizabetha said. "Not Elizabeth. And it's Katherina. Bauer, not Bower."

"Move on," he said, "get on with you."

Katy passed across the gangplank with Abraham, Peter and the Merks, Rosannah and Conrad. Behind them came Lorentz and Molly, and Conrad's sister Anna Maria Schade with her husband.

From the other ship came Karl and Philip Bauer, Katy's son, young John Frietz, Henry Siteman with his wife Barbara and their five children, Christian Zange with Juliana, John Dorris, Chambers Blakeley, Nick Cruhm and eight Webers, Georg and Mary with their sons and daughters.

Their possessions, such as they were, were piled in an untidy heap near the warehouse wall. It seemed, and was, a pathetically small pile. The little man with his papers thought so, too.

"Is that all there is?" he asked skeptically. "Perhaps it's as well. A New York family arrived here with a boatload of things, including a pianoforte. Can you imagine?" He looked at them sharply, down his nose. "There is, of course, nowhere to put it. And I fancy it will be broken up for firewood soon enough, soon's the winter sets in for good." He gave them another sharp look. "A faggot's worth gold in this town, as you'll see."

An hour later their little procession left the quay and straggled up through the town. The place resembled an agitated anthill. It was filled with soldiers and civilians, many of them clutching small parcels. Lodging houses and taverns were crawling with men and women. Half the houses had sentries posted outside, presumably to guard against the homeless simply rushing in and taking possession. Every shop had its door guarded and its windows barred. They came up over the shoulder of the citadel's hill and crossed a foul-smelling ditch onto the common. There was a chill wind coming out of the northwest; clouds were scudding across the sky. They could see white smoke from some distant fire. On the common itself were neat rows of flimsy huts and teepees, cobbled together from skinny tree trunks, brush and old boards, their canvas doors quivering in the wind. There was firewood neatly piled outside each door. On the fringes of this army-regimented "village" were more miserable sights: families huddled in torn and discarded army tents, people crouching over smoky fires under deckhouses ripped from boats and set down in the mud.

Katy pulled her shawl tightly about her, huddling against the cold, and stared. There must be hundreds of these huts! A tent city for thousands of people! A sudden gust made the nearest teepee rattle. Her heart sank.

We'll freeze! Spring is five months away, they say, a hundred and fifty days and nights in a tent, ice on the soul, frost settling on the bones, they'll tell us we'll be all right but the soft snow will fall on the words and blur their meaning and . . . oh, God, will we still be here, in the spring?

Ahead of her Heinrich strode with his children and his plump wife. One of his hands was on Eve's shoulder, the other hefting a bulky pack. Isabella stumbled on the rough ground and he reached out to steady her. How strong he was!

There were people everywhere, laboring, parading, standing in line, waiting to be assigned lodgings, to receive clothing, salt meat, flour, peas. In the center was the Provost Marshal's quarters. There were two rows of sentries guarding its entrance. Those sentries would be greatly needed in time, the little man said. Six thousand people in town now, and five thousand refugees on their way. Maybe more. Many more, how many he couldn't say. It was going to get worse, much worse.

He led them past the Provost Marshal's. They already had lodgings assigned, their guide told them. He consulted another paper. Those wigwams, over there . . .

Wigwams? Tents. Teepees. So it was true. They'd come to roost in tents again, after all.

They'd have to endure, again. Katy steeled herself. Endure they would. For four months, six, a year, whatever it took. They'd huddle around the fires at night. By day there'd be gatherings, work to do, schooling to arrange, they'd be warm, they'd be together, they would come through.

And in the spring, what?

There'd be land, again, land to till, a house to build . . .

God help us, let this be the last one!

In the morning, having burned an alarming proportion of their meager ration of firewood, Abraham and Peter went in search of a secure supply. They came back late in the afternoon with a cartload, but looking grim.

"It's frightful," Abraham said as he stooped to rekindle the blaze. "A desolate sight. There's wood here and there, on what they call the Arm, and other places. But for thirty miles, forty, north and south, there have been fires. Blackened trunks of trees, jumbled everywhere, impenetrable save by the roads the army has pushed through, everything black and covered with ash, except here and there some brush, and a few small oaks that escaped the heat, the earth rocky, the soil thin, no farms, not anywhere, no one can cultivate this land . . ."

"Remember how different Ninety Six was from the swamps around Charlestown," Katy said in a reasonable tone, trying to quieten him down.

"What if the whole place is rocky like this? You can't grow anything in rock!"

"You got wood," Katy said, heading him off.

"The fires that swept through didn't entirely burn the trees. Only enough to kill them. The wood's still good. For this year, anyway."

"Why so much fire?"

"Some Hessian soldiers told us the Indians burned the place down, I suppose in indignation at having their land taken from them. Burned everything around. For almost a week in the late summer, they said, you couldn't see for smoke, clouds of black smoke filled the sky, choking everything." He looked up. His own little fire was burning clean, a brisk and bright little blaze to chase away the Indians' spirits. "Someone else told us there were but three fires, two set by hunters and one by a sawmill, and the woods had been tinder-dry after a rainless summer."

"Are there Indians about?" Katy asked.

"Yes. In town there are Indians, called Meegamaag, or Micmacs by the soldiers, friendly enough, and treated fairly, though inclined, so they say, to public drunkenness and lewd behavior. If they'd burned everything around, they'd be more feared, I think."

"No Indian attacks?"

"No, not any more."

"Well, that's a blessing." She thought for a moment, staring into the cheerful fire. "Where will they send us, do you think?"

"How do I know?" Abraham said irritably. "I spent the day looking for firewood."

In truth, he had asked, but had gotten no satisfactory reply. He didn't think it prudent to pass this on. It seemed the Nova Scotia authorities, having had no detailed instructions from London, were inclined not to do very much. The governor, Parr, aided by his aged Surveyor General, Charles Morris, and his son, also called Charles, had taken a set of provincial maps, and laid out for settlement the unoccupied areas of the province. But everyone knew they couldn't go yet, not until the spring. The land would have to be properly surveyed, first, for town lots, garden lots and big lots for farms. And the settlers would have to be supplied from Halifax, at least for the first two years, and maybe longer.

Abraham had probed his informants as much as he could. It seemed hardly anyone within a day or two of Halifax actually cultivated any land. It was too rocky, too sour, too thin. The townsfolk were all just townsfolk, and engaged in trade of one form or another, some of it petty, some of it quite substantial, with the Islands as well as with England itself. But no one grew anything. There were said to be good farms across the province on Fundy Bay, farms stolen from the French, expelled to who knew where—Stumpel had boasted of his small part in that. And there were pockets of good land around some of the southern bays, around Lunenburg, LaHave and other places. Jacob Strum had told Abraham he'd been talking to a few farmers from that part. Germans, he said, mostly Palatines like us, or from Schwabia and the southern border. Zwicker. Mader. Hartel. Becker. They'd brought a boatload of cabbages and turnips up to town to sell. Also, Abraham was told, there were still great forests along the shore. But except for a very few places, no substantial farming. Fishing was what they mostly did.

A most curious place. It was cheaper, it seemed, to burn coal from England than to cut fuel from the forests that everywhere surrounded the city. Except, of course, for the forty miles burned, the whole place was one gigantic forest. But everyone shunned it. It wasn't natural.

No garrison city is natural, Katy told him when he'd said all this.

They fell silent. Katy thought of Halifax, as far as she had seen it earlier that day. How wretched it was! The streets a mix of half-frozen muck and stones, churned into a porridge by the boots of the soldiers and the restless wandering of refugees. The place stank of the codfish drying on the roofs of the warehouses, the slops thrown carelessly into the roadway and the open sewers flowing down the hill to the harbor. Shops were poorly stocked, but the taverns were doing a roaring trade, with reeling men going out and in, raucous laughter, drunken brawls and retching in the streets. Tucked into corners and alleys between houses were crude board tables, on which stony-faced and freezing refugees had laid out what trinkets they had for sale, trying to raise money for lodging by passing off their jewelry and silver oddments.

She thought of the shrieking and screaming she'd heard from the taverns. Someone had told her afterward that Halifax was garrisoned with three regiments of artillery and three of whores. Huh! She could believe it.

Endure, yes. It's the proper word.

In January, the governor wrote to the Right Honorable Thomas Townsend: "Five Hundred Refugees arrived here in November from Charlestown.

Every thing has been done to ajust [sic] them in settling themselves in the Province and I flatter myself they will be a great acquisition to it."

"Every thing" wasn't very much. Rations were provided to heads of families a week at a time. Clothing and blankets were distributed when available, but there were never quite enough. Promises were made about land, but no allotments, and no surveying was done in the winter. Apart from that, Parr simply waited for someone to tell him what to do. He seemed to fret more about the livery of his servants than the fate of his wretched charges.

The days slipped by. The women and children stayed near the common, cooking on the great open fires the army provisioners maintained, boiling clothing in the large cauldrons, gossiping, sewing, shopping the meager shops or on the wharves with what money they could scrounge. The men spent their days scavenging for firewood, for which there was a constant, relentless need. Many of them hunted, till there was hardly a rabbit, a chipmunk, a porcupine within ten miles, much less a deer. Peter Frietz and Christian Zange had discovered the northern pastime of ice fishing. Halifax harbor never froze, but Northwest Arm did. They hacked a hole in the ice and lowered their lines, easy as fishing in a barrel. Sundry fishes—no one knew their names. They would cook these in the smoke from the camp fires, eat them with kraut and potatoes from Lunenburg, more German food than they'd had in twenty years.

It was cold, unbelievably cold. And damp.

Heinrich Strum spent the daylight hours on the ice, fishing, or in the woods. Sometimes he'd take the children, but most often just Eve, a solemn, wordless, determined girl who followed her father everywhere. She seemed to like ice fishing, and would spend hours staring into the jagged hole, waiting. Isabella's laughter and good humor were unable to penetrate their quietness, though she never seemed to notice. Young Henry roamed with his cousins, the Michler boys. Katy worried about Eve. And she worried about Heinrich's long silences.

He's the strong one! He can't give up on us now!

At night, they huddled in their tents and teepees, a dozen, fifteen, twenty to each, sleeping on top of each other or nested like spoons for warmth, bundled in their blankets and clothing and what furs the hunting had provided. When they could buy tobacco, they smoked. They gossiped. And they worried about where they were going.

In the middle of the first month, Colonel Hamilton, virtually the only refugee with enough social panache to get himself invited to the Governor's rather pretentious little mansion, ran into a visiting New Yorker, Joseph Pynchon, who was in Halifax to negotiate with Parr on behalf of a group called the Port Roseway Associates. These were Loyalist officers and what Hamilton called "men of substance" who had formed themselves into an association and were jointly petitioning the Crown for an attractive parcel of Nova Scotia land. They would be granted the land collectively, and would later draw lots to divide it up. Hamilton had met Pynchon briefly in New York, and had developed an interest in the putative settlement. Now he proposed in earnest that his Carolinians be invited to join. Pynchon hesitated. Parr had indicated that they were to be sent elsewhere, though he didn't yet know where. Besides . . . He would see . . . They would talk further . . .

Hamilton wasn't daunted by Pynchon's hesitancy. He had determined to find a place for "his" refugees, and departed for New York to discuss the matter with Carleton directly. His directness, his bluff military manner and his eloquent exposition of the sufferings of the Ninety Sixers prevailed. He came away with what he wanted. He would get his land. Provisions and other supplies were ordered for his refugees "in the same manner and in equal proportion" to the allotments to others still on their way to Nova Scotia, and "as soon as the season renders it advisable" they would leave their tents and move down the coast to their new lands. The commissary at Halifax would assign them a full year's provisions. Hamilton was given a paper allotting him "a full allowance to 129 men, 130 women and youths, and 24 Black servants, and a half allowance to 65 children."

Among those who would go were all the Strums, Heinrich and his family, Jacob with his, Eva Michler with Daniel and their children. Katy Frietz and her family would go, including Peter and his wife-to-be, Frances Hater, and her daughter Rosannah, with husband Conrad Merk. All the Bauers would go. The balance of the refugees from Charlestown would go to Ship Harbour, on the Eastern Shore.

They would all move when spring came, they were told.

It was something to look forward to.

One morning around ten, Katy burst into a teepee where Isabella and some of the girls were sitting.

"I've seen him!" she said. "I've seen Stumpel!"

"Who's Stumpel?" Isabella asked.

Who's Stumpel? Stumpel's the bastard! Stumpel's the one who . . . But Isabella knew none of that. Why should she? None of them had cared to discuss the past.

"He's the one who caused our ruin," she said, wondering if it were any longer true, or if it really had been true, even then.

"How can he be here?" Isabella asked skeptically after Katy told her the tale. "From what you say, he's either in some prison somewhere or living off the fat of the land. Not marching around a frozen village in the middle of winter."

"I don't know," Katy said. "But I know it was him. Walking around with other soldiers. Going somewhere. But it *was* him."

That evening she told the men, and in the morning Heinrich Strum went looking for *the miserable bastard*, though what he'd do if he turned him up, even Heinrich didn't know. But how could he not look?

He came back a few hours later. "No one seems to know," he said. "It's possible he was with a regiment recently disbanded here. Some of them were Hessian mercenaries. The army's paying them off in land. I'm told it's somewhere south of here. Around Lunenburg. The LaHave River."

"Is that near Port Roseway?" Katy asked. *Will we be neighbors, after all this time? There's a dish of coincidence, fit for a king!*

"No, I don't think so," Heinrich said.

"What will you do if you find him?"

"I'll think of something," he said, staring at her expressionlessly.

But there was no sign of Stumpel, then or later, though years afterward, someone told them there'd been a land grant in his name near New Dublin, at the mouth of the LaHave River. He'd never taken it up. He'd vanished, as he'd done before. Had he even known they were in the province?

Would he have cared, had he known? she wondered.

And then she thought, *Would he even remember?*

It grew colder, even colder.

Hamilton spent a good deal of his time with the Governor's cronies. Campbell, who would lead them to Port Roseway, went with him. Heinrich Strum spent even more time alone, in the bush. Katy herself endured, as she had promised herself she would. Abraham looked worn out. But she found herself inexplicably cheerful much of the time.

I always knew I'd come through.

For the first time in ages, she thought of Anna.

Is she glad? When she thinks of us, is she glad? Has she got the joy of a victor, or the guilt of a survivor?

In Carolina, no one confiscated or appropriated the Frietz land. Once or twice, Peter Dorst chased squatters off and re-sealed the house. He couldn't have said why he did it. It was just something he had to do, with Anna's unspoken encouragement.

The Merk land, too, remained their own. Old Balthazar was still alive. He spent his days in bitter quarrels with his youngest, Johan, over his part in the late lamented war, and waited without hope for the return of his family. Johan, for his part, made sure Conrad's farm was secure and tended. Lorentz's fields reverted to wilderness.

No one went near the Strum land. Not even squatters.

Anna visited once or twice, but it was full of ghosts, and she could hear their silent cries in her mind. Going there made her sad for the might-have-beens.

Afterward, she always stopped with Maria Elizabeth, who was living in her old home with Rosena and her husband David Rush. They would sit on the bench down by Cuffeetown Creek. They usually talked about the children. That was a comfortable thing. Sometimes they held hands, for warmth, for contact and because of what had passed.

On the 12th day of January came a blinding storm and . . . Katy was never afterward able to think of it without anguish.

Why?

The elements, the weather, the universe, were never fair. But this seemed so . . . grotesquely arbitrary.

Even by the standards of what they had gone through.

She remembered it all, suddenly. Twenty years of it. Seduced and cheated, then abandoned. Beset by fever, banditry, evil quarrels, war, betrayals, death. Almost five hundred when they started, down to what, fifty?

And now this . . .

Young Henry Strum slipped into their teepee as they were preparing for sleep. His face was white, but whether from cold or fright Katy couldn't tell.

"What is it?" she asked.

"It's Pa," he said. "Pa and Eve. They went out this morning and they aren't back. They should be back by now. Isabella sent me."

Katy listened to the wind. It wasn't blowing as hard, but it was still blowing, and the snow was still driving down the smoke flap, through the cracks and drifting against the doorway. There was two, maybe three feet of it fresh on the ground, and still coming down.

She remembered Heinrich leaving that morning, before it started. It had been a queer day, the air startlingly clear and still, as though everything was being viewed through a magic glass. Every stone of the citadel stood out, every grain of the clapboard houses below. The black spruces seemed blacker than ever, every needle sharp and clear. The sun was a barely perceived disk, a white disk in a white sky, turning leaden. Those ships that could reach harbor did so; mariners battened down everything loose. The Indians vanished from town. And Heinrich Strum went ice fishing with his daughter.

He strode off along the path to the Northwest Arm. Katy saw the two of them disappearing over the rise. The girl's small hand was in his. His head was bare. She remembered thinking he was going to need a head-covering, and hoped there was one in his pack. She had noticed his head, because although he had been going gray, that morning his hair had seemed as ominously black as a raven's wing.

The shiny black of a beetle's back, she thought. Black as a crow. Black as fate. Then she caught herself.

I'm rambling! It's just hair.

The storm descended quickly, first a gust, then a steady, howling wind, and with it the snow, coming in horizontally, driving into every crack and cranny of every tent and every teepee; the gray vanished and the world turned white.

The storm had lasted all day and showed no signs of abating.

She'd huddled close to the fire and hadn't thought of Strum and his daughter again.

Henry stood rigid in the doorway. She pulled him in and hugged him to her, trying to get him to unbend.

"We'll find them," she said. "Wherever they are. I'm sure they're safe."

"They should have been home by now," he said, pulling himself away.

Abraham, Peter and John were pulling on extra coats and wrapping their heads and bodies in shawls.

"We'll find them, you'll see."

They roused Karl Bauer and Heinrich's brother Jacob. They tied themselves to a long piece of rope and set off into the driving snow in the direction of the Arm. Isabella came into the teepee as they left, ashen and, for once, silent. She sat with her stepson and waited. As they all did.

An hour went by, two, three. The wind kept up. Katy built up the fire and they huddled around it, staring into the flames, trying not to think. Henry fell asleep, head in Isabella's ample lap. Katy herself dozed off, awaking shivering when the fire died down and the cold seeped into her unconscious. She built it up again.

What are we waiting for? He's strong, a survivor! Of all of us, he'll come through!

But she wasn't sure. This northern land was so unforgiving. Perhaps it was because they hadn't yet seen a spring, but there seemed a rawness to the landscape, a savagery that was impersonal, even vengeful. And they were going to have to put down roots here.

How can we survive in a land without flowers?

At sunup, or what would have been sunup, there was a mournful, muffled bugling from the fortification, the sound strangled by the snow. Soldiers getting up for parade? What for? No one will see them in this weather, not even the mustering officer. Not a weather for invaders, either.

Stop it!

The boy Henry cried out in his sleep, and she shivered. Where were they?

She began to worry anew then. Could something else have gone wrong? You couldn't lose five men on a string! But perhaps there was something else out there . . . It was easy to believe in some malevolent force when there was no sound and visibility was reduced to an arm's length.

Stop it!

Without warning the canvas doorway was hurled aside and a gray monster filled the opening. Isabella screamed. Henry sprang to his feet. Katy stared. It was Karl and Peter, backing into the teepee, dragging a heavy bundle behind them. They were panting, gasping, like a horse after a thirty-mile dash.

They dragged the bundle nearer the fire, scattering the others. It was Heinrich, with Eve clasped in his arms, covered with snow, frost in his hair, on his lips, in his eyes, his nostrils clogged with it. Eve was invisible, wrapped in his coat, locked in his embrace.

Jacob and Abraham staggered in after them, with the boy John following. Jacob was breathing raggedly, half wheeze and half gasp. He moved forward, then began to laugh, a queer, high, nervous giggle.

"They're frozen together," he said, the giggle almost strangling the words. "Need an ax to chip 'em apart . . ."

Stop it!

"Are they alive?" Katy demanded.

"No, yes, they're frozen, found 'em near the path down by the Arm, going the right way in the end, never knew it, lost in the blizzard, not knowing which way was which. They were very close to the path, could have made it back, we should have looked earlier, could have helped them . . ."

"Stop it," she screamed.

Isabella moved forward. "Everyone not needed, out," she commanded. "Leave us to do what we must."

The bundle had been dropped close to the fire. Someone had added kindling and split wood, and the fire blazed fiercely. The snow started to fall away in wet clumps. Their skin was pale, the colorlessness of frost, very cold to the touch.

Katy retreated, near where Henry was standing rigidly, staring. Isabella had taken charge, was doing what had to be done. Stripping away the clothing, drying, wrapping in blankets, rubbing the extremities. Peter's Frances, who had appeared from nowhere, began warming gruel on the fire. It would get something hot inside them, if they could swallow.

If they could swallow! If they were alive!

They can't be dead! Too much death already! Started out as five hundred hapless Palatine Protestants, dying on a London heath. She remembered the shrouds slipping overboard on the *Dragon*, so many bodies wrapped in canvas that there was scarce a scrap left for sails. Anna trapped below, giving birth in the shit and the stench. Death and life. Maybe the Cherokee spirits had seen them coming, had sent angels with raven's-feather wings to greet them, stop them before they could make their rigid furrows in the sacred land, but had been confused by the death and life, life and death. Poor Heinrich! Elizabeth, her body torn and bleeding. Catherine, killed by her own neighbors in a moon-madness frenzy. His children, scattered, taken by fevers and fluxes. And Isabella! Didn't he deserve Isabella at last, with her jolly laughter and big, warm breasts, maybe she should push a nipple in his lips, fill him with the milk of human kindness!

Isabella was on the ground, Heinrich in her arms, rocking back and forth, rubbing, chafing, crooning.

They had pried the girl from his arms, with great difficulty, and laid her out. But it was no good. No point in chafing there. She was an icicle. He had taken her in his arms out there in the blind, fumbling blizzard, wrapped her in his greatcoat next to his great heart, but it had been for nothing, she was frozen through, the breath ice in her lungs, her limbs rigid, poor little thing.

Henry, dry-eyed and blind with staring, was all that was left.

Heinrich, though, was alive, clinging to life by the thinnest of fraying threads.

Clinging to life? No, life was clinging to him. It knew where it had been most at home.

They stayed like that until midday. No one moved. Adam Bauer came by several times to inquire, and left to spread what meager news there was. Their hopes were centered on that thinnest of threads.

In the middle of the afternoon, Heinrich trembled, ever so slightly, in Isabella's embrace. Katy stared at his face, lined and seamed, carved by his long weariness. As she stared, his eyes flickered once, maybe it was pain, maybe grief, maybe nothing but her imagination, but then he was gone.

Isabella, feeling the life drain from him at last, started to wail.

Henry, too, breaking their hearts.

Katy took Abraham's large, comforting paw.

She felt despair clutching at her, fought it off.

No! No! The bucket of our story is empty, but it will fill up again. Conrad's children, Peter's children, they will fill up the bucket with new life.

Port Roseway! Maybe I'll spend my last days in a cabin by the sea!

She felt a sudden yearning for the Carolina Back Country. Among the odors of damp cloth, smoke and old sweat, she thought she smelled crushed oak and sweet grass, and caught a sudden vision of Cuffeetown Creek, drifting placidly past the barn.

She squeezed Abraham's hand.

Could we have made it work, had we done things differently?

The creeks would flow, the grass would grow. The land didn't care, in the end. To the land, the human blood, shed in fear and anguish, the blood that flowed into the cracks and crevices of the earth, was just more nourishment for the wild things that grew there.

Perhaps that was the only lesson after all.

Not the pointlessness of savagery and violence. That was obvious

Just endurance.

Twenty

For a long time, neither of them said anything. They simply sat and stared at the sluggish creek. There was no sound from the farmhouse. Even the children were quiet. It was so still that they could plainly hear a bee, a dozen paces away; and when Katy stirred, the creaking of her shoe was as loud as the rattling of a passing cart.

Silence creeps in like a fog, when you least expect it.

At length, Anna sighed, stirred, shifting her bones on the boards. A sadness welled up in her, at the back of her throat, but there were no tears. She had used up her tears.

I wish I could mourn, just a little. Then it would be over.

"So that's how he died," she said at last. "Not from the sword, not from a bullet or a bayonet, not in the saddle, not with comrades, not from his wounds . . ."

"His wounds, yes," Katy interrupted, more sharply than she had intended. *Damn the woman! Why does she make me do this!* "His spirit was wounded, and in the end, that's what killed him, the grievous hurt he had sustained . . ." She stopped. The words sounded false to her, self-righteous. Why was she accusing Anna now?

But Anna conceded the point. "Perhaps you're right," she said. "Who wouldn't be wounded, losing two wives and six, no, seven, of his eight children?"

"And his country!"

Anna was still conciliatory. "That, too."

The concession mollified Katy, and when the silence returned, it seemed less fog-like and more . . . companionable. Anna sat quietly. After a few minutes, a single tear did squeeze itself from her eye and rolled down her cheek.

"I loved him, you know," she said. Then, because that sounded too stark, she added, "in my way."

"We all did," Katy said.

"No, you don't understand," Anna said, impatient that her little confession hadn't been understood. "I loved him in . . . in that way."

"I know," Katy said, smiling a little. "We all did. You, me, Maria . . ."

"No, you still don't understand. I . . . wanted him . . ."

"I know. And Maria got him . . . in that way."

"Maria!"

"Yes, our dear, sweet Maria. She told me, once. Probably a lot of other people got him too. Ah, he was a sweet boy!"

"I should have!" Anna said. "Even if just once!"

They looked at each other and almost started to laugh. Anna thought, *Eighty years old, and there's juice yet!* She wanted to reach out for her sister's hand, but refrained. No, not yet.

"Katy," she said, "tell me what happened. Tell me what happened to the rest, after that great storm."

Katy got up, and went over to the creek, where she teetered on the bank, staring down into the brown water. She scuffed a leaf into the stream, watched it float away. After a minute, she returned to the bench.

"They buried him," she said at last. "Even there in Nova Scotia, even in January, when the ground is frozen. They dug and they dug and they chipped at the ice, and then we covered him with rocks and clumps of frozen earth. Others who died they took to sea and abandoned to the Atlantic, but Isabella wouldn't let them, and the boy Henry supported her."

She paused. Isabella! How quickly the jolly Isabella had found another man! By the spring, already. Arthur McRae, former King's American Dragoon, a nice enough man, poor fool. He moved on to the Saint John River. Got land at Kingston. Isabella herself got two half lots on Belle Isle Bay in 1786. Somewhere near John Hamilton, Katy believed.

Spring had come at last, even to Nova Scotia, and Halifax's icy streets turned to deep muck as the winter's slops washed down the hill into the harbor.

And like the spring runoff, the families that remained in their teepees were sent into the hinterlands, hither and yon, the final scattering of the "poor, wretched Palatines."

She ticked them off for Anna.

"Christoph and Margaret Ruppert, with their children and niece Barbara, along with many others followed John Hamilton to the Saint John River area. The Rupperts settled on the Kennebecasis River, but I believe they didn't stay there more than a few years.

"Some of the others went to a place called Ship Harbour." She thought for a moment. "Among our people, Christian Zange with Juliana, Nick Cruhm, Lorentz Merk, Georg Weber and all his family. I heard the Webers moved not long afterwards to Clam Harbour. Others went to a place they called Rawdon, named after . . ."

"I know who Rawdon was," Anna said impatiently.

"Damned insult, naming a Loyalist settlement after that man."

"I thought he was one of yours?"

Katy ignored her. Rawdontown, ironically named, was too complicated to explain.

In November '83, the South Carolina Royalists and King's Rangers arrived in Halifax from East Florida. "In the spring they went to a place called Country Harbour. Fritz Henn was among them. He didn't stay long either. I'll tell you about him . . ."

"Never mind Fritz Henn," Anna said. "Where did you go?"

"Shelburne," she said, a world of contempt in the word. "Shelburne, though it wasn't called that then. Port Roseway."

No sooner had they got to Port Roseway than Governor Parr renamed the place. Later he'd proudly caused to be published his toadying letter to Shelburne himself, and she could still recall every word. She mimicked the tone in her head, for the umpteenth time. Wretched little man! "I had," he had written, "the heartfelt satisfaction of shewing a small mark of my gratitude, by naming the first Harbour in the world after Your Lordship, and I flatter myself that the Town will in a very few years, be worthy of so fine a Harbour . . . My being so particular may seem trifling, but it proceeds from the joy and pleasure I felt, at the universal satisfaction that appeared, upon my naming Your Lordship aloud and the immediate firing of the Guns in the Town, the Fort, and the *Sophie* Frigate."

Just thinking of Parr made her angry all over again. What a choice for a name! They had all resented it bitterly. By then they had all read the Articles of Peace—hadn't a copy signed by Lafayette been found on a captured vessel, bound for Marblehead? It had been printed in the *Nova Scotia Gazette*. And hadn't it been perfectly clear from that document that Lord Shelburne, as Prime Minister of England, had signally failed to protect the Loyalists' interests?

It was a bitter blow to be betrayed, yet again, by their own side!

Well, at least the ship that had yielded up the Articles of Peace provided some sweeter fruit, too—lemons in boxes, raisins in cakes, sherry and Malaga wine and about four thousand bushels of Cadiz salt. She and Abraham had joined with a few other families to buy one of those raisin cakes at public auction.

Anna watched the play of emotions across her sister's face with some bemusement. At length, she interrupted the reverie.

"When?" she asked. "When and how to this Port Roseway? What did you do when you got there? What was it like?"

Ah, but it seems so long ago! We marched down through the muck to the dockside, Hamilton assuring us all the way that this was our last move, we were going home at last . . . But how were we to be sure that the rapacious Americans wouldn't want a fourteenth colony? There was plenty of sentiment in Nova Scotia for the American cause.

They climbed the gangplanks with their small bundles of necessaries, along with Colonel Campbell, whose family and slaves were already on board, and set sail, in the general direction of South Carolina, back past the Islands, back past the light, and on south . . . Hamilton stayed in Halifax. He was going to New Brunswick . . .

Of course, Heinrich Strum stayed in Halifax, too. We left him there, for the spring worms. For him, it was over. For us . . . Not yet.

They sailed all day in a favorable wind, a warm day with patches of light fog. Skirting the coast, a line of dark green forest punctuated by occasional cliffs the color of healing bruises. They fetched up that night in the town of Liverpool, where Sam Campbell went ashore.

A local merchant and man-about-village, Simeon Perkins, made a note the following morning in his diary: "1783, 7 May. Two small schooners from Halifax, with people for Roseway, came here in the Night. A Colonel Samuel Campbell (of the North Carolina Militia) is one of them. He is said to be a man of Property, has several black slaves with him. They go out again this morning."

They arrived at Port Roseway the next morning about ten. It was a warm spring day; the sun was glittering on the water and there was a gentle breeze from the southwest. To the east and north there were jumbled shoals, great granite boulders and tree-covered hills. She remembered the creaking of the rigging and the gentle slap of the waves as they eased their way into the harbor.

But what a shock, then! There were upward of thirty ships already there, and on the shore, thousands of people. Not a building in sight. Not a dock, not a wharf, not a warehouse, not a house, not a church, nothing. Just confused mobs, milling about apparently aimlessly. There *was* no town.

How to explain the chaos to Anna? And how disheartening it was, to discover that this final refuge was barren scrub and rock, that nothing had been done to prepare for them, and then to discover that thousands more were coming, that there was a tidal wave of misery approaching from New York, threatening to swamp everything?

They were rowed to the shore with their small baggages, and then the oarsmen rowed away, leaving them looking bewilderedly around.

Three thousand and thirty-seven people, it turned out, were already there, in the same situation as themselves.

God-damned Parr!

The surveyors, Benjamin Marston and William Morris, had only arrived in Port Roseway five days earlier with Thomas Pynchon. With the first New York fleet due in two days, and the Halifax contingent a few days after that, they'd quickly settled on a town site, but when the Associates arrived, they hated it and insisted on looking again, to Marston's great irritation, and appointed three men from each of their sixteen "companies" to accompany him. "That is to commit to a mere mob of sixty what a few judicious men found very difficult to transact with a lesser mob of twenty," Marston grumbled to his diary. "This cursed, republican, town-meeting spirit has been the ruin of us already . . ."

Anna was staring at her. "And was it freezing cold all this time?" she asked.

"It was summer, or at least spring," Katy said impatiently. "They do have summer in the north, you know."

Although she remembered mostly the fogs, in the first couple of weeks, heavy fogs that rolled in unexpectedly from the ocean, shrouds of gray trailing beads of damp.

For a while, they had stayed in temporary shelters and tents provided by the army, set up in the public square, or what was to be the public square when the town somehow got itself built. And they were set to work clearing trees, stumps, loose rock. How they worked! It gave no time for resentment at once again living under canvas.

"At least *we* worked," Katy said, remembering the soft New York towns-folk. "We were used to working. The others worked a few days and then left it to the surveyors to clear the roadways and prepare their lots for them."

Eventually the town lots had been prepared, each sixty feet by one hundred and twenty feet, sixteen lots to a block, each lot large enough for a considerable house and a small garden. They were to draw for these lots starting May 22.

How anxious they were, and how right to be anxious! Because the Associates, resentful of what they regarded as interlopers on "their" land, insisted that they and only they be allowed to draw lots, even though some, it became clear, were there to speculate in land, not to settle it. At least one was a Yankee skipper who just happened to be in town. One tried to bribe the surveyors by "sending one of them a green turtle."

In the last week of May, they were rudely pushed from their temporary shelters. Not, it turned out, to make way for the erection of public build-ings, at least a worthy cause, but for a more devious purpose, "to accom-modate sons of Favour . . . that go to Halifax with full pockets of a mettle well known in Mexico."

"And this," said Katy, still indignant at the memory, "before we had any place to go to. They hadn't drawn us any lots yet."

Anna said nothing. All this talk of speculators privately confirmed her already well-tested suspicion that many Loyalists were merely opportunists who had been found out by their neighbors. Her suspicion would have turned to certainty had she access to Marston's diary of the time, in which he recorded sourly that the Associates seemed "a set of Licentious villains whose only motive for coming here seems to have been the King's Provi-sions and a short respite from that Fate which must ever attend men of their character." It was a great victory for civility when she managed to hold her tongue and let Katy talk.

"Meanwhile," her sister said, oblivious to Anna's hidden act of generosity, "nothing had been done about surveying farms. It was another two years—two years!—before proper surveys were done. Meanwhile, ships kept coming, more and more people dumped in the common, with nowhere to go, hundreds of them, thousands . . ."

"Thousands?" Anna asked skeptically.

"Carleton sent another eight thousand Loyalists to Nova Scotia. Not all of them came to Roseway, but . . . enough did."

She paused, stirred, picked at her dress that lay heavy, heavy on her legs. Perhaps it wasn't so good to remember. It was over. And Abraham . . .

I lay against him at night, laying my hands on his back, that broad, comforting back, trying to infect him with energy, give him comfort and hope, but he was weary, much wearier than I. Heinrich's death took the stuffing from him. He was never the same after that.

On August 19, they finally got their town lots, in Parr's division on the northern side of town.

I—we—drew Lot A8, good enough.

She had gone to the lottery with her son John. Abraham had stayed in the small shed near the water in which they had been sheltering for the past few months. "You go," he'd said. "It'll be all right, you'll see." She had tried to cajole him into going, but he wouldn't. She'd been angry with him, she remembered, senselessly angry because you can't fight the dark with anger, you can only fight the blackness by lighting a candle and shining it into the shadowed corners of the heart. But weariness is contagious, and she hadn't the strength, then, to forego her angry words.

The surveyors were sitting at a table on the public grounds. They had written the lot numbers on scraps torn from sheets of paper, each scrap twisted into a roll so the number was obscured. She pulled her paper from the pile, smoothed it out and Marston noted her name and the number in his Book of Locations.

She'd taken the paper back to show Abraham, and in a burst of enthusiasm they'd moved the same day to their new home. There, with furious energy, he'd hewed and hacked and hammered, and well before the summer's end, their cabin was built and their little garden prepared for spring planting. In the back corner of the lot they left a maple sapling, at her insistence.

"It was my totem for the future," she told Anna, somewhat ruefully.

Once the cabin was built, Abraham lapsed again into his quiet. On warm days he would drag his chair to the porch and stare gloomily down upon the harbor.

That was when she decided she'd have to keep them alive. Abraham was never going to begin and improve yet another farm, he was too weary, it would fall to her to put food on their table . . . She had Peter and Daniel Michler build her a small shop.

"What sort of shop?" Anna asked, nonplussed. Her sister a shopkeeper!

"It doesn't matter," Katy said. "Whatever people wanted. Notions, small goods, anything . . ."

To her surprise, she remembered that little shop with considerable pride. *I did it, I kept us, me, and we did well, we had a little money . . .*

It also gave her something to do, in the face of Abraham's silence. Busy with her bookkeeping, so she didn't see him . . . disappearing . . .

Three more transports arrived, and with them another ninety families. There were no surveyed lots for them, and no one would help without "exorbitant pay," the surveyors reported disgustedly.

Disillusion was spreading, and squabbling broke out. People bought their way into the choicer lots. Families were rudely shoved aside from land they had already started improving, and no one listened to their complaints.

In September, the fall fleet arrived, further dramatically expanding the population. The Port Roseway Associates made some feeble efforts to keep what they considered undesirable riffraff from the town, but it was a losing battle. Carleton was swamped, complaining that "the violence of the Americans, which broke out after the cessation of hostilities, encrease the number of their Countrymen who look to me for escape from threatened destruction." So he paid no attention to these pleas "not to allow all sorts and ranks of men" into Shelburne. He had to do what he had no escape from doing. The town filled with disbanded soldiers, widows and orphans, freed slaves trying for the first time to make a life of their own. By the end of the year, a head count put the population at eight thousand eight hundred and ninety-six individuals, including one thousand five hundred and thirty-one free blacks living in town and in a small community on the northwest arm called Birchtown.

Rowdiness increased, and unrest, and belligerence.

Taverns opened, and brothels.

Lower orders of men were blamed. So were the "negros."

Katy kept her head down, and a large stick by the door for the truant children who would steal her blind.

In the late fall, they heard that some of the southern states had issued proclamations relaxing the laws of confiscation and banishment, and that the forced sale of former Loyalist estates had stopped. In a few cases, the right of Loyalists to return and own property was explicitly granted. Hardly anyone believed in this spirit of forgiveness.

But it didn't stop them wishing.

There was another long silence. Katy was lost in her memories. *It wasn't so bad there. There was a stove, and plenty of wood, and the house was tight. There was civility as well as unrest. Rosannah visited often. So did Peter and John. Daniel and Eva. That December, we went all the way to Lunenburg, to the Lutheran church on the hill, for a christening . . . little Anna Maria Barbara Strum, Jacob's third daughter. Young Henry came too, at thirteen a miniature Heinrich . . . It broke our hearts to see him, solemn little man . . . Jacob seemed to be living in Lunenburg, then, blacksmithing, coming back often enough to prove his grant and make babies. It was clear he and Anna didn't really get on.*

And so the winter came.

Poor Abraham! Grew smaller and smaller . . .

On January 30, 1784, almost a year to the day after Heinrich Strum perished in the great storm, Abraham slipped away. It was a sparkling winter's afternoon, the sun glittering on the fresh snow, the smoke from the chimneys ascending straight into the blue, for there was no wind. Abraham was staring out at the yard, squinting a little against the glare, then he gave a great sigh, and slipped sideways in his chair, and was gone.

"I saw him go," she said, looking at Anna. "The air just went from him, poof, gone, like that . . ."

Anna reached over, laid her hand on Katy's knee. It was the first time she'd touched her sister in, what, forty years? The fabric of her dress was rough-textured. She pressed too lightly to feel the bones beneath.

"No, it's all right," Katy said. "It was a long time ago."

In truth, she had mourned, but not for his death. She had mourned for his life, for all the things he had been forced to do, against his nature and his spirit. He had been a farmer who became a soldier, and she mourned for the farmer in him.

Yes, it was Heinrich's death that did it. Heinrich wasn't supposed to die. He was the hero of our story, and was supposed to last until the final word . . . He was supposed to be there still, resolute, at The End . . .

"What did you do, after that?" Anna asked.

"I ran my shop and visited my family and life went on . . ." She stopped. Life had gone on, but Shelburne was in trouble. Too much disorganization, no help from the government, too many wastrels and then . . . The blacks of Birchtown, most of them skilled workmen desperate for food and money, hired themselves out at discount rates, enraging the New Yorkers. There were still no farm lots. It all came to a head by mid summer, as Simeon Perkins, up the coast in Liverpool, recorded in his diary: "An extraordinary mobb or Riot has happened in Shelburne. Some thousands of People Assembled with Clubbs, and Drove the Negroes out of the Town and threatened Some people." Within days, Parr, alarmed, had rearmed the disbanded soldiers. Jacob Strum, given a gun one more time, left it in the parlor, took himself off to Lunenburg and didn't come back. Others just . . . drifted away. Newly built houses stood empty.

It was then, Christmas Day 1784, that the King's Rangers arrived in Halifax, up from St. Augustine via New York. There were about nine hundred of them in all, men, women, children. Among them were Georg Schildnacht Jr., George Dawkins and Fritz Henn.

Had she already mentioned Fritz? Katy could no longer remember. She was adrift between her memories and the recounting of them.

Fritz and the rest were sent up the coast to a bleak place called Country Harbour. Somewhere along the Eastern Shore, the ship carrying timber and nails for their shelters foundered and was lost; of the nine hundred, fully a third died of scurvy and cold that first winter. The stories filtered down to Shelburne. Some of the men bartered their town lots, and sometimes even their wives, for rum and food. In the spring, most of the survivors returned to their original homes in the United States, preferring to take their chances with their victorious former neighbors rather than with the cruelties of another northern winter. Georg Schildnacht moved to Ship Harbour to join the others from Ninety Six who had settled there. Fritz Henn made his way to Lunenburg. There, at last, a happy story!

"I went to his wedding," Katy recalled. "In Lunenburg it was, in Zion Lutheran, up on the hill. Local girl, Anna Mary Heb, saw him in church and fell in love . . . What a dashing young Dragoon he was! I think Jacob Strum, who was Fritz's brother-in-law, got them together after that. First they lived with her father, then I heard he bought some land of his own and planted apples. Still there, I believe."

She paused, picked at her skirt and fanned herself idly. Anna was sitting primly again, both hands in her lap, her brief feather touch forgotten. She wasn't looking at anything in particular. Clearly she wasn't interested in the Henns. *Keep to the point, woman!* But how hard it was to remember those years! Everything blurred together and became confused. She'd heard about then that the folks in New Brunswick, Hamilton and the Rupperts and, she supposed, the McRae woman, had run into trouble and had fired off a petition to His Excellency the Governor in Chief of New Brunswick. It had been some complicated thing about their stores and clothing being thieved, put into the hands of some person who made some unspecified improper use of it, "whereby your memorialists and families are totally deprived and now find themselves nearly destitute of cloathing."

"Still, not everything was bleak, there were good times too," she told Anna. "With family, and all the children . . ."

What else happened in those years? Oh yes! Some colonel took Adam Bauer to court "for purchasing the necessarys of one of complainant's soldiers," and old Adam temporarily lost his license—courts always preferred a colonel's word to a tavern-keeper's, especially one who had been trading in all kinds of merchandise of unknown provenance. A year or so later he was charged again, along with a crony, the buxom Mrs. Hewett. This time he was accused of buying stolen goods. Of course, he professed the most innocent (and justified) bewilderment, "having bought these things in public and in Open Day, with not the least suspicion they were stolen." After all, the distress of the winters induced many to sell their property to keep from starving, didn't they? The case was dismissed, and she remembered Adam getting indignantly but triumphantly drunk afterward. Hadn't he carefully brought his rum cup from the Carolinas with him, a small possession, but precious enough? And useful!

On June 11, 1786, her son Peter and his new wife Frances christened little Elizabeth at Christ Church, Shelburne. Sometime after that, maybe a year, Jacob and Anna had another baby, a son, Johann Peter. Anna had by then joined him in Lunenburg, and they moved to Mahone Bay, to a property owned by someone else, she couldn't remember who. It didn't matter. Anna had left Shelburne mostly because their house burned down. Katy remembered that because just afterward, sometime in June '85, she thought, an order went out directing "the taking down and removal of all wooden funnels and wooden chimneys on houses within the town." Damned stupid thing, wooden chimneys. Not so bad in Carolina, perhaps, but in this frozen north . . .

I'm rambling, she thought. *Nobody cares. Anna doesn't care. Why does it matter?* Was it important except to himself that John Snell, old Barnet's youngest, was killed by a falling tree? What did it matter that some ship's captain let go a few convicts off Shelburne, and they came swarming ashore, terrorizing everyone? There were more riots around then. Karl Bauer married Margaret Hamilton. Certainly important to them. Handbills were distributed forbidding "negro dances, and negro frolics in the town of Shelburne." She had been ordered to post one in her store, and had grudgingly done so, but behind the stove where no one could see it. She looked over at her sister, who was looking at her, her head cocked. *Why should she care, really?*

More peaceable citizens drifted away, one at a time or in families. A few went to London; a few to the West Indies, to Barbados, New Providence or Jamaica; one went to Cape Breton and others traveled to Quebec. Many remained in Nova Scotia, pushing along the shores to the villages settled by New Englanders—westward to Barrington and to Yarmouth, eastward to Liverpool. Some went to Chester, others to Lunenburg and still others to Halifax; some were attracted to farm land in the Annapolis Valley, or to New Brunswick.

Many returned to the United States.

"Why did you stay?" Anna asked. *What a litany of woe! But not to forget the destruction back here in Ninety Six, and the bands of orphans and beggars, and the struggle we have had to make our way too . . . Winners don't always savor victory, after all.*

"I sold my goods and kept my head down," Katy said. "What else was I to do?"

The next spring, 1786, a group of thirty-nine families from the Carolinas (among them "Charles" and Adam "Bowers," Daniel Michler,

Katy herself and her son Peter, Conrad Merk and others) was given a collective grant of seven thousand five hundred and twenty-eight acres on Pell's Road, the route across the province to Annapolis. Katy was granted lot #34, one hundred and sixty acres, between William Dorris and Karl Bauer, and next door to Conrad. Jacob Strum drew lot #6, one hundred and ninety-seven acres, although, in effect, he had already left for good.

But it didn't help. Too many of them were restless. Conrad and Rosannah were unhappy to see their children roaming this blighted place. The Michlers were ready to move. And young Henry . . . It was the Claims Commission that settled it, in the end.

"What was that?" Anna asked, curious.

"It was in the spring of '86. The British parliament was to compensate Loyalists for losing their American properties . . ."

Anna made to speak, bit her tongue.

". . . and sent commissioners to hear our stories."

And how fast we filled up the buckets of our stories then! And such stories! Death and terror, pain and loss, but plainly told, always plainly told. Some stories need no ornament. They only needed retelling.

They were scribbled down into some book, no doubt to be hidden in a vault in some dusty warehouse in London, lost forever.

Well, maybe the recording angel would remember.

Poor, wretched Heinrich!

Commissioners Jeremy Pemberton, Esquire, and Colonel Thomas Dundas appeared in Shelburne early in the spring. In June, Henry Strum was given his chance to say his piece.

"1786, 22 June, Shelburne, Henry Strum, (jr.), infant son of Heinrich, late of South Carolina.

"Infant appears. He is about 16 years of age. Daniel Migler, uncle to the Infant, appears with him, as his guardian. Adam Bauer, Wits. Sworn Saith: Knew Henry Strum, Father of Claimant. Came from Germany with Wits. about 24 yrs ago. Was settled in 96 District. Was a Loyalist, went to Florida as a soldier with Captn Murphy, served all the war, was a Seargint under Col. Ferris; came to Halifax from Charles Town, died last Jany, 3 year. Infant is his only child."

The commissioner, hardened after all these months to stories of woe, was nonetheless impressed. The lad was steady, his black eyes coolly assessing, curiously adult and very calm in demeanor. He scribbled a marginal note, to remind himself: "N.B.—They seem all very fine people."

The commissioner reserved judgment, not that it much mattered. Once Henry had said his piece, it was clear he wanted to return to Carolina to see his father's land. He was only sixteen but a masterful lad, and his determination was all they needed, the small incremental puff of wind that filled the sails. His cousins Peter, Daniel and Jacob Michler would go with him, and so would Daniel and Eva, though they prudently kept their Shelburne land. Jacob Strum, Henry's uncle, decided to remain in Nova Scotia, but Conrad and Rosannah Merk would leave, too. So would Peter and Frances Frietz. In fact, all the Frietzes would go.

Even me!

Katy stood up from the bench, and turned to face Anna.

"I wanted to come home with my family," she said.

She rose and went down the bank to the creek again. Carefully, mindful of her back and unbending limbs, she got down on one knee and scooped up water, splashing it on her face. It was cooler than the air, but not by much. She let it trickle down into her bodice, enjoying the tickling on her skin.

Then she got up, and planted her feet in front of Anna.

"Your turn, sister. Tell the tale."

"No," Anna said. "First finish what you began."

Katy sighed. "There's little left to tell. We came back. Charlestown was calling itself Charleston but it was the same wharf nonetheless, the same wharf, the same town, the same horses, the same journey up to the Back Country. Old Balthazar Merk had been ill, as you know, but Conrad and Rosannah got back in time. Johan was there, and they fought for a while, but then it was over, for their father was dying, and he made them clasp hands before he went. So they settled onto their land and raised their children, and . . ." She paused. So much meaning in a few words! "Their" land!

I went to "my" land, but only once. It was overgrown and the roof had fallen in on the house, and there were rats and wild things living in the rooms, and my heart started to beat faster and faster, and I fled, spent a day wandering in the woods, alarming my children, but it terrified me, that house, all I could smell was my beloved, rotting in the sour soils of Shelburne! After that my

Rosannah found a corner for me in her house, and I settled down to become the
Widow Frietz and . . .

"And I visited with Maria," she said. "She and her son had sold her
place to David Rush by then, and Rosena, of all people, wild Rosena and
he were raising a family of their own. Maria and me, widow women."

Anna bit her lip, but still said nothing.

"I thought of you, sometimes," Katy said.

"Did you?"

"But my heart was hard. I blamed you, you see, for so much . . ."

"Do you still?"

Katy took a long time to respond. Did she? Did she really? The answer
was yes! Yes! She did . . . Ah, but the tocsins of war were so long ago! The
rattle of armies and the cries of the dying were fading into history, and she
remembered only Abraham's blank look and his sinking into hopelessness.
There was no one to blame for that, except fate.

Finally she said, "It's all over, over, we're in a new century, it's our children's world, now, our grandchildren's world. It's time to let it go . . ."

"So it isn't too late?" Anna asked.

"No."

Katy sat down again. It was hard to stand for any time, now, the weight
of her body ground her legs into her hips, and they ached. The sun was
sinking rapidly, and the shadows were lengthening. They sat for a while,
in silence.

What of the others?

Daniel and Eva had stayed only until '91. They kept some acreage for
their sons' use, but they sold the rest on Cuffeetown Creek and went back
to Shelburne. Why? Too many ghosts, Eva had said, hugging Katy, too many
wretched emotions, too many hurtful stories told by too many people with
memories that were too long. She couldn't stand the sidelong glances, the
mean-spirited innuendoes, the pointed reminders of *who she'd been*. So they
went back, to Shelburne of all places, and Katy had heard nothing more of
them, except that Daniel had died just before the turn of the century.

And Heinrich's boy, Henry?

They'd gone with him to his father's farm when first they were back.
The memory made her shiver. The farm was neglected, as might be
expected, but the house was in good repair. No one had damaged it. No, it
was more than that—someone had been looking after it, had repaired the

chimney, secured the door. There was sign of new work on the fences. One of the outbuildings had been rebuilt. They never discovered who it had been. No one was living in the house.

Inside, it was untouched.

You could still see the boards from which Heinrich had scrubbed his murdered wife's blood.

The boy decided to stay there. He said he felt no ghosts. "In any case," he said, "they would be my ghosts, and friendly to me."

She had tried to argue, but he was a willful young man and wouldn't listen.

After that, she had hardly seen him. He never visited, but she kept up through her children and grandchildren. He had repaired the farm, brought it back to, well, if not abundance then at least to comfort.

"I know," said Anna, unexpectedly. "I saw him."

Katy looked at her sharply. "You went to see him?" Her voice rose to a squeak, which irritated her.

"Why not? He didn't know who I was. I was just passing, and stopped in for a visit. He wasn't at all curious."

"And what did you find?"

"He *was* just like his father . . ."

"And you fell in love with him, I suppose?" Even to herself, she sounded stupidly sarcastic, and silently criticized herself for it.

"Katy! I could be his grandmother!"

"So?"

"Well, I could have," Anna said, laughing.

"I know," Katy said sheepishly, giving in a little.

They both chuckled, startling themselves with the unexpected sound.

Henry had stayed until '96 and then, abruptly, left. Of course, he was married by then, to Sara, whom people called Sally. They went to Georgia, she heard.

Catherine's ghost must have been laid to rest, by now. Don't ghosts forget, too? Surely they have better things to do after twenty years than to rattle bones and scare owls. Although she had heard stories about recent hauntings in the old house, none of which surprised her very much.

"So there you have it," she said to Anna. "That's the tale. After that, I grew old, much to my surprise. And I came here, to visit with Maria. This bench became my friend. We didn't say much, you know. We old never do. We're too wise to say much, except to ourselves . . ."

Anna smiled. As if no one else ever grew old! How like Katy! "You were never much for silence, sister."

She reflected. What to tell of her own story? So little had happened! They stayed, her daughters grew up and married and scattered, her sons became men and married and scattered, she grew old, and after a long while, in 1805, Peter had died. But he died in his bed, peacefully, with his wife and his children around him, and it was a good death as these things went, for he was eighty years old, and it had been hard to weep much for him. He had escaped the war unwounded in body or spirit, and had been reconciled with his sister. She, too, had visited Maria, and this bench, but only on days she knew Katy wouldn't be there.

What else? Katy knew the rest. Ninety Six was no longer. The last decade of the century had been hard times in Edgefield County, as it was now called. Every Sunday, the parsons described the place as a Pandemonium, the capital of Hell, a locus of wild disorder. Why? Because although times were hard, there was a grog shop at every crossroads and sometimes in between, and the sins of the county hadn't changed, whiskey and rum, gambling, loose women . . . But at least there were parsons now. In 1788, all the German-Protestant congregations in the Back Country were incorporated. One of the fifteen churches represented was the German Lutheran Church of St. George on Hard Labour Creek. Among those who had brought about this union were some familiar names, Philip Zimmermann, Philip Kiess, Balthazar Merk, Philip Knaab, Peter Zimmermann, Fritz Knaab, Peter and Dietrich Utz. Later, of course, it all sort of fell apart as sixteen thousand people flocked to join the Baptists in a frenzy of revivalism. In 1805, the Methodists acquired St. George and renamed it Tranquil Church, but it was always popularly called Swamp Meeting House.

There was still lawlessness and thievery, starving beggars, bands of orphans. It was wise to travel fully armed; there were outlaws in the Long Canes, and the Law didn't venture too far off the roads. Those roads were thronged for a time with people heading north and west into the open lands of Georgia; the crossing at Swancey's Ferry on the Saluda was often jammed with wagons and herds of cattle as settlers went off looking for fresh opportunities, paying no mind to the wagons heading back the other way, having failed to find any such thing.

No, nothing much happened, those years.

The land went on, of course. Summers came, winters went. The more or less united States elected senators, presidents. Politicians roared and blustered.

Her children had done well, were becoming a . . . presence . . . in the Carolinas.

The Zimmermanns prospered. So did the Merks, those who had stayed.

LeRoy Hammond became a justice of the peace, sometime around the middle of the '80s.

Patrick Cunningham came back to Charleston, as it was now called, and successfully petitioned to be allowed to remain. He was fined twelve percent of his property and denied political rights for seven years. Still, he managed to serve two terms in the legislature during this time.

In '86, Columbia was established as the capital of South Carolina, which delighted all the Back Country, who had no love for the snobs of Charleston.

Well, and in 1811, there was the great earthquake.

The year after that, war broke out again between the United States and Britain. There was privateering, and shipping was blockaded. The President's home in Washington was burned by Redcoats. The United States attempted to invade Canada, but was repulsed. Carolina sent troops off to New Orleans. In the Back Country, they tried to turn out the militia again. Hardly anyone joined up. No one seemed to care. The Back Country was done with war.

Good!

And in June 1813, the past finally caught up to the present.

No great earthquake, no great war, no cataclysm . . . but Maria, dear, sweet, lovely, *dead* Maria . . . She died at last, that great heart, gone to her husband, wherever he was.

Anna had gone to the funeral, of course.

And afterward, she had gone down to the creek to sit on the bench where she and Maria had been so companionable so often.

To find Katy already there, staring at the sluggish water, lost in her thoughts.

Anna had felt a sudden upwelling of anger and resentment. How dare she!

But she'd been ashamed of the anger, and after a while had sat down on the end of the bench.

Two toothless old crows, indeed, in our black plumage and with our bloodless limbs!

They sat there in silence for a while.

Sometimes silence isn't so bad, Anna thought.

Sometimes silence can be a beginning.

Twenty-one

June 1813
The Rush Farm, Cuffeetown Creek, South Carolina

Rosena Rush and Rosannah Merk peered guiltily around the corner of the barn, down toward the creek. It was dusk, and the old women hadn't returned. They were consumed with curiosity.

What do they talk about, after forty years? Two old women, whose stories are almost used up?

They strained to see through the gathering dark. The bench was empty. Where were they?

There!

They were coming slowly back up across the field. Katy was hobbling a little, her bad hip giving her trouble. Anna, who was a head taller, was behind her. As they came closer, the two younger women could see that Anna had her hand on Katy's shoulder.

Rosannah stared. *So it was all right! In the end, the past always drowns in the future . . . It's true, wounds do heal, scars do fade . . .* She started to say something, but she was interrupted. Somewhere up at the house, a child was shouting something, imperiously. She turned away, leaving the old ladies to their stately progress.

The children. It was always for them. Everything, always. What else counted, in the end?

Chapter notes

Chapter One (September 1763—Idar-Oberstein, German Palatinate)
The material in this chapter came from general histories of Germany (for which see bibliography), from travel books on Germany (for which see bibliography), from personal visits on site, from contemporary London newspapers, from the Goethe Institute's genealogical research, from other German family history sources (see Genealogical notes) and, for the specific family names, from Janie Revill, from the ever-valuable archives of the Genealogical Project, Church of the Latterday Saints, from various family sources (see them listed in the Thanks section, for many of them went far beyond courtesy in responding to our pestering), and from *The Stroms of South Carolina*, by Samuel and Martha Strom. All the information on Johan Christian Stumpel came from contemporary newspaper accounts.

Chapter Two (August 1764—Whitechapel, London)
The chapter was sourced from the British Library newspaper collection (the "poor, benighted Palatines" were a major story in the penny press in London for several months), from on-the-ground visits to Whitechapel and to the Lutheran Church of St. George, from correspondence with its Pastor, the Rev. A.B. Muller, from Lloyds of London shipping registry archives, from *Shipping News*, and from Winthrop Bell (*The Foreign Protestants and the Settlement of Nova Scotia*, by Winthrop P. Bell, published by the Centre for Canadian Studies and Mount Allison University). The quote in the final paragraph in the chapter, on the arrest of Stumpel, is from Bell.

Chapter Three (February 1765—Charlestown, South Carolina)
The material in this and all subsequent chapters set in the Carolinas came from personal visits to the sites mentioned, from archives and libraries in

Charlestown, Columbia and Ninety Six, and from the kindness of Park Rangers, librarians, residents and archivists, in addition to those descendants mentioned in the genealogical credits. Many books were useful—see Sources. Several passages were adapted more directly, with permission. Details of Lieutenant Governor Bull's disposition of the immigrants were adapted from *Greenwood County Sketches*. The story of Calhoun was adapted from many sources, most particularly *Greenwood County Sketches* by Margaret Watson and *The History of South Carolina*, edited by Edward McCrady.

Chapter Four (August 1765—Cuffeetown Creek, South Carolina)

Especially valuable in this chapter were *Greenwood County Sketches* and Robert Bass's most excellent and indispensable *Ninety Six*. The recounting of the Indian wars and the attack on Goudy's Fort at Ninety Six was adapted from many sources, including particularly the *History of South Carolina*, Vol. 2, and from *Greenwood County Sketches*. At least one passage owes its provenance to *The Carolina Backcountry on the Eve of the Revolution* by Charles Woodmason.

Chapter Five (August 1768—Dutch Fork, South Carolina)

Several passages have been loosely adapted from Woodmason's fascinating reminiscences, and there are also some direct quotes, used with permission of the publishers.

Chapter Six (November 1775—Ninety Six, South Carolina)

As in the previous chapter, Woodmason has proved an indispensable source, and we are grateful to the publishers for permission to quote from his writings. Several other passages in this chapter owe their provenance to *Greenwood County Sketches*, Charles Botta's history of the revolution, *Colonial and Revolutionary History of Upper South Carolina* by J.B.O. Landrum and the *History of South Carolina*.

Chapter Seven (January 1776—Great Cane Brake, South Carolina)

Here, as in so many other places, Robert Bass's *Ninety Six* proved indispensable. Also useful was Carole Troxler's ever-reliable dissertation and her ongoing work in the field, and one passage from the *History of Edgefield County*.

Chapter Eight (September 1777—Charlestown, South Carolina)
Several details in this chapter have been adapted from Carole Troxler's dissertation, from Charles Botta, and from the *History of Edgefield County*.

Chapter Nine (December 1778—Cuffeetown Creek, South Carolina)
Kinloch Bull's *The Oligarchs in Colonial and Revolutionary Charleston* proved a useful source for this chapter.

Chapter Ten (August 1779—Cuffeetown Creek, South Carolina)
The recounting of the taking of Savannah and Prevost's (and therefore Heinrich Strum's) campaigns along the coast, and also the inland campaigns, including the battle at Kettle Creek, was adapted from many sources, principally *Ninety Six*, Charles Botta and *Campaigns of the American Revolution* by D.W. Marshall and H.H. Peckham. The tale of Jacob Strum's imprisonment comes from Samuel and Martha Strom in *The Stroms of South Carolina 1765–1983 and Certain Allied Families*.

Chapter Eleven (October 1779, Savannah, Georgia)
The description of the siege of Savannah was adapted from many sources, including *Ninety Six*, *Atlas of the American Revolution*, *Campaigns of the American Revolution*, *A History of the War in America* by Botta, *The Siege of Savannah* edited by Franklin Benjamin Hough, *South Carolina Loyalists in the American Revolution* by R.S. Lambert and (in the Hough book) an extract from the *Journal of a Naval Officer in the Fleet of Count d'Estaing*, 1782.

Chapter Twelve (June 1780—Charlestown, South Carolina)
The story of "Purves List" was adapted from Leonardo Andrea's work,

which can be found in the files of the Church of Latter-Day Saints. The passages about Clinton's and Tarleton's journey south was adapted from Charles Botta, *Oliver Wiswell* by Kenneth Roberts and *Ninety Six*.

Chapter Thirteen (August 1780—Ninety Six, South Carolina)

Much of the military maneuverings of the period were adapted from Andrea's work in the files of the Church of Latter-Day Saints, from Trox-ler, from various histories and from the excellent recounting in *Ninety Six*. Debts in this chapter are also owed to the *History of Edgefield County*, *Greenwood County Sketches* and *South Carolina Loyalists in the American Revolution*.

Chapter Fourteen (May 1781—Ninety Six, South Carolina)

Some passages in this chapter have been adapted from *South Carolina Loyal-ists in the American Revolution*, the *History of Edgefield County*, *Campaigns of the American Revolution*, and *Ninety Six*. The story of the "Mountain Men" is derived from many sources, but we have borrowed particularly from Charles Botta. The King's Mountain battle was adapted from the detailed account in *South Carolina Loyalists in the American Revolution*.

Chapter Fifteen (June 1781—Ninety Six, South Carolina)

The story of the siege of Ninety Six was adapted from many sources, but among the most useful were the *History of Edgefield County*, the splendid *Ninety Six*, *Greenwood County Sketches*, *South Carolina Loyalists in the American Revolution*, *A History of South Carolina* and *Oliver Wiswell*. The novel, *Oliver Wiswell*, brilliantly cast the siege in terms of human drama; much good detail came from the *History of Edgefield County* and especially from the *Colonial and Revolutionary History of Upper South Carolina*.

Chapter Sixteen (July 1781—Ninety Six, South Carolina)

Again, the sources for the events following the siege of Ninety Six are many and varied. Among the best are the novel *Oliver Wiswell*, the *His-tory of Edgefield County*, *Ninety Six* and the *History of South Carolina*.

Chapter Seventeen (September 1782—James Island, South Carolina)
Troxler's excellent work was an indispensable source for this chapter. So
was *Ninety Six*. "Bloody Bill's" September foray into the Back Country,
and especially his attack on Hayes' post, owes much to *Ninety Six*. His
raids on Edward Hampton's plantation and the home of Dannett Abney
were adapted from the *History of Edgefield County*.

Chapter Eighteen (October 1782—James Island, South Carolina)
The account of Bloody Bill's last raid was adapted from *History of Edgefield
County*. Other stories in this chapter owe much to *South Carolina Loyalists
in the American Revolution* and the *History of South Carolina, Vol. 4*.

Chapter Nineteen (January 1783—Halifax, Nova Scotia)
Troxler, again, was a rich source. So was the fourth volume of the *History
of South Carolina*, and *Charleston, the Place and the People*, by Harriott
Harry Ravenal (Rutledge). Johann Gottfried Seume's first-person memoir
yielded up some good detail about Halifax in winter in the period. The
story of Hamilton, Joseph Pynchon and the Port Roseway Associates was
adapted from *King's Bounty* by Marion Robertson, used with the permission of the Nova Scotia Museum.

*Chapter Twenty (June 1813—The Rush Farm, Cuffeetown Creek, South
Carolina)*
Much of the material in this chapter has been adapted from family histo-
ries, from the files of the Public Archives of Nova Scotia, from Troxler,
from the Nova Scotia Gazette, from the Ontario Bureau of Archives, from
King's Bounty, from Shelburne town records, from *Greenwood County
Sketches*, and from the *History of Edgefield County*.

Sources: a select bibliography

The histories of the period are too numerous to mention, ranging as they do from encyclopedias to specialist histories of this or that regiment. For our enquiry, the following books proved particularly useful:

GERMANY
Acton, Lord, Ed. *The Cambridge Modern History*. Cambridge: Cambridge University Press, 1904.

Blanning, T.C.W. *Reform and Revolution in Maintz 1743-1803*. Cambridge: Cambridge University Press, 1974.

Bruford, W.H. *Germany in the 18th Century: The Social Background of the Literary Revival*. Cambridge: Cambridge University Press, 1935.

Elkins, T. H. *Germany*. London: Chatto & Windus, 1968.

Hugo, Victor. *The Rhine*. New York: Worthington, 1886.

Kelly, Arthur C.M. *Hessische Truppen in Amerikanischen Unabhangigkeitskrieg*. New York: Rhinebeck, 1991.

Mathern, Willy. *Du Unser Naheland*. Bad Kreuznach: Pandion Verlag, 1992.

Murray, John. *Handbook for North Germany*. London: John Murray, 1877.

Petry, Dr. Ludwig. *Handbuch Der Historischen Statten Deutschlands V.* Stuttgart: A. Krner, 1964.

Stieler, Karl. *The Rhine From Its Source to the Sea*. Trans. G.C.T. Bartley. Philadelphia: J.P Lippincott & Co., 1878.

Tucker, Rev. Bowman W. *The Romance of the Palatine Millers*. Montreal: Rev. Bowman W. Tucker, 1929.

Archival material:
Seume, Johann Gottfried [1789]. "Adventures of a Hessian Recruit." [First published in *Neue Literatur Und Volker Kunde*.] Boston: Massachusetts Historical Society Proceedings 1887-1889, Vol. IV.

ENGLAND
Crane, R. S. and F. B. Kaye. *A Census of British Newspapers and Periodicals 1620-1800*. Chapel Hill: University of North Carolina Press, 1927.
Owen, Sir David. *The Origin and Development of the Ports of the United Kingdom*. London: Allman, 1948.
Rudé, George. *The History of London: Hanoverian London 1714-1808*. London: Secker & Warburg, 1971

Archival material:
Acts of the Privy Council, Ser 4, 1745-66. Toronto: Robarts Library, University of Toronto.
Acts of the Privy Council, Ser 4, 1766-83. Toronto: Robarts Library, University of Toronto.
Carleton Papers, Vols. 1-4. Halifax, Nova Scotia: Public Archives of Nova Scotia.
Colonial Office Papers, Part 2 [August 1782]. Vol. 41 [misc. docs.], Vol. 54 [misc. docs.], Vol. 56 [docs. 1, 40, 60, 62, 66, 281], Vol. 59 [misc. docs.]. Halifax, Nova Scotia: Public Archives of Nova Scotia.
Index to Reports from Committees of the House of Commons (Britain). Toronto: Robarts Library, University of Toronto.
Journal of the Commissioners For Trade and Plantations: Jan. 1764-1767. Toronto: Robarts Library, University of Toronto.
Lords Papers, General Index: 1714-1805. Toronto: Robarts Library, University of Toronto.
Reports of the House of Commons, 1764. Toronto: Robarts Library, University of Toronto.
The Unbound Papers [of the Privy Council]. Toronto: Robarts Library, University of Toronto.

SOUTH CAROLINA

Bass, Robert D. *Ninety Six: The Struggle for the South Carolina Back Country.* Orangeburg, South Carolina: The Sandlapper Press, 1978.

Bull, Kinloch Jr. *The Oligarchs in Colonial and Revolutionary Charleston.* Columbia: University of South Carolina Press, 1991.

Burton, Orville Vernon. *In My Father's House Are Many Mansions: Family and Community in Edgefield South Carolina.* Chapel Hill: University of North Carolina Press, 1988.

Chapman, John A. *History of Edgefield County From Earliest Settlements to 1897.* Newberry, S.C.: Elbert H. Aull, 1897. Rpt: Spartanburg, S.C.: The Reprint Company, 1988.

Dykeman, Wilma. *With Fire and Sword: The Battle of King's Mountain 1780.* Washington, D.C.: National Park Service, undated.

Hemphill, J.C. *Men of Mark in South Carolina.* Washington: Men of Mark Publishing Co., 1907.

Hough, Franklin Benjamin. *The Siege of Savannah in 1779: As Described in Two Contemporaneous Journals of French Officers in the Fleet of Count Charles d'Estaing.* Albany, New York: Joel Mansell, 1874.

Hudson, Patricia L., et al. *The Smithsonian Guide to Historic America: The Carolinas and the Appalachian States.* New York: Stewart, Tabori & Chang, 1989.

Kovacik, Charles and John Wineberry. *South Carolina: A Geography.* Boulder: Westview Press, 1987.

Lambert. R. S. *South Carolina Loyalists in the American Revolution.* Columbia: University of South Carolina Press, 1987.

Landrum, J.B.O. *Colonial and Revolutionary History of Upper South Carolina.* Greenville, S.C.: Shannon & Co., 1897.

McCrady, Edward, Ed. *History of South Carolina, Vol. 2: Under the Royal Government 1719-1776.* New York: Macmillan, 1899.

—— *History of South Carolina, Vol. 3: American Revolution 1775-1780.* New York: Macmillan, 1899.

—— *History of South Carolina, Vol. 4: American Revolution 1780-1783.* New York: Macmillan, 1899.

Meriwether, Robert L. *The Expansion of South Carolina, 1729-1765.* Philadelphia: Porcupine Press, 1974.

Moss, B.G. *Roster of South Carolina Patriots in the American Revolution.* Baltimore: Genealogical Publishing Co., 1983.

Ravenel, Harriott Harry (Rutledge) ("Mrs St. Julien"). *Charleston: The Place and the People.* New York: Macmillan, 1906.

Revill, Janie. *A Compilation of the Original Lists of Protestant Immigrants to South Carolina 1763-1773.* Columbia, S.C.: The State Company, 1939. Rpt: Baltimore: Genealogical Publishing Co., 1974.

Rogers, George C. Jr. *Charleston in the Age of the Pinckneys.* Columbia: University of South Carolina Press, 1980.

The South Carolina Synod of the Lutheran Church in America. *A History of the Lutheran Church in South Carolina.* The Lutheran Church, 1971.

Stokeley, Jim. *Fort Moultrie.* Washington, D.C.: National Park Handbook, U.S. Department of the Interior, 1985.

Stoney, Samuel Gaillard. *Plantations of the Carolina Low Country.* New York: Dover, 1989.

Uhlendorf, Bernhard Alexander. *The Siege of Charleston.* Ann Arbor: University of Michigan Press, 1938.

Watson, Margaret. *Greenwood County Sketches: Old Roads and Early Families.* Greenwood, South Carolina: Attic Press, 1982.

Weigley, Russell F. *The Partisan War: The South Carolina Campaign of 1780-1782.* Columbia: University of South Carolina Press, 1970.

Woodmason, Charles. *The Carolina Backcountry on the Eve of the Revolution.* Ed. R.J. Hooker. Chapel Hill: University of North Carolina Press, 1986.

NOVA SCOTIA

Bell, Winthrop P. *The Foreign Protestants and the Settlement of Nova Scotia.* Sackville, New Brunswick: The Centre For Canadian Studies and Mount Allison University, 1990.

Conrad, Margaret, et al. *No Place Like Home.* Halifax: Formac, 1988.

Conrad, Margaret, Ed. *Making Adjustments: Change and Continuity in Planter Nova Scotia 1759-1800.* Fredericton: Acadiensis Press, 1991.

DesBrisay, M.B. *History of the County of Lunenburg* [1870]. Rpt: Bridgewater: The Bridgewater Bulletin, 1976.

Devolpi, Charles P. *Nova Scotia: A Pictorial Record 1605-1878.* Toronto: Longman Canada Ltd., 1974.

Hartling, Philip. *Where Broad Atlantic Surges Roll.* Antigonish. N.S.: Formac, 1979.

Heritage Trust of Nova Scotia. *South Shore: Seasoned Timbers, Vol. 2*. Halifax: Heritage Trust of Nova Scotia, 1974.

Hilchey, Doris. *Refuge: The Loyalists Come to Nova Scotia*. Seabright: Four East Publications, 1985.

Kirkconnell, Watson. *The Loyalists of Nova Scotia*. Halifax: The Loyalist Gazette, 1969.

Macdonald, Ronald. *Report On Selected Buildings in Mahone Bay: A Paper Prepared for the Historic Research Section of the National Historic Parks Department*. Ottawa: National Historic Parks Department, 1977.

Macnutt, W. S. *The Atlantic Provinces: The Emergence of Colonial Society 1712-1857*. Toronto: McClelland & Stewart, 1965.

Pacey, Elizabeth. *Georgian Halifax*. Hantsport: Lancelot Press, 1987.

Robertson, Marion. *King's Bounty: A History of Early Shelburne*. Halifax: The Nova Scotia Museum, 1983.

Roth, D. Luther. *Acadie and the Acadians*. Philadelphia: Lutheran Publication Society, 1890.

Spendlove, F. St. *George: The Face of Early Canada*. Toronto: Ryerson Press, 1958.

Zinck, Hilda M. *Green Shutters Cook Book* . [Handwritten manuscript.] Tantallon, N.S.: Four East Publications, 1982.

Archival material:

Arndt, Karl J.R. *Halifax and Lunenburg, 1782*. In *German-Canadian Yearbook 1978*. Halifax, Nova Scotia: Public Archives of Nova Scotia.

Gilroy, M. *Loyalists and Land Settlements in Nova Scotia* [1937]. Halifax, Nova Scotia: Public Archives of Nova Scotia.

Griffin, Clare. *Stormont: A Town Unbuilt, 1784-*. [Handwritten manuscript.] Halifax, Nova Scotia: Public Archives of Nova Scotia.

Nova Scotia Historical Review [misc. vols.]. Halifax, Nova Scotia: Public Archives of Nova Scotia.

Westhaver, Evalina. *Childhood Reminiscences of Evalina Westhaver 1866-1882*. [Handwritten manuscript.] Halifax, Nova Scotia: Public Archives of Nova Scotia.

LOYALISTS AND LOYALISM

Allen, Robert S. *The Loyal Americans*. Ottawa: The National Museums of Canada, 1983.

Allen, Robert S. *Loyalist Literature*. Toronto: Dundurn Press, 1982.

Antliff, W. Bruce. *Loyalist Settlements 1783-1789: New Evidence of Canadian Loyalist Claims*. Toronto: Ontario Ministry of Citizenship & Culture, 1985.

Belcher, Henry. *First American Civil War*. London: Macmillan, 1911.

Blakeley, Phyllis R. and John N. Grant, Eds. *Eleven Exiles*. Toronto: Dundurn Press, 1982.

Brown, Wallace. *The King's Friends: The Composition and Motives of the American Loyalist Claimants*. Providence: Brown University Press, 1965.

Callahan, North. *Flight from the Republic*. Indianapolis: Bobbs Merril, 1967.

Clark, Murtie June. *Loyalists in the Southern Campaign of the Revolutionary War*. Baltimore: The Genealogical Publishing Co., 1981.

Demond, Robert O. *Loyalists in North Carolina*. Hamden, CT: Archon Books, 1964.

Rubincam, Milton. *The Old United Empire Loyalist List*. Baltimore: Genealogical Publishing Co., 1969.

Ryerson, Egerton. *Loyalists of America*. Toronto: W. Briggs, 1880.

Sabine, Lorenzo. *Loyalists of the American Revolution*. New York: Putnam, 1897.

Stewart, Walter. *True Blue: The Loyalist Legend*. Toronto: Collins, 1985.

Troxler, Carole Watterson. *The Migration of Carolina and Georgia Loyalists to Nova Scotia and New Brunswick*. [Unpublished dissertation.] Chapel Hill: University of North Carolina, 1974.

Wright, Esther Clark. *The Loyalists of New Brunswick*. Wolfville, N.S.: E.C. Wright, 1981.

Wright, Esther Clark. *The Petitcodiac: A Study of the New Brunswick River and of the People Who Settled Along It*. Sackville, N.B.: Tribune Press, 1945.

Archival material:

Coldham, Peter Wilson. *American Loyalist Claims, Vol. 1: Abstracts From the Public Records Office [Series 13, Bundles 1-35, 37]*. Washington, D.C.: National Genealogical Society, 1980.

Peterson, Jean, et al. *The Loyalist Guide: Nova Scotia Loyalists and Their Documents*. Halifax: Public Archives of Nova Scotia, 1983.

Town of Shelburne Records 1769-1868. Halifax, Nova Scotia: Public Archives of Nova Scotia.

HISTORIES OF THE REVOLUTION

Atlas of the American Revolution. Chicago: Rand McNally, 1974.

Botta, Charles. *History of the War of the Independence of the United States of America, Vols. 1 and 2*. Trans. George Alexander Otis. New Haven: Nathan Whiting, 1834.

Hibbert, Christopher. *Redcoats and Rebels: The American Revolution Through British Eyes*. New York: W.W. Norton, 1990.

Higginbotham, Don. *Daniel Morgan, Revolutionary Rifleman*. Chapel Hill: University of North Carolina Press, 1961.

Katcher, Philip R. N. *Encyclopedia of British, Provincial and German Units 1775-1783*. Harrisburg, PA.: Stackpole Books, 1973.

Marshall, D. W. and H. H. Peckham. *Campaigns of the American Revolution*. Ann Arbor: University of Michigan Press, 1976.

Weir, Robert M. *A Most Important Epocha: Coming of Revolution*. Columbia: University of South Carolina Press, 1970.

Wood, W. J. *Battles of the Revolutionary War 1775-1781*. Chapel Hill: Algonquin Books, 1990.

FICTION

Collier, James Lincoln and Christopher Collier. *My Brother Sam Is Dead*. New York: Scholastic Inc., 1974.

Haliburton, Thomas Chandler. *The Clockmaker*. Toronto: McClelland & Stewart, 1990.

Roberts, Kenneth. *Oliver Wiswell*. New York: Doubleday Doran and Co., 1940.

NEWSPAPERS AND MAGAZINES

Daily Advertiser. London: 1764.

Gentleman's Magazine. London: 1764-1780.

Lloyd's Evening Post & British Chronicle. London: 1764.

The London Chronicle For the Year 1764: Vol. XVI, July 1-December 29. London: Burney Collection of the British Library.

The London Gazette. London: The Burney Collection of the British Library.

Nova Scotia Gazette and Weekly Chronicle. Halifax: Public Archives of Nova Scotia.

GENEALOGICAL INFORMATION

Boyer, Carl. *Ship Passenger Lists, The South 1538-1825.* Newhall, CA.: Boyer, 1980.

Burgert, Annette Kunselman. *Eighteenth Century Emigrants, Vol. 1: The Northern Kraichgau.* Myerstown, PA.: AKB Publications, 1995.

Clark, Murtie June. *Colonial Soldiers of the South 1732-1774.* Baltimore: Genealogical Publishing Co., 1983.

Clemens, William Montgomery. *North And South Carolina Marriage Records.* New York: E.P Dutton & Co., 1927.

Cobb, Sanford. *The Story of the Palatines: An Episode In Colonial History.* New York: Putnam's, 1897.

Das Neue Testament [Inscribed, "June 20th 1836 John Peter Strum His Book"].

"Daughters of the American Revolution Index of the Rolls of Honor (Ancestor's Index)" in *The Lineage Books of the National Society of the Daughters of the American Revolution, Vols. 121-160.* Washington, D.C.: Judd & Detweiler, 1940.

Filby, P. William, Ed. *Passengers and Immigration Lists Index: Vols. 1-3.* Detroit: Gale Research Co., 1988.

Jones, Alice, Rita Bower and Mark Bower. *Twice A Refugee: The Bower Story.* Barrington Passage, Nova Scotia: Alice Jones and Rita Bower, 1979.

List of Private Claims to the House of Representatives of the United States From the 1st to 31st Congress. Baltimore: Genealogical Publishers, 1970.

Meynen, Emil. *Bibliography On German Settlement In Colonial North America.* Leipsig: O. Harrassowicz, 1937.

Paul, Roland, et al. *300 Jahre Pfalzer In Amerika Landau.* Pfalz: Pfalzische Verlagsanstalt, 1983.

Pension Roll of 1835: Vol. III, Southern States. Baltimore: Genealogical Publishers, 1968.

Punch, Terrence. *Genealogical Research in Nova Scotia.* Halifax: Petheric Press, 1983.

Rupp, I. D. *A Collection of Upwards of 30,000 Names of German, Swiss, Dutch, French and Other Immigrants In Pennsylvania From 1727 -1776.* Philadelphia: Leary, Stuart, 1927.

Strom, Samuel T. Sr. and Martha J. Strom. *The Stroms of South Carolina 1765-1983 and Certain Allied Families.* Union, South Carolina: S. and M. Strom, 1984.

OTHER DETAILS

Bruhn ,Wolfgang. *Das Kostumwerk.* Tbingen: Wasmuth, 1955.

Hofstatter, Hans H. *Das Grosse Buch Der Volkstrachten.* Eltville am Rhein: Rheingauer Verlaggesellschaft, 1977.

Hottenroth, F. *Le Costume Chez Les Peuples Anciens et Modernes.* New York: E. Weyhe, undated.

MacGregor, David R. *Fast Sailing Ships 1775-1875: Their Design and Construction.* Annapolis, MD: Naval Institute Press, 1988.

MacMechan, Archibald, Ed. *Sagas of the Sea.* New York: Dutton, 1924.

McMaster, F. *Soldiers and Uniforms: South Carolina Military Affairs.* Columbia, S.C.: University of South Carolina Press, 1971.

Racinet, A.C.A. *Le Costume Historique.* Paris: Firmin-Didot et cie, 1888.

Worsley and Griffith. *The Romance of Lloyd's.* London: Hillman-Curl, 1936.

Archival material:
Lloyd's Register of Shipping. London: Lloyd's of London Archives.